THE GLOBAL ENTREPRENEUR

Taking Your Business International

THIRD EDITION

James F. Foley
Jamric Press International

ii

This publication is designed to provide accurate and authoritative information in regard to the subject matter covered. It is sold with the understanding that the publisher is not engaged in rendering legal, accounting, or other professional service. If legal advice or other expert assistance is required, the services of a competent professional should be sought.

First printed in the USA by Dearborn Financial Publishing - (ISBN 1-57410-124-2)

Printed in the United States of America

Library of Congress Cataloging-in-Publication Data

Foley, James F.
The global entrepreneur : taking your business international /
James F. Foley.
p.   cm.
Includes index.

13-digit ISBN 978-0-9753153-1-6 (pbk.) Previously ISBN 978-0-9753153-0-9
10-digit ISBN 0-9753153-1-5

1.Export marketing-United States.2.International business
enterprises-United States-Management. 3. International trade.
I. Title.
HF1416.5.F65 1999
6589.049-dc21 99-16595
                 CIP

v2

Dedication

To my parents – for giving me love, courage,
and the wings to go global.

CONTENTS

Detailed Contents

SECTION TWO   GETTING GLOBAL 91

7. TWO KEY DECISIONS BEFORE GOING GLOBAL   92

SECTION FOUR   SUSTAINING GLOBAL SUCCESS 267

17. SETTING A PACE FOR YOUR EXPORT GROWTH-ASSESSING YOUR EXPORT PROGRESS AND SUCCESS 269

18. MANAGING INTERNATIONAL CHANNELS OF DISTRIBUTION 286

19. INTERNATIONAL ADVERTISING, PUBLIC RELATIONS, AND TRADE MISSIONS/SHOWS 297

LIST OF FIGURES

Forward

"Cleveland and Cincinnati will never be the same after Hong Kong and Rio!" remarked Eduardo. I was shocked by what I had heard from my colleague, a Latin American sales manager and never one to hold back emotion. "Hold on," I replied, "I like Cleveland and Cincinnati!" I had only been to Cleveland, but as a Midwesterner transplanted in Los Angeles I was determined not to let a typical Southern Californian beat up on my home, even if the remark missed home by a few hundred miles. Eduardo continued, "Obviously the point is not Cleveland, Cincinnati, or anywhere U.S. You don't understand, but you will."

I understood. Only days before, I had returned from my first business trip to Europe. I was the technical support representative. My boss was the European manager. We sold computer components on behalf of U.S. manufacturers that were too small to directly export. It was a wonderful trip. Early on I decided I could get used to travel if I did not have to pay.

I also experienced how exciting international business can be. There is a challenge in dealing with different cultures, new competitive challenges, new cities, and new customers. In my company, the international sales staff primarily travelled, not the technical staff. And though the company had suggested I consider a move from technical support to sales, I was inclined to stay in technical support. I had been in sales before, but now enjoyed the relative calm of technical support.

That changed upon my return from Europe. The European manager abruptly announced he had taken another sales position and his boss suggested I reconsider going back into sales. If I did, I was promised a trip back to Europe. The prospect of further international travel got the best of me. I accepted the offer and within two weeks I was back in Europe. It was upon my return from that trip that Eduardo decided to test how much the international bug had bit when he hit me with the Cleveland/Cincinnati remark. Was I going to be a wanna-be international sales manager or a true pro? What was my motivation? What was my potential?

Eduardo explained his remark. "Ultimately it's not the hotels, the food, or the tourist spots. Those are motivations for the wanna-bes. Get caught up in those aspects and you'll miss the bigger picture. The fun and challenge is in the size of the game. The U.S. market is only a handful of all the customers in the world. The game played locally soon becomes too small. The real fun is when you take on the world."

At the time I didn't understand that part of Eduardo's argument. I knew the U.S. represented only a small portion of the world's population. What I didn't understand is what a wonderful and intricate challenge there is in going after the rest of the world. I figured the difference would be the hotels, the food, and the tourist spots. Eduardo knew otherwise and wanted to share that knowledge. He soon became my mentor, one of many mentors that have helped me along a path that eventually led me to many years of exciting opportunities in international trade.

Though I had mentors, I never had a book. The books I found were a bit too obvious and did not seem to include many of the aspects my colleagues were teaching me. I did find dense textbooks with important fundamentals, but nothing I could see myself reading on a flight between the U.S. and London.

Hence this book. If you are just starting off in international trade, I hope you'll find this a useful framework to use when formulating your plan. If you are currently involved in international trade, I trust you'll find plenty of new ideas and concepts you can apply today in your ongoing international opportunities.

They are not all my ideas. These days, working with the Illinois SBDC International Trade Center at Bradley University, I have the opportunity to speak with companies on a daily basis about how they trade - import or export, small or large, newcomers or old pros. It is a chance to see into industries and products much more diverse than my own computer industry experience. And it also lets me see the mistakes. That can be costly. Fines for the improper use of a NAFTA certificate of origin can run into thousands of dollars, and not just for the company. The individual signing the document can also be fined. But let's not begin on a low note!

Use this book as your mentor. Use it to encourage yourself to find your own mentors. Then do not forget to mentor those after you. It is one of the rules of international business. I hope you will find other rules in this book and truly become a global entrepreneur.

Good luck.

Jim Foley
Bradley University
Peoria, Illinois

Acknowledgments

The reviewers, Judith Benton of ED>Net, California; Ruperto Chavarri, formerly of the Louisiana International Trade Center SBDC; Dr. Sara Jackson of University of the Incarnate Word; Jack Nettis, Jr., of Lake County Economic Development Center, International Trade Assistance Center; and Jon Richards of Southwest Oregon Community College, provided excellent feedback, ideas, and inspiration. This book has come along way from the original manuscript thanks to their comments. Judith Benton also provided most of the forms in Appendix B and greatly assisted with Chapters 14 and 15.

Several people provided information about their international trade course offerings. Their responses were valuable in the creation and success of this title. Thanks to Bidhan Chandra, Empire State College (New York); John Charles, Winston-Salem State University Small Business Technology Development Center; Michelle Cunningham, City of Denton, Texas; George Flemming, North Carolina A&T State University; CED Flores, Virginia Economic Development Partnership; Jeanette Miller, University of Delaware; Ph Qin, North Carolina A&T State University; and Brent Rondon, Duquesne University SBDC.

The following individuals from the private sector provided information and advice for specific chapters: Catherine Merz, Oak Park, Illinois, on intellectual property rights; Bill Major of McGladrey & Pullen, LLP, Chicago, on tax and accounting; Clifford Vadnais of Bank One, Chicago, on finance, Sumner Bourne, Peoria, Illinois, on legal; and Michael Richter, Germany, on marketing. Chris Welsh, past Chief Executive of C H Jones Ltd., West Midlands, England, reviewed the original manuscript and offered a number of suggestions from his perspective in a large, publicly traded British company.

My thanks to Dearborn Financial Publishing for printing the first version of the book. Their help and guidance during the writing of the manuscript, and their expertise in creating a great book helped achieve the strong success of the first edition. Particular thanks to my editor, Robin Nominelli Bermel and Project Editor Trey Thoelcke. Other members of the team were Jack Kiburz, Lucy Jenkins, and Scott Rattray of Rattray Design for the cover work. For the second edition, extra thanks to Richard Tomic who assisted with layout and production.

This book would not have been possible if it were not for my experiences and learning at Bradley University. Special thanks to our team at The Turner Center for Entrepreneurship, Ken Klotz, Jennie Hale, Jim Ryan, Beatriz Poloney, and Ross Miller and past colleagues including Dave Williams, Tony Cambas, John Kolmer, Heather McCord and others who helped me learn so much. My thanks as well to Chuck Stoner, Larry Weinzimmer, Raj Iyer, and Ed Bond, all of the Foster College of Business. Student assistance came from Peigen Tao, Heather Loresch, and Nicole Byard. And a very big thanks to Bradley University Emeritus Faculty Dr. James Goodnow who's mentorship greatly helped my career here at Bradley.

A final thanks to other global entrepreneurs and mentors that have made this book possible. They include Brownie Cocke de Ursua, Susan Forgie, Vic Cowley, Tom VanOverbeek, Larry Finch, Joella Brown, S. Logan Brown, Rick Hayes, Kelly Murphrey, Barbara Moebius, and Tom Collins. It also includes my friends and colleagues at the Illinois Department of Commerce and Economic Opportunity, the U.S. Department of Commerce (including our own Shari Stout based in Peoria), International Association of Trade Training Organizations IATTO.

NASBITE International

A final thanks to NASBITE International which years ago took the steps to develop the Certified Global Business Professional (CGBP). I was fortunate enough to serve on the NASBITE Board of Governors during its development, and for a time, as Director of the CGBP Certification. Little did we know how well this professional qualification would be accepted. So many individuals have now been certified and it has become the widely accepted standard for international trade excellence including employees of the U.S. Department of Commerce, U.S. Small Business Administration, and individuals and organizations outside the U.S. (More information at www.nasbite.org)

The first two editions of this book pre-dated the CGBP exam, but because the text was already very practical, it aligned well with the exam. For this third edition, I have aligned the topics even closer to the training standard of the CGBP. So if you are reading this to prepare for the exam, I think you'll find it very helpful. Pay particular attention to Sections 1, 2, and 3.

SECTION ONE

Before You Go Global

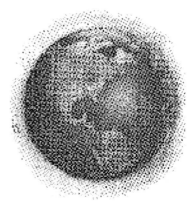

T aking your business international is a long-term process that involves a number of steps. It also requires some initial planning. Section One is about that planning - the steps a company should take before expanding its international business. Even if a company is already selling internationally, there are a number of issues developed in these initial chapters that will apply to any company, no matter how internationally developed.

This section begins by exploring in Chapter 1 why a company goes global, including some strategic issues that will impact the whole international planning process. Chapter 2 will help you determine when a company is ready to go global and what factors have to be in place.

Chapter 3 details harmonized codes, which are numbers assigned by the U.S. government to all products. This may seem an odd point to begin a technical discussion of statistical numbers, but many of the subsequent chapters discuss harmonized codes and there is a need to introduce them early in the text.

Chapters 4, 5, and 6 tackle the topic of choosing foreign markets, ranking them, and finding marketing data upon which to base such decisions. There is an in-depth discussion in Chapter 6 regarding how to determine the competitive position of a company in international markets. It will be particularly useful to anyone who is not familiar with some of the very helpful databases reporting international trade activities.

Finally, Chapter 7 discusses two fundamental decisions a company must make before any further international planning is done: (1) how to enter foreign markets that are being targeted, and (2) whether to adapt or standardize products to meet foreign customer needs and expectations

CHAPTER 1

Why Go Global?

Who is a global entrepreneur? Someone who brokers used jeans to Eastern Europe? Someone who imports textiles from Asia? Someone who develops software utilities and begins selling internationally through the Internet?

Of course, all of these are global entrepreneurs - those who see the opportunities to either sell or purchase goods internationally to enhance their business. However, the vision I have in mind of a true global entrepreneur is not just an individual selling or buying goods and services internationally. It is not limited to a one-person shop. A true global entrepreneur can work in a one-person shop, a ten-person small company, a 500-person manufacturing company, or a giant Fortune 500 corporation. The size of the company is not the issue. The issue is the role of the individual in that company.

A global entrepreneur has the vision and knowledge of how to fully involve his or her company in the global market. Not just a one or two foreign market player. Not just an importer or just an exporter. Not just a company with apathy toward international market differences. A global entrepreneur leverages the strengths of his or her company to achieve even greater success by looking way beyond our 50 states.

So what does all that mean? To be the global entrepreneur in your company, whether you are the only employee or one of many, you must first set an international vision for you and your company and that vision must begin with the fundamentals that will be outlined in this chapter.

Skip this chapter and you could lose your job! Why? Because unless you fully understand the motivation behind international business, you risk underestimating the full potential of both yourself and your company. It is not only about adding new international markets to your domestic sales. It is not only about buying cheaper input materials for manufacturing. As Eduardo told me, it is about the size of the game, and the game of international business is more than just increasing international sales.

• GLOBAL MOTIVATIONS

There are a number of motivations for going global. Let's start with the traditional reasons companies trade outside their domestic borders.

Sales to Other Markets

The fundamental reason companies trade internationally is to access markets beyond their home base. With 95 percent of the world's population living outside the United States, it seems obvious to expand your domestic success to other markets.

Selling to Canada is a perfect example. Canada shares many common needs and economic opportunities with the U.S. As a well developed country with a strong infrastructure (roads, telecommunications, education), U.S. companies can access its strong consumers almost as easily as those in the U.S. (OK, maybe not so easy if you have to complete a NAFTA certificate of origin.)

Sometimes sales to other countries are necessary for a company to be profitable. For example, imagine the research and development costs of developing a new passenger jet or pharmaceutical drug. Each requires massive expenditures for research and development (R&D) and initial start-up costs for the manufacturing facility. Without access to world markets, sales would be significantly lower, which in turn limits the ability to spread these massive costs over the life of the product. This spreading of costs, or economies of scale, motivates many companies to sell internationally.

Diversification and Reduced Risk

A second equally compelling reason is that a company with international sales diversifies its customer base. This means changing conditions in a company's domestic market, such as decreased demand or poor economic conditions, won't have as much impact. One of our clients was able to avoid any employee layoffs during the 2008-2009 recession mostly because of its strong international sales base. Global sales also means diversification of market conditions, such as a product with strong seasonal demand. Selling to markets in both the northern and southern hemisphere helps balance demand. This market diversification then leads to overall reduced risk for the company.

Avoid Changing Domestic Conditions

In some cases the issue can be more than just economies of scale. A company may need to find new buyers when their existing domestic customer base diminishes.

For example, when a product is at the end of its life cycle domestically, there may still be opportunities in foreign markets. Volkswagen continued to sell the original VW Beetles in Latin America for years after the last one was produced in the U.S. This meant their investment in R&D and manufacturing could be extended beyond the normal product life domestically. Another example would be when products have outdated technology for the domestic market, such as printing presses, but find new life in other markets. (This does not always apply. In some industries, such as telecommunications, foreign markets are demanding technology that is more advanced than that widely used in the U.S. market.) Product obsolescence issues can be a strong motivation for going global.

Some companies also look to international markets when facing increased regulations or other government or societal concerns that hamper domestic sales. The U.S. cigarette industry, for example, faces reducing consumer demand and increasing government regulations so U.S. cigarette manufacturers have aggressively pursued an international expansion strategy.

A company may also access foreign markets to take advantage of seasonal differences between their domestic market and foreign markets. By doing this, a manufacturer of summer-related products that sell well in the U.S. between May and August can turn to customers in the southern hemisphere that would purchase these products during the months of September through April, thus using international sales to offset domestic purchasing cycles.

Access to Lower Cost Structures

Another motivation often cited as a reason for going global is to improve a company's competitive position by lowering their costs. Specifically, this refers to lowering the costs associated with making products, such as raw materials, labor, and manufacturing overhead. While this relates to improved economies of scale as previously mentioned, it is more often a motivation to import materials for use in local manufacturing. It would also be a motivation to invest in foreign manufacturing facilities to access lower labor costs and cheaper raw materials. This could then involve producing components to be imported for use in domestic manufacturing or even wholly manufacturing the product overseas for eventual import into the U.S. This would also create the opportunity to sell to foreign markets close to the overseas manufacturing facility. The products may be more cost competitive if produced closer to the consumer due to lower freight costs and lower labor and materials costs.

• BEYOND THE TRADITIONAL MOTIVATIONS

These three motivations - more markets, avoiding local conditions, and lower costs - seem to imply the motivation to go global is increased sales. Certainly the overall motivation is increased sales, but that is the simple answer. A more complex analysis opens the door to the real fun - the larger game. Ultimately the goal of global trade is to expand the scope and reach of your company so that the tools and resources available to fight your competition give your company an unbeatable edge - an edge that renews and transforms itself faster than the competition can keep up.

This may begin to sound like MBA mumbo jumbo, so let's break it down into two basic principles: (1) exploit global presence, and (2) global money flows.

Exploit Global Presence

Access to foreign customers is certainly a strong motivation to go global. But to frame the argument in terms of sales misses a larger point. Going global means that all sorts of issues related to a company's operation can be internationalized and leveraged.

Ultimately, it is about sales, but getting to those increased sales is what exploiting global presence is all about.

Gary Hamel has written extensively about this subject.[1] His key concept is strategic intent - an objective that will hold the organization together over a long period of time while the company builds its global competitive abilities. From an international perspective, this has three important components: (1) global brand awareness, (2) worldwide distribution and manufacturing capacity, and (3) extranational scale economies and experience effects.

Global brand awareness. A truly global company, such as a Starbucks, Microsoft, or Caterpillar, has a unique opportunity to build brand awareness globally that can become an extremely powerful competitive tool. A truly global brand allows all sorts of marketing opportunities smaller players do not have.

For example, consider the cost of sponsoring the Olympics, the World Cup, or even the Super Bowl. A company with a global sales and marketing base can justify (and profit from) the expenditure. These events reach millions of consumers internationally-all different types of buyers. This worldwide exposure makes little sense for a product that is only traded in a few markets. However, a global player, such as a Microsoft, will easily profit from such international exposure much to the frustration of a smaller, domestic-oriented competitor.

This is not to imply that global brand awareness only means advertising at huge international events with equally huge costs. If that were the case, only large companies could pursue a global brand strategy. To the contrary, the concept can be applied by any size company within the framework of its industry. Each industry has its own Super Bowl. The validity of a global brand strategy applies just as well to a niche industry as it does to computer software and photographic film. The key is to exploit a company's global position through unique brand (marketing) opportunities only available to a global player.

Worldwide distribution and manufacturing capacity. A second aspect of exploiting global presence is to establish a global distribution system and integrated manufacturing capability. All the excellent sales and marketing attempts will be in vain if the manufacturer cannot get the product to the consumer. This point is obvious in a domestic market but it gets more complicated internationally. From a manufacturing perspective, a company must always be aware of international opportunities that can enhance its cost structure. It can then modify its products to satisfy unique foreign market needs.

Global distribution and manufacturing is not a problem to be solved, but a competitive advantage to use against competitors who simply view global distribution and manufacturing as a problem. In other words, establishing worldwide distribution not only gets products to your foreign customers, it can help keep out competing products. The same can be said of global manufacturing. It is the competitive strategy aspect of worldwide distribution and manufacturing that is important.

Extranational scale economies and experience effects. While international manufacturing and sales improves economies of scale, the effects of international business on all of the company's operations creates extranational scale economies. Virtually all the activities of a truly global company-purchasing, manufacturing, sales, marketing, human resource management, public relations, cost control, taxes, technology, logistics, government relations, and customer services - can be leveraged into stronger, more effective activities because of the scale offered by being global.

These economies also build toward internal learning and experiences which will contribute to continued successes in dealing with emerging markets, moving from distribution to direct selling internationally, and adapting products to local needs without increasing costs. These are all experience issues that become competitive advantages when compared to other companies ignoring their international potential.

All of which leads to . . .Combining the three issues - global brand awareness and dominance, worldwide distribution and capacity, and extranational scale economies and experience effects - creates a competitive edge. It creates barriers for your competition that may be extremely difficult for them to beat. It may even keep new competitions from entering the market because they see the strength of your global company. And it adds value to your company (shareholder wealth). To really understand the importance of exploiting international presence you must view it as a competitive strategy, not an issue-specific strategy. While it is about creating more sales, seeing it as an overall competitive strategy leverages all aspects of the company globally and makes going global potentially profitable and value-building for your company.

Global Money Flows

One other aspect of going global is so important that it requires separate treatment. A global company has the ability to play an international game not just with product and service flows between countries, but also money flows. It is not just about shipping goods to Europe or Asia, it is about the potential to invest in Europe or Asia, especially if that is where your competition resides.

Gary Hamel refers to this as cross-subsidization - using cash flows internationally to fight your competitive battles. Hamel cites the example of using cash flow from one's home market (domestic base of operation) to cross-subsidize an attack in that market by a foreign-based competitor. So if an Italian firm decides to enter the U.S., a U.S.-based competitor does not respond directly to the threat by attacking the Italian company in the U.S. market. Rather the attack is made on the home ground of the Italian company. The reasoning behind this action is that the Italian company is funding its entrance into the U.S. market with the cash flow from its domestic operations.

Of course one could argue that the Italian firm is doing the same thing - entering the U.S. market to hit the profits generated by the U.S. company in its domestic market. The strategic element of this action is to be the first to establish worldwide presence so your company is in the position to cross-subsidize any potential threats. In other words, by proactively entering international markets, you are in a position to participate in not only the product and service fulfillment part of the game, but also the cash flow part.

• WHAT ABOUT SMALL COMPANIES?

With all this talk about exploiting global presence and global cash flows, a small company may think, "What about us? We just want to enter Canada and Mexico!" I understand the concern.

At the Illinois SBDC International Trade Center I work all the time with companies just beginning their international expansion. Their concerns are basic: How to find a good foreign representative, how to get the product there, and how to get paid. Those are important questions and the very issues this book addresses.

However, the distinction I make throughout this book is that problems must always be viewed strategically. You must always consider the problem to be an opportunity. For example, instead of questioning how to get paid, find a payment method that includes acceptable risk and maximizes benefits for both seller and buyer.

Is this just restating the problem in a positive perspective? Perhaps, but by reframing the questions, the answers will be quite different. If a company only focuses on how to get paid, rather than how to reduce risk while maximizing buyer benefit, they risk missing a competitive opportunity to establish some very real competitive barriers that will sustain their success.

The issues and ideas presented in this book are suitable for small and midsize firms as well as large companies. Throughout each issue, from selecting a foreign market to the use of technology, my focus will be on the strategy involved in building long-term success, not just solving today's problems. This perspective is helpful to any size company.

• USING THIS TEXT

A text is sequential; going global is not. A text starts with Chapter 1 and moves through each topic, as if each topic should follow the one before it. Going global is a process. Some issues will need attention in the beginning, others at the end. However, most issues will continually need to be addressed. In planning a text on taking a business international, there is a danger that the process will appear to be sequential like the text. It is not.

The Text in a Course: When this text is used in a course for students or executives, the sequence of the chapters will probably have a natural flow that will easily match the topics of the course. Section One establishes the foundations of international business and how to choose foreign markets. Section Two details the initial steps and considerations. Section Three identifies the procedures and documentation required to move products internationally. And Section Four discusses how to sustain initial success.

The Text on Its Own When using this text as a reference to go global or expand globally, it will probably be more appropriate to view the book as a collection of topics. Figure 1.1 presents an overview of the issues of international trade and how they fit into this book's topics. The figure details the six major topics associated with going global:

Figure 1.1 Issues of International Trade

	Your Company
1	Getting Ready to Go Global
1	Why Go Global?
2	When Is a Company Ready to Go Global?
	Going Global
10	International Business across Cultures
12	Legal Considerations
13	Tax and Accounting Issues
16	Financial Risk, Payment Methods, and Trade Finance
22	The Internet and International Trade
	Foreign Markets
4	Which Foreign Markets Will Be Successful for Your Product?
5	Selecting Foreign Markets
6	Sources of International Marketing Data
7	Foreign Market Entry Mode Selection
	Your Customers
8	Finding Your Partners for Indirect Exporting
9	Finding Your Partners for Direct Exporting
	Your Products
3	Harmonized Codes - Classifying Your Export Products
11	International Product Strategies
	Moving Your Products Internationally
14	Logistics
15	Documentation
	Sustaining Success
17	Setting a Pace for Your Export Growth-Assessing Your Export Progress and Success
18	Managing International Channels of Distribution
19	International Advertising, Public Relations, and Trade Missions/Shows
20	Key to Success: A Customer Orientation
21	Sustaining Success through Clear Communication and Managing Change
	Resources
6	Sources of International Marketing Data
22	The Internet and International Trade

1. Company - issues relating to your company (Why go global? How to get global?)
2. Foreign market - identifying which foreign markets will be successful and how to enter them
3. Customers - finding foreign buyers for your products
4. Products - getting your products ready, pricing them, and moving them internationally
5. Sustaining success - how to sustain initial global success
6. Resources - identifying resources to use when going global

If you are reading this book as a reference, you may want to first review these six major topics and then refer to Figure 1.1 to find the particular chapters that may be of interest. For example, a company that is already exporting to a number of countries will find the topic of sustaining success, and its related chapters, to have a number of issues and suggestions directly related to expanding international sales.

The key is to view the book as a collection of issues relating to taking a business international and determine which topics and chapters most apply to the opportunities and challenges facing your company.

• NOTE

1. For more information on Gary Hamel's writing, begin with one of his most important writings, "Strategic Intent," Harvard Business Review (May-June 1989): 63.

CHAPTER 2

When Is a Company Ready to Go Global?

A frequent criticism of U.S. industries is that many companies which have the potential to export don't export. That always comes as a surprise to me because most companies that I know with the potential to export do export. Companies often find it difficult to avoid at least some exporting. Foreign buyers attend U.S. trade shows and read U.S. industry press which generates inquiries and some sales. And U.S. companies near Canada or Mexico see obvious opportunities and export to the neighboring country. Even without proactively seeking export sales, successful domestic companies tend to do some level of exporting.

The more important issue is how many companies with the potential to really succeed in a global market do so. How many have a true global strategy? For the small to midsize company, that number is probably too small. The purpose of this chapter is not to establish the conditions that are necessary for a company to export, but to highlight when a company is ready to go global and achieve the strategic benefits discussed in Chapter 1. Assuming a company has a product or service that at least some international buyers want, then that company is ready to go global when the following four conditions exist:

1. Management commitment
2. In-depth experience with the product or service
3. Adequate cash flow
4. Capacity and capability to produce international products or services

I will also detail conditions that do not necessarily have to be in place before exporting. Surprisingly, many of the perceived barriers to international expansion, such as international expertise or language capabilities, should not stop a company from expanding globally. Instead the company needs to acknowledge such shortcomings and factor them into their international business plan.

• MANAGEMENT COMMITMENT

I remember a sad story from a salesperson of a manufacturer in the medical equipment industry. Though he was hired to be the Latin America sales manager, he was also given a number of U.S. sales accounts. Management made it clear the U.S. accounts needed to be a priority. He soon found his domestic sales responsibilities occupied a great deal of his time and attention. Though he continued prospecting contacts in Latin America, he was never able to visit them. Time after time his foreign trip requests were denied. In fact, after more than two years not a single market visit to Latin America was authorized.

Before his hiring the company sold some equipment in Latin America without a salesperson ever making a trip. The average sale was $200,000, though sales were infrequent. The sales rep understandably felt he needed to visit the market to develop the potential. Management didn't agree, saying, "We sold by fax before, why can't you?" Yet, domestic customers were never expected to sign a deal without a visit from a salesperson.

After numerous attempts to change the attitude of the company's president, the sales rep eventually quit. I felt it was a great loss to the company because their potential in Latin America was strong. But the general style of the management was to micromanage and in the end they weren't really willing to commit to international business.

Sadly, I have heard a number of stories in which employees face greater barriers internally than externally. The reasons vary from management's lack of understanding the company's international potential to poor delegation. Whatever the reason, the outcome always seems the same; the company underachieves its international potential and the employees who recognize the potential grow frustrated. This is why management commitment is a factor that should definitely be in place before exporting.

What Does Management Commitment Establish?

A strong management commitment to international expansion is more than simply approving trips to Latin America. Management commitment ultimately translates to strong resource commitments. It means the budget, personnel, and time commitments will be there to support the activities of the international department. It also means the whole company - from accounting to freight - will adopt its own commitment to the international strategy. Without the stated support of management and company stakeholders toward international goals, individual departments may not make the required investment in time and resources to help the international department succeed. Interdepartmental cooperation will be poor.

By clarifying management commitment to international business, you also establish risk and payback parameters to use in your business plan which will in turn establish budget limits. Without identifying these parameters and incorporating them into the international strategy, you risk developing an international strategy that ultimately will fail because it will contradict management goals and expectations. It may lead to establishing an international business plan that is underfunded - a common cause of international business failure.

Management commitment to international expansion also establishes a framework for hiring new employees to support the company's international efforts. If management has made it clear that international expansion is a priority, the international experience or expertise of an applicant could be an important factor in the hiring process. For example, it might justify hiring a sales manger with international experience even

Figure 2.1 Management Issues and Corresponding International Business Plan Implications

Management Issues	International Business Plan Implication
What payback period is required for market expansion incentives?	Develop a timetable for activities that reflects payback expectations or justifies why they depart from the company's normally accepted payback period.
What payback period is required for capital expenditures? (For example, machinery that may be required to manufacture product to different foreign standards.)	Establish market potential required to justify capital expenditure.
How are resources allocated?	Detail assignment of resources in the plan.
How is overhead allocated?	Full overhead allocation will require a longer payback period.
How will future staff/personnel decisions be affected by the international expansion?	Priority may need to be made in hiring and promotion decisions based on the international expertise of the individual. Positions may also need higher salaries to attract staff with international experience.
How decentralized is the company's decision process?	Feedback and control mechanisms need to be in place.
What is the company attitude toward failure? If there is consensus that a particular market expansion should be made, which ultimately fails, what are the repercussions?	Should one country fail, will further expansion be permitted? The plan should indicate the process for dealing with failed markets.
What is management's attitude toward risk?	Business plan should be in line with management risk attitude.

though his salary package may be higher. It also could mean that particular support staff positions, such as customer service or order fulfillment, require foreign language capability.

The issues associated with management commitment and their impact on the international business plan are summarized in Figure 2.1. The benefits of strong management commitment and support of the international strategy cannot be overstated. It ensures the international team will be engaged in fighting external competitive wars, not internal ones!

• PRODUCT EXPERIENCE - UNDERSTAND YOUR COMPETITIVE ADVANTAGE

A company with a product or service that is successful in the U.S. market will probably have some initial international sales very early in their development. But to really succeed internationally a company needs to develop its international strategy and the business plan to execute that strategy. To do this, the company must have experience in developing, marketing, and servicing its product domestically. You will realize why this is important once you understand the steps to developing and implementing a strategy.

Your international strategy will be based on aspects of the competitive position of your company. For example, how does your company compete? What emphasis is placed on strategies such as low-cost production, product differentiation, or market/customer focus? What are the basic strengths of your company? What really makes the company excel? What is your industry structure and how does your product offering compete in that industry? Which activities are internal and which are contracted out?

The answers to these questions will focus your international strategy. But developing those answers will probably be difficult until you have some domestic experience with your product or service. That is not to say an international strategy cannot be developed for a new business or product that grows out of an existing company or product range. In that case, the competitive nature of the new venture will be clearly understood by management, and a strategy can be developed. But when entrepreneurs are still in the initial stages of forming a company, launching a product, and generally getting their domestic business in order, they should remain focused on establishing their domestic business.

Wait until you really understand what makes your product or service a success before you embark on international planning and expansion. As alluring as foreign travel may be, keep your focus on achieving domestic experience that can form the basis for a successful international strategy and international business plan. You want to begin international planning, but not at the expense of domestic success.

How much domestic experience is enough before going global? Figure 2.2 lists the six most important issues you need to explore before developing your international

An Exception to the Rule

There are some exceptions to the need for domestic business experience prior to developing an international strategy. One is if the company's main strategy is to conduct international business. For example, I know a consultant who specializes in developing concrete manufacturing in foreign countries. He likes to travel and prefers the challenge of dealing with international customers versus U.S.-based clients. His techniques and knowledge are less known outside of the U.S. and thus more valuable. In his case, the very core of his business is to conduct international business. Thus his international business plan was written before the company had any domestic business. It should also be noted that he had a thorough understanding of how to compete prior to starting the business.

Figure 2.2 Six Questions to Answer before Developing an International Strategy

1. Who are the end-users and why do they need your product? Detail the demographic profile of your customers. Identify the role the product plays for each consumer.

    Purpose: To help identify which foreign markets are suitable for your products and what potential product modifications will be required.

2. What is the basis for your company' competitive advantage? What role do each of the following have in the competitive nature of your product: price, features, quality, customer service, brand and product image, technology.

    Purpose: To help identify which foreign markets are suitable and determine the marketing approach.

3. What is the most effective distribution channel for your product? Do you typically sell to agents, distributors, or direct to end-users?

    Purpose: To assist in choosing your foreign market entry method and profile suitable customers.

4. What role does your company play in the value chain? What are the value-added activities? For example, of the following, which are areas of excellence in your company and which of these functions are outsourced?
    - R&D
    - Purchasing
    - Human resource management
    - Technology
    - Manufacturing
    - Marketing and sales
    - Customer service

    Purpose: To clarify what functions will later need to be duplicated overseas, either by your company or your foreign partner.

5. Did you conduct an analysis of your industry and its profitability structure? A common analysis is the Porter Five Forces model, discussed in Michael

(continued)

Figure 2.2 Continued

Porter's book Competitive Strategy. It presents an analytical framework for understanding industries and competitors particularly by describing five competitive forces that determine industry attractiveness:

1. **Bargaining power of buyers** - how much leverage do buyers have?
2. **Threat of substitute products or services**-what are other products or services outside the core industry that can be substituted?
3. **Bargaining power of suppliers** - how much leverage do suppliers have?
4. **Threat of new entrants** - what are the entry barriers?
5. **Rivalry among existing firms** - how competitive is the industry?

Purpose: You will intuitively understand these forces in your own industry but by detailing them and using the framework as a basis for a management discussion about the competitive advantage of your company, you'll better understand issues and decisions related to your international strategy. The importance of each force will also be used when you develop indicators for foreign market success.

For example, in the domestic market your product's primary challenge may come from competing products from other companies within your industry. However, in a given foreign market, where perhaps the product isn't even used, your primary challenge may not be competitors within your industry, but substitute products. The frozen foods industry would be a good illustration. In the U.S., consumers chose between highly competitive firms attempting either price or product differences to compete. Meanwhile, consumers in developing economies won't yet have the need for frozen foods because the use of home freezers is likely to be limited. Plus, the market's infrastructure would probably make distribution expensive. In this case, the primary competition comes more from substitute products (locally grown, fresh produce) more than direct competitors. When choosing indicators for potential foreign markets, a greater priority might be placed on usage of refrigerators rather than just population.

6.   When and how will you know if your international expansion must either be stopped or scaled back? How much investment in time and resources (cash) will be allowed before the company acknowledges it cannot continue its international strategy?

Purpose: International expansion is often exciting. Even minor successes get the attention of staff and company stakeholders (owners, shareholders). But its very nature can also lure a company to keep investing and expanding without the necessary profit returns. The push and excitement to go global may also blind the company, including management, to the reality that the investment may become too great and retrenchment is necessary. Thus a company's international business plan must address indicators that eventually force the issue of addressing further investing in the global expansion. These may be on a market by market basis, or the whole of the international expansion plan.

strategy. When you can answer fully and accurately the six questions in Figure 2.2, your company is ready for international expansion.

• CASH FLOW

I can always tell that a company's chance to succeed internationally will be limited when I mention the need to invest in international strategy and the response is, "I'm not sure we'll have the budget for that." Assuming they have a good product and management commitment this response typically means they have no spare cash flow.

Like your domestic business, cash flow greases the wheels of international business. It may not reach the level of financing needed when the company was created or even the cash it takes to maintain your domestic business. But to be under the illusion that you can accomplish successful international expansion without the appropriate investment will simply lead to mistakes, missed opportunities, and probably failure.

But how much cash flow (investment) is required? Clearly the amount is determined by your international strategy and the opportunities it identifies. For example, for every market a company enters directly, versus indirectly, more cash is required. Equally, the more direct your involvement in those markets, the more cash required. The timing of your plan will also dictate your cash requirements - the more aggressive the expansion plan, the greater cash requirement. Each of these cash requirements (investments) must in turn be balanced against the expected payback (profit) opportunities and their impact on building long-term owner/shareholder value of the company.

The good news is that through good planning and leveraging of resources, an international strategy can often be effective even with budgets smaller than those for your domestic operations. Just be sure your strategy fits your financial resources.

• CAPACITY AND CAPABILITY TO PRODUCE INTERNATIONAL PRODUCTS

Nothing is more frustrating to a sales department than not being able to fill an order due to lack of inventory. Equally frustrating is having a product foreign buyers want, but not being able to sell it to them because the product does not meet local market regulations or standards. International expansion without product capacity or the capability to adapt your product will lead to channel frustration. Channel frustration is a situation in which foreign distributors, buyers, or end-users want a product but cannot buy it due to lack of supply or local usage issues. Channel frustration leads to unhappy customers and eventually could lead to an exporter's retreat from the market.

Capacity and Capability for Manufacturers

Regarding your company's capacity to produce your products, be sure your international strategy adequately addresses these issues:

• What would be the impact if sales increased by 20, 40, or even 100 percent within the next 12 months?

• How would the company respond if one month's production level had to be produced in half the normal time?

- What would be the logistic challenges if manufacturing had to track product produced for international buyers separately from that of domestic buyers throughout the manufacturing process?

Regarding product capability, review your company's ability to:

- Make technical modifications to the product as required
- Respond to R&D challenges that may require redesigning the product or offering different features without significant cost impact
- Document your product's features, maintenance, and repair for the purpose of adequately training your customers, many of whom won't speak English as their first language

Capacity and Capability for Service Companies

If your company is primarily involved in services, rather than products, the concerns are similar to those of manufacturers. First, do you have the necessary staff and support services to accommodate a significant increase in sales? Service companies depend on their employees to offer their services. If domestic customers are already exceeding the limits of the current staff, additional international sales could lead to lost domestic business potentially risking the viability of the company.

Second, just as the uses and standards of products vary internationally, so do services. To be ready to go global, a service company must ensure they have the expertise to adapt and change their service to adjust to international differences in how the service is used. For example, an accounting firm would be poorly prepared to offer international accounting service if they did not first acquire expertise in international accounting standards, financial statements, and tax laws.

• WHAT DOES NOT HAVE TO BE IN PLACE BEFORE GOING GLOBAL

In an ideal world, when a company plans its international expansion, employees will already speak a second language and the budget will be available to travel the ends of the earth searching for new markets. This is unlikely. So the question remains, how important are issues such as international expertise and language before international expansion? Though certainly desirable, this section will clarify that three typical barriers to international expansion - experience, language, and travel - should not be barriers at all.

International Expertise

Many times when I am speaking with executives about requirements for a successful international strategy, they are puzzled that I do not mention international expertise. This is not a requirement because the skills necessary for conducting international business can either be learned or outsourced. I always hope an executive will take on the challenge of learning international business skills rather than outsourcing the work because, after all, that is what this whole book is about. However, if time or resources are tight, a strategy of indirectly entering foreign markets eliminates the need to learn many of the traditional international skills because your indirect partner, such as a broker, will have the skills.

A company's level of international skills and knowledge will determine its international strategy. An international plan that calls for significant overseas market involvement, for example, a foreign sales office or R&D alliance, would probably not be a realistic plan for a company that has yet to develop some internal international experience and institutional learning. Ultimately a company's success will be determined by how well it identifies and leverages its core competencies, which most likely are not uniquely international skills but deeper industry or organization skills such as R&D, logistics, partnering, or technology. These competencies will most impact their global success. Over the long term, their growing international experience will enable continued international expansion, but the lack of international experience should not be a barrier to beginning global expansion.

Which skills would be the most important to develop internally? The profile of the Certified Global Business Professional (CGBP) offered by Nasbite International is an ideal model and available directly at www.nasbite.org (search for CGBP tasks and knowledge document.) It shows the four primary functions (expertise) are global management, global marketing, supply chain management, and trade finance.

Product expertise versus international expertise. The most successful ambassadors of a company as it expands internationally will be the employees who have significant company experience and know the product, the company, and its culture. They take on the challenge of international business because they find it interesting and challenging. I'd rather teach a product manager who has a deep passion for the company's product and capabilities how to use the Paris Metro than send a seasoned European traveler who doesn't share the same inner passion for the product.

The right people will learn the most important international skills very quickly and will find that their international people skills almost come naturally. I have seen this numerous times at international trade shows - the watering holes for the newly initiated. The individuals that will never get it always stand out. They never leave behind their American ways, insist on having everything their way, and generally want the universe to reflect their view of the world. The successful ones - whether it is their first or one of many trips abroad - embrace differences and encourage new experiences. Their overseas customers will sense this from the first meeting. Foreign buyers and partners respect, above all else, an American who genuinely demonstrates an openness to their culture. They also respect someone knowledgeable about the products that can adequately represent the company.

Thus a company should not let its own internal lack of international experience hinder its commitment to an aggressive international strategy. It does mean they will have to be committed to fast, organizational learning to compensate for the lack of skills. Fortunately, there are plenty of resources to assist a company in acquiring that knowledge. At the very least, a company can pursue a strategy of indirect market entry until the management and organizational international skills are attained.

Language

The need for language skills in international business is an ongoing debate, especially within academic circles. Most insist that it is a necessity because it separates the wanna-bes from the pros.

I remember attending a reception during my first European trade show in Germany and meeting a number of potentially important contacts. After a few minutes of polite conversation in English, many would naturally return to speaking German when the conversation would stray. I found it frustrating. Not because I felt uncomfortable, but because I realized important competitive interchanges were occurring and I was missing the chance to really learn more about the German computer market.

A language experience in Italy was more successful. I was traveling with the president of our company to visit the Italian company Olivetti who had become an important customer. Upon arrival in Ivrea, a small town outside Milan where the company is headquartered, we were to telephone our contact at Olivetti. We thought it was going to be a simple task but the only phone was at the reception desk. The owner was more than eager to help us but our frustrated attempts to explain in English what we wanted to do failed and after some time we gave up. I finally decided to try Spanish. Though communication was slow because only a few words were understood by each of us, within a few minutes we were speaking to our contact at Olivetti. I was glad I had some foreign language experience, and it was a perfect opportunity to impress the president of my company on my first trip with him!

No one will argue that the ability to speak a foreign language does not make a difference in international business. The advantages are obvious. But for those who speak English as their first language, the issue appears to be less significant because English is widely considered the language of international business.

The core issue when developing a business plan is to determine what extent language should influence your international strategy. A related issue is your human resource decisions. Should your decision about who travels to the market to represent the company be made on the basis of language ability?

Regarding strategy formulation, language should be a factor but certainly not a determining one. For example, if you already have Spanish capability within your company because of strong business with Mexico, your European expansion should not necessarily be focused on Spain. Rather, market opportunity should dictate your strategy. The strength of the market opportunity will justify expenditures, such as translators, to compensate for language barriers.

Compared to international strategy issues, the impact of language abilities on human resource decisions is trickier. Some people are simply not adept at learning a language, especially if they have never mastered a second language by adulthood. This would imply that language ability is an important factor when choosing which individuals within a company should be sent overseas, especially for long-term assignments.

Yet research on Americans working in foreign markets does not indicate that language alone determines the success or failure of such assignments. Instead, a variety of factors influence a person's ability to cope with foreign assignments. These include relationship skills, family situation, technical skills, personality, and work ethics. Thus even a bilingual employee with perfect language skills may not succeed if other factors are a negative influence.

When forming your international strategy, internal language capabilities should probably not play a significant role in market selection or in assigning responsibilities, but any person traveling abroad, especially for the purpose of international business, should at least learn basic phrases which will not only make travel easier but score important cultural points with your foreign customers or even your boss!

Will You Need to Visit Foreign Markets?

On a daily basis, you probably know more about the country in which you live than any other country. From newspapers and television to conversations in the office, it is easy to remain informed of local economic conditions, government activities, and consumer attitudes. You are also aware of happenings in your particular industry and the priorities and concerns of your customers. Internal meetings in the company and interaction with customers during visits or trade shows provide you with the information to develop an effective strategy that hopefully leads to domestic success. Without this same hands-on knowledge of a foreign market, how can you hope to develop an equally effective international strategy?

Given a choice between traveling and not traveling - which is essentially a question of the company's available time and money - the clear choice is to travel. There is no equally effective method of learning about the real opportunities and challenges of your product in a foreign market than to go there and speak with potential foreign buyers (distributors/agents) and end-users.

However, are market visits a necessity for success? Not always. I know a company that has been quite successful internationally in a variety of markets but never in China. It felt the investment was greater than it wanted to make and expanded instead in regions where it was already successful. So when the company was approached by a U.S. broker (who already had significant sales in China) to represent them in China, they agreed. In less than two months, they sold over $80,000 in products with no travel to China.

Thus, visits may not always be necessary for your international strategy, especially for indirect strategies in which sales are made through U.S. intermediaries (for example, brokers) who in turn export the product on behalf of the manufacturers. However, even in cases of an indirect strategy, travel will only enhance your knowledge and your success. It builds and strengthens your relationship with your distribution network, ensures your international strategy is credible and reliable, and provides an ongoing feedback mechanism for improvements. In this way, when possible and justifiable, travel should be encouraged.

CHAPTER 3

Harmonized Codes - Classifying Your Export Products

This may seem an early point at which to discuss the rather technical issue of classifying your export products by their harmonized codes. Most people think of the harmonized code as a documentation issue and relegate the problem to their freight department or outside freight companies.

In fact, the harmonized code is an important tool for international planning. It will be used to identify potential foreign markets, the activities of competitors, and foreign import tariffs. Before you can proceed with the issues discussed in the following chapters, you'll need to determine the harmonized code of the products you plan to export.

Even if your company is involved with providing services rather than manufacturing products, knowing about harmonized codes will be helpful. Research on international service opportunities is often more limited than information relating to product opportunities. However, much can be learned about providing international services if research is done on products that complement the services. For example, a company involved in software design and development may be interested in research on the exports of computers and related equipment. In this way, knowing how to find the harmonized codes for computers would be important.

This chapter covers the background of harmonized codes, how to use the system to classify products, and where to get assistance. I will also compare the harmonized code system to the Standard Industrial Classification (SIC) system, the North American Industry Classification System (NAICS), and the Standard International Trade Classification (SITC) system.

• WHY HARMONIZED CODES ARE NEEDED

Imagine the potential problems of shipping goods internationally if the exporter considers its product one thing, but the foreign customs authority considers it another - especially if the foreign authority's opinion leads to a significantly higher import duty. For example, suppose a U.S. manufacturer exports bicycle seats made out of leather to Brazil. Let's further assume Brazil wants to give their local producers of leather seats protection from cheap imports by enforcing a 30 percent duty on leather seats of all types. However let's further assume Brazil does not care about protecting its bicycle industry, so a bicycle seat has no duty applied. The U.S. manufacturer considers its product a bicycle seat, and indicates as such on the export documentation. But when the items are imported, the customs agents in Brazil consider them leather seats. The answer is Brazil slaps on a 30 percent duty. Clearly there is a significant impact on the export potential if the product receives a 30 percent duty rather than duty-free status.

Though these sorts of disagreements still occur between countries, they have been greatly reduced through the implementation of the **Harmonized Commodity Description and Coding System** (harmonized system). Internationally it is known as the International System of Numbering or **International Harmonized Codes**. Essentially most trading nations have agreed on a system of describing all products through the use of a ten-digit number. By agreeing on both the format of the numbers, and most importantly, how to classify products, disagreements such as the bicycle seat example should no longer occur.

• HOW THE HARMONIZED SYSTEM WORKS

All products are described by a ten-digit number that is broken down by chapter, heading, subheading, and commodity code. The **chapter** represents the first two digits. The **heading** represents the first four digits. The **subheading** is the first six digits. And finally, the full ten-digit number is called the **commodity code**. These distinctions will become clearer to you as you work with the harmonized system.

The first step to understanding the system is to recognize the breakdown of the ten-digit number by chapter, heading, subheading, and commodity code. Figure 3.1 breaks down the harmonized code.

Sections and Chapters

The harmonized system consists of 22 sections divided into just under 100 chapters that correspond to the International System of Numbering. Each section and chapter is a very general grouping of common products. For example, Section 1 is "Live Animals and Animal Products." As shown in Figure 3.2, Section 1 is then broken into five chapters.

As you can see from the chapter titles in Section 1 shown in Figure 3.2, a live sheep would probably be in Chapter 1, but lamb meat would probably be in Chapter 2. And though you might consider salmon a live animal, you can see that it would belong in Chapter 3, not Chapter 1.

Figure 3.1 Breakdown of Harmonized Codes

Code	Definition	Example
03	Chapter in which a commodity is classified	Fish and crustaceans, molluscs and other aquatic invertebrates
0302	Represents the heading in that chapter	Fish, fresh or chilled, excluding fish fillets and other fish meat of heading 0304
0302.12	Represents the harmonized system code subheading	Pacific salmon, Atlantic salmon and Danube salmon
0302.12.0012	Represents statistical subdivisions	Commodity code for Chinook (king) Salmon

These examples demonstrate some of the principles used when choosing the harmonized code for a product. First, you must look at all chapters that might apply to a product before deciding on a particular chapter. For example, you might misclassify salmon as belonging to Chapter 1, but upon further review, it is clear that salmon belongs in Chapter 3. The chapter - and the descriptions within each chapter - with the best description of a product is the one to be used. Fish and crustaceans better describes salmon than live animals. If you were to look at the introductory notes for Chapter 1 you would find the notice:

This chapter covers all live animals except:
(a) Fish and crustaceans, molluscs and other aquatic invertebrates, of heading 0301, 0306, and 0307;
(b) Cultures of micro-organisms and other products of heading 3002; and
(c) Animals of heading 9508.

Figure 3.2 Breakdown of Harmonized Code by Chapters

Section 1 - Live Animals and Animal Products
Chapters 1-5:
01 Live animals
02 Meat and edible meat offal
03 Fish and crustaceans, molluscs and other aquatic invertebrates
04 Dairy produce; birds' eggs; natural honey; edible products of animal origin, not elsewhere specified or included
05 Products of animal origin, not elsewhere specified or included

The notes help you avoid the mistake of placing salmon in Chapter 1 by pointing out that it really belongs in Chapter 3.

The second point to observe are the dreaded words not elsewhere specified or included. You will sometimes see these words abbreviated as n.e.s.o.i. I say they are dreaded because often you will have a product that never really has a place in the harmonized code except to be lumped into this catch-all category.

Headings

After finding the correct chapter for a product, the next step is to identify the correct heading. The heading incorporates the first four digits of the ten-digit code; the first two denote the chapter. For example, in Chapter 3, there are seven headings:

0301 Live fish
0302 Fish, fresh or chilled, excluding fish fillets and other fish meat of heading 0304
0303 Fish, frozen, excluding fish fillets and other fish meat of heading 0304
0304   Fish fillets and other fish meat (whether or not minced excluding fish steaks), fresh, chilled, or frozen
0305   Fish, dried, salted, or in brine; smoked fish, whether or not cooked before or during the smoking process, flours, meals, and pellets of fish, fit for human consumption
0306   Crustaceans, whether in shell or not, live, fresh, chilled, frozen, dried, salted, or in brine; crustaceans, in shell, cooked by steaming or by boiling in water, whether or not chilled, frozen, dried, salted, or in brine; flours, meals, and pellets of crustaceans, fit for human consumption
0307   Molluscs, whether in shell or not, live, fresh, chilled, frozen, dried, salted, or in brine; aquatic invertebrates other than crustaceans and molluscs, live, fresh, chilled, frozen, dried, salted, or in brine; flours, meals, and pellets of aquatic invertebrates other than crustaceans, fit for human consumption

By looking at the headings, you get a sense of the priorities in a chapter, and thus some general direction as to how to classify a product in that chapter. For example, by reviewing the seven headings in Chapter 3, you can see that classification of products in this chapter can be broken down into two general rules:

1. Fish is classified in headings 0301 through 0305, crustaceans are under heading 0306, and molluscs and other aquatic invertebrates are under heading 0307.
2. The state of the fish (live, whole, in fillets, or dried) will determine which of the five fish headings to use (crustaceans are always in 0306 and molluscs in 0307).

From this simple analysis, you can already get a pretty good idea of where to classify salmon. Salmon will be in headings 0301-0305 depending on its condition. Live salmon will be in 0301, whole nonfrozen salmon in 0302, whole frozen salmon in 0303, salmon fillets in 0304, and dried, salted, or smoked salmon in 0305.

This also illustrates another consideration. There appears to be an emphasis placed on products that are fit for human consumption because this wording is used in three of the seven headings. This raises the question, where would crustaceans not fit for human consumption be classified? There does not seem to be any appropriate heading.

When you came across these types of inconsistencies, it is important to read the section and chapter notes. It is good practice to always read these notes when you begin researching a particular product. For example, the chapter notes for Chapter 3 state:

> *This chapter does not cover:*
> *(a) Marine mammals (heading 0106) or meat thereof (heading 0208 or 0210);*
> *(b) Fish (including livers and roes thereof) or crustaceans, molluscs, or other aquatic invertebrates, dead and unfit or unsuitable for human consumption by reason of either their species or their condition (chapter 5); flours, meals, or pellets of fish or of crustaceans, molluscs, or other aquatic invertebrates, unfit for human consumption (heading 2301); or*
> *(c) Caviar or caviar substitutes prepared from fish eggs (heading 1604).*

From these notes it is clear that any fish, crustaceans, or molluscs that are unfit for human consumption cannot be classified in Chapter 3. Generally, the notes will give you some indication of where to classify these exceptions (known as 'redirection'). For example, the notes indicate that Chapter 5 would be the correct chapter for crustaceans not fit for human consumption. In Chapter 5, you can find heading 0511 Animal products not elsewhere specified or included; dead animals of Chapter 1 or 3, unfit for human consumption. If you neglect to read the notes, you risk incorrect classification.

When you see a reference to an exception in the chapter notes, it is crucial to read the reference heading to make sure you understand the exceptions. For example, the notes in Chapter 1 mention, "This chapter covers all live animals except . . . animals of heading 9508." Heading 9508 covers:

> *Merry-go-rounds, boat-swings, shooting galleries, and other fairground amusements; traveling circuses, traveling menageries, and traveling theatres; parts and accessories thereof.*

What does that have to do with Chapter 1, live animals? Well, if you had horses or lions that were part of a traveling circus, they would be classified in 9508, not Chapter 1. It may seem strange, but for whatever reason, traveling circuses are treated separately from live animals on their own. This demonstrates that the chapter notes are important parts of the harmonized code system.

Subheading

Once you have found the heading, you move on to the subheading. The subheading incorporates the first six digits of the ten-digit code, the first two of which is the chapter and the first four of which is the heading. When writing the subheading, it is the convention to place a period between the heading and the last two digits of the subheading.

Returning to the salmon example, let's assume we are exporting whole, fresh salmon, which would fall under heading 0302. It includes these subheadings:

Salmonidae, excluding livers and roes:
0302.11 *Trout*
0302.12 *Pacific salmon, Atlantic salmon, and Danube salmon*
0302.19 *Other*
  Flat fish, excluding livers and roes:
0302.21 *Halibut and Greenland turbot*
0302.22 *Plaice*
0302.23 *Sole*
0302.20 *Other*
  Tunas, skipjack, or stripe-bellied bonito, excluding livers and roes:
0302.31 *Albacore or longfinned tunas*
0302.32 *Yellowfin tunas*
0302.33 *Skipjack or strip-bellied bonito*
0302.30 *Other*
0302.40 *Herrings, excluding livers and roes*
0302.50 *Cod, excluding livers and roes*
  Other fish, excluding livers and roes:
0302.61 *Sardines, sardinnella, brisling, or sprats*
0302.62 *Haddock*
0302.63 *Atlantic pollock (coalfish)*
0302.64 *Mackerel*
0302.65 *Dogfish and other sharks*
0302.66 *Eels*
0302.69 *Other*
0302.70 *Livers and roes*

As you can see in the subheadings for 0302, once you reach the level of subheading, the descriptions are pretty complete. In our example, the correct subheading would be 0302.12 - Pacific salmon, Atlantic salmon, and Danube salmon. The heading includes all fish, but the subheading details the specific type of fish.

International harmonization of codes. The fairly specific nature of the subheading is not a coincidence. It is at the level of subheading that the codes have been harmonized globally. In other words, no matter what the exporting or importing country, all whole, fresh Atlantic salmon would be under the subheading 0302.12. This is the basic concept behind the international harmonized codes - the first six digits of the ten-digit code are the same for all products in all countries that have adopted the international harmonized code system. These would be member countries of the World Customs Organization (WCO).

The Commodity Code

So what about the final four digits that make up the ten-digit commodity code? This is where the classifications for each country will vary. Each country may choose four digits to round out the commodity code. If the country doesn't care for additional classification to detail products beyond the subheading, they will simply add four zeros. Other countries create many different commodity codes under a particular subheading.

For example, the full ten-digit U.S. commodity codes for exporting fresh, whole salmon are:

0302.12.0003	*Atlantic - farmed*
0302.12.0004	*Atlantic - not farmed*
0302.12.0012	*Chinook (king)*
0302.12.0022	*Chum (dog)*
0302.12.0032	*Pink (humpie)*
0302.12.0042	*Sockeye (red)*
0302.12.0052	*Coho (silver)*
0302.12.0062	*Other*

When exporting fresh, whole salmon, you must be able to further classify by one of seven types. If your salmon is not on the list, then you would export it under the catchall other code of 0302.12.0062.

In contrast, the subheading 0302.21 Halibut and Greenland turbot has only one commodity code, 0302.21.0000. When exporting whole, fresh halibut or Greenland turbot, the U.S. government does not care whether it is Greenland turbot or any other type of turbot.

To complete your harmonized code you will need to determine what commodity codes, if any, are under the particular subheading. Whether there is no commodity code or several codes, remember that only the subheading will be consistent from country to country.

The commodity code - importing versus exporting. As previously discussed, the subheadings in the harmonized system are the same between countries, but the commodity codes will vary. Not only can the commodity codes be different between countries, but they may also vary between codes used for exporting products and those used for importing products. In the U.S., for example, the purpose of the codes is different for importing and exporting. For import purposes, the commodity code is used to determine what import duty, if any, is applied to the product, as well as tracking import statistics. Because no duty is applied to U.S. exports, the primary use of the commodity code for exporting is statistical reporting and export compliance. Most shipments leaving the U.S. are recorded through AES Direct which includes the commodity code, so the U.S. is able to track each product that has been exported and to which country. (See Chapter 15.)

The U.S. has established two sets of commodity codes to distinguish between commodity codes for exporting and importing. Both are based on the harmonized system, so they share identical chapters, headings, and subheadings. The differences are in the full ten-digit commodity codes. This distinction between exporting and importing often leads to confusing terminology, but it is important to understand the differences.

When exporting from the United States, the system of classification is called the **Schedule B**. The system is managed by the U.S. Census Bureau. Schedule B refers to the actual book in which the export classification codes are published. The precise wording of the classification number you will use when exporting is called your Schedule B number. The AES Direct EEI filing has a section labeled Schedule B Description of Commodities where you enter the Schedule B numbers.

When importing into the United States, the system of classification is called the **Harmonized Tariff Schedule of the United State (HTSUS)**. The HTSUS is managed by the Office of Tariff Affairs and Trade Agreements within the U.S. International Trade Commission. The primary purpose of the HTSUS system is to assist in the application of import duties and track import statistics. These import statistics are used to determine the impact of imports on U.S industries.

If you import and export the same product, it will actually have two harmonized codes. Its HTSUS number is used when the product is imported, while the Schedule B number is used when exporting. Under subheading 0301.12 - Pacific salmon, Atlantic salmon and Danube salmon, the following are the HTSUS and Schedule B commodity codes:

HTSUS	Schedule B
0302.12.0003 Atlantic - farmed	*0302.12.0003 Atlantic - farmed*
0302.12.0004 Atlantic - not farmed	*0302.12.0004 Atlantic - not farmed*
0302.12.0013 Chinook (king) - farmed	*0302.12.0012 Chinook (king)*
0302.12.0014 Chinook (king) - not farmed	*0302.12.0022 Chum (dog)*
0302.12.0022 Chum (dog)	*0302.12.0032 Pink (humpie)*
0302.12.0032 Pink (humpie)	*0302.12.0042 Sockeye (red)*
0302.12.0042 Sockeye (red)	*0302.12.0052 Coho (silver)*
0302.12.0053 Coho (silver) - farmed	*0302.12.0062 Other*
0302.12.0054 Coho (silver) - not farmed	
0302.12.0062 Other	

Note that there are two differences between the Schedule B and HTSUS numbers for subheading 0302.12. In Schedule B, it didn't matter if Chinook and Coho were farmed or not farmed. But for the HTSUS code, you must distinguish between farmed or not farmed Chinook and Coho. The U.S. government is indicating that when importing, it is important to maintain such a distinction.

The distinction between a product's Schedule B and HTSUS number is often lost on an exporter. Exporters frequently refer to the Schedule B number as the harmonized code. But in fact, simply saying harmonized code doesn't clarify if it is the Schedule B or HTSUS number. To be precise, you should refer to your export harmonized code as your Schedule B code. In practice, as discussed in Chapter 15, the exporter may use either their Schedule B or HTSUS for their export documentation (except for a selection of Schedule B as detailed in the AES Direct manual).

• LOCATING THE CORRECT HARMONIZED CODE

Having clarified the distinction between a product's Schedule B and HTSUS number, we return to the task of classifying products. It is important to emphasize that properly classifying products can at times be a difficult task. To learn all of the various intricacies involved in choosing the correct code takes practice. Don't assume that you will be able to find the correct code the first time without some outside help. Fortunately, there is plenty of assistance available.

Obtaining Copies of the Schedule B or HTSUS

Whether you are searching for the Schedule B number (when exporting), or the HTSUS number (when importing), the process is the same though you will be using a different source for each number. The Schedule B number is located in the Schedule B book, which is published by the Census Department within the U.S. Department of Commerce. The HTSUS book is published by the Office of Tariff Affairs and Trade Agreements within the U.S. International Trade Commission. The Schedule B and HTSUS numbers are available on the Internet. The advantage of this source is immediate access and no cost. However, I highly recommend purchasing one or both of the books in the printed format. Not only will the books always be handy, but the process of classifying products is much easier if you can flip through a book rather than looking at your computer screen or printouts. The key to correctly classifying products is not only finding what you think is the correct number, but also eliminating what is not correct. This process of going back and forth, reading notes, and cross referencing chapters is much easier when the whole of the book is in front of you.

For the sake of immediate access, however, the Web versions can be found at:

Schedule B: http://www.census.gov/foreign-trade/schedules/b/
HTSUS: usitc.gov (http://usitc.gov/tata/hts/index.htm)

From these sites you can download chapters and other miscellaneous information. If you are attempting to classify your products without the full book, be sure to download enough of the Schedule B or HTSUS to ensure you have all the relevant information.

First Step - Check the Index

To find your harmonized code, you may be tempted to look at all of the chapter titles to find a category that fits your product. However, you can potentially save a lot of time by first looking at the cross-referenced indexes that have been prepared. Both Schedule B and the HTSUS have product descriptions listed alphabetically, rather than by chapter. For example, when looking for the correct Schedule B number for salmon, you can look at the index and see that many of the various types and states of salmon are all presented in one area, which can be used for the sake of comparison. However, it is important to understand the index is only a guide. You should use it to refer to the specific number in either Schedule B or the HTSUS to confirm that it is accurate for your product. The indexes only refer to the correct subheading, not the full ten-digit commodity code. You will need to refer to the subheading in the book to get the full number. Still, the indexes offer a quick method of getting an idea of where your product is classified.

The index of Schedule B is particularly helpful because it includes many of the everyday words for products that may not appear in the body of Schedule B. For example, the word *billfold* does not occur anywhere in the actual Schedule B classifications. However, it is included in the index where it indicates billfolds are likely classified under either 4202.31 or 3202.32. These are subheadings for articles of a kind normally carried in the pocket or in the handbag, which would include billfolds. Even though the word *billfold* does not appear in the classification, the index guides you to the likely proper classification.

The Internet versions of Schedule B and the HTSUS include the ability to search for key words. For example, the Schedule B site offers a screen for searching both Schedule B and the index. There is also a helpful classification search engine offered by U.S. Census. Try it at https://uscensus.prod.3ceonline.com/.

Schedule B versus HTSUS Subheadings

Another trick to finding your correct harmonized code is to remember that you can use either Schedule B or the HTSUS to find the subheading. Because both systems are harmonized to the subheading level, products must have the same subheading in either classification. Thus, if you are having problems finding the right Schedule B number, refer to the HTSUS book, and vice versa. For example, neither the HTSUS nor its index includes the word *billfold*, but it is included in the Schedule B index. Thus you can use each as a tool, as well as their respective websites.

I've also used this trick when calling for assistance from the various government agencies. For example, if I'm having trouble classifying a product for export, I'll call the U.S. Census help line for their advice because they answer Schedule B questions. I'll also call U.S. Customs for their advice. The commodity code may vary between agencies, but the subheading will be the same.

Resolving Difficult Classifications

It may seem odd that you have to call more than one department for assistance in classifying your products, but it is important to remember that classification of products under the harmonized system is kind of like a puzzle; you have to piece all the bits of information together to arrive at a definite answer. Not all classifications are as easy as the salmon or billfold example. There are six guiding rules that will help you determine difficult classifications. Figure 3.3 summarizes these six rules known as the **General Rules of Interpretation**.

Some examples may help to clarify the rules in Figure 3.3.

Figure 3.3 The Six General Rules of Interpretation for Classifying Products under the Harmonized Code System

1.   The titles of sections and chapters are only a guide. Classification should first be based on the wording of the heading (four-digit number).

2.   Incomplete or unfinished articles are to be classified as if they are completed or finished, as long as the item has the essential character of the complete or finished article. Goods made of mixtures or composites should refer to Rule 3.

3.   When a good is classifiable under two or more headings, classification is as follows:
      a. The heading that provides the most specific description shall be preferred to a heading providing a more general description.
      b. If both headings are equally descriptive, the heading of the material component that gives the essential character should be used.
      c. Goods that cannot be classified by rule 3a or 3b should be classified under the heading that occurs last in numerical order among those that equally merit consideration.

4.   Goods that cannot be classified through rules 1-3 should be classified as you would a good that is the most similar that does have a clear Schedule B number.

5.   Packing and containers:
      a. Specifically shaped and/or fitted, suitable for repetitive use, and presented with the goods, classified with the good. Otherwise on their own merit.
      b. Normal packing classified with the goods.

6.   Rules 1-4 are to be used to determine the heading. You would then repeat the process to get the subheading.

Product: the metal base plate of a clothes iron
Issue: classified as a miscellaneous metal part or as an iron for pressing clothes?

Based on rule 2, the metal base of an iron for pressing clothes is classified as an iron (Schedule B number 8516.40.0000). This is because the only real use of this part is for it to be made into a full iron. Thus the metal base is still classified as a clothes iron because it maintains the essential character of an iron.

In contrast, metal screws shipped to a manufacturer of irons are not classified as an iron. Even though the screws will be used in the manufacturing of the iron, and thus become an iron, they clearly do not retain the essential character of an iron. There are many purposes for such screws, which would instead be classified under the heading 7318 Screws, bolts, nuts, coach screws.

Product: a jar of half peanut butter and half jelly (known as 'Goober PB and J).
Issue: classified as peanut butter, jelly, or something else?
Schedule B numbers: peanut butter - 2008.11.1000
  jams, fruit jellies - 2007.10.0000

This example involves rule 3. If the jar contains exactly one-half peanut butter and one-half jelly, you cannot use rule 3a because no one heading is more specific. In other words, peanut butter is no more specific a description than fruit jellies. Nor could you use rule 3b because who is to say a jar of half peanut butter and half jelly is more peanut butter or jelly? Neither the peanut butter nor the jelly gives the contents its essential character. So in the end, the good would be classified as 2008.11.1000, peanut butter, because according to rule 3c, it is the last numerical heading.

Seek Assistance in Classifying Your Goods

These two examples illustrate that classifying goods can be a tricky issue. When your exact product is listed in the index or the body of the Schedule B or HTSUS, your harmonized code is clearly correct. When the description of the commodity code exactly describes a product, I call it a 'good' harmonized code because it unequivocally describes the product. For example, 8418.69.0020 is Drinking water coolers, self-contained, and 9201.20.0000 is Grand pianos. Such good harmonized codes are not only good because they are easy to find and confirm, but also because if you use that harmonized code for marketing research, the results will track well with your product.

But more often than not, you will find your product and the exact Schedule B or HTSUS commodity code are not a perfect fit. Or worse, it fits into Not elsewhere specified or included (n.e.s.o.i) or an Other category. In these cases, your product is grouped into a catchall category that does little to precisely describe it.

When classifying your products, be sure and get outside assistance. Some suggested contacts are:

- *Schedule B*: U.S. Census Bureau of the U.S. Department of Commerce. As the Census Bureau has the responsibility of managing Schedule B, they must assist exporters in locating correct Schedule B numbers. I find they can be extremely helpful, especially if you get them to take the time to really answer all your questions about why they would suggest a particular commodity code. Be sure and do as much research as possible before you call so you have a better idea of what to expect and what questions to ask.
- *HTSUS*: U.S. Customs. Though the HTSUS is managed by the U.S. International Trade Commission, I find U.S. Customs, which has offices throughout the U.S., a better source for HTSUS assistance. Be sure and realize before you call that when you are looking for an HTSUS number, you are looking for the import commodity code. Don't forget the distinction between importing and exporting commodity codes. Also remember that the first six digits of your HTSUS number should match the first six digits of your Schedule B number. When I have a really difficult product to classify, I call both U.S. Census and Customs to double check that the numbers agree.

- *Local international trade resources.* You should also consider contacting your local resources, such as your local Small Business Development Center (SBDC), a state international trade center, or similar export assistance center. Though you should do your own product classification, these centers can offer second opinions and advice.

Binding Rulings and the Customs Rulings Online Search System (CROSS)

What do you do if you still can't find a Schedule B or HTSUS number that seems appropriate? Or what if you feel your commodity code is correct, but your foreign buyer's government is insisting it should be a different commodity code?

One option is to obtain a **binding ruling**. This is a free service of U.S. Customs in which they review your literature and all relevant product information to make a final determination of what the commodity code should be. It will be a determination of your HTSUS number because that is the domain of U.S. Customs. This is a service primarily for importers that have difficult goods to classify. Each time the customs agent questions the HTSUS number can lead to delays. The advantage of a binding ruling is that once a manufacturer receives such a ruling, all future imports reference the binding rulings and the customs agent won't question the validity of the commodity code.

Binding rulings are published and available to view at no cost at http://rulings.cbp.gov/. This database can also be a great help in classifying products because if the specific product already has a binding ruling, your work is essentially done for you! The other day I was researching iPad covers of leather and found it not as easy as I thought it was going to be. Then I figured, surely someone has already requested a binding ruling. I found one quickly which confirmed exactly which HTSUS to use. Another important aspect of the CROSS database is that each ruling includes the specific justification of why the HTSUS was selected, and often why another one was not selected. It can be a very helpful learning tool to read binding rulings.

• HARMONIZED CODE VERSUS SIC AND NAICS

We have looked at the harmonized code in some detail because it is generally the most important product code number used by U.S. companies involved in international trade. But there are some other important product and industry classifications that you may encounter in your international documentation or research requirements. The most important are the Standard Industrial Classification (SIC) and the North American Industry Classification System (NAICS).

Standard Industrial Classification (SIC). The SIC system has been around for some time. In fact, it has now been replaced by the NAICS, but many people are still accustomed to the SIC code. The **Standard Industrial Classification** for a company is a four-digit number used to describe the type of activity in which they are engaged. Where the harmonized code describes products, the SIC code describes what a company does. For example, 7378 is the SIC code for companies "primarily engaged in the maintenance and repair of computers and computer peripheral equipment." Such a company may not have a harmonized code because they don't produce anything, whereas 0273 is the SIC code for companies "primarily engaged in the production of finfish and shellfish." In other words, 0273 would include companies that grow fish. If the company raises salmon, regardless of the type of salmon, their SIC code remains 0273. Thus, a company with one SIC code may have many harmonized codes.

North American Industry Classification System (NAICS). A new system has been adopted that replaces the SIC system. It was developed jointly by the United States, Canada, and Mexico. One benefit of the **NAICS** system (pronounced "nakes") is that it identifies many new industries not included in the SIC system. The code also has been expanded from a four-digit system to a six-digit system. This offers a larger number of sectors and allows more flexibility in designating subsectors.

An example of this increased flexibility would be the classification of casino. The SIC system did not have a code for casinos. Instead such establishments were classified under the catchall SIC code 7011 - Hotels and motels. The NAICS not only has a separate category for casinos (713210), it also has one for casino hotels (721120). This increase in subsectors greatly improves the usability of the data tracked by NAICS versus that of the old SIC system.

A final benefit is the comparability of data between the U.S., Canada, and Mexico because all three countries share the NAICS. Though not all codes are common to all three countries, the NAICS offers much greater comparability than the SIC system.

For further information on the NAICS, consult the census site which includes tables showing both the NIACS codes and the correspondence between NAICS and SIC: www.census.gov/naics.

CHAPTER 4

Which Foreign Markets Will Be Successful for Your Product?

Determining the potential of your product in a market is a bit like determining IQ. Is it determined by heredity or environment? Heredity relates to one's inherited ability, a non-controllable variable. Environment relates to one's childhood living conditions, a controllable variable. The relevance of each, heredity or environment, has been an ongoing debate. Though no consensus has been reached, one view is that heredity establishes a certain minimum and maximum range, and environment determines where, within that range, the IQ is developed.

In much the same way, your product inherits certain characteristics that you probably can't change. For example, if your product is X-ray film, an inherited characteristic is that users of your product need to have X-ray equipment. Thus, in a country with limited X-ray equipment usage, your market potential is limited by the population of X-ray machines that fit your type of film. Using the same marketing expenditure in a country with more X-ray equipment usage would no doubt yield better results.

The key to a successful international strategy is prioritizing markets based on how they fit with your products and company strengths and then properly controlling the variables (environment) such as marketing and customer service to maximize your success. You find the markets with the greatest maximum potential and then set forth a plan to reach that potential. And just like developing one's IQ, reaching your product's potential may take time and investment. The key is prioritizing opportunities against your resource constraints, time frame, and corporate goals.

This chapter will discuss how to choose and prioritize foreign markets as part of your international strategy. Part of developing that strategy will be a decision to take either a reactive or proactive strategy in your market selection. A reactive market selection strategy places an emphasis on choosing markets that have already demonstrated success for your type of product. This approach typically uses past sales or competitive sales as indicators for potential markets. A proactive strategy places a greater emphasis on your own market analysis independent of past sales, or those made by your competitors. In either case, the goal is to develop market-related indicators that are used to predict foreign market success. This chapter also includes a detailed discussion of trade barriers such as tariffs and nontariff barriers and their potential impact on market selection.

Once markets have been selected, they should be ranked and grouped to give an overall direction to your international business plan. This process will be discussed in Chapter 5.

• DEVELOPING INDICATORS BASED ON PREVIOUS EXPERIENCE

You may already have a good idea which foreign markets will be suitable for your products, especially if your products have been successful domestically. Success tends to attract buyers from overseas markets and generates sales even without a formal international sales strategy. Actions of your competitors are also good indications of which markets should be favorable.

Thus, even before a company formalizes its international strategy, it will receive numerous indicators of potential success. Identifying indicators based on previous experience is the first step toward determining which foreign markets should be successful for your company. This involves reviewing past leads, sales, and competitive behavior, attending trade shows, and talking with experts and customers.

Past Leads

Leads you have received from overseas markets during the course of your domestic marketing are an excellent indication of foreign market potential, especially if the leads indicate trends. One or two leads may simply be aggressive foreign distributors looking for a new line to represent without regard to the real potential of your product in their market. They are sometimes referred to as line collectors because they just gather as many brands as possible to enhance their company's image. They could also be competitors seeking further information. However, if you can notice a trend, for example, the majority of the leads coming from a particular region or from non-adjoining countries that share similar characteristics, then this information can be extremely useful when choosing foreign markets for your international plan.

Past Sales

An even better indicator of market potential is past sales you have received from foreign markets. Actually making a sale to a country virtually establishes that your product can compete with whatever is offered in that country. Presumably the foreign buyers have done their own research and, notwithstanding the freight costs, have determined your product is better than others. You should also look at your past sales for any trends that may indicate a particular region or market profile.

Competitor Behavior

One of the best indicators for determining the foreign market potential of your products is to look at what your competitors are doing. Assuming they have done their own homework before choosing their markets, you may be able to save time and money by following them. Of course this comes with certain risks which will be discussed later.

How do you determine where your competitors are selling? See Chapter 6, Determining Your Competitive Position.

Domestic Trade Shows

For many industries, the U.S. trade show for that industry may be the single most important international gathering. Even if participation by foreign buyers is not particularly significant, virtually all U.S. trade shows have some foreign visitors.

Trade shows can be used in a number of ways to investigate your international sales potential:

- *Participant profile.* During the show, notice if certain countries tend to have more visitors than others. In particular look for regional trends such as Europe versus Asia (though the U.S. location of the show could easily impact regional participation).
- *Talk to participants.* When a foreign visitor comes to your booth, don't simply answer their questions. Ask them about their market, the competition, and local conditions. Use it as an opportunity to learn as much as possible, especially if the visitor already imports from the U.S.
- *U.S. Commercial Service International Buyer Program.* Many U.S. trade shows are designated as International Buyer Program shows. This means the U.S. Commercial Service pre-arranges meetings during the trade show between foreign visitors and potential U.S. exporters – at no cost to the U.S. company! More details at www.trade.gov/cs/.

Discussions with Industry Experts

International business tends to be a topic people like to discuss. As you develop contacts within your industry, such as with the press or companies with related but not competing products, never miss the opportunity to learn what they think of the international potential for your products. They may have spent considerable time abroad and can offer firsthand experiences from which you'll gain knowledge without the time or expense.

Once you find a really good expert, develop the connection as best you can. He or she could become a mentor. In other cases, the exchange goes both ways. However you characterize it, don't take it for granted. Such contacts can often provide inside information on markets and customers that could otherwise only be learned by months of work in that market. For example, when I first started selling in Europe, I searched for the assistance of the international sales director of a related computer company that everyone seemed to respect. It was easy to develop an ongoing alliance because we were always at the same trade shows. At first I basically sought his advice about markets and customers, but as I became more successful and experienced, our sharing was much more equal. More than once the information we shared kept both companies out of trouble. It was definitely one of the keys to my success. Often the international community within an industry is surprisingly small, and a few well-placed contacts can cover a lot of ground!

Input from Customers

Finally, remember to ask your customers, both domestic and foreign, for their input. They will have attended trade shows, read trade press, and be able to provide some input that you may have missed. Foreign customers can be particularly helpful because their professional contacts are typically international and potentially very helpful. For example, even if your distributor in England doesn't have any sales on the continent, he will have met other European distributors during distributor meetings and trade shows. He may also be able to provide some industry-specific details on trade regulations or market conditions.

The first step in developing your list of foreign markets is to gather and analyze all the information you may already have within your company. Your goal, beyond simply noting that a particular country may be a good market, is to develop indicators of success. These indicators will be factors that are shared by all the countries/markets that you identified as potential markets. They will probably be obvious indicators of success and ones you already use domestically. But factors for market success overseas are not always the same as those for the U.S. You'll use this list of indicators as you research new markets.

• PROACTIVE VERSUS REACTIVE MARKET SELECTION

Reviewing all the known indicators for foreign market selection (past sales, leads, competitor actions, and talking with experts and customers) is an important step toward defining your list of potential foreign markets, and you could stop at this point. The list you have identified will no doubt include some of the very markets that, no matter how much more research you continue to do, will remain top choices.

However, without further research, the list only represents countries/markets that you have found from a reactive selection basis. There may be other markets that have not yet ordered products from you or that your competitor has missed that represent tremendous potential. You will only find these markets through a more proactive selection process.

Understandably, a reactive market selection process is very appealing. It offers a low cost, and a fast low-risk approach to selecting your foreign markets. Because the list includes markets in which you have already sold product, or where your competitor has been successful, you have some strong indications that your product or service will be successful. You have indications that your products are needed because your competitor would not continue in the market if the sales were not there. You also can learn from your competitors by analyzing their entry methods, marketing campaigns, and pricing policies.

But is it the right list for you? Maybe not, and your international business plan will be incomplete if you stop here. Relying on a reactive selection process is attractive, but also has significant disadvantages.

Pitfalls of a Reactive Market Selection Strategy

Assuming your product has the potential to be a leader in a foreign market, one of the greatest disadvantages of following your competitors into a market is you lose first mover advantage - benefits you gain by being the first foreign supplier in a market. Being first means you establish the rules and the framework of the foreign-supplied products in that industry. One only has to look at the Coke versus Pepsi war to see the advantage each has in markets where one of the two gained the foothold first. Success by your competitor means the market could be successful for your product, but is not a guarantee of that success.

Your competitors and initial overseas customers also may mislead you. The most important markets may be elsewhere. This is particularly true if your competitive analysis only included U.S. competitors. Foreign competitors may have long known of other markets of significant importance in your industry. Their markets may still be missing from your selection process. The markets they have selected actually may not be that good for you. Perhaps your competitors have found their choices were not very profitable but continue to pursue them rather than lose their investment.

Finally, product selection and product life cycle have an important impact on foreign market selection. If your company manufactures a range of products, your market selection process will have to be duplicated for each of your products. If you have many different products, you will want to screen them for the best prospects. You may then decide to delay foreign sales of the less competitive products in favor of products that will be more competitive.

Global product life cycles also will impact your product and market choice. Some foreign markets will be in the initial usage stage of your product's life cycle with plenty of growth potential (introduction stage), while other markets may be reaching saturation. Depending on how your company competes (cost leadership, differentiation, or focus), your product can be better placed based on each market's position in the product's life cycle.

Your foreign market selection has really just begun if you have only researched known indicators. The next step is to identify indicators that will be used for a global assessment of your product's potential and then integrate all your findings into a model to rank markets based on the results. A global assessment, independent of previous sales or competitor actions, avoids missing markets that might otherwise be overlooked. Integrating the results with your known indicators will eventually allow you to rank your results, and avoid further research on markets that have poor potential. This model will be discussed in Chapter 5.

Figure 4.1 Questions to Help Identify Global Indicators for Foreign Market Success

Basic Issues:	Examples:
Who uses the product (the end-user)? Who supplies the product to the end-user?	Companies, institutions, individuals Retail stores, catalogs, direct from the distributor
Why is the product used? What are the benefits?	Health benefits, manufacturing needs Cost savings, access to technology
Would the use of the product vary by the market?	Sunglasses can be beachwear in resorts, ski accessory in winter areas, fashion in urban areas.
What triggers the purchase of the product? Do other events or conditions need to be present?	Products linked to technology may or may not be used in that country.
Will cultural differences limit sales?	Cosmetics may not do well in markets where society does not place a value on the benefits of cosmetics.
What infrastructure is needed for this product to succeed?	Telephone, Internet, cheap national distribution, human resource requirements
Local Market Characteristics: Is the market growing, decreasing, or stagnant?	You may have a product that only tends to do well in a maturing market, where you primarily compete based on low cost. This would mean searching only for mature markets.
What is the U.S. industry structure? (Very competitive? Strong substitute products? Entry barriers?)	Depending on the basis for how your products compete, you may seek or avoid competitive foreign markets.
How dependent is product usage on environmental conditions (climate, geography)?	The U.S. has a wide variety of climates and geographic features not available in other countries. This could dramatically impact the success of your products or services.

- ## GLOBAL ASSESSMENT - A PROACTIVE MARKET SELECTION STRATEGY

Given that a reactive selection process has potential disadvantages, most companies will consider a more proactive selection process. This involves blending information already known to the company (past sales and competitive behavior) with marketing research data from indicators that can be applied on a global basis. This section will discuss how to identify indicators you can use to scan all the world markets for suitable targets for your international expansion plan.

Global Indicators

Which indicators should you use for a global assessment? Population? Gross domestic product (GDP)? Per capita income? The answer clearly depends on your product, services, and industry. To identify indicators suitable for your company, hold internal and external discussions to focus on factors that will help predict which foreign markets would be the most successful for your products. Questions you should address are summarized in Figure 4.1. Identifying specific indicators that will accurately predict the potential of your product in a foreign market is more important than finding indicators that simply indicate relative size to the U.S. domestic market but actually have no bearing on the potential for your product.

For example, assume a company that manufactures high-end furniture for commercial use in leisure applications has a primary base of customers that includes hotels and resorts. The driving force behind their sales potential will be new construction and remodeling opportunities. The sales potential may have nothing to do with the actual number of people living in the market. Instead, the annual level of business and vacation visitors will be more important. Thus, for the global analysis, indicators such as population and per capita income will be less helpful than number of hotels and resorts and new office and resort construction. In this example, a country such as Fiji, with a population less than .3 percent of the U.S. population, may represent (on a proportional basis) a better sales potential than .3 percent of the U.S. market, because the density of hotels and resorts in Fiji is much greater than the U.S.

There are five types of indicators suitable for a global assessment of your product's international potential:

1. *Demographic*. These are indicators that directly describe characteristics of the individual consumer. Their relevance depends on the role the consumer plays in the purchase decision of your products or service. Demographic indicators would be very important to a manufacturer of consumer goods such as Apple and General Foods, but less important to other manufacturers, especially if their products are typically purchased by a few customers, such as Boeing.

2. *Macroeconomic*. No matter how strong a market appears to be by the demographic indicators, the overall economic condition of the market will no doubt determine the potential for success. Though their relative importance will de-

pend on your particular product and industry, macroeconomic indicators are used to identify issues such as inflation, potential for economic recession, economic growth potential, and currency stability. They are especially useful to separate emerging markets from mature markets.

3. *Government policies*. Many policies of foreign governments directly impact the potential for your international success. Obvious examples would be import controls, tariffs, and regulations concerning the use of your products. Other policies such as currency exchange controls or labeling standards may be less obvious, yet still hamper your efforts in the market. Many countries impose a number of barriers restricting the potential for the success of foreign imports of products and services. These are discussed later in this chapter. Government policy indicators are used to help identify market where these challenges are significant.

4. *Environmental*. The U.S. market enjoys a wide range of climates and terrain, as well as an advanced infrastructure in such areas as telecommunications and transportation. Clearly this is not the case in all countries and such differences could dramatically impact the potential for your products. Environmental indicators are used to identify differences such as weather, geography, and infrastructure that will impact your potential sales.

5. *Import/Export Data*. Chapter 3 discussed the harmonized code classification system. Countries track their imports and exports by harmonized code. These statistics are available via the web at no cost. This trade data can be a critical resource for selecting foreign markets. Though the data is historical and thus based on what has happened in the past, it can confirm existing demand for a product and establish trends, such as growing demand. Chapter 6 discusses use of trade data in more detail, including complementary product substitution which is useful when the harmonized code is not particularly description of your product.

6. *Industry-specific*. The structure of your industry may be entirely different in the U.S. than in other countries. For example, in the U.S., usage of your product may be widespread with many competitors in the market. In other countries, your type of product may not be used at all and the market is characterized by the use of substitute products. There also may be different risks and threats against your industry in specific countries that don't exist in others. Industry-specific indicators are used to identify these differences that only occur at the industry level.

Once you have brainstormed the use of your product and the characteristics of your industry, develop a list of global market potential indicators. A summary of the typical indicators in the five groups is shown in Figure 4.2. Don't worry at this point about the

Figure 4.2 Indicators Suitable for Global Assessment

Demographic Indicators
Population including growth and density
Gender makeup
Literacy rate
Education levels
Per capita income and distribution

Macroeconomic Indicators
GDP and GDP growth rates
Inflation rate

Government Policies
Import tariffs (especially if there are strong local competitors)
Currency exchange controls
Nontariff trade barriers (technical standards, labeling requirements, documentation)
Intellectual property rights protection (patents, copyrights, trademarks)
Political risk (stability)
Investment policies and protections
Labor practices and restrictions
Taxation

Environmental Indicators
Climate
Geography
Infrastructure (transportation, telecommunications)

Trade Statistics
Imports by country of U.S. goods
Imports by country of goods from competing countries

Industry Indicators
Entry barriers (obstacles such as local branding, access to distribution, expected retaliation)
Rivalry (number of competitors, intensity of the competition, market shares)
Supplier power (concentration of suppliers, switching costs)
Buyer power (maturity of distribution channel, access to consumer)
Substitute products (use of products not directly competing but used as a substitute)
Growth of the industry
Stability of the industry
Risks in the industry

difficulty in finding the data for a particular indicator. It would be fortunate if all of the indicators could easily be found by secondary research means using little time and money, but Chapter 6 will discuss in greater detail how to find the data for each indicator.

• TRADE BARRIERS

Trade barriers are an important consideration for international companies as they expand globally. Their impact may be relatively minor, such as increased documentation or routine testing to demonstrate compliance with standards. The impact can also be dramatic - for instance, when import tariffs make importation prohibitive.

Fortunately, the trend globally is away from such restrictions. The U.S., with its generally open borders, has joined with other countries to sign massive trade agreements reducing trade barriers. The most significant multilateral agreement was the Uruguay Round of the GATT (General Agreement on Tariffs and Trade), which also established the World Trade Organization (WTO). Regional trade agreements have also been signed to remove trade restrictions among members. The North American Free Trade Agreement (NAFTA) and the European Union are two recent examples.

Despite global reductions, import barriers can still impact a company's international business planning. Though tariff barriers continue to be reduced, nontariff barriers may remain a challenge in particular markets, especially nontariff barriers that are difficult to quantify, such as poor access to distribution or labeling requirements.

This section is intended to highlight the issue of trade barriers as they impact a company's global expansion and its section of foreign markets. This subject is highly complex. Interested readers seeking further details are encouraged to seek more information in international economic and political books.

Tariff Barriers

One of the most common ways governments have traditionally protected local industries and their locally produced products was to impose a tax or import duty on either all imported goods or those within industries needing protection. Taxes applied on imported goods are known as **tariffs**. In some cases, countries have also imposed tariffs on exported goods. But generally, when the word tariff is used, it implies import duties.

Tariffs are often calculated as a percentage of the value of the product, known as an **ad valorem duty**. For example, foil with a harmonized code heading 7607.19 from the U.S. exported to Chile will be assessed an 11 percent import duty. This is applied against the CIF value (Cost + Insurance + Freight), not simply the selling price. The tariff will still be applied on the CIF value, even if the importer paid the international freight. Chapter 11 includes an example of import duty calculation.

When the duty is assessed on a per unit basis - independent of the value of the good - it is a **specific duty**. This is often the case for alcohol products in which the duty is by the liter or gallon regardless of the invoice value.

When comparing import duties between countries, be careful that you distinguish between import duties and local taxes that are applied to all goods, domestic and foreign.

For example, people often mislabel value added tax (VAT) as an import tax. Normally, it is not. Rather it is a consumption tax applied to products purchased by the consumer, regardless of origin. This is similar to the Imposto Sobre Productos Industrializados (IPI) tax in Brazil. It is applied to industrial products regardless of the country of origin.

Nontariff Barriers

Tariff barriers get all the attention because they are easy to measure and track. For example, when NAFTA's goal was to reduce virtually all import tariffs to zero, the concept was easy to understand and quantify.

Nontariff trade barriers are much more complicated. Essentially, **nontariff barriers** are all discriminatory barriers, other than import duties, facing imported products and their foreign producers. Some straightforward examples of nontariff barriers are quotas - government imposed limits on the import quantity of specific products - and standards - product specifications or testing requirements such as the European Union CE Mark or U.S. Food and Drug approvals.

Nontariff barriers also include much less obvious obstacles that are established by foreign governments. For example, a U.S. trade case brought to the World Trade Organization (WTO) on behalf of Kodak alleged that the Japanese government protected Fuji Photo Film Company by blocking foreign competition. Many of the practices cited in the case would be considered nontariff barriers because they did not specifically involve import duties. Kodak indicated the Japanese government would not allow certain price discounting promotions, such as two-for-one offers. (Since the filing of the case, the Japanese government lessened its enforcement.) The case was rejected by the WTO, a loss to both the U.S. and Kodak. However the U.S. believes statements made by the Japanese government in its legal briefs can be used as binding trade obligations.[1]

Can such nontariff barriers result in a complete ban of your products from a market? Just ask Evan Segal, president of Dormont Manufacturing Co. His company manufacturers gas hoses for use in connecting gas supply to appliances. After his hoses had already been installed in the EuroDisney theme park outside Paris, French inspectors stated they would have to be replaced by French-approved equipment. This came after Segal had been selling his products throughout Europe. He had even received approval from the British Standards Institute, but the approval was withdrawn after a complaint was filed with the European Commission by a German competitor. Segal believed his hoses would never meet the required standards. Committees that included his competitors apparently created the design requirements leading to Segal's opinion that his competitors basically wrote the rules to describe their own products. There was no real rhyme or reason to the regulations, which included requirements for the color of the plastic components. These regulations were in contrast to the U.S., where safety and performance issues form the basis for regulations.[2]

Given that nontariff trade barriers have the potential to keep your products out of a market, you can see why reducing them has become increasingly important to the U.S. Nevertheless, many nontariff barriers exist in various countries throughout the world. The most significant types are:

- Import licenses
- Product labeling
- Government procurement barriers
- Government standards and testing
- Quotas
- Service and investment barriers

Import licenses. Foreign governments may require that the importer receive an **import license** in order to import the product. Import license requirements are commonly associated with exchange controls. Exporters should be aware of any import license requirements because if the importer fails to get one, it may not be able to pay the exporter.

Government standards and testing. As seen from the Dormont Manufacturing case, industry standards adopted by governments are especially insidious because the standards themselves may have been fashioned by local competitors. Rather than simply designing standards to protect consumer health and safety, their hidden agenda may be to keep foreign products out of the market.

Regardless of the motive, government imposed standards for both products and services are reality in all countries (including the U.S.). One of the best examples of a government standard is the **CE Mark** of the European Union (EU). This standard applies to many industrial and consumer goods offered for sale within the EU. The certification process may require independent testing of the products by a laboratory approved by the EU. Fortunately, for many products, the manufacturer can self-certify their products to be in compliance with the CE Mark directive. However, understanding the various directives (technical specifications) of the CE Mark and internally testing for compliance can be difficult. Manufacturers often are required to hire outside consultants familiar with the requirements of the CE Mark. All of this leads to increased costs and delays to market entry for the manufacturer. The same complaints have been leveled at the U.S. with its myriad product standards, which often vary from state to state. The CE Mark and other government standards can be a serious and expensive barrier facing U.S. companies.

Testing differences can also be a barrier. Brazil has not recognized the USDA poultry meat inspection system, so imports of fresh U.S. products are prohibited. In Malaysia, all imported beef and poultry products must originate from facilities which have been approved by Malaysian authorities as halal, or acceptable for consumption by Muslims.

Product labeling. Labeling is another important nontariff barrier. A good example comes from our neighbor to the north, Canada. Canada requires most products to have bilingual labeling (English and French). Labels for products to be sold in the province of Quebec must give the French language equal prominence with any other language on the label. Given the costs of changing printing plates or manufacturing dies, such requirements can be costly for the unprepared exporter.

Quotas. Government imposed limits on the import quantity of a particular product are known as **quotas**. An **absolute quota** restricts additional product from entering the country once the quota has been filled. A **tariff-rate quota** allows the product to enter the country after the quota has been reached at an increased tariff rate.

In some cases, countries will establish quotas that discriminate based on the country of origin of the goods. These are called discriminatory quotas. For example, the U.S. imposes quotas of sugar on various nations. Each specific country is allowed a specified level of sugar exports to the U.S.

Government procurement barriers. Though the Uruguay Round has helped reduce government procurement barriers, many still remain, especially in state-controlled sectors. Barriers to foreign competition for government procurement tenders can take a variety of forms from outright exclusion of non-national firms to requirements that a specified percentage of the products used in a procurement project or tender must be locally produced. Often the restrictions are quite complicated. For example, in certain sectors Brazil allows a price differential of up to 12 percent of the winning bid over rival bids as long as the higher bid qualifies for preferential treatment. But qualifying for the preferential treatment relies on results of a price and technology model utilizing indicators such as Brazilian-owned companies, Brazilian technology or products, and a minimum local value-added content.

Another growing barrier is the ISO 9000 standard. As distinct from the CE Mark, which is product related, ISO 9000 is a group of nonindustry-specific quality assurance standards to be used by companies that supply goods and services internationally. It was developed by the International Organization of Standardization. Increasingly, many companies are finding that they must comply with the relevant ISO standards to qualify for international business opportunities, especially within the European Union.

Services and investment barriers. Import barriers are often associated with duties and quotas applied to products imported into a country, but governments also discriminate against the import of services or investments. The barriers can be absolute, disallowing the service or investment altogether. For example, foreign firms are not allowed to provide legal services in India. In other cases, the barriers can be so restrictive as to effectively eliminate the opportunity to offer the service or invest in the country. Restrictions may be specific to services, to investing, or to both.

Service barriers, typically utilized to protect local industries, take a variety of forms. Examples include arbitrary application of regulations, administrative nontransparency, prequalification of foreign firms, and standards requirements.

Sometimes the service barriers affect outsourcing options. For example, it is common in the airline industry for one airline to utilize the on-airport services of another (even competing) airline. Yet in Greece, the local carrier, Olympic, has a monopoly in the provision of ground services to other airlines. Foreign airlines serving Greece must provide their own ground handling services or obtain them from Olympic, but not from each other.

In some cases, service restrictions will impact marketing efforts. In Brazil, foreign-produced advertising materials are restricted. Two-thirds of any film footage must be produced in Brazil, and 100 percent of any sound tracks must be produced in Brazil.

In some countries, the service can only be offered if it is deemed important for the good of the nation. For example, Brazil may refuse entry of consultants or service providers if their service does not provide new technology, increase productivity in Brazil, or attract new investment.

Investment restrictions impact service providers, manufacturers, and investors. Restrictions impact the types and characteristics of allowable investments for particular countries and may involve limitations on foreign ownership, the number of foreign boards of directors, or capital participation.

• FINDING COUNTRY DATA ON TRADE BARRIERS

Given the potential impact of import barriers on your international planning, adequate research must be done for all markets prior to entry. This is particularly important for markets with traditionally restrictive trade regulations such as Brazil or China. Preplanning will hopefully reduce the cost impact of such barriers.

For both tariff and nontariff barriers, the best place to begin is with the Country Commercial Guide (CCG) reports from www.export.gov, discussed in Chapter 6. For example, the section titled "Trade Regulations & Standards" generally includes the following information for each country:

• Tariff barriers	• Government procurement barriers
• Services barriers	• Investment barriers
• Barriers to trade	• Customs valuation
• Typical import steps	• Tariffs and import taxes
• Internal taxes	• Other imports
• Imports subject to special control	• Import of used material
• Labeling and marking requirements	• Prohibited imports
• Standards	• Free trade zones/warehouses

As this list demonstrates, the CCG reports not only provide information on import barriers, but also local taxes, import procedures, and logistics.

Another useful resource for trade barrier information is the Export Reference Library offered by the Bureau of National Affairs (commonly known as BNA). This web- and print-based resource includes their Country Prolife reports, which includes detailed information on regulations, laws, and other issues impacting trade with over 200 foreign markets. The International Trade Reporter is a weekly report containing current analysis and updates on trade issues across the globe. More information on the BNA resources may be found at www.bna.com.

How do you find what the duty rate will be on your products going into a country? Getting up to date import duties for a particular country used to require quite a bit of time as most of the duty tables were only available in print, and often only in the local language. For U.S. companies, the method in the past was to call the Country Desk Officer within at 1-800-USA-TRADE (872-8723), which still is available. However, many countries and regional economic unions now publish their duty rates online and at no cost. As an example, see the European Union online customs tariff database at ec.europa.eu or the Asia-Pacific Economic Cooperation (APEC which includes over 20 countries including China, Australia, Japan, and Korea.) import duty database at http://www.apec.org (search for 'tariffs and ROOs'. The export.gov website also includes direct link to a number of country-specific online customs tariff resources.

There are also for-fee resources which can be very helpful for larger companies needing a single source for import duty rates across all harmonized codes countries of origin. An example is the Customs Info Database (www.customsinfo.com) which not only offers duty rate calculators, but other trade related resources such as product classification assistance.

If you are not able to find a suitable resource and need assistance in determining the duty rate of your product into a foreign market, or non-tariff barrier information, contact your local export assistance partners. Assisting with this type of information is a routine service offered by most trade centers or export assistance centers.

• NOTES

1. Bob Davis and Laura Johannes, "Kodak and U.S. Government Team Up for New Drive on Japan's Film Market," The Wall Street Journal (February 4, 1998): A4.

2. Source of Case: Timothy Aeppel, "Europe's Unity Undoes a U.S. Exporter," The Wall Street Journal (April 1, 1998): B1.

CHAPTER 5

Selecting Foreign Markets

With so many prospective countries, which do you choose for your international expansion plan? Do you invest in countries that have shown success in the past before you enter a new country? Do you enter the top prospects independent of their location or should a regional focus be established? If an entire country such as China seems too large for complete market entry do you focus on cities or regions within a country which may be more manageable while still offering a greater opportunity than many other countries?

Does your company even make these decisions? Many do not. Instead their market expansion decisions are made independent of a global analysis. Previous experiences and industry norms create a prejudiced view that dictates market selection. That could be a big mistake. Unless you try to quantify and rank the global opportunity for your company, you risk expensive mistakes like missing an important market or pursuing markets that ultimately waste your resources.

As discussed in Chapter 4, market selection should be based on indicators you have developed from both a reactive study (past sales, competitive activities, etc.) and a more proactive, global assessment method. By combining both sets of indicators, you will develop a comprehensive list of market indicators that eliminates blind spots.

Once you have found the data for each indicator, the data needs to be analyzed to assist with decisions such as which markets are selected for entry and in which order. Given the variety and scope of all the data, you may find it helpful to develop an analytical tool, such as a spreadsheet model, to clarify the process. Such a model incorporates the data from each indicator and applies relative weights based on the importance of each indicator. This chapter discusses how to develop a model. It would normally be developed before researching the data so that you understand the relative importance of each indicator and can make cost/benefit decisions regarding how to get the data for each indicator. The outcome of the model will rank each market. Though it is unlikely the ranking will be the final order used in your international plan, it can serve as a useful tool when discussing the final order of foreign markets you will choose for your international expansion.

I will also detail the importance of looking beyond political (national) borders to define your market analysis. Rather than focusing on countries, your research may be better served by looking at regions defined by opportunity rather than historical borders. Such regions may be a collection of countries, such as the European Union, or they may be an area within a country.

• WHY RANK MARKETS?

Ranking potential foreign markets is a bit like having to write an outline for a school paper before writing the paper; you know you should do it but hate the process. Many companies ignore this important step when developing their international business plan. More accurately, many companies do a poor job of properly evaluating their market selection process and rely too much on assumptions never tested. This is especially true if hidden agendas are operating among members of the team - agendas that may dictate market selection based on personal preference rather than competitive advantages.

The process of market selection should be a series of informed decisions made with the international team's consensus using information derived from indicators linked to characteristics, strengths, and weaknesses of the company and its products. Ranking markets based on such indicators is a good starting point for a consensus-oriented discussion.

The ranking of potential markets is normally not the sole justification for selecting a market. There may be other considerations that determine which foreign markets are pursued and in what order. Budget constraints and specific strengths of the company, such as prior experience in particular markets, may in the end be the most important considerations when choosing a market. For example, an analysis and ranking of markets may indicate the top five markets for a company are all in Asia. However, due to the close proximity, prior experience, and relative ease of entering Canada and Mexico, the company may enter those markets before pursuing Asia. Nevertheless, as summarized in Figure 5.1, the process of ranking foreign markets based on specific indicators can be extremely helpful when developing your international expansion plan.

It is important to note that analytical models are merely tools to help narrow market selection. You should not base your decision solely on the outcome of a model. Also remember analyzing indicators is a process, not a one-time exercise. Your models should continually be updated and improved as the company enters new markets and gains more international experience.

TOOL FOR SELECTING FOREIGN MARKETS: AN ILLUSTRATION

MasterFitness is a manufacturer of exercise equipment used in both home and commercial applications. Unlike its competitors which have become name brands in health clubs throughout the U.S., MasterFitness primarily competes on the basis of simple, no-nonsense exercise equipment of extremely high durability. Its products do not compete with the high-tech features of its competitors' products. Rather, MasterFitness prides itself on placing equipment in a facility and knowing it will continue to operate without service or repair for years. The durability of its products has led to the company

Figure 5.1 Reasons for Ranking Foreign Markets Using an Analytical Model

Ranking foreign markets based on specific indicators results in a number of benefits, even if the company eventually enters foreign markets in a different order than implied by the ranking. Justification for ranking market opportunities include:

• The process of developing and improving the analytical model helps highlight factors for success in a market. It provides an easy mechanism to encourage team input regarding important factors to consider before entering a market.

• Applying the model to markets you have already entered provides a benchmark for your success in that market.

• Much of the data researched for the model will be useful for the market-entry plan for each market.

• Ranking is an important way to highlight non-industry and product-specific barriers in a particular market that a company may not have previously been aware of. For example, comparisons of government controls or political risks between markets will be much easier after analyzing the indicators.

• As the company's international experience increases, the model can be refined and used as a sales projection tool.

doing particularly well in the hotel (hospitality) market, educational facilities, and prisons. The relatively low prices of its products makes them ideal for home use, although the brand is not well known.

In assessing its international potential, the company wanted to determine which foreign markets would show the most potential for its products. Because the company is extremely small compared to the name-brand competitors, MasterFitness knows it needs markets that are relatively easy to enter and do not require massive investments in advertising and promotion. They also feel a market that is already using sports equipment, preferably imported from the U.S., would be easier to enter than a market that has yet to mature in its use of sports equipment.

For the purpose of this illustration, a fairly simple model has been adapted from the original MasterFitness model developed for its international planning.

Step One: Developing Indicators

Based on past sales, leads, competitive research, and discussions with industry leaders, MasterFitness feels the following indicators are important:

Product Specific Indicators

• *Level of U.S. exports of exercise equipment (harmonized code 9506.91.0000 - articles and equipment for general physical exercise, gymnastics or athletics).* Rationale: The company competes primarily on price and product durability. It historically has done well in mature markets in which U.S. competitors are successful. Thus an important indicator is the level of exports of the U.S. competitors into foreign markets. The harmonized code 9506.91.0000 is a good match for MasterFitness' products because it closely describes its product range.

• *World imports of exercise equipment (9506.91).* Rationale: The indicator above will be useful to indicate which countries purchase significant amounts of U.S. exercise equipment. But what if important competitors to MasterFitness are foreign-based companies, such as in China or Mexico? It would be helpful to also research total imports of harmonized code 9506.91 regardless of which country is exporting. This indicator will help determine the total import market of exercise equipment for a foreign country.

Industry Size Indicators

• *Population.* Rationale: Generally its product usage depends on individuals, so the larger the population the larger the market potential.

• *Per capita income.* Rationale: Because exercise equipment tends to be used by the middle to upper class, population numbers need to be qualified to account for income levels.

• *Total market for sporting goods.* Rationale: Though the total market for sporting goods encompasses a tremendous number of products not directly competing with exercise equipment (such as basketballs, tennis rackets, and golf clubs), it serves to indicate the overall priority the market places on sports, which indirectly indicates a need for exercise equipment.

Market Growth Indicators

• *Average annual growth projections of the total market for sporting goods.* Rationale: Though the company does well in a mature market, it knows that to find new distributors without prior commitments to a U.S. product, the market needs to be growing.

It is worth emphasizing that these indicators only represent a sample of indicators that would be helpful to MasterFitness. The number of hotels, educational facilities, or prisons in each market would also be useful indicators because they represent specific customer segments that have historically been strong users of MasterFitness products. Your company's model should use indicators that closely match your company, product, and industry. For more tips on selecting indicators, see Figure 5.2.

Figure 5.3 shows the data for these indicators. In this fairly simple model, all of the data was attained through secondary research methods. Sources for these types of indicators will be discussed in Chapter 6.

Figure 5.2 Tips for Selecting Indicators for Market Screening[1]

1) Find indicators that relate to the total size of the market: Any list of indicators must include at least one indicator that, it is hoped, predicts the total size of the market. An example for a firm that sells auto insurance would be "total number of automobiles." For a company that produces wine, the indicator might be "total population of legal drinking age." For a medical device manufacturer, it may be "total number of clinics and hospitals."

2) Use a single source for each indicator: Because the indicator must be comparable across all countries, the same data source should be used for all countries. This ensures the definition and measure are the same for all countries.

3) Incorporate trade statistics: The level of imports into a country of a specific product may be a good indicator of demand. Import statistics are particularly useful if there is not a strong local industry. For example, high-tech medical equipment is primarily manufactured in a few countries (United States, Japan, Germany, Netherlands), so the level of imports in other countries would be a good indicator of demand.

4) Research demand for comparable products: A firm may manufacture a product that is not specifically defined in the trade statistics and instead is classified with allied products. This could mean import statistics are misleading because they are not for the specific product. In these cases, a comparable product could be substituted. (For MasterFitness, this could be 4203.21.000 – *Articles of apparel and clothing accessories …specifically designed for use in sports.*)

5) Avoid general or vague indicators; quantitative indicators are best: Indicators used for the selection criteria have to be numbers. It is problematic to use qualitative indicators because they are difficult to compare across multiple countries. "Cultural attitude toward technology" may be an important concept to a manufacturer of high-tech gadgets, but perhaps better would be "Internet users per 1000 population." Important qualitative indicators should be examined in the post-screening market research phase.

6) Determine foreign market entry mode: The entry mode a company is planning to use can have an important impact on the suitable indicators. Generally speaking, if a company is only exporting and does not anticipate any overseas assets, then political and economic risk indicators are not as important. However, if the entry mode will include foreign direct investment (sales office, distribution warehouse, manufacturing facility), political and economic risks are much more important.

7) Investigate tariff and non-tariff barriers: When considering market barriers as suitable indicators, a firm also should consider the level of local production of the particular product. If, generally speaking, most consumption of a product is imported (for example, fresh fruit in Canada, where there is some local production, but the majority is imported), market barriers are not as important.

Figure 5.3 MasterFitness Initial Research Data[2]

Country	U.S. Exports of Exercise Equipment - HS 9506.91 U.S. $	World Imports HS 9506.91 U.S. $'000	Population	Per Capita Income U.S. $	Total Market for Sporting Goods U.S. $ Millions	Average Annual Growth for Sporting Goods
Argentina	1,820,428	59,456	41,086,927	11,558	776	17%
Brazil	12,090,259	70,315	198,656,019	11,340	775	5%
Canada	177,531,368	337,324	34,880,491	52,219	1,153	5%
Chile	4,683,985	39,426	17,464,814	15,363	201	10%
France	7,663,108	271,559	65,696,689	39,772	594	2%
Germany	40,197,607	389,296	81,889,839	41,514	5,460	3%
Japan	28,379,321	242,013	127,561,489	46,720	15,400	13%
Mexico	43,495,177	130,766	120,847,477	9,742	354	15%
Singapore	10,962,720	44,563	5,312,400	51,709	131	7%
South Korea	12,851,895	74,492	50,004,000	22,590	330	15%
U.K.	53,946,898	362,682	63,227,526	38,514	850	7%

Step Two: Converting the Data into Comparable Indicators

The next step is to convert the data for each indicator into a point score so the performance of each country can be numerically ranked against the other countries. Various methods can be applied and some judgment will need to be used to ensure comparability between indicators.

In the case of MasterFitness, the best performing country established the benchmark by which all other countries were evaluated. The best performing country in a specific indicator received ten points as leader and all other countries received points based on their relative performance. If the data were to be loaded into a spreadsheet, this calculation would be: value of each country indicator / value of the top indicator X 10. *(See note 3 at end of chapter.)* You should not spend too much time trying to develop the model to end all models. Remember, the model is to be a discussion tool, not the sole basis for market selection. The model can be refined as you continue to learn the dynamics of which market indicators best predict your product success and how to use them.

Step Three: Weighting Each Indicator

Not all indicators will be equally important as predictors of foreign market potential. Some will be considerably more important than others. For a medical equipment manufacturer, the number of hospitals and per capita expenditure on medical procedures may be much more important than a country's gross domestic product or even population. For a publisher of English-only textbooks, the use of English in a specific market will obviously be more important than the current level of books imported into that country. For some industries, trade barriers, such as those discussed in Chapter 4, will be so significant as to warrant heavy weighting.

Each indicator in the model should be assigned a weight that represents the relative importance of each indicator. For the MasterFitness example, Figure 5.4 shows the weight for each indicator and the points resulting from multiplying the indicator by its weight. In this model, the maximum number of points a particular country could score for each indicator was 10. Each indicator was then multiplied by a weight between 1 and 3 (3 being the highest). U.S. exports of exercise equipment was given the greatest weight, reflecting the company's view that a market that already imports U.S. exercise equipment would be a very good prospect for its products. World imports, population and the total sports market growth projections were also weighed slightly higher than the other three indicators because both are excellent indicators of market potential, yet independent of previous U.S. success. In this model, the perfect foreign market would receive 10 points for each indicator resulting in a total of 110 points.

The assignment of points and weights is somewhat arbitrary because a model appropriate for your company may look very different from one for another company. This model's perfect market would score 110 points. Another model's perfect score might be 50 or 200. The key is to be consistent when assigning point values.

I also encourage you to make decisions about points and weights prior to conducting too much research on each indicator. Real value can be gained by having an extensive internal discussion on these issues prior to knowing the results of the market ranking. Once the research on each indicator has been conducted and the market ranking calculated, it will be much more difficult to honestly assess the importance of each indicator.

Figure 5.4 MasterFitness Market Selection Model

Country	Indicator 1	Weight	Points	Indicator 2	Weight	Points	Indicator 3	Weight	Points	Indicator 4	Weight	Points	Indicator 5	Weight	Points	Indicator 6	Weight	Points	Total
Argentina	0	3	0	2	2	4	2	2	4	2	1	2	1	1	1	10	2	20	31
Brazil	1	3	3	2	2	4	10	2	20	2	1	2	1	1	1	3	2	6	36
Canada	10	3	30	9	2	18	2	2	4	10	1	10	1	1	1	3	2	6	69
Chile	0	3	0	1	2	2	1	2	2	3	1	3	0	1	0	6	2	12	19
France	0	3	0	7	2	14	3	2	6	8	1	8	0	1	0	1	2	2	30
Germany	2	3	6	10	2	20	4	2	8	8	1	8	4	1	4	2	2	4	50
Japan	2	3	6	6	2	12	6	2	12	9	1	9	10	1	10	8	2	16	65
Mexico	2	3	6	3	2	6	6	2	12	2	1	2	0	1	0	9	2	18	44
Singapore	1	3	3	1	2	2	0	2	0	10	1	10	0	1	0	4	2	8	23
South Korea	1	3	3	2	2	4	3	2	6	4	1	4	0	1	0	9	2	18	35
U.K.	3	3	9	9	2	18	3	2	6	7	1	7	1	1	1	4	2	8	49

It could easily turn into a case of changing the model to justify a desired ranking. You need to bring some objectivity into the process, which might warrant outside assistance such as peers, consultants, or public trade assistance professionals.

Step Four: Analyzing the Results

Figure 5.5 lists the results of MasterFitness' model ranked by point total. When you first analyze at the results of a model, question the results. In this example, is it reasonable that Canada is the top market? Equally, is it reasonable that Chile is the lowest ranked market? Look for obvious errors. They may indicate mistakes in your data (research or entry), or suggest that the model needs to be modified.

Also conduct a what-if analysis. For example, change some of the weights and see how the results vary. Pay particular attention to significant changes in country ranking. This will indicate where your weighting may be inappropriately skewing the results. It may also point out data problems.

Your goal is to perfect both the model and the data. As you continue your international expansion, the model can be improved and expanded to include a greater understanding of the markets and the dynamics of your products. All of this will improve the accuracy and usefulness of the model for use in selecting future markets.

Beyond use as a market selection tool, the statistical model can be modified to assist in projecting sales. This would require incorporating sales experience from foreign markets into the model using statistical techniques such as regression analysis.

• HOW TO USE YOUR MARKET SELECTION MODEL

Once you have developed and perfected your model, how should it be used? Sometimes the process of developing the model and researching the data will give you a pretty good short-term idea of which markets you are going to enter. Hopefully, it will provide a useful perspective that the international team can use as a discussion tool when the final markets are chosen. At the least, the data collected will be useful when you develop marketing plans for the individual markets.

Figure 5.5 MasterFitness Market Ranking

Rank, Country, Total Points			
1) Canada	69	8) Argentina	31
2) Japan	65	9) France	30
3) Germany	50	10) Singapore	23
4) U.K.	49	11) Chile	19
5) Mexico	44		
6) Brazil	36		
7) South Korea	35		

Some points to consider when using market potential ranking models include:

- Use the model as a tool and as a starting point for market selection. Be wary of placing too much emphasis on statistics because they may be susceptible to various data errors.
- Determine how sensitive the outcome of the country ranking is to indicators that may be inaccurate or inappropriate for your company. For example, if the U.S. export levels of a particular product are used and they are heavily influencing the outcome of the country ranking, be sure that the harmonized code used was a good match for your product. Obviously the model is only as good as the indicators, but there is a tendency to accept the indicators as fact once the data is assembled even if one or more of the indicators has only marginal value.
- As discussed in Figure 5.2, be sure to only include indicators that will really impact your company's potential and your market decision. For example, some market selection statistical models tend to include a variety of macroeconomic or government-related indicators such as inflation rates, exchange rate controls, and cultural similarities. These can be very helpful indicators or they can be misleading depending on your company, your strategy, and your products and services.
- When you analyze the results, look for patterns that may guide your planning. There may be geographic groupings such as a high number of European markets in the top percentile. Or there may be economic or demographic groupings that transcend an individual indicator. An example would be a high number of markets that share a common demographic indicator, though the particular indicator wasn't used in the model.
- These models are particularly useful for evaluating the potential of existing products to be exported into existing markets - markets that already use similar products. However, market selection models can be particularly difficult to use for new, revolutionary products. In such cases, many of the most common indicators, such as U.S. exports or current levels of product usage in a foreign market, will not apply because the product does not yet exist and potential buyers may not fully understand the benefit of the product. Instead the model may need to utilize indicators which parallel (track with) other products that are either complementary to the new product or exhibit similar sales potential.

Using Two Models as a Screening Tool

You may want to develop two models. First, a very simple model that uses only a few indicators to screen all potential markets. For example, you may determine that there is a minimum per capita income and population threshold to consider a market. The second model would then perform a detailed analysis on the markets that passed the first screening. This is particularly useful for your initial international business plan because the field of potential markets could be 200 countries or more.

• COUNTRY VERSUS MARKET ANALYSIS

In his provocative book The End of the Nation State, Kenichi Ohmae persuasively argues that international business strategies should no longer be described in terms of countries defined by historical and political borders (nation states), but rather by focused geographical units.[4] As examples, Ohmae cites Hong Kong and the adjacent stretch of southern China, or the Kansai region around Osaka. Both are significant economic powerhouses larger than many countries. Ohmae refers to these markets as region states. They may be a region within a country, or a region overlapping many countries.

What determines these new business units? Ohmae argues it is the flow of four Is; investment, industry, information technology, and individual consumers.

1. Investment. Prior to the mid-eighties, the majority of foreign investment flowed either between governments or multilateral lending agencies to governments. Now most of the foreign investments are corporate transactions driven by business opportunities with little or no government control or interference. The better the opportunity, the more money will be invested.

2. Industry. In the past, a company's foreign market selection decisions were influenced by a host of government incentives designed to induce investment. Now the industry makes strategic decisions with a priority placed on the market and resource opportunities.

3. Information technology. One of the fundamental opportunities offered by recent developments in technology is the ability of a business to operate globally without necessarily establishing local infrastructure in each market. A good example would be pan-European call (telephone) centers for marketing or customer support that years ago would have required separate facilities in each country. Today one center can support all of a company's European efforts, thus blurring the lines between nations.

4. Individual consumers. Purchase decisions, once dictated by national preference, are now driven by cost and features. Today consumers are better informed and seek the best products for their requirements, independent of the product's country of origin. A consumer's home nation no longer exerts the dominant pressure on the consumer to only purchase locally manufactured products.

Each of these four has diminished the influence of governments on international business planning. It is increasingly important to look beyond political borders (or within them) to define your market opportunity.

The implication for your market selection model is that rather than focus your model on data from indicators of a whole country, it may be more relevant to choose part of a country or to combine countries. The decision should be based on the size and scale offered by a market, independent of political borders. This process or methodology is called **market segmentation**: defining a market opportunity by focusing on a subset of prospects that share a common need or similar characteristic. Common ways to define the subset would be geographic (city, region), demographic (age, income), psychographic (behaviors, value), and behavioralistic: (brand loyalty, first adopters). Market segmentation helps with large markets to identify most profitable or easiest sales opportunities

However, most data continues to be grouped by country, especially for foreign markets. For example, data is readily available that tracks the exports of a particular product from the U.S. into a foreign country; but it would much more difficult to determine the importation level of only the Kansai region around Osaka. It could be difficult to supply accurate data for a model based on geographical units independent of political borders.

Despite the data collection challenge, Ohmae's thesis should be incorporated into your international strategy. The global changes outlined by Ohmae, especially the technology opportunities, dictate that your marketing plan should to some extent ignore political borders. Specifically it means:

- Entry into a particular country may be the most effective if initially limited to a particular area within that country.
- Entry into a particular country may be the most effective if the country is grouped into a regional market-entry plan.
- When selecting the order of market entry, final ranking should be done on overall market opportunities rather than individual countries. In the case of MasterFitness this could mean entering Western Europe before Japan, even though Japan was ranked highest.
- Value chain decisions (such as purchasing, distribution, marketing, and customer service) should adopt a borderless view of a market.

• NOTES

1. Adapted from "Table 7-4 Tips for Selecting Market indicators", Vern Terpstra, James Foley, Ravi Sarathy; *International Marketing* 11th Edition. (Naperville, Naper Publishing Group, 2012). Used with permission.

2. Data Sources: U.S Exports HS 9506.91 (2012) USA Trade Online; World Imports HS 9506.91 (2011) UNComtrade; Population (2012) World Bank Databank; Per Capita Income (current US$ 2012) World Bank Databank; Total Market for Sporting Goods and Growth Rate for Sporting Goods (Best Market Report 2004) Export.gov.

3. In Figure 5.4 example formulas using the data from Figure 5.3 would be:
   Canada U.S Exports: $177,531,368 / 177,531,368 * 10 = 10$
   U.K. U.S. Exports: $53,946,898 / 177,531,368 * 10 = 3$
   Singapore Population: $5,312,400 / 198,656,019 * 10 = .26$ rounded to 0
   (Note how each country's indicator is divided by the value of the top performing indicator and multiplied by 10.)

4. Kenichi Ohmae, The End of the Nation State (New York, NY: The Free Press, A Division of Simon & Schuster Inc., 1995).

CHAPTER 6

Sources of International Marketing Data

F inding useful data for your international plan will be an ongoing challenge, but it is getting easier as more and more data is published on the web, and private companies continue to offer up-to-date, detailed data on markets and opportunities. Of all the changes since writing the first edition of this text, the availability of good international marketing data has probably been the greatest. And the best news for you is that increasingly, much of this great data is free! For example, all trade statistics between countries at the six-digit level is available at no cost from the United Nations. The World Bank publishes over 1300 indicators for about 200 countries. And whereas good marketing data on emerging countries was often out of data or incomplete, such data now is very good and increasingly accurate. Even where the data is not available at no cost, the private sector is doing a great job publishing critical marketing insights that with a bit of investment, can pay great marketing dividends.

This chapter will analyze the challenge of collecting international marketing data in a cost-effective manner by first discussing the issue of primary versus secondary data research. Next, the variety of international data sources, many of which are free, will be detailed. Finally, we'll look in depth at how to determine your competitive position in foreign markets.

I should emphasize that the research goals and resources identified in this chapter are not meant to replace the very valuable information and data that can be obtained through a visit to a potential foreign market. The direct interaction with potential customers, distributors, peers, and the media will always be worth the investment of time and money. If travel is not an option, especially for a small company, the need for outside research is critical to the market selection process. And for companies that intend to visit potential markets to research, their pre-travel planning should include the research described in this chapter.

• PRIMARY VERSUS SECONDARY DATA

In a perfect world, all decisions for a marketing plan would be based on **primary data** - original information collected specifically for a particular requirement. Primary data is generally more accurate, relevant, and timely compared to **secondary data**, which is based on information that already exists from third parties. But primary data is also more costly than secondary data, especially for foreign markets.

Typically, a company starts a domestic research project using as much secondary data as possible before resorting to costly primary data. The same is true for international marketing decisions, but international secondary data may be considerably more difficult to find, incomplete, and perhaps even wholly inaccurate.

Obstacles to Collecting International Secondary Data

When collecting secondary data for international marketing decisions you must always be aware of potential pitfalls:

- *Comparability.* Often the data available for one country or market will not compare with the same data of another country. This leads to problems when the data is used to compare one market to another, such as in market potential models discussed in Chapter 5. Comparability problems arise from differences and errors that occur when collecting the original data. This is especially true if the various studies were not conducted by the same organization and therefore don't have a common goal.
- *Lack of current data.* In the U.S. market, we are accustomed to having access to data that may be as current as the day you request it. With increased use of technology, the longest time-lag for data may only be a few months to a year. However, for many foreign markets, especially emerging markets, the frequency of surveys and data collection is considerably less and may only be collected every five or ten years, if at all.
- *Cost of international secondary data.* Given the challenges of collecting accurate, timely international data, it is often very expensive. This is particularly true for markets where government spending on statistical reporting is low and the burden falls on private industry. Such markets tend to be difficult to survey due to infrastructure challenges. When a private company does collect the data, they can command a premium price for their products.

Obstacles to Collecting International Primary Data

Given the challenges facing international secondary data, it may seem attractive to emphasize primary data for your international marketing decisions. However, conducting your own primary research can be extremely time consuming and expensive because marketing research is based on responses from people, and communicating with people in foreign markets may be considerably more difficult than in the U.S. Generally, there are three issues that make primary data collection difficult and expensive:

1. *Language.* The most obvious challenge is language. Any survey instrument needs to be translated, and then checked to be sure the data collected is con-

sistent with the research goals. Because each translation creates a new survey tool, it needs to be tested before use in a full study, which leads to increased time and costs.

2. *Infrastructure*. The local infrastructure may dictate data collection techniques completely different (and perhaps more expensive) than used domestically. For example, you may have commissioned a web-based survey in the U.S. through a third party research company with sophisticated software and technology that resulted in a very affordable and accurate survey. The same study in a foreign market may have to rely on person-to-person surveys - which are more prone to error - because local web usage may not be widespread. Even in instances where internet usage is comparable, the profile of the web users may be different leading to results which may be less comparable. Other examples of infrastructure constraints would include a poor postal system, lack of good mailing lists, and lack of support companies to assist with the research.

3. *Cultural*. A number of cultural considerations complicate primary data collection. A common problem is the difference in cultural attitudes toward research surveys. Some societies shy away from sharing personal data or opinions. Or the cultural attitude may be to always be polite, which could result in the respondents answering questions with responses they believe would please the interviewer but don't reflect their true opinions. Respondents may also fabricate answers when they don't know what to say or misunderstand the questions.

• RESOLVING PRIMARY VERSUS SECONDARY INTERNATIONAL DATA CHALLENGES

Given the variety of problems and potential costs of both types of international data, how do you incorporate international marketing research into your international planning? Fortunately, it is a problem that all firms encounter and a couple of tricks and shortcuts are available.

Segment the research task/define budgets. The most important step is to break the marketing research requirements into realistic short-, medium-, and long-term goals that correlate to your international strategy. The more aggressive the goals for a given time frame, the greater the budget requirement. If your short-term goal is to identify your top three markets and enter them within the next year, you should easily be able to make your market decisions using secondary data at little to no cost. If your goal is to identify more than a dozen markets and enter them within the short to medium term, you will need to invest more money and rely on a greater degree of primary data. If your strategy includes targeting emerging markets, your marketing research costs also will be higher. The key is to put your research goals into perspective as they relate to your international strategy.

Utilize resources. Governmental agencies, industry associations, and private companies alike offer a wide range of international data products designed to assist companies in international business planning. Successful global entrepreneurs know to access these resources when conducting their international marketing research.

The wealth of affordable data is not limited to secondary data. Many organizations, in particular the U.S. Department of Commerce (USDOC), offer extremely cost-efficient primary data collection services. The USDOC offers **Customized Market Analysis (CMA)** reports which provide targeted marketing research conducted by commerce department employees based in U.S. foreign offices (most often embassies). These reports can be very helpful in filling gaps left from secondary research options without an unreasonable expense. When conducting international research, always utilize all local, state, and federal resources. It will lower costs and reduce the time frame required to complete the research.

• DEALING WITH DATA PROBLEMS

International data is rarely complete or fully accurate no matter how much time and investment is dedicated to your international market research. The infrastructure is not in place in many international countries to ensure timely and complete reporting of economic, demographic, and industry data. When data is available, it is often difficult to compare with data from other markets. Commissioning primary research to fill the gap is often too expensive or difficult for even the most experienced international company.

Problems with international marketing data can have an important impact on the selection of foreign markets. Because data is often available for industrialized, mature markets, a bias toward those markets can develop. If no attempt is made to deal with data problems, a company risks making the wrong market selections.

Faced with the problem of incomplete or inaccurate data, what options are available? There are a number of tricks that can greatly lessen the impact of data problems. The most common are easy to implement even for small companies. Four techniques that can be effective include:
1. Complementary product or industry substitution
2. National statistics substitution
3. Ratio comparisons
4. Timeline comparisons

Complementary product or industry substitution. The most common method of dealing with the lack of data needed for a particular research goal is to substitute another available indicator that will hopefully track as well as the original. Such an indicator would be called a complementary indicator.

An example is a company trying to find data for a product with a bad harmonized code. A harmonized code is considered 'bad' when it does a poor job of accurately describing the product even though it is the correct harmonized code for that product. For example, a medical instrument manufacturer in Chicago produces a very specific medical instrument used only in particular medical procedures. The harmonized code for this product falls into a catchall category for medical instruments, so their product is grouped with many other products that it is not in competition with. The export data for this harmonized code is misleading because so many other products are tracked by the same harmonized code.

The solution was to use the harmonized code for magnetic resonance imaging (MRI) apparatus because MRI apparatus is usually used in conjunction with this product. This complementary data gave a more accurate picture of which foreign markets may be suitable for these medical instruments. It is not a perfect substitution because the high cost of MRI apparatus may be a barrier in a particular market that may not hesitate to buy this medical instrument. Nevertheless, the data was useful to the company in its initial foreign market potential model. Primary research was later used to more accurately define market potential.

Substitution is not limited to products. It also may be helpful to substitute indicators from a completely different industry. For example, if your product is considered a luxury item and no data is available, the data for another luxury product may be substituted even if it is from a different industry.

National statistics substitution. When data is not available for a product or industry, correlating national demographic and consumption statistics to the product may be useful. Nearly all countries have at least broad demographic data such as per capita income, number of households, number of companies, percentage of literacy, and government spending on items such as healthcare and education. They may also have consumption statistics such as number of telephones per household or average number of automobiles. Both demographic and consumption statistics can be suitable substitutions to help approximate the potential market for your product. In the medical instrument example, indicators such as number of hospitals and number of hospital beds were useful for the company's initial market screening.

Ratio comparisons. Utilizing a ratio comparison is also a very common technique for dealing with data problems. The concept is to create a ratio using the data that is available for two markets to predict the data for a third market. The assumption is that consumption in one market is proportional to another based on some known indicator for both markets, such as population. For example, if the foreign market has 25 percent less people than the U.S., the foreign market is arguably 75 percent of the U.S. market. If only one indicator is used, the results could be misleading because such a comparison ignores differences in consumption patterns. But ratio comparisons do well when used in conjunction with other indicators that reflect differences in consumption patterns.

Timeline comparisons. Use of timeline comparisons can be a helpful tool when dealing with incomplete data. The assumption behind comparing the timeline of a known market to that of an unknown market is that the unknown market will have the same level of consumption as the known market at the same level of development. You must assume that as a market develops and the GDP and per capita income increase, consumption will increase. The current level of consumption in a particular foreign market would then be the same as the consumption in another market when its GDP and/or per capita income was the same. This approach has limitations because it does not account for differences in consumption behavior, but it can be a useful substitute when better options are not available or when timeline comparisons are done in conjunction with other indicators.

• SOURCES FOR COUNTRY AND MARKET DATA

The most fundamental data you will probably use when researching foreign markets is economic and demographic data such as population, GDP, per capita income, inflation, and literacy. This is generally the easiest data to find, especially once you know where to look. There are numerous agencies, websites, and databases you can contact for information, as well as local, state, and federal resources.

www.export.gov

If you haven't encountered export.gov during your international business journey, this chapter will prove to be very beneficial. This website, managed by the U.S. Department of Commerce, is by far the single most important research tool available to the global entrepreneur - experienced or not. Best of all, the reports and data are available for free and contain thousands of documents relating to international trade. The site also includes a number of training videos and webinar links many of which are useful if you are studying for the NASBITE CGBP exam.

For the purpose of selecting international markets and researching data to support your statistical market potential model, you want to read the ***Country Commercial Guides (CCG)***. These guides are available for most countries and generally follow the same outline. Figure 6.1 shows the table of contents for a typical CCG.

The CCGs are updated annually and contain reports on a country's economic, political, marketing, trade regulation, investment, financing, and travel conditions. The appendices include country data, domestic indicators, trade and investment statistics, and a list of contact points. Figure 6.2 lists the types of questions you would be able to answer with the information you can find in a CCG.

There are a number of other features at www.export.gov including directories, trade leads, training event calendar, and webinars so be sure and take the time to review all the sections. The single source for most of the reports is found in the Marketing Research Library. Export.gov also allows you to register for updates on markets and industry so when important reports or insights are released, it will be emailed to you. For more information, visit the 'Connect' tab on the www.export.gov site. That tab also has links to other government agencies involved in trade promotion, and a listing of the U.S. Commercial Service offices in the U.S. and overseas.

Figure 6.1 Table of Contents of a Typical Country Commercial Guide (CCG)

I. EXECUTIVE SUMMARY
II. ECONOMIC TRENDS AND OUT-
LOOK
Major Trends and Outlook
Current Trends and Outlook
Banking
Additional Reforms
Management
Macroeconomic Trends
Foreign Trade
Financial Services
Investments and Privatization
Forecast for upcoming years
III. POLITICAL ENVIRONMENT
Political System
Political Parties
Nature of Bilateral Relationship
with the U.S.
Major Political Issues Affecting the
business climate
IV. MARKETING U.S. PRODUCTS AND
SERVICES
Distribution and Sales Channels
Import Channels/The Retail Network
Direct Marketing
Use of Agents and Distributors
Identifying a Partner
Market Research
Franchising
Licensing Arrangements
Joint Ventures
Steps to Establishing an Office
Structures Commonly Used by
Foreign Investors
Selling Factors and Technologies
Advertising and Trade Promotion
Pricing Products
Sales Service/Customer Support
Government Procurement
Electric Current
V. LEADING SECTORS FOR U.S. EX-
PORTS AND INVESTMENT
Best Prospects for Non-Agricultural
Goods and Services
Best Prospects for Agricultural Prod-
ucts
Significant Investment Opportunities

VI. TRADE REGULATIONS AND
STANDARDS
Trade Barriers
Non-Tariff Barriers
Price Banding
Used Capital Goods
Imports of Equipment by
Governmental Institutions
Customs Valuation
Tariff and Import Taxes
Illustrated Study of Direct
Import Costs
Fines and Penalties
Methods of Payment for Imports
Drawback
Temp. Admission Regime
Standards and Conformity
Assessment Legal Framework
Standards
Accreditation
Product and System Certifi-
cation
International Agreements
Information Sources
Agricultural Products
Anti-Dumping and Counter-
vailing Duty Laws
Labeling Requirements
Import/Export Documenta-
tion
Shipping Documentation
Commercial In
voices
Bill of Lading
Packing Lists
Insurance Certifi-
cate
Samples and Advertising
Matter
Sales Sample
Customs Brokers
Free Trade Zones/Special Customs
Area/Warehouses
Customs and Tax Advantages
Bonded Warehouses
Membership in Free Trade
Agreements   (Continued)

Figure 6.1 Continued

VII. INVESTMENT CLIMATE
    Openness to Foreign Investment
        Right to Private Ownership
         and Establishment
    Protection of Property Rights
    Performance Requirements and
     Incentives
    Transparency of the Regulatory System
    Corruption
    Labor
    Efficient and Capital Markets and
     Portfolio Investment
    Conversion and Transfer Policies
    Expropriation and Compensation
    Dispute Settlement
    Political Violence
    Bilateral Investment Agreements
    OPIC and Other Investment
     Insurance Programs
    Major Foreign Investors
    Direct Investment
VIII. TRADE AND PROJECT FINANCING
    Foreign Exchange Controls
     Affecting Trading
    General Financing Availability
        Private Sector Banks
    Export Financing and Insurance
    Small Business Administration
    Multilateral Development Bank
     Operations
        Overseas Private Investment
         Corporation
        Multilateral Investment
         Guarantee Agency
        U.S. Trade and Development
IX. BUSINESS TRAVEL
    Geography and Climate
    Time
    Business Customs
    Language
    Currency
    Visas
    Work Permits
    Business Infrastructure
        Lodging

        Communications
        Health
        Holidays
        Security Assessment
X. APPENDICES:
  A.   COUNTRY DATA
      -Profile
      -Government System
      -Language
      -Work Week
  B.   DOMESTIC ECONOMY
      -GDP Growth Rate
      -GDP per Capita
      -Unemployment Rate
      -Foreign Exchange Reserve
      -Exchange Rate
      -Public Debt
      -Current Account Balance
      -Labor Force
      -Domestic Savings
      -Investment as Percent of GDP
      -Consumer Price Increase
  C.   TRADE
      -Total Exports
      -Total Exports to U.S.
      -Total Imports
      -Imports from U.S.
      -Trade Balance
  D.   INVESTMENT STATISTICS
  E.   U.S. AND COUNTRY
      CONTACTS
      -U.S. Government
      -Government
      -Market Research Firms
      -English Speaking Law Firms
      -Telecomms Consultants
      -Intellectual Property Consultants
      -Country Commercial Banks
      -Multilateral Development Bank
      Offices
      -Customs Brokers
      -Bonded Warehouses
      -Inspection Company Contact In-
      formation
  F.   MARKET RESEARCH
  G.   TRADE EVENT SCHEDULE

Figure 6.2 Questions You Can Answer with the Country Commercial Guides

- What is the forecast for the country's economic growth?

- What are the key issues currently facing the country's government?

- How are relations between the U.S. and the country?

- How do U.S. companies generally sell products into the country?

- How extensive is the use of distributors and agents in the country?

- What would be involved in setting up a company in the country?

- What considerations are important when pricing my products for sale in the country?

- What U.S. products and services have the best opportunities in the country?

- What trade barriers exist in the country?

- What types of taxes/duties are applied to imports?

- What is the legal structure?

- Does the country belong to any trading pacts or free-trade agreements, and if so, what is the impact on my products?

- What labeling and documentation issues are needed when export to this country?
- Are free trade zones available in the country?

- What is the investment climate like in the country?

- What issues are important regarding trade and project financing?

- What should I know about traveling to the country on business?

CIA World Factbook – www.cia.gov

The Export.gov site contains summaries of important statistics for each country, but the **CIA World Factbook** goes into much greater detail. Here you will find data on geography, resources, population demographics, government, infrastructure, military, and economic indicators. Don't let the source agency mislead you; though the CIA manages the report, data for each report comes from dozens of agencies. It is one of the most useful resources available for foreign country research.

World Bank Development Indicators – data.worldbank.org

The data available through the World Bank is remarkable. What makes it so powerful is that all the data is comparable and up to date across the more than 200 countries in the database. This means when you research indicators such as GDP, rural population, income share held by highest 20%, etc., you know the way it is calculated is the same for all countries. Plus this database also offers analysis by regional groupings or income such as 'high income' countries, or 'Arab world'.

Due to the size of the database, it can seem a bit difficult at first to use. But take the time to learn how to use it – there's a tutorial online. To unlock the full potential you need to use the full access website shown by a blue box 'DATABANK' or look for the link "To access the full WDI, visit the World DataBank". Once you get there look for 'more countries' which takes you to the full dataset. Figure 6.3 shows the correct screen with full access. Once you have your data, you can map it or even download to a spreadsheet. All at no cost!

OECD.StatExtracts – stats.oecd.org

This a good companion site to the World Bank offering some of the same indicators such as population and economic projections. It is maintained by the Organisation for Economic Co-Operation and Development (OECD). The OECD database can be useful to fill in with indicators not available through the World Bank such as data relating to education and training, science technology and patents, transport, and a number of other sectors. The OECD also publishes some of its data monthly which may provide more up-to-date indicators than the World Bank, especially those relating to the economy. The StatExtract database is a subset of OECD's larger statistical database which has a subscription fee. For most companies, the StatExtract database would suffice, and it free.

Country Desk Officers

For a more personal touch, contact the U.S. Department of Commerce's country desk officers. Each officer is assigned one or more countries or markets and maintains a wealth of information that either has yet to be coded into a report or is not included in other formats due to the changing nature of the data. Begin by contacting the Trade Information Center at 800-USA-TRADE (872-8723) or your local U.S. Department of Commerce Export Assistance Center.

globalEDGE from Michigan State University – globaledge.msu.edu

This is a well-researched and thorough site with information on many countries. Each country website is organized in the same way with a top-level view of the key indicators and links to other key resources for each country. These links can be very helpful because they help to identify many other resources for a country.

Figure 6.3 Screen Shot of World Bank's World Databank

Private Resources

A number of companies specialize in foreign marketing research data. Euromonitor International is a good example (www.euromonitor.com). Unlike its name implies, the data available is global, not just Europe. Euromonitor is probably best known for its product Passport which offers a vast number of indicators by country associated with consumer behavior such as number of microwave ovens per home, or fruit juice consumption. Their statistics and reports are primarily based on in-country research conducted by local researchers. This means most of the data from Euromonitor is proprietary. There is a fee for the data, but a number of universities subscribe to Euromonitor. Other private companies with country data include D&B (www.dnb.com), Bureau of National Affairs (www.bna.com), and Datamonitor (www.datamonitor.com).

• INDUSTRY DATA

Demographic and economic indicators of each country are helpful, but even the least expensive widget won't sell if a market doesn't need widgets. There is no getting around the need to combine demographic and economic data with industry and product-specific information.

With industry-specific research, you hope to answer questions such as:
- Is my product considered to be in the same industry as it is in the U.S.?
- Is the industry growing?
- What are the specific barriers to entry for this industry? What about tariffs, distribution challenges, strong local branding, or lack of differentiation with local

products?
- How receptive are local consumers to foreign products?
- How receptive are local consumers to U.S. products?
- How mature is the local industry? How competitive is it? How active are local manufacturers?
- What are the levels of U.S. exports of my products, my industry, or complementary goods?
- What is the level of imports into the market of non-U.S. manufactured goods?
- What are the government- or industry-mandated technical standards or requirements in this market?
- Will transport times or costs make my product noncompetitive?

It may seem these detailed, industry-specific questions can only be answered through primary research conducted in each foreign market, but if your products or services fall within a broad industry classification, significant research may have already been conducted and summarized in various resources. Before setting out to conduct expensive primary research, determine what information may already be available.

• WHERE TO GO FOR INDUSTRY DATA

As with country data, there are numerous sources for industry-specific information about products and services.

www.export.gov

The export.gov site is not just a source for demographic and economic data but also a tremendous resource for hundreds of reports on particular products and services. Some of the most important ones are:

- *Market Research Reports and insights.* The website is organized by industry sectors such as aerospace & defense, consumer goods, health technologies, manufacturing industries, travel and tourism, etc. Within each industry section is a variety of marketing insights and reports, as well as key international trade shows. The website also provides direct links to U.S. Commercial Service experts in that industry. See Figure 6.4 for selected industry reports.
- *Best Market Report.* These reports put into one document the best foreign markets for U.S. goods and services. Each report covers one industry sector. Many include subsectors within that industry. For example the safety and security products best market report breaks the industry down to 13 sectors including video surveillance systems, physical security, scanning equipment, and consultancy services. Within each sector, and by country, the report then assigns a number from one to four in which one represents little opportunity for a U.S. company to succeed in that country and industry, to a four indicating a high probability of success. These are tremendous reports. Even if your specific industry is not included, there is a good chance a related industry will have a report.

Figure 6.4 Sample Market Research Reports on www.export.gov

Regulations for the Importation of Used Vehicles and Trucks into Mexico
Turkey: Medical Technologies Market
Building Products Import to Japan
Housing Starts in Japan
China: Medical Devices Market and Healthcare Reform
Air Pollution Control in Guangdong
Motorcycles – Czech Market Brief
France: Motorcycles Market Brief
Accessing Government Procurement Opportunities in Canada
Brazilian Airport Privatization – Second Round of Concessions
Outbound Travel of Southern China
Pleasure Boats Industry and Market in China
Renewable energy in the EU
China: Guangdong Education Report
EU Regulations on Food Supplements, Health foods, herbal medicines
German Travel & Tourism to the United States
Housing Starts in Japan
Peru: Mining Projects Portfolio Taiwan: Cable Television Equipment
Vietnam: Textile Industry
Switzerland: Fitness Equipment
Canada: Management Consulting Services
Venezuela: Radio and TV Broadcasting Equipment
Israel: Footwear
Mexico: Portable and Personal Digital Assistants
Mexico: Natural Gas Conversion Technologies
Philippines: Railroad Equipment
Japan: CAD/CAM/CAE Application Software
Taiwan: Coatings and Paints
Taiwan: Personal Computers and Peripherals
Germany: Solid Waste Recycling Equipment
Spain: Paper Packaging
Singapore: Medical Devices
Pakistan: Food Processing and Packaging Equipment
Hungary: Automotive Parts and Service Equipment
Vietnam: Household Consumer Goods
Turkey: Materials Handling Machinery
Greece: Residential Natural Gas Equipment
India: Wireless Communications
Germany: Automotive Parts and Service
Vietnam: Aquaculture Industry
Colombia: Oil and Gas Field Machinery
Ecuador: Fast Food Equipment

Industry Desk Officers and Industry Teams

When you get tired of reading all the reports, try phoning the U.S. Department of Commerce industry desk officers. They are particularly helpful when you need an outside opinion of your market indicators and resource sources. Often they will identify new sources for data or simply give you their opinion of the global market. They are in contact with other industry experts and competitors and can generally give you more anecdotal information that may not have made its way into the press. Be prepared before you call so you don't spend time asking questions that have already been addressed in the market research reports at export.gov. And when you find a good desk officer, cultivate your relationship and don't tell your competitors! Try 800-USA-TRADE or your local U.S. Export Assistance Center (locations listed on export.gov).

The U.S. Commercial Service has organized their trade specialists into teams by industry. They attend important industry trade shows and maintain the industry profile resource pages at export.gov. For more information visit www.export.gov or contact your local U.S. Export Assistance Center.

Trade Associations

Historically, trade associations have watched out for the domestic industry issues such as government regulations and public opinions. Many also play an important role in coordinating industry-specific data and information to increase exports. Such associations conduct market data surveys regarding member international activities - specific information that otherwise could be difficult to find. They nearly always are involved in international standards issues which can become a nuisance to small firms without guided assistance.

Publications, Industry Journals, and Periodicals

Other good sources of international data specific to your industry are domestic and international publications. These sources provide insights and perspectives not available elsewhere. This is particularly true for competitor information, especially that of private companies. When looking for competitive information on a small, privately held company, the best information may come from a write-up in a local newspaper. Generally, management is less guarded when speaking to a hometown newspaper.

International industry magazines and journals are also valuable. Not only will their editorial content provide important insights on regional industry trends, companies, and trade shows, but the advertisements are a good source of information about competitor activities. And when you travel to the market, the editorial staff of industry publications will be a good resource for a local perspective of the market, barriers, and customers.

Where do you find obscure hometown newspapers and international publications? Years ago it may have been impossible, but these days the Internet provides a number of online publication search engines. I have come to rely on two sources: Dow Jones Factiva (www.dowjones.com/factiva) and LexisNesix (www.lesixnexis.com). Both contain the same-day full text of many U.S. periodicals such as The Wall Street Journal,

New York Times, and Forbes. But their power for international trade research are the hundreds of international publications they include such as the Financial Times, Economist, and World Reporter. They even have more obscure publications such as Chemiefasern Textilindustrie, Jane's Defense Weekly, Far Eastern Economic Review, or Agence France-Presse. They also have some hometown international newspapers such as Canberra Times, South China Morning Post, Hindustan Times, or The Toronto Sun. Though annual subscriptions can be expensive, you can go to your local library or university to see what sources for online searching they may have available to the public free of charge.

Networking

Last but not least, go up and down your supply chain and even horizontally to other noncompeting companies in your industry for information and data. Ask vendors, customers, and anyone else you can trust for their opinion of indications for foreign markets for your product. Get their suggestions of where to find the data. Suppliers and customers can be particularly helpful because they understand your industry and probably deal with your competitors. A good insider can save you time and money. More importantly, networking can help you avoid mistakes. Networking is especially important during international trips such as to trade shows. These events offer daily opportunities to get new insights into the local markets.

• DETERMINING YOUR COMPETITIVE POSITION IN FOREIGN MARKETS

No discussion on researching international marketing data would be complete without highlighting how to research the activities of competitors in foreign markets. However, competition is an odd thing because it is different in each industry. I have worked in the computer industry which seemed very competitive to me. However, the tremendous growth rates of the 1980s made our battles seem much easier compared to battles in maturing industries, which I later had the chance to study.

For example, here in Peoria, IL, one of the most interesting corporate battles was between Caterpillar, a manufacturer of heavy equipment, and Japan's Komatsu Ltd. After decades of outstanding growth and performance, Caterpillar found itself in a fierce battle during the 1980s with its Japanese rival. Komatsu's ambition was summed up in its simple slogan "maru-C," which roughly translates as "encircle Caterpillar."[1] Komatsu's strategy essentially was to identify the weaknesses of Caterpillar and attack those market segments. (In MBA jargon, this is known as the loose brick strategy, where one attacks one's competition by finding loose bricks in the competitor's wall that it can remove in hopes of eventually taking out the whole wall.) Komatsu's attack on Caterpillar in the 1980s came at a bad time for Caterpillar, which was facing enormous labor problems, a high dollar-yen relationship, and extremely high overhead costs, eventually leading to a $1 billion loss during 1982-84.[2]

The competitive pressure put on Caterpillar by Komatsu, combined with other issues such as labor costs, eventually led Caterpillar to a corporate turnaround now envied by many corporate leaders. It soon regained market share, and by 1995 was number one in every market it served, except Japan where it was second.[3] Throughout the 1990s, Caterpillar continued to set record earnings. The turnaround is an interesting story of both competition and corporate reorganization.

The point here is that competition can be good if it leads to change and improvements. However, you must be aware of your competition before it is too late. Had Caterpillar ignored Komatsu, its eventual turnaround may have come too late. There are a number of unique tools available to the international manager to increase awareness of what is happening internationally. This next section looks at these tools.

• COMPETITIVE INFORMATION IS NO ELIXIR FOR SUCCESS

It should be stressed that the volumes of data and information you collect about the activities of your competitors could be misleading if their strategy is wrong. This is particularly important if you plan to use the information to develop your international strategy or expansion plan. If too much priority is placed on the international activities of your competitors, you run the risk of creating a reactive strategy that may result in an ineffective international expansion plan poorly suited for the future. Your competitors may actually be losing money, and their international strategy decisions may not suit your company or products.

On the other hand, the more information you gather about your competitors, the better position you'll be in. It is important not to ignore your competitors' international behavior, especially if your competitors tend to be more experienced internationally. The key is to determine if the information is reliable and then use it within the right context. Knowing exactly what your competitors are doing is not the key to international success. It could, in fact, lead you down the wrong road. However, used appropriately, this information can be an important addition to your international planning.

• THE GOAL OF COMPETITIVE INTERNATIONAL RESEARCH

There are five issues you should research with regard to the international activities of your competitors:

1. Where are they selling? Which markets and regions?
2. To whom are they selling?
3. How are they selling? Direct, through distributors, agents, retail?
4. How much are they selling and at what price?
5. What is their international strategic plan?

You will not find information to answer all these questions for all competitors, but you should find as much information as time and resources allow and then maintain an ongoing program of tracking competitive activities. In the final analysis, the results may be of little impact on your strategic planning and internal decisions, but because many of the methods used to get answers to the above questions involve little to no cost, it is better to have the information rather than ignore it altogether.

• KEY SOURCES OF INTERNATIONAL COMPETITIVE INFORMATION

There are four categories of sources for international competitive information:

1. Databases - public and private
2. Company information
3. Public information
4. Interviews - direct contact

Within each of these categories are specific sources of information. Some are better than others for particular questions. Some are very expensive. A summary of sources is shown in Figure 6.5 including a comparison of how each can be used to answer the five questions concerning competitors. Which ones you use and to which extent will depend on your specific requirements and budget.

• TRADE STATISTICS

One of the most helpful ways to know where competitors are selling is through import and export trade statistics. This data would commonly be used as one or more indicators in the foreign market selection matrix discussed in Chapter 5. Since the data is the combined imports and exports of all companies, it does not provide the trading activites of a single company. But trade statistics do provide an overall picture of supply and demand of products.

As first discussed in Chapter 3, all products have a harmonized code. Countries track the import and export of commodities using those harmonized codes. This data is then reported to the United Nations at the six-digit level. (U.N. can only be summarized at the six-digit level since the final four digits vary by country.) Many countries also publish their import export data at the ten-digit level. Trade statistics report the value of trade (for example in U.S. Dollars), and the volume (such as total number of grand pianos) as shown in Figure 6.6.

U.S. Trade Online - usatrade.census.gov

U.S. Trade Online is the official site for U.S. export and import data. It is maintained by U.S. Census. This is a monthly compilation of virtually all U.S. exports and imports and offers monthly, year-to-date, and past year trade to and from all countries. There is a low annual subscription cost, or you may get a report from your local international trade assistance provider such as a state trade center or a U.S. Export Assistance Center.

As the data is available at the ten-digit harmonized code, it can be very precise in indicating demand for U.S. goods (U.S. exports), or showing where U.S. companies are buying products (U.S. imports). As discussed in Chapter 3, some products have very exact matches to their harmonized code, such as 8418.69.0020 drinking water coolers,

Figure 6.5 Comparison of Sources of International Competitive Information

Sources of International Competitive Information	Where are they selling? Markets, Regions?	To whom are they selling?	How are they selling? Direct distributors, retailers?	Sales levels and pricing information?	International Strategic Plan?
DATABASES (PUBLIC & PRIVATE)					
U.S. Exports by Commodity	Excellent No assuming a good harmonized code to use	No	No	Aggregate information available at harmonized code level for both quantity and total export values, but not at the company level	No
PIERS or Datamyne	Excellent - potentially outstanding depending on match with exporter's name/product	Excellent - potentially outstanding depending on match with exporter's name/product	Unlikely	Potentially useful for quantity, at both industry and company level. Not useful for pricing or shipments values.	No
Directory of U.S. Exporters	Limited	No	No	Very limited quantity information, no pricing.	No
UN COMTRADE Database	Good but limited to data collected at the level of general commodity codes	No	No	Aggregate information available at very general commodity codes for export values but not quantities and not at company level	No
COMPANY INFORMATION					
Company Literature, Web sites	Potentially excellent	Potentially excellent	Potentially excellent	Potentially excellent but unlikely	Unlikely
Company Advertising	Excellent	Excellent	Very Good	Unlikely	No
Industry Associations	Excellent	Depends on association	Depends on association	Excellent No	

(continued)

Figure 6.5 Continued

Sources of International Competitive Information	Where are they selling? Markets, Regions?	To whom are they selling?	How are they selling? Direct distributors, retailers?	Sales levels and pricing information?	International Strategic Plan?
PUBLIC SOURCES					
Press (including electronic databases of popular and industry press)	Outstanding when available	Outstanding when available	Outstanding when available	Potentially some very good information	Potentially may have to look hard
INTERVIEWS/DIRECT CONTACT					
Interview: Industry Contacts (Press, Advertising)	Excellent depending on knowledge + openness of contacts	Excellent depending on knowledge + openness of contacts	Excellent depending on knowledge + openness of contacts	Potentially very good, but strong chance of misinformation	Perhaps
Government Contacts	Excellent	Probably limited	Good	Potentially good for aggregate information. Unlikely at the company level	No
Foreign Customers/ Distributors	Excellent	Excellent	Excellent	Limited	Unlikely
Employees from Competitors	Excellent	Excellent	Excellent	Excellent	Excellent

self-contained, and 9201.20.0000 Grand pianos. Other products are classified in catchall categories that do a poor job of describing the product. Trade statistics may be less helpful in those circumstances.

When you have a good harmonized code the information can be particularly useful. Figure 6.6 shows a sample report for harmonized code 9201.20.0000 Grand pianos. (The report has been reformatted for clarity.) The report is divided into two sections. The first part shows the dollar value of exports (the five columns after the country names). The second part shows the quantities of units exported (the last five columns). For each country, the current year-to-date is shown first and next the previous year-to-date. Census also reports by economic groups such as APEC or European Union. The last few rows of Figure 6.6 show some of these groupings.

Assuming you were a manufacturer of grand pianos and you wanted to know to where the other U.S. competitors were shipping, this report provides quite a bit of information. For example, regardless of the year, the largest market by far is Canada. In second place for shipments for the calendar year 2012 is Japan with $1,216,543 exported from the U.S. to Japan. Note that some countries were significant buyers in 2012, but had yet to import any through May – such as South Korea and Indonesia. You can also calculate the average price per grand piano to a country by dividing the value by the quantity. The database in fact offers that average price as one of its standard fields along with calculating the growth rate (or decrease) of exports to a market over a period of time.

As shown by the example, export data can be very helpful. When looking at a report, analyze the following areas:

- *Ranking*. One of the key indicators is the ranking, primarily by dollars. (The units section may not be helpful depending on the units. Most often, the unit is weight, which may not have as much relevance.) Be sure to do the ranking analysis for both the year-to-date column and each of the full year columns. Often the rankings will change.
- *Growth*. Another important analysis is growth rates which identify trends of either increasing or decreasing markets. For example, though Brazil is proportionately a much smaller market compared to Mexico or Japan, it shows much more steady growth. This could be an indication that it would be a good time to enter the market if the exporter is not yet there.
- *Complementary Products*. Don't just research the export statistics for your products. Look for complementary products as well. For grand pianos this could be 9201.10.0000 (upright pianos), or even all of Chapter 92 which are musical instruments and parts. USA Trade Online allows you to report at various levels of the harmonized code, including the chapter level. In this respect, a country's total imports of Chapter 92 would provide a high-level overview of to what extent a particularly country prefers U.S. musical instruments.
- *Statistically significant*. Another concern is that if the numbers are small compared to other data, they may not be reliable. For example, Venezuela is the seventh market as ranked by the Jan-Aug 1998 data. But the data from the other time periods indicates there is no ongoing justification to place it as the seventh most important market.
- *Transshipments*. One of the greatest problems with this report is that it does not accurately indicate the country of the final consumer. For example, Germany is consistently the number one country in Europe receiving grand pianos from the U.S. However, it is also a major sea link for U.S. shipments, and German companies often act as master distributors for other European destinations. If a shipment of pianos was consigned to Germany, the export documentation would indicate Germany as the destination. If some time later the pianos were re-exported to Austria, Poland, or Denmark, that would not be reflected in this report.

The data found at USA Trade Online is also available at the U.S. International Trade Commission website (dataweb.usitc.gov). This site is free but the interface is not as powerful as the Census site. However, for low-volume research, it's a great alternative to the Census site.

Figure 6.6 U.S. Exports of Harmonized Code 9201.20.0000 *Grand Pianos*

	Dollar Value or Exports (in $1,000's)					Actual Number of Units Exported				
	May 2013 YTD	2012	2011	2010	2009	May 2013 YTD	2012	2011	2010	2009
World	$7,720	$16,996	$17,190	$16,674	$14,575	742	1,526	1,628	1,591	1,438
Canada	3,959	9,407	11,214	8,565	7,811	386	860	1,063	877	801
Japan	258	1,217	785	1,021	804	22	97	83	88	72
South Korea		1,182	145		138		58	14		8
Mexico	450	765	317	367	328	44	83	38	38	51
China	391	562	570	1,651	725	39	55	56	166	72
Poland	17	506	220	203		2	37	16	23	
Germany	1,054	441	881	1,105	1,254	100	42	76	71	117
Hong Kong	59	347	69	218	137	6	47	6	22	15
U.K.	78	334	188	341	264	6	34	18	35	28
Australia	139	240	479	169	35	13	22	44	12	4
Indonesia		154	52	31	154		15	5	3	15
Brazil	30	140	379	801	805	5	16	33	74	73
Singapore	60	137	82	109		6	14	7	11	
Regional Groupings										
APEC	5,846	14,275	14,439	12,630	10,415	559	2,277	1,385	1,261	1,066
North Amer	4,410	10,163	11,531	8,931	8,139	430	943	1,101	915	852
E.U.	1,463	1,573	1,758	1,483	1,684	141	140	154	183	236
20 Latin Markets	520	1,447	1,198	1,357	1,365	78	148	111	133	147

UN Commodity Trade Statistics Database (UN Comtrade) – comtrade.un.org

The USA Trade Online database is useful to determine where your U.S. based competitors export. But what if you have significant non-U.S. competitors? Their export activities would be missing completely from these reports. For example, in the case of grand pianos, the U.K. has at least one important exporter, Steinway, yet their export activities are not readily available because they export from the U.K.

The data from U.N. Comtrade tracks import and export activities for all countries on an annual basis. It is essentially an international version of U.S. Trade Online. However a significant difference is the U.N. data only goes to the six-digit harmonized code. In the case of grand pianos this is not an issue as grand pianos are classified at the six-digit level. However many products are not fully described at only the six-digit level. For example row boats, canoes, and outboard motorboats are all classified as 8903.99. It is only at the ten digit level that row boats and canoes are tracked separately from outboard motorboats. Even with the limitation of data at the six-digit level, the U.N. data offers excellent insights into trading activities between non-U.S. countries. And there is no cost to use the site. The site can be a bit challenging to learn how to use. However, for quick access, use the steps summarized in Figure 6.7.

Figure 6.7 UN Comtrade Database: Quick Guide

The following instructions will guide you through how to research the import values for all countries for a particular harmonized code. Using this site helps identify top importing countries of a particular product.

1) Visit the website comtrade.un.org
2) Click on the link for 'Database'
3) Under the tab "Data Query" select "Express Selection"
4) You'll then get a screen with a number of boxes to complete. In the upper right click option HS07
5) Under "Enter Commodity Codes / Text" enter the six digit harmonized code using number only, such as 920120 for 'grand pianos'
6) Leave next box blank.
7) Under "Enter Partners Codes / Text" type the word 'world'.
8) Put a year in the 'Enter Years' box. (You can put the most recent full year but if not all countries have reported data, you may miss significant countries.)
9) Click the 'import' box at the bottom and accept the terms and conditions.

You'll then get the report. To have the report sorted from largest importing country, use the drop box to the right of 'Sort Order' and select 'TradeVal'. You should see a report similar to the screen shown in Figure 6.8.

Figure 6.8 UN Comtrade: Total Imports by Country of 920120 Grand Pianos

UN comtrade
United Nations Commodity Trade Stati

| Home | Data Query | Data Availability | Metadata & Reference | Subscription & Support | Fast tracks |

Home › Data Query › Express Selection › Query Result

Basic Query Results:

Statistics: 112 rows returned in 0.80 seconds.

Quick filter [?]   [Search] [Clear]   [Clear] [Apply]

Selected classification: HS2007
Selected commodities: 920120 (Grand pianos, incl. auto. pianos)
Selected reporters: All
Selected years: 2011
Selected partners: World
Selected trade flows: Import

Sort Order TradeVal;   ▾ [Refresh]

Direct Download SDMX Download Printable Format

Modify Selection View Graph & Map View Explanatory Notes View Not-Available-Data
Switch to any HS classifications

1 2 3 4 5 6

Period	Trade Flow	Reporter	Partner	Code	Trade Value	NetWeight (kg)	Quantity Unit	Trade Quantity	Flag
2011	Import	USA	World	920120	$71,787,770	1,957,317	5	11,728	4
2011	Import	China	World	920120	$37,996,413	1,035,984	5	5,074	4
2011	Import	Germany	World	920120	$32,685,353	940,995	5	2,511	2
2011	Import	France	World	920120	$21,959,479	598,732	5	1,512	4
2011	Import	Canada	World	920120	$20,798,436	567,076	5	2,497	4
2011	Import	Japan	World	920120	$14,777,668	262,839	5	837	0
2011	Import	Australia	World	920120	$13,646,263	585,068	5	1,871	4
2011	Import	United Kingdom	World	920120	$13,499,097	371,378	5	1,032	0
2011	Import	Russian Federation	World	920120	$10,813,216	244,144	5	717	0
2011	Import	Switzerland	World	920120	$9,916,404	131,812	5	400	0
2011	Import	Rep. of Korea	World	920120	$9,123,671	340,820	5	980	2
2011	Import	Italy	World	920120	$8,157,159	397,699	5	893	4
2011	Import	Poland	World	920120	$6,823,538	137,891	5	558	0
2011	Import	Malaysia	World	920120	$6,133,875	167,242	5	2,107	4
2011	Import	China, Hong Kong SAR	World	920120	$5,648,429	154,006	5	710	4
2011	Import	Singapore	World	920120	$5,412,043	147,561	5	798	4
2011	Import	Austria	World	920120	$5,197,128	93,600	5	260	0
2011	Import	Brazil	World	920120	$4,244,859	175,492	5	633	0

PIERS & DATAMYNE

So far we have research trade statistics to get trade flows of products such as 'what are the largest countries importing grand pianos'? However, none of the previous resources tell us the export (or import) activities of specific companies. This data can be very difficult to obtain. However, private companies have been offering select import/export activities of companies. Their data can tell you 'Where is Nike exporting its shoes?"

PIERS (www.piers.com) has long been the brand leader in this field. It has been publishing trade data since 1970. PIERS is the abbreviation for the Port Import Export Reporting Service and is is a proprietary database affiliated with the Journal of Commerce It is similar to the U.S. Exports by Commodity in that the database is based on shipping documents; however, the PIERS data comes from the manifests of vessels loading international cargo outbound from the U.S. (It also includes all inbound shipments for imports.) The advantage of this database over USA TradeOnline is that PIERS includes much more specific details of each shipment, including the name of the shipper. Figure 6.9 shows the data tracked by PIERS. Note that the data is ocean only so air shipments are not reported.

Datamyne (www.datamyne.com) is the new kid on the block. For years it has only had import data on companies. But more recently it has added exports as well. Datamyne also has significant data on all imports and exports (ocean and air) for a number of Latin countries.

PIERS and Datamyne offers very unique data. Because the data originates with vessel manifests, it removes the harmonized code constraints of USA TradeOnline. For example, these databases may capture trade names, brand names, and other product related descriptions lost in the harmonized code.

The transshipment problems still exist as described earlier. U.S. companies can make a shipment to one port and the product may eventually ship onward to consumers in different countries. Also, the ship manifest often lists the freight forwarder rather than the manufacturer as the shipper. Thus ABC Manufacturing may be the exporting company, but their name never appears in the reports because their shipping is done through a consolidator. Or if the export is through an intermediary, such as a U.S. broker or export management company, the original manufacturer's name will not appear. As good as it is, it is still not the panacea for competitive information. Air shipments also are missed.

If knowing the export or import activities of specific companies is important to your international strategy, investing in the PIERS or Datamyne data will be worth it. You do not need to purchase all the data. They offer custom reports or database access parameters to make it more affordable.

Figure 6.9 Data Tracked in the PEIRS Database

Shows combined list including both imports and exports. Not all fields are complete for each transaction.
- Product description
- PIERS product code
- Harmonized tariff code and description
- U.S. and overseas port name
- Container size, quantity, TEU count, and cubic feet
- Steamship line, vessel name, and Manifest number
- Cargo quantity and unit of measure
- Cargo weight
- Voyage number
- Estimated cargo value
- Payment type and bank name
- Shipment direction
- U.S. and overseas origins and destinations
- Marks and numbers
- Name and address of U.S. importer (imports only)
- Bill of lading number
- Name and address of U.S. exporter
- Container number
- Name and address of foreign shipper (imports only)
- Customs clearing district (imports only)
- Name and address of notify party
- Arrival and departure dates in U.S. ports
- Refrigerated, NVOCC, Ro/Ro, hazardous materials, and financial indicator flags

• COMPANY INFORMATION

Company Websites and Literature

Sometimes the easiest source of competitive information is directly from the competitors themselves. It may take some work, but at least you can rely on the information because it comes straight from the competitor.

Websites have become particularly useful because you can access websites of distributors and agents worldwide at no cost. Companies are increasingly putting more information on their websites. Though the information may be publicly available, it is easier to access than contacting the company directly. Be sure to investigate the sites of overseas distributors and customers. Often they will be more forthright with competitive information.

Company International Advertising

The reason to seek out the international advertising of your competitors is to try and answer some basic marketing questions. Though it may not be a helpful source for information about competitive pricing or strategic plans, it will offer some important insights. For example, you can probably determine if the advertisement was placed (paid for) directly by the manufacturer or by their foreign distributor in the local market. Some clues that tip off the fact that the advertisement was placed by the manufacturer would include:

- Ad is not translated
- Contact details include U.S. addresses and phone numbers
- More than one local distributor is listed on the ad
- A foreign office of the manufacturer is listed

Clues that the ad was placed by the local distributor:
- The only contact details are the local distributor with no details of how to reach the U.S. manufacturer
- Poor ad quality - looks like U.S. ads were pieced together
- An emphasis on the distributor rather than the manufacturer
- Products featured from more than one manufacturer

These clues are useful because the greater the likelihood the manufacturer is directly involved in placing the advertisement, the stronger the signal that the manufacturer sees that market as an international priority. Direct placement of international advertising into a market implies a high level of commitment and involvement in the market. These are generalizations, and circumstances can be constructed that contradict these assumptions, but the number of ads annually and the total advertising space offer positive signs about the viability of the market.

Ads also can provide an insight into how a competitor competes in a particular foreign market versus the U.S. market. You may find more of an emphasis on price or a particular feature compared to their competitive positioning in the U.S. This may be helpful information when you position your own products in that market.

Global Directories

There are a number of companies that provide detailed information about companies around the world. Kompass (www.kompass.com) is probably the most well known because it has been doing it for many years. It offers basic searching for free, and if the company is also an advertiser, all their details are also free. It also allows for searching by harmonized code and also the nature of their business such as producer, distributor, importer, etc.

OneSource (www.onesource.com) is actually larger than Kompass, though not as well known. They do not offer free online searching. However their for-fee database is very powerful and offers some unique features such as corporate trees, LinkedIn connections, and industry reports. They also offer free trials.

Two other databases are worth a look. Solusource (www.solusource.com) is from the well-known Thomas Register which for years was the printed version of a 'manufacturers yellow pages'. But now they have gone global and have listings in about 30 countries. Access is free. Alibaba (www.alibaba.com) is fast establishing itself as a significant player in this area. However, they have even more limited (about 20 countries) and much if not all the data is self-reported by the companies. So be sure and double-check any details obtained through Alibaba.

Industry Associations

Sometimes companies within industries realize they are stronger working together than against each other and they share sales and pricing information which many times includes international details. Because this data is considered extremely confidential, participants give the sales and pricing details to a third party, such as an industry association, that in turn summarizes the data and releases it in aggregate form with no company details. It is a simple, reliable, and cheap method of getting very good competitive information. Normally, you can only get the report if your company is both a member of the association and participates in providing sales details.

Though not all associations provide this service because it is not demanded or desired by the membership, most trade associations do track international trends and data. Associations can be helpful in augmenting your other research.

• PUBLIC SOURCES

Public sources such as newspapers and industry magazines have only recently been recognized as valuable sources of competitor details. Now that most major periodicals and trade press have full-text searching and retrieval capabilities, the ability to search for articles specific to particular companies, products, and industries is easy and affordable.

Industry Press

The benefit of industry press is its specificity to particular industries. You are no doubt familiar with your domestic industry press, but there are probably other magazines or journals for your industry in other significant international markets. Not only will they provide useful industry data, but also distributor lists, advertisements, and other company-specific information. Even if you don't understand the local language, you may be surprised at how much information you can garner from browsing the industry magazines from foreign markets. You can obtain these magazines often through the internet, or database search such as Factiva (Chapter 5). If all else fails, try to find out if the magazine has a U.S. editorial or advertising representative. He or she can send you a copy of the magazine. Even just one issue can provide quite a bit of useful competitive information.

Newspapers

You might not consider the popular press an important source of competitive information but it can be extremely useful. This is particularly true of closely held, private companies. When trying to get competitive information on such companies, I have often found that the local newspaper in the city where the corporate headquarters is located will feature interviews or other news about the company not reported by other sources. I remember once trying to find the annual sales figures for a small company in Colorado. Even credit agencies did not have sales information. Finally, through one of the electronic newspaper retrieval systems (Factivia, LexisNexis), I found an interview with the owner conducted by a local journalist from his hometown. In the article, the owner made a passing comment about the company's sales figures. While it may not have been rock-solid data, it was very useful.

• INTERVIEWS AND DIRECT CONTACT

The best and most reliable source for competitive information is direct contact with individuals that have personal knowledge of your competitors' activities. As shown in Figure 6.5, these sources are typically good to excellent for information on all types of competitive issues.

Industry Contacts - Press and Advertising

The importance of maintaining good contacts within the industry has been previously emphasized. I mention it again because initiating and maintaining strong contacts takes time and effort and it is easy to allow your efforts to slip. Companies also tend to avoid outside assistance, remaining insular in their strategic approach. Though this may suffice domestically, it dramatically limits a company's sources of international competitive information.

Keep a strong focus on developing good, reliable international contacts within your industry. As previously suggested, when traveling overseas, always include at least one visit to a magazine or journal's office, even if the appointment is made with short notice. Editorial staffs rely on fresh input and appreciate the opportunity to hear perspectives from outside their country. In turn, they will offer insights and answers to your questions that never may have appeared in print.

One important caveat in dealing with editorial or advertising industry contacts is that they are also in contact with your competitors so you never know if the information is entirely true. It is very easy to put misinformation into the market via these contacts, so always treat this information with close scrutiny and try to get second confirmations of any important data.

Government Contacts

Closely related to industry-specific private sector contacts are U.S. and foreign government contacts in the public sector. Government contacts are highly unlikely to offer any company-specific information other than what would already be in the public arena. But government contacts are particularly helpful for gaining aggregate competitive information such as competitive trends, challenges, and opportunities. Though they are not able to discuss specifics such as company names, they are a good source for initial research issues such as where competitors are selling internationally and how (distributor, agent, etc.).

Foreign Customers and Distributors

Because your foreign customers and distributors are constantly immersed in the day-to-day activities of their local markets, they are in a good position to tell you what your competitors are doing. Most good distributors will closely monitor the activities of other distributors. Their sales reps and customers also keep them informed of what is happening in the market, including prices and sales volume information.

Your customers and distributors are your eyes and ears in the foreign market, so constant contact with your distributors, agents, and customers (especially key accounts) is also important. They are an excellent source of very specific and detailed competitive information, and because it comes from a number of sources, it can be quite reliable.

Like most sources of competitive information, maintaining a good flow of information from customers and distributors has to be an ongoing effort. It is not enough to expect the information to make its way back home. Time and investment must be made in travel to the foreign market to visit with distributors and customers. When well developed, it may easily be one of the most consistent methods of determining what your competitors are doing.

Employees from Competitors

If you're lucky, you can hire an employee from a competitor. Then even strategic information will be available to you. There are some significant barriers to hiring competitor's employees, including provisions in their employment contracts (non-compete clauses) which prohibit them from accepting a job with a competitor for a specific period of time after leaving their current employer, so your options may be limited. Nevertheless, it is important to investigate all options because as shown in Figure 6.5, this is the only source that provides excellent competitive information for all the various issues to be researched. Of course employees may also be bound by trade secrets – which are inside knowledge and procedures that are to be kept confidential outside the company. Violating these can be a serious issue and one that must be carefully watched if an employee is hired from a competitor.

• NOTES

1.Both of these articles provide further insight into the competitive turnaround at Caterpillar:

J. P. Donlon, "Heavy Metal-Interview with Caterpillar CEO Donald Fites," Chief Executive (U.S.) (1 September 1995): 48.

Robert S. Eckley, "Caterpillar's Ordeal: Foreign Competition in Capital Goods," Business Horizons (1 March 1989): 80.

2. Eckley, "Caterpillar's Ordeal: Foreign Competition in Capital Goods."

3. Donlon, "Heavy Metal-Interview with Caterpillar CEO Donald Fites."

SECTION TWO

Getting
Global

In Section One, you learned why you should go global, when you should go global, and where to go. By now, you are probably eager to either start or expand your current global activities. There may be pressures other than from yourself to begin sooner than is appropriate. After all the market research, internal assessments, and consensus building internally, your colleagues are probably anxious to see if all their work and support will pay off in increased sales. Externally, there may be existing customers or contacts in foreign markets pressing to be appointed as the exclusive representative for your company. These are constant reminders that the foreign opportunities are ready to be developed. Is your company ready?

Many are not, even though the indicators suggest that their global expansion will be successful and profitable. Planning beyond the initial stage is needed to avoid costly mistakes, the most important being the appointment of the wrong foreign representative. And legal mistakes such as violations of the Foreign Corrupt Practices Act can result in fines.

Section Two will cover various considerations that should be made prior to any significant international activity. I start with selecting your foreign market entry mode in Chapter 7 followed by Chapters 8 and 9 discussing the process of finding your foreign partners. In Chapter 10, I discuss the impact of cultural differences on international business. The critical issues of international pricing and product policy is addressed in Chapter 11, including a detailed presentation of international pricing escalation.

Finally, Chapters 12 and 13 present the legal and tax considerations involved in international business.

CHAPTER 7

Foreign Market Entry Mode Selection

How a company enters a foreign market is one of the most critical strategic decisions it makes. There are a number of considerations in selecting a marketing entry mode. At its most basic, the decision of which type of entry mode focuses on the question of how close does the company need to be to its foreign customers versus the increased risks? This is because entry modes that keep the exporters more or less away from the final user (buyer) such as indirect exporting, carries little to no risk. But is also means the exporter has little control of the sales process, and limited to no feedback from the foreign customers. On the other hand, utilizing foreign direct investment as part of the entry mode selection, with the opening of a foreign sales and marketing office, bring the company much closer to the foreign buyer, greater control, and excellent feedback. But foreign direct investment also brings a whole new set of challenges and risks not associated with less-direct forms of market entry.

Balancing the risks versus rewards of each entry mode is what may make selecting your entry mode difficult. The higher your risk tolerance (not only in terms of financial risk, but time and management attention), the more likely you can justify a more direct foreign market entry mode. The less tolerance for risk you have, or international management experience, the more likely you select an entry mode that pushes most of the sales and marketing challenge to other partners. And the risk is also linked to the specific foreign market: a market with relatively low political risk, such as Canada, would generally favor a more direct approach. A higher risk country, such as Russia, would favor more indirect.

In this chapter I'll discuss balancing these risks, and explain the types of entry modes available for a company as it grows internationally.

• FOREIGN MARKET ENTRY - INDIRECT, DIRECT, OR FDI?

I know of a well-established manufacturer of a wide variety of accessories and enhancements for construction equipment. Its traditional customer base is local and state transportation departments and commercial firms involved in infrastructure construction. The firm delivers high quality products customized for the particular application at competitive prices which are kept low by maintaining a tight overhead.

Though the company has suspected their international potential could be significant, a short- to medium-term decision was made not to pursue international sales. Their, president, explains, "For the time being, we must keep our attention on domestic sales, manufacturing enhancements (including ISO registration), and marketing campaigns. International sales would be too distracting for the next two years while we continue to focus on consolidating our domestic success."

But rather than completely ignore its international potential, a combination of piggyback sales and indirect exports through domestic dealers has led to some very profitable international sales - all without a single international invoice, foreign currency risk exposure, or trip outside the U.S. The company has successfully entered a number of markets indirectly.

This is an excellent example of a company identifying its strengths and priorities and applying the analysis to its entry mode decisions. Eventually, it will pursue an aggressive international strategy that will include direct exporting and probably some overseas alliances. And rather than miss some important opportunities for both profit and institutional learning in the meantime, the company pursued a policy of indirect market entry.

Risk is directly tied to entry mode: Figure 7.1 demonstrates the related risk associated with five foreign market entry modes into a hypothetical country. Overall risk, as shown by the shaded boxes, increases from little risk associated with indirect exporting, to significant risk if a company elects to open a sales, marketing, and manufacturing subsidiary in the country. Don't be overly concerned at this point about the specific risks associated with each entry mode. These will be discussed in chapter 11. For now, just notice that risk is directly connected to the entry mode and the specific country being entered. A company with little international experience and low risk tolerance may elect an entry mode more toward the left of the. A company with great experience and risk tolerance would be more comfortable with modes toward the right.

The Progression of Foreign Market Entry Modes

The various foreign market entry modes can be seen as a range of options for companies as they increase their involvement in a foreign market. Some are more appropriate for the early stage of market entry, others for a later stage when more time and investment can be justified. The choice of mode is not determined by the size of the company. Each mode can be used by small or large companies.

Most companies begin their international expansion using direct exporting. As we will discuss later, though indirect exporting can be an attractive option in certain circumstances, it also has significant disadvantages. With **direct exporting**, a company sells

Figure 7.1 Foreign Market Entry Modes and Risk

				FX Translation Risk
				Commercial Risk
			Commercial Risk	FX Econ Risk
		Commercial Risk	FX Econ Risk	FX Transactional Risk
	Commercial Risk	FX Econ Risk	FX Transactional Risk	
	FX Econ Risk	FX Transactional Risk		Political Risk
	Political Risk	Political Risk	Political Risk	
Political Risk				
- - - - Export Sales / No Foreign Direct Investment - - - - -			- - - Foreign Direct Investment - - - -	
Indirect Export Sales (EMC, Piggyback)	**Direct Export Sales** - all sales denominated in the home currency of the seller	**Direct Export Sales** - sales denominated in the foreign currency of the buyer	**Overseas Sales and Marketing Office and Staff**	**Overseas Manufacturing, Sales and Marketing and Staff**
Scenario 1	**Scenario 2**	**Scenario 3**	**Scenario 4**	**Scenario 5**

The above figure helps to demonstrate that foreign market entry mode is directly tied to risk. As a company moves away from indirect export (least risk) to direct export, and later foreign direct investment, risk increases. In exchange, the company gains additional control and feedback from the market.

its products to an overseas buyer. The foreign buyer, typically a distributor or agent depending on the product, represents the manufacturer in the foreign market. A foreign distributor purchases a product in large enough quantities to make the overseas shipping costs affordable. The distributor warehouses the product and sells it into the distribution channel which may include retailers, dealers, or direct sales to the end-users. The distributor acts as an extension of the manufacturer and in some cases will feature the manufacturer's logo and branding in its local literature.

During this initial stage of direct exporting, the manufacturer relies on the foreign distributor to market and sell its product into the distribution channel. Though the manufacturer is dealing directly with the distributor, the day-to-day activities of getting the product to the market are the responsibility of the foreign distributor, backed by the marketing resources and product experience of the manufacturer. Direct contact between the exporter and the foreign distributor is through foreign sales trips by the domestic-based manufacturer, trade shows, manufacturer-sponsored international distributor meetings, and functions held at the manufacturer's facility. In this initial stage, the manufacturer makes no direct investment in the foreign market.

As the manufacturer gains international experience, it will seek greater control and feedback. This can be accomplished by establishing a marketing subsidiary in the foreign market. This would typically represent its first overseas investment – or foreign direct investment (FDI). The purpose of a marketing subsidiary is not to bypass the foreign distributor by selling directly into the market, but rather to increase the control and feedback by getting closer to the end-users, even if the manufacturer doesn't directly sell to the end-users. Subsidiary staff , who would be employees of the exporter, might join the distributor on sales calls to key accounts. They might also directly control marketing, such as advertising, public relations campaigns, and foreign trade shows. And if the manufacturer eventually sells directly to the market, the marketing subsidiary would become a sales office. Many companies, including very mature global companies, remain committed to selling only through their distributors/dealers even though they have established marketing subsidiaries in foreign markets.

At this point to improve profits, delivery times, and product adaptation for local needs, the manufacturer may opt to begin some type of foreign manufacturing. Legal, government, or consumer needs may also be a consideration. Foreign manufacturing may be local assembly using parts manufactured in the company's home market or it may involve full, local production using foreign sourced inputs. If the U.S. manufacturer owns 100 percent of the foreign production, it is referred to as a wholly owned operation. If ownership is split between the manufacturer and an overseas partner, a joint venture would be created. If no ownership is desired but proprietary technology is required to manufacture the goods, then overseas licensing would be initiated. The goal of each of these variations of foreign manufacturing is to bring the manufacturing closer to the consumer in order to improve the product and its profitability, or mitigate local market barriers such as government import tariffs and consumer purchasing preferences.

Figure 7.2 summarizes the advantages and disadvantages of select foreign market entry modes. Refer to this figure as you read the next sections on each entry mode.

Figure 7.2 Advantages and Disadvantages of Select Market Entry Modes[1]

Entry Modes						
	Indirect Export-ing	Direct Export-ing	Direct Export-ing with FDI	Foreign Manufac-turing / Foreign Sales & Dis-tribution	Licens-ing	Joint Venture / Strategic Alliances
Advantages	No experi-ence re-quired	Greater control	Greater control	Full control	Low in-vestment require-ments	Can have some control and feedback depending on contract
	Faster to market	Greater feedback	Greater feedback	Greater feed-back	Fast market entry	Access to local knowledge and market ex-pertise
	Low cost	Gain mar-ket knowledge	Better meet customer needs	Keep all profits	Use local partner	Shared risks
Disadvantages	Limited control	More costly	More com-plex	Most expensive	Limited control	Actual con-trol may be limited by foreign part-ner
	Limited feedback	More time and effort required	More time and effort required	More time and effort required	Potentially less profits compared to other modes	May lead to lower profits due to shared risks
	No gained market knowledge	More risk	More risk	Most risky	May be creating future competitor	Can be diffi-cult or ex-pensive to disengage from partner
Likely stage in a firm's globalization	Early stage or never	Early stage	Maturing	Mature firm with strong international experience	Depends on industry and market.	Depends on industry and market

• INDIRECT MARKET ENTRY

An **indirect market entry** strategy essentially involves turning over the foreign market entry to a third party. In most cases, this third party does the exporting for your company, so for the purpose of this chapter we will refer to this process as indirect exporting. Keep in mind that a third party also can help you enter a market via other traditional entry modes, such as overseas licensing, local sales and marketing, and even manufacturing. The essential difference between an indirect and direct market entry is that a third party is coordinating the entry on your behalf and assumes the risk.

Types of Indirect Exporting

If you are not familiar with indirect exporting, you may be surprised at the variety of companies and sales arrangements available for indirect exporting. The most traditional methods/types are:

- *Export management company*. This is the most common way to indirectly export. Different industries call these companies by different names, but essentially they are companies whose primary purpose is to sell and market products and services internationally on behalf of other companies. The most common types are **export management companies** (EMCs), **export trading companies** (ETCs), and export commission agents and brokers. They all accomplish the same thing - making the international sale. The main differences are their level of involvement in completing the sale, such as invoicing, shipping, and collecting payment. The distinctions between each type are blurred, especially between differing industries, but the general nature of each type is summarized in Figure 7.3.
- *Piggyback exporting*. **Piggyback exporters** manufacture their own products and sell them internationally. To expand their international distribution network and expertise, they also represent products they do not manufacture. (The same would apply to international service providers.) As a manufacturer, you can piggyback onto the success of another company. For example, a small software company might sell its products to a much larger software company with international distribution while maintaining its own direct domestic sales program.

  Suitable partners for piggyback exporting are manufacturers whose products are enhanced by your products or companies within your industry that do not manufacture competing products but sell to the same customer base. The key is to find a company already successful internationally that fits well with your product and is willing to sell products from outside its own company.

  The outcome of piggyback exporting is essentially the same as that of EMCs because your piggyback partner becomes your export department.
- *Domestic distributors and gray marketing*. Often products from U.S. manufacturers are sold to domestic distributors, dealers, or even customers that redirect the products to foreign customers. In some cases, the manufacturer is

Figure 7.3 Clarification of the Types of Export Management Companies

Export Management Company - EMCs can be considered replacements for your own in-house international department. EMCs are typically involved in the whole international trade process including sales, marketing, invoicing, shipping, foreign receivables risks, and in some cases customer training, support, and warranty issues. Often the representation arrangement is on an exclusive basis, meaning the manufacturer will not sell directly into any markets covered by the contract with the EMC. Because these contacts are generally exclusive, most EMCs will not represent competing products. However, a particular EMC will likely focus on specific industries and regions of the world.

Export Trading Company - ETCs are much like EMCs and for the purpose of this text will be treated as the same. The distinction often lies in the size of the company. Traditional export trading companies are massive such as Mitsubishi International Corporation. The term became more common after the 1982 U.S. Export Trading Company Act, which helped eliminate fears of antitrust violations between companies joining together to export their products or services. Thus ETCs are more likely than EMCs to represent competing products. They are also more likely to import as well as export products and may even own or control the transportation methods.

Export Commission Agents and Brokers - The basic difference between an agent or broker and EMCs and ETCs is that agents typically don't fulfill the order; they simply pass it on to the manufacturer. The arrangement is similar to that of domestic sales reps. They act as sales agents for a company but don't invoice the customer or coordinate the logistics. It is also common for an agent or broker not to disclose details of the international sale. In this case the agent invoices and collects the foreign receivable for fear that once each party is aware of the other future sales will be conducted directly between the manufacturer and the customer to avoid the agent's profit margin. Agents and brokers are typically smaller companies, if not one-person operations, and generally have limited capital to finance such transactions. Thus, any ongoing relationships between manufacturers and foreign customers tend to be out in the open and the manufacturer simply pays the agent a commission. As an agent becomes more involved in the export process, it becomes an EMC.

aware that its product is being exported and supports the sale. The manufacturer may even assist with the sale, such as supplying a particular document associated with export sales. This use of domestic distributors is extremely effective and would be an example of indirect exporting.

However, if the export is not authorized by the manufacturer, especially if the export is into a foreign market where the manufacturer already has representation (either directly or indirectly), it is considered gray marketing. Though theoretically gray marketing is indirect exporting, it is not desired because it disrupts the authorized export channels.

Benefits of Indirect Exporting

Regardless of the method, indirect exporting can be an important addition to a company's sales and marketing strategy and considering all the benefits, it can be an attractive option. The following benefits are generally attributed to using an EMC where 100 percent of the export activity is outsourced.

No international experience required The most important benefit of indirect exporting is that a company can indirectly export as soon as it has a product to sell that can compete internationally. No internal international experience is required. You don't have to know which foreign markets should be targeted, how to sell to those markets, and most importantly, how to fulfill the order and get paid internationally. Your indirect export sales are simply like domestic sales that are re-exported.

Management is not distracted. This is a particularly important benefit for companies during their initial stages of growth when their domestic goals may be more important than international opportunities. Because indirect exporting typically turns over the international sales and marketing to a third party with little to no handholding by the manufacturer, management's time and resources are not diverted from other priorities. This can be important for a company that is still developing its R&D, manufacturing, or sales and marketing strategies. As discussed in Chapter 2, a company is only ready to go global when there is adequate experience, cash flow, management commitment, and capacity. Until these are all in place, management needs to focus on achieving stronger domestic success, and consider indirect exporting.

Faster to the international market. Because a strategy of indirect exporting utilizes the experience and strengths of the exporting partner, the manufacturer gets its products into the international marketplace faster than other entry modes. Tasks such as hiring additional international staff or training existing employees are not required. Nor will time be lost finding international distributors because the export partner will have already identified the potential distributors. The company doesn't have to develop banking, legal, transport, or accounting resources because the export partner also will coordinate these international aspects. All of this adds up to considerable time savings and means your products reach the international market faster. You essentially draw on the years of international experience and contacts of your partner.

Little to no increased financial commitment. The export partner typically covers most incremental expenses associated with international sales. This would include costs such as international travel, telecommunication, and sometimes even marketing expenditures, all of which are considered part of the EMC's cost of doing business. And because all of your international sales are treated as domestic sales, there is no foreign exchange risk or international collection problem.

Low risk. Indirect exporting involves low risk for the manufacturer. With no increased costs in resources and expenses, the sales from indirect exporting are incremental to your existing business. Management is able to pursue domestic priorities and remain focused on its cash producing priority - domestic sales. What could be better than additional sales with little to no additional work?

Indirect exporting seems to be the lowest risk, easiest decision a company could make. But is it actually a low-risk decision? The whole picture won't be clear until you analyze the disadvantages of indirect market entry.

Disadvantages of Indirect Exporting

Though the benefits of indirect exporting are significant, so are the downside risks, which is why many companies will not consider indirect market entry.

Poor control. Because all of the export activities are coordinated by your export partner, you essentially have little control over the fundamental sales and marketing decisions for those markets covered by your indirect exporting contracts. Typically, the EMC will make all the important decisions, including which companies will be chosen as overseas distributors and which markets receive the most attention. The aggressiveness of the sales campaigns and the personal attention your overseas customers receive will all be factors out of your control. Even the number of times personal sales calls are made will be determined by your EMC or piggyback partner.

Why wouldn't your export partner make the right decisions in your best interest? Because the EMC or piggyback partner is also working for other companies and its marketing decisions impact more than one company and product. Budgets can also constrain their activities.

For example, when a sales trip to a foreign market is planned, the EMC attempts to accomplish sales objectives of several companies. Due to its time and budget constraints, it will visit various buyers and contacts on this trip that may have nothing to do with your products and goals. Like all companies, EMCs have to justify the time and expense they will incur to make your product successful as well as the other products and manufacturers it represents. Some of these decisions, including which countries to visit, may be contrary to your goals. Because you have no control, you may experience the same frustration you encounter with the independent reps who handle your domestic markets. This very lack of control often forces companies with independent reps to change to in-house representation.

Wrong market, wrong distributor. EMCs and piggyback companies usually have a stronghold on particular markets and countries. The markets that have historically been successful for the EMC will likely be the markets they use for your products, even if they are not the best markets. This is particularly true if you have a worldwide, exclusive contact with your export partner. Because of the expense, an EMC rarely will be truly global so its markets become your only choices.

Are these the right choices? You may never know. You'll generally receive poor feedback about your real foreign market potential from your export partner. For example, if you have a worldwide contract with an EMC strong in Europe and Asia but weak in South America or Africa, it is unlikely that it will tell you that you should be focusing on Brazil or South Africa, even if those markets should in fact be the priorities. The specific international markets EMCs choose for your products may not be the right markets.

Your lack of control also may lead to your products being assigned to foreign distributors who are not the most effective for your products. I know because I spent a number of years working for an EMC. When we would agree to represent a new manufacturer, my first inclination was to see if any of my existing distributors would be appropriate for the new product line. One of the most expensive and time consuming tasks of international business is establishing an international network of distributors and agents and getting to know how to work with and manage them, so it is understandable that an EMC will try and utilize its existing network. At times, I would give the product line to one of our established distributors even though the fit of the new product wasn't perfect. This was not done to harm the manufacturer that I represented. It was simply the reality that the cost of establishing a new relationship with a different distributor was too high to justify. Though I never gave a product line to a distributor that I felt would not do its best to represent the new product, there were instances where more time and money spent on the distributor selection process may have resulted in a more effective distributor. Indirect exporting does not ensure the use of overseas distributors that are the most effective for your products.

Inadequate market feedback. You'll probably not be surprised if I tell you that indirect export partners do not provide the manufacturer with many details concerning their international activities. In some cases, such as with international brokers, this may include not revealing the names of international customers.

The reasoning is simple; if the manufacturer is kept from knowing many details it will continue to need its indirect partner. If the manufacturer receives too much information it will take over the business itself once the contract expires.

Not receiving specific details such as customer names is only one of the challenges of indirect exporting. This inadequate feedback from the market and your customers may affect the international success of your company. Important information comes from customers including product enhancement suggestions and competitive information. Yet all of this information may never be relayed to you. And it's not always because your export partner is trying to keep you in the dark. They simply may not recognize the relevance of a particular piece of information to your company. When a problem arises in a market, your EMC or piggyback partner may not even know the right questions to ask to determine what the problem is. And your partner may not have the technical expertise or knowledge of your R&D to know what product development and enhancement information should be relayed to you even if they want to pass the information onward.

Clearly, I cannot generalize about EMCs. Many provide excellent feedback. However, because they are not your employees, the communication between you and your export partners will rarely be as thorough as that between you and an internal department. (Chapter 8 will discuss ways to mitigate this problem.)

Potentially lower sales. Indirect exporting may lead to missed sales opportunities and lower overall international sales because your indirect export partner may not have chosen the ideal mix of markets and distributors. Lack of control and poor feedback also contribute to overall lower sales than you would achieve if you used a direct market entry method. Indirect exporting is not the preferred entry mode if market dominance and top market share is your overall international strategy. However, indirect exporting does play an important role within many types of international strategies.

Higher risk? Poor control, inadequate feedback, and potentially lower sales would indicate that indirect exporting has higher risks than direct exporting. This is particularly true if your export partner fails in its international sales and marketing efforts with your product. If the wrong distributor is chosen, the overseas customer base may never truly understand the real strength and benefits of your products. The distributor may so poorly represent your products that local customers have the wrong image of your brand - too expensive, too difficult, or poor quality. If the distributor has a bad reputation, your brand could be tarnished. Recovering from these perceptions can be costly and time consuming.

Missed opportunities due to poor control and feedback could also allow your competitors to become so entrenched and successful in particular foreign markets that you effectively lose any chance of success without significant investment.

When faced with the risks of indirect exporting many manufacturers never choose this entry method. But before you can rule out indirect exporting, you must first explore the issues associated with direct market entry.

• DIRECT MARKET ENTRY

It is considered direct market entry when a company deals directly with an entity in the foreign market rather than through another domestic company. The foreign entity may be an agent, representative, distributor, or even a subsidiary of the company. Though the most common mode of direct entry is through direct exporting, other direct entry modes include: licensing, overseas sales and marketing offices, overseas joint ventures and alliances, and overseas manufacturing. With direct market entry, the manufacturer is in direct control of the international expansion, even if particular tasks of the expansion, such as marketing and research, are outsourced.

Benefits of Direct Exporting

The advantage of direct exporting over indirect exporting is that it overcomes the problems of control and feedback.

Direct control. A manufacturer pursuing a strategy of direct exporting is in direct control of all major decisions, including two critical decisions. The first is direct involvement in the selection of which foreign markets to enter. The second is actively choosing the foreign companies to represent the U.S. company. Both decisions have tremendous impact on the future international success. Of course being in control of these decisions and achieving international success are still two different issues. But with adequate planning and investment, directly exporting offers an excellent opportunity to make the right market and foreign representation decisions.

Direct control of the international process also means the timetable for international expansion is under the control of the manufacturer, not an outside, third party. When utilizing indirect exporting partners, expansion beyond the initial target markets is often slower than desired by the manufacturer. This relates to the earlier point that EMCs and other indirect export partners have more than one "boss" and must relate expenses to overall goals and timetables, which may not be in sync with one particular manufacturer.

Excellent feedback. Unlike indirect exporting in which the export partner may avoid giving too many specifics of their international activities, a company directly exporting may receive an overwhelming amount of feedback. The very nature of direct exporting involves close contact with the foreign market. Feedback from the market is typically immediate and abundant. Through my experiences, I found that everyone constantly gave me advice about my company's products, the industry, and the marketplace. Most other international executives I have spoken to have had the same experience.

The key is to listen and not ignore this valuable feedback. Nurture your good foreign contacts the same way you do your local industry contacts to gather inside information.

Greater sales? You would assume a company's sales will be greater than through indirect exporting because the manufacturer has complete control and good feedback. Certainly a company would only pursue direct exporting if it believed it offered the best sales potential. However, the success of the strategy will depend on its execution. A poorly conducted market selection and distributor search could lead to very disappointing results and sales that are lower than if the company had chosen indirect exporting. Greater sales through direct exporting cannot be determined until the actual sales results are compared to the sales budget.

Disadvantages of Direct Exporting

Though the advantages of direct exporting are tremendous, manufacturers should not utilize this entry mode without fully understanding the requirements and potential drawbacks.

Greater investment required than indirect exporting. Because the manufacturer is in control of the entire export process, from market and distributor selection through sales fulfillment and payment collection, the financial and nonfinancial resource requirements are significant. The pace and intensity of international expansion will determine the level of investment required by the company. I don't want to dissuade a company from a direct export strategy simply because of the resource commitments because utilizing resources and setting an appropriate pace can lower the risk. However, no company should pursue a policy of direct exporting without recognizing that some level of commitment needs to be made toward the international effort.

Time-to-market may be higher. Depending on a company's international expertise and contacts, direct exporting may result in a longer time-to-market than an indirect method. This is because a manufacturer will need to establish an existing international distribution network, and that takes time. It is a relative matter because an ineffective indirect export partner will also result in a long time-to-market delay. You need to be aware that launching products into foreign markets, especially without prior experience and contacts, will take time.

Higher risk. Risk is often defined in financial terms. How much money will be lost if this strategy fails? What financial investment is required? Because direct exporting involves a higher financial commitment, not to mention nonfinancial resources such as management time and support resources, direct exporting may be considered a higher risk than indirect exporting.

Because high risk was also listed as a disadvantage of indirect exporting, this may appear to be a contradiction. It is not. Both methods are risky. They just involve different types of risk. A direct export strategy involves a greater financial commitment, so it is easier to identify the risk in a specific dollar amount. For indirect exporting, the risk is related to missed opportunities due to inappropriate decisions made by the indirect export partner. Both strategies have elements of risk, but the significance of each risk depends on many factors.

With an indirect export strategy, the level of risk is directly related to the quality of the match between the manufacturer and the indirect export partner. If the indirect partner has an established distribution network ideally suited for the manufacturer, the risk is minimal. With a direct export strategy, the level of risk is directly related to the company's commitment and ability to expend the necessary time and resources. With a strong commitment, risk is minimized. The company that chooses directly exporting sees indirect as risky. The company that chooses indirect exporting see direct as risky. The company's view of which risk suits them will determine which method to use.

• CHOOSING BETWEEN DIRECT AND INDIRECT METHODS

The decision to choose direct or indirect exporting can be narrowed down to deciding which of the risks are relevant to the company and how each risk could impact the international and domestic goals of the company.

For example, a company that feels its international potential is a crucial part of its short- to medium-term strategy would probably view financial risk as a necessary component of pursuing that strategy. This company would likely favor direct exporting. A company whose short- to medium-term goals do not emphasize its international potential would view the financial risk as a threat to its other goals and would favor indirect exporting. This difference in view may exist even if each company had a long-term goal of fully developing its international potential.

Figure 7.4 summarizes these two different views of risk. The left axis indicates the level of control and feedback a company has in a particular foreign market. Increased resource commitments are shown on the bottom axis. Generally, to increase control and feedback, there must be an increase in the financial and nonfinancial costs such as staff time. The optimal position of maximum control and feedback with little financial or resource costs is represented in the upper left. Though desirable, it is unlikely that a company can attain such a position, especially in a foreign market where strong control and feedback most often means employing direct exporting, which requires financial and resource investments. A company would not want to be in the lower right area where significant resource commitments have been made but little to no increase in control and feedback is received.

The most likely scenario is that the company must choose between the payoff of control and feedback and the investment required. This is where the two different views of risk are evident. Some companies will find it increasingly risky to move out along the resource axis. Due to either domestic priorities or financial constraints, they will not risk making an investment beyond a certain point even with the benefit of increased control and feedback. They see too much risk operating beyond line A.

On the other hand, other companies will make the necessary financial and nonfinancial commitments as long as a minimum level of control and feedback is attained. This minimum level is shown by line B. For these companies, they will not accept market control and feedback under line B because it is too risky.

One view is not better than the other. Studying these views helps clarify the tendency for some companies to favor indirect market entry over direct market entry. Companies who are not willing to go beyond line A are well suited for indirect exporting. Companies who are not willing to accept levels below line B are well suited for direct exporting. An indirect exporter finds itself in the lower left - less control and feedback in exchange for less financial and time commitment. A direct exporter finds itself in the upper right - control and feedback in exchange for more financial and time commitment.

This view of which risk is greater and why is based on many aspects of a company. In some cases, simply lacking international expertise and experience may push a

Figure 7.4 Risks and Rewards of Indirect and Direct Exporting

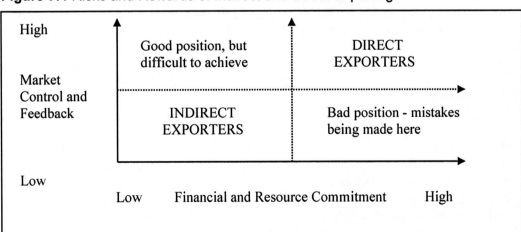

company toward indirect exporting. In other cases, the corporate culture of a company and an aggressive view of resource risk may push the company toward direct exporting.

Companies may also find their views of international risk change as they expand internationally. Significant international success, combined with increased international experience, will lead the company from line A to line B. This helps explain why companies often begin with indirect exporting and move to direct involvement.

Is It All or Nothing?

A key point to make at this point is that the decision between indirect exporting and direct exporting is not all or nothing. A company should not choose only one or the other. Rather the decision should be made on a market-by-market basis.

For example, if a company has a strong market in Europe with some internal strengths and experience in Europe and a view that the investment is worth it, it will no doubt choose a direct entry strategy for the European market. The same company may have no experience in Asia and view that market as somewhat risky in terms of the investment in time and money. Rather than ignore this market, a strategy of indirect exporting to Asia would be more profitable than no exporting at all. One company can pursue direct and indirect exports at the same time.

A company also may choose to use both strategies if it has different product lines with different customer profiles. For example, if a company manufactures products for the agricultural industry and they know the industry inside and out and have a pretty good international network of resources and potential customers in the international agricultural industry, it would choose a direct export strategy. If that company also has a spin-off technology suitable for the manufacturing-technology industry and a widely dispersed customer base that spans many types of manufacturers in various industries, it may be best to piggyback the product with a company that specializes in manufacturing-technology products and already has the vast international network. Again, one company employs both indirect and direct strategies.

A company should consider both direct and indirect entry modes in order to maximize its international potential. Many companies ignore indirect options and forsake whole international markets because they feel it is better to wait until they can afford to enter those markets. Though this may be true, companies need to constantly assess the situation to determine if a blended approach of direct and indirect exporting is more appropriate.

It also should be mentioned that if a company's medium- to long-term strategy in a market is to go direct, it may not be wise to go indirect in the short term. Often a change from indirect to direct can be very difficult, especially if the indirect partner did not represent the product effectively. For example, if customer support for the product is poor, the poor image of the product created by the indirect partner will be difficult to reverse when the manufacturer switches to direct market entry. Also, if inadequate efforts of the indirect partner result in significant gains for competitors, any future opportunities in that market may be lost. The decision to use indirect export must be made within the overall strategy of the company.

• FOREIGN DIRECT INVESTMENT (FDI)

Foreign direct investment (FDI) is an investment made by a company in a facility or asset in a foreign country to market and/or produce a product. The initial phase of a company's international expansion typically does not involve FDI. Instead, a company begins selling to foreign markets using local agents or distributors that represent the U.S. manufacturer or service provider. The obvious benefits of a non-FDI strategy are its relatively low investment and low risk. By employing a non-FDI strategy, you avoid having to establish and manage foreign facilities, hire international staff, and deal with the foreign exchange risks as well as the increased political and economic risk exposure.

The question addressed in this section is whether a successful export-only company must eventually move beyond exporting and make foreign direct investments. For example, do companies ultimately have to open overseas sales and marketing offices? Is foreign manufacturing inevitable?

The answer relates back to our earlier discussion of risk versus reward shown in Table 7.1 For a number of reasons I will discuss, companies do choose to move into foreign direct investment even with the greater risk. It is important issue to understand why FDI may be important even if you believe it will be some time before your company is ready for such activities. The importance of FDI lies in the significant competitive advantages that come from increasing your foreign market involvement. A company should always be questioning its foreign market entry methods to look for ways to improve. Even with significant export success, management must continually address the issues of foreign offices, foreign assembly, and foreign manufacturing.

• WHY COMPANIES GO BEYOND EXPORTING

It is not an easy decision for a company to move beyond exporting. Once a company crosses the line from simply exporting to making direct foreign investments, the company takes on new risks. When a company opens an overseas sales office, it acquires foreign assets, faces new human resource management issues, and increases the international tax considerations. The risks only increase in number and magnitude if the foreign investment involves a more significant foreign market investment, such as an overseas manufacturing facility.

However, in practice it may actually be more risky for a company not to pursue foreign direct investments. Despite the increased risks associated with FDI, such a strategy may be necessary if the company is to achieve its international potential. I will discuss three instances in which moving beyond exporting is justified: (1) barriers to exporting success, (2) a need for increased foreign market control and feedback, and (3) access to foreign resources.

Barriers to Exporting Success

For some foreign markets, the cost of transportation or local import barriers may prevent exporting as a viable long-term option. Even if a company wants to pursue exporting to avoid the cost and risks associated with overseas investments, it may not be possible. In such markets, foreign goods may face significant import barriers or landed costs that are so high that they limit sales and reduce the market's attractiveness. In these cases, a company may be forced to make a foreign direct investment.

Transportation costs. Depending on the product, the added expense of international freight and related costs may make the product noncompetitive in foreign markets. Despite the improving efficiency of international transportation options and the resulting decreases in freight costs, some products are not well suited to exporting because the transportation costs remain too high. This is particularly true of products that have a low value relative to the freight costs, for example heavy or bulky raw materials.

It also holds true for products that could easily be produced in the target foreign market as long as product differentiation isn't based on the origin of the product. For example, Coca-Cola and Pepsi traditionally produce their soft drinks through local manufacturing in each foreign market. It is not practical or necessary to produce the drinks in the U.S. On the other hand, Perrier bottled water differentiates itself because the water is bottled in France using natural mountain water. Clearly, Perrier would lose this differentiation if it was produced outside France. For Perrier, the increased logistics costs are offset by the ability to get a higher price for the product.

Import barriers. Even in cases where the transportation costs are reasonable, import barriers may keep the product from being competitive in the local market. As discussed in Chapter 4, import barriers take the form of either tariff or nontariff barriers. Tariffs are taxes applied directly to the products by foreign governments to give locally produced products a competitive advantage. Nontariff barriers include quotas and product standard requirements. Nontariff barriers can be even trickier than tariffs because the effect is more difficult to quantify. Both types of barriers have the effect of making imported products more expensive than they would otherwise be without the barriers. This can result in the imported product being priced too high to be competitive in the local market. Sales are either not possible or so low that the market is unattractive.

Need for Increased Control and Feedback

As a company gains experience exporting to a particular foreign market, it may become evident that to really achieve success, more control of and feedback from the foreign market is necessary. Compared to the issue of import barriers and transportation costs, which are challenges that exist from the time you enter a market, the need for increased control and feedback may only become apparent over time.

Generally, most companies find that the initial effort of their foreign buyers (agents and distributors) leads to a particular level of success. Over time, as the agent or distributor gains more experience with the product and continues to invest in the local marketing efforts, sales will continue to expand. As the manufacturer receives feedback from its foreign distributor, it adapts its product and marketing strategy to enhance sales in that market.

However, many manufacturers find that over time, there is increased pressure for them to become more involved in the foreign market. This may initially take the form of a foreign sales and marketing office, but could eventually lead to a distribution center, customer support/repair center, and foreign manufacturing. The point at which this pressure becomes significant enough to warrant the manufacturer investing in the foreign market will vary by company, industry, and even product. The following triggering events may force the issue.

Moving from exclusive distribution to nonexclusive distribution. Companies typically establish exclusive distributors/agents on a market by market basis, often using country borders to define territories. The benefit of an exclusive relationship is that the distributor or agent is motivated to invest in local marketing activities. It knows the sales generated by its work will benefit it because it has exclusive representation.

It is usually impossible for any single distributor to fully exploit the potential of a particular market. A distributor may be strong in particular segments of the customer base, but not all. For example, it may have good contacts with 50, 60, or even 80 percent of the key accounts in the market, but not 100 percent. It may have a sales and marketing style that works well for some categories of customers, but not all. It may have a geographic focus on one part of the market, but not the entire market.

I faced this challenge in Germany. Of the potential distributors, each had a geographic strength based on its headquarters. Each was strong in one region - northern, mid, or southern Germany - depending on where it had offices. None could offer true coverage of the entire country. I knew I had to appoint only one distributor so an exclusive distributorship could act as a motivator to encourage the necessary investment in our product line. The distributor, in turn, would have to appoint sub-distributors to cover the other parts of the country. I expected this and knew it would also add extra costs to the product potentially resulting in a higher price to the final buyers. Nevertheless, our company was not in a position to conduct the required marketing activities (translations, advertising, and trade shows) so we had to begin with one distributor. Our long-term plan was to move to non-exclusivity.

Because most distributors will not be perfect, there is an increasing need to consider appointing more distributors in the market. Once this happens, the previous exclusive distributor will probably no longer make significant marketing expenditures such as local advertising or trade shows. Thus, the manufacturer will be required to step up its own marketing activities which may lead to setting up a local sales and marketing office. In this way, the move to nonexclusive representation may be a triggering event that forces the manufacturer to make a foreign direct investment in a local sales office.

Increasing customer support requirements. For some products, as the number of customers increases in a market, so does the customer support requirements. These may be warranty and repair needs, training requirements, or other product support needs. Generally, these needs are met by the appointed distributor or a third party service company.

However, over time, the U.S. manufacturer may find that the ability of the distributor or third party service company to adequately address the needs of the customer base is not sufficient. This is particularly true if the manufacturer continues to directly support its U.S. domestic market. If the company has never had to turn over its domestic customer support to its U.S. distributors or a third party, it may find it difficult to do so overseas.

The initial indications of international customer support problems vary. The average warranty repair time may increase to an intolerable level. It could be that increased complaints from customers regarding the service they are receiving from the distributor or third party service firm may increase. Or inappropriate procedures or activities by the distributor or service company may result in a lawsuit.

Whatever the reason, exporting companies may eventually find that they are at a disadvantage by not being able to service their foreign customers directly, which may trigger the need to open a foreign customer service facility.

Strong buyer-seller relationship. Another need that would trigger FDI is if the nature of the buying process in the industry dictates that the supplier be readily accessible to the buyer. For example, the printing industry is inherently local because of the close relationship between the buyers (advertising agencies, manufacturers, service providers) and the printers. Each buyer must work closely with its printer during the entire process, from initial specs to the proofs and final inspection. It is difficult to work this closely if you are separated by thousands of miles and time zones, especially if the printing job is urgent.

This also is the case if there is a strong research and development linkage between buyer and seller. For example, many manufacturers provide products that are directly related to the buyer's products, such as product packing for food products. The supplier must work very closely with the buyer to make sure that the packaging works technically, cosmetically, and functionally. Mistakes could lead to severe problems for the buyer if the packaging fails - spoiled food, lost sales, upset customers.

When the relationship between supplier and buyer must be very close, a U.S. company may find it must establish some overseas presence in order to directly interface with the buyer. Though some initial export success may have been achieved through an export only strategy, the full potential of the market may not be reached without a local presence by the U.S. company.

Increased competition - export stagnation. Often the pressure to increase the involvement in a foreign market comes from the competition. During the initial entry into a foreign market, the exporter may find that initial success is easy. The product or service is well received and gets the attention of particular segments of the distribution channel and customer base, and exports increase. However, over time, the sales growth rate declines and exports level off or perhaps even decrease. Depending on the industry and the particular product or service, this decline can be attributed to any number of issues.

For example, buyers may have readily accepted the product regardless of the price. This activity may attract other foreign manufacturers to enter the market. It may also trigger a strong response from local competition or other foreign suppliers already located in the market. Whatever the reason, sales become harder and exports stagnate.

This situation could lead to more aggressive activities in the export process, such as increased advertising, promotional activities, or foreign travel by the U.S. company. Or it may lead to direct involvement in the market, such as establishing a local (regional) sales and marketing office. This does not necessarily mean a change in distributors or distribution method. The same exclusive distributors may still be used after opening the overseas sales office. The sales office simply allows greater control and feedback from the market, which should lead to increased sales. In this way, increased competition, or export stagnation, may lead to the need to pursue foreign direct investment.

Access to Foreign Resources

A final justification for a company to pursue foreign direct investment is access to foreign resources. The most common example is a company that establishes overseas manufacturing to access lower labor costs or raw material inputs. Another example is a company that opens a foreign sales office and hires a local director. In this way, it is accessing a different type of resource - expertise. Companies may also try to acquire local technology.

• FDI: A STRATEGIC FRAMEWORK

Ultimately, a company's decision to pursue foreign direct investment revolves around the cost-benefit analysis of the particular investment. Be it a foreign sales office, distribution center, or full scale overseas manufacturing, the long-term benefit needs to outweigh the risks.

Figure 7.5 demonstrates this balance between risk and reward. The reward of FDI is the increase in control, feedback, and access to local resources. These rewards should eventually lead to increased profits. However, the rewards come at the expense of increased financial and company resources. In pursuing FDI, whether through one foreign sales office or many overseas manufacturing facilities, the company must increase its money, time, and resource commitment. Such expenditures lead to increased risk.

Companies that are only exporting have relatively low levels of control, feedback, and access to foreign resources. By the same token, the financial and resource commitment is also low. Such companies would fall in the first band of the graph in Figure 7.5. By contrast, a company operating an overseas manufacturing facility has considerably greater control, feedback, and access to foreign resources. They also have tremendously increased financial and resource commitments. These companies operate in the third band. FDI activities involving less investment and risk than manufacturing facilities, such as a sales and marketing office, would fit into the second band.

An exporting-only company in band one may eventually be pressured to move out towards band two or three by a need to lower export barriers, a need for increased control and feedback, or access to foreign resources. In an ideal world, the company would like to receive the benefits of FDI without making the necessary financial and resource commitments. This is demonstrated by the path of arrow A - increased profits with little to no increased financial or resource commitments. Essentially path A is an unlikely situation. Bypassing export barriers, increasing control and feedback, and accessing foreign resources will almost always involve an increase in financial and resource commitment. However, if an FDI decision follows path A, you should clearly pursue the opportunity.

On the other hand, path C should be avoided. On this path, the increased involvement in the foreign market does not lead to any of the benefits. All risk and no reward. An example of this might be establishing a sales office in an extremely expensive foreign city and hiring an expensive director with little or no increase in sales. This would result in high risk, but no reward.

Most FDI decisions follow the path of B - increased financial and resource commitments with a corresponding increase in the rewards. Risk with reward. If an FDI decision follows path B, the move forward is probably justified. As the path moves closer to path A, the decision becomes easier. However, as the path moves closer to C, the decision is more difficult.

Figure 7.5 Risks and Rewards of Foreign Direct Investment

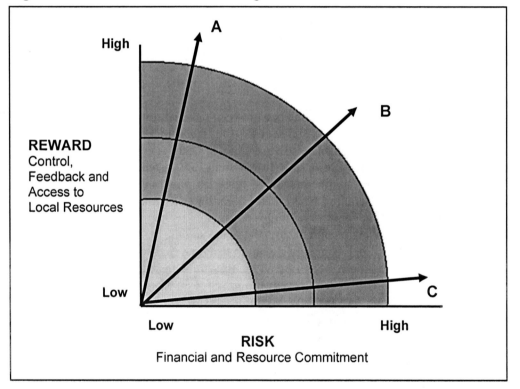

Figure 7.5 summarizes the strategic basis for foreign direct investment - the increase in control, feedback, access to local resources, and lower export barriers is achieved through investing in the foreign market. Though such an investment leads to increased financial and resource commitment which increases risk, total profit potential for the company also increases.

• FDI OPTIONS

Foreign direct investments can involve a variety of scenarios, as summarized in Figure 7.6. At one end, increased control and market feedback is achieved simply by having one overseas salesperson based in the foreign market. He or she would be a full time salesperson devoted to that market. This could eventually lead to an increased level of involvement such as a sales, marketing, distribution, or customer support center. Eventually, overseas manufacturing or assembly may be required. In this final section, I will discuss the option most companies choose as they expand internationally - an overseas sales and marketing office.

Foreign Sales and Marketing Offices

One of the single most powerful techniques for improving your international sales success is to establish a foreign sales and marketing office. Travel to a market, no matter how frequent, cannot match the wealth of knowledge and increased control offered by creating an overseas sales and marketing office. It does not have to be a big

Figure 7.6 Range of Foreign Direct Investment Options

Overseas salesperson

Overseas sales office

Overseas marketing office

Overseas distribution

Overseas customer support, training, warranty repair

Overseas joint venture: partial ownership of a distributor

Overseas product finishing (labeling, packaging)

Overseas assembly

Contract manufacturing

Overseas manufacturing joint venture

Overseas manufacturing, wholly owned foreign production

Note: Each of the above represents an investment overseas. Those at the top represent the least involvement in the foreign market. As they descend they represent increased levels of the investment required.

operation. It can begin with one person working from home. This can be surprisingly affordable, especially if a local salesperson is hired rather than moving someone to the market.

Establishing a foreign sales and marketing office does not necessarily mean a change in the distribution strategy. If sales to the end-user or distribution channel are previously through an exclusive distributor, that strategy can still be used. In this case, the purpose of the foreign sales office would be to increase the support to the distributor. It would allow for greater participation in trade shows, training events, and public relations activities. It essentially means the manufacturer's sales representative is available at all times instead of only when an international trip is planned.

A move from exclusive to nonexclusive distribution also can trigger the necessity for a foreign sales and marketing office. Once the distributor loses its exclusive protection, it will naturally decrease its local marketing activities. The foreign sales office would then take on those responsibilities.

Specific considerations when starting a foreign sales and marketing office include: location, facility size, staffing, market perception, tax and accounting, and reporting and control.

Location. The location of the foreign office is very important. It may be in a metropolitan city. It may be in the country with the greatest sales success in the past. Or it may be where the individual (or staff) would have the greatest impact on the market. This could be a location central to the cities or countries that person will cover. It could also be near the largest distributor.

When choosing a location, utilize your resources. For example, if your state has a foreign office in or near the country, visit it for suggestions and assistance. Your bank or freight forwarder may also operate a facility in the country. Each of these would be a very important resource to use when planning the office. They can give you the inside perspective on where to locate in the country as well as other important factors to consider.

Facility size. The size of the office will depend on the responsibilities of the office. If the office will only coordinate sales, a small facility may suffice. It could even be a temporary office, such as those offered by companies where a membership fee gives access to the overall facility, and individual offices are used on an as-needed basis. For some examples, visit the Executive Suite Association's website at www.execsuites.org.

If the office will coordinate sales and marketing, perhaps for a large area, the facility may need to be larger and include support staff such as a receptionist. Fortunately, such facilities form the backbone of office space in most metropolitan areas and should be fairly affordable, especially if there is no specific need to locate the office in a prime area of the city.

Even if the facility will have some inventory and distribution responsibilities, the cost may still be lower than expected. Called light-industrial facilities (or estates), they are not intended for manufacturing but will have a separate area for inventory (unfinished floor, freight doors) and one for offices. These are typically located outside a city center.

Staffing. One of the most difficult decisions is how to staff the facility. It involves a range of issues, from immigration to tax, culture, and control issues. The basic decision is whether to send an individual from the U.S. office (headquarters) to work in the facility. This involves greater cost but probably offers better control and feedback because the individual is already known to management. It also means the company's knowledge and expertise will be more easily transferred to the foreign market.

This could also be expensive and a resource drain on the headquarters. Thus, a consideration should be made to hire a local sales or marketing person. The tax and legal implications are reduced and the total cost should be lower. However, the advantages of control, feedback, and communication through an individual from the U.S. office are lost. If a foreign salesperson is hired, consider trying to mitigate some of these disadvantages by having the person spend considerable time in the U.S. learning about the company's products, domestic procedures, management, corporate culture, and other issues that will empower the individual to effectively represent the U.S. company.

Market perception. The launch of the foreign sales and marketing office should be well planned and executed. The perception of the market regarding why the facility is being opened is critical. For example, if no major change is made to the distribution network, it should be made clear to the press and customers. On the other hand, if distributors will be changed, it should be carefully managed so problems do not arise. An upset local distributor could end up ruining the market perception.

Tax and accounting. Unfortunately, the tax and accounting implications of even a small sales operation are not easy. There are a number of issues that must be addressed. The most difficult is the specific legal structure that is chosen for the overseas entity. The choice of structure will impact the tax consequences of its activities.

Related to tax is the issue of transfer pricing. Assuming the foreign office will purchase product from the U.S. office and then sell onward to the distribution channel, the transfer price is the price paid by the foreign subsidiary. You might think that a company should be able to charge whatever it likes. The U.S. company should be able to invoice its subsidiary at a normal distributor rate, or one higher or lower.

However, under tax regulations adopted by many countries, including the U.S., a company cannot invoice whatever it likes. It must be able to justify the price and show that the price is essentially a hands-off price - a price that an unrelated party would pay. In other words, the company should export to its subsidiary at the same price it would if it was selling to a foreign buyer not owned by the company. This issue I known as 'transfer pricing'. You should seek the advice of a professional international accounting firm to ensure compliance with local and foreign tax laws.

Reporting and control. Establishing a foreign sales and marketing office also comes with the challenge of how to manage and control the operation. This is especially true if the foreign office will not include any individuals from the home office.

It will not be as easy to duplicate the reporting and control system in place in your domestic offices. These systems will help form the basis of a system for the new office, but they must still be adapted to take into account the unique challenges and issues facing the foreign office. For example, a foreign bank's account and spending authority will be more complex than that of a U.S. office.

Outside expertise should be consulted, especially if someone familiar with the specific needs of your industry can be used. His or her expertise will be very helpful in developing an effective reporting and control mechanism that addresses the needs of the home office and the foreign office. The International Executive Service Corps would be an excellent source of advice. It offers a not-for-profit service that links executives with international experience directly with U.S. companies expanding internationally. The executives are typically retired and work at no charge. The company is simply required to reimburse travel and overhead expenses. Visit the International Executive Service Corps website at www.iesc.org.

This brief discussion of an overseas sales and marketing office serves to highlight only a few of the issues a company will face as it pursues foreign direct investment. Just as initiating exporting required planning and outreach to resources, so will initiating overseas investment. The challenge is even greater because the potential risk is higher.

If you choose to begin foreign direct investments, be sure and network extensively with all international resources, including industry peers. They will prove invaluable. However, do not let the challenge dissuade you from starting the process. Going beyond exporting to foreign direct investment may prove to be the critical step in reaching your company's long-term international potential.

Overseas Distribution

As a company grows its export business, it may find a need to warehouse product in foreign markets. This can be particularly important if to be competitive, the product needs to be shipped in large quantities, such as full ocean containers. If a foreign distributor is unwilling to purchase such a significant quantity, the exporter may be forced to consider some type of overseas distribution. Owning warehouse overseas would be an example of FDI and would be used to support its other sales and marketing efforts.

Increasingly, as an option before FDI overseas distribution would be the use of **third party logistics (3PL)** in which some part of the supply chain task is outsourced. In this case, it would be the warehousing. Many companies offer the service of warehousing on a contractual basis: you pay for what you use with little to no fixed costs. Beyond warehousing, these companies also break apart the large ocean shipment into smaller shipments the company then ships for the manufacturer (called **pick and pack**). The Netherlands has positioned itself as an ideal location for outsourced warehousing and logistics. The Holland International Distribution Council is an great example. Their membership offers outsourced logistics throughout Europe. For more information visit http://www.ndl.nl.

Overseas Manufacturing

One of the best known forms of foreign direct investment is overseas manufacturing. In many cases, overseas manufacturing is not selected as a form of foreign market entry for marketing purposes, but as a means to lower the costs of producing a product that is then imported back into the home market of the manufacturer. In such a case, it is often referred to as **off-shoring**: taking the whole of a manufacturing facility overseas and closing the domestic facility. An example would be when a furniture manufacturer closes its facility in the U.S., moves all production to China, and imports the product from China into the U.S.

Within the context of foreign market entry mode, **overseas manufacturing** is when some or most of the manufacturing of a product is done overseas to serve overseas customers. This is actually quite common. For example, when Caterpillar opened one of its largest manufacturing facilities in China (outside Shanghai) it did so primarily to manufacture products to be sold within Asia. Significant parts of those products use components manufactured in the U.S.

If a company has determined some type of overseas manufacturing is needed, it has a number of options as discussed next.

Contract manufacturing. This is when rather than make any foreign direct investment in a manufacturing facility, the company outsources the manufacturing to a foreign manufacturer. This has the benefit of lower costs and risks since no employees or fixed assets are held by the company seeking the overseas manufacturing. A well-known example is Foxconn in China which manufacturers Apple's iPhone and iPads. The disadvantage is control and communications since the company has no employees in the overseas manufacturing facility. Indeed with Foxconn, a recurring concern has been their labor conditions.

Joint venture. Often a company will join with a local company in a foreign market to form a partnership to manufacture products. **Joint venture** is a term used for a number of cooperative arrangements in which two companies work together. In this case, it would be a new entity partly owned by the local company and partly owned by the manufacturer seeking to have the product produced. When Caterpillar first entered China, this was the only method to enter the country because the Chinese government did not permit foreign companies to have 100% ownership of Chinese companies. Caterpillar was forced to use a joint venture. (Chinese regulations have since changed and wholly-owned foreign enterprises known as WOFEs, are now permitted.)

Joint ventures offer a number of advantages for overseas manufacturing. The local partner brings market knowledge, connections, government relations, and local manufacturing know-how, all of which leads to lower risk. And in some case, joint venture may be the only government approved option. However the significant disadvantage is loss of control and shared profits. Many companies may accept the shared profit requirement because there is also less risk. The loss of control may be a more significant barrier, which is why companies often avoid manufacturing joint ventures.

Joint ventures are not limited to manufacturing joint ventures. Companies routinely use partnership arrangements when expanding internationally. Some joint ventures do not involve ownership and are simply cooperative arrangements. These are sometimes referred to as **strategic alliances**. An example would be airline alliances such as Oneworld or Star Alliance. When shared ownership is involved, the jv may be called an **equity joint venture**.

Wholly-owned foreign production. When a company wants full control of its manufacturing process in a foreign country, it would select **wholly-owned foreign production**. The advantages over a joint venture are full control of operations and no shared profits. The disadvantages are lack of a local partner for expertise and connections. It also represents greater risk since the company must bear the full responsibilities of the investment and management.

Licensing. A final method of overseas manufacturing is **licensing**. In licensing, the right to use technology by a third party is given by the holder of the technology. Let's assume a company has a patent on type of cell phone technology. It may decide it does not want to manufacturer products using that technology, or if it does, only in its home market. In this case, the company would enter into a legal contract giving the right to use the technology to a **licensee** (the company receiving the right). Within the context of foreign market entry, licensing may be a very cost-effective way to create revenue with little to no work on behalf of the holder of the technology. Licensing comes with risks. It may create a new competitor and ultimately the profits may be lower than if the company did its own manufacturing.

Another type of licensing is **franchising** in which the whole of a business process is licensed to another company. An example here would be if Subway was looking to expand internationally but did not want to own its corporate sandwich stores in a foreign country. It may decide FDI would be too risky or distractive to its overall mission. Instead, it would license its brand, marketing tools, store operations manual, and other related knowledge and techniques associated with running a Subway store. In exchange for the license, Subway would receive franchise fees from each store including a share of the revenue.

Summary: Which is the right choice when a company is seeking overseas manufacturing? There is no easy answer. In some cases, government regulations may dictate the choice. In other, local market conditions would be the top consideration such as a high risk market favoring contract manufacturing or joint venture. The selection of manufacturing entry mode revolves around balancing the risks versus rewards.

• NOTES

1. Adapted from "Table 8-1 • Advantages and Disadvantages of Selected Market Entry Strategies", Vern Terpstra, James Foley, Ravi Sarathy; *International Marketing* 11th Edition. (Naperville, Naper Publishing Group, 2012). Used with permission.

Finding Your Partners for Indirect Exporting

Clearly you will only be searching for an indirect partner if you intend to utilize an indirect market entry method. If not, you can skip this chapter and proceed to Chapter 9. Given the attractiveness of indirect market entry for particular markets, as discussed in Chapter 8, many companies need to find at least one or two indirect partners.

The first step to finding a great partner is to clarify your requirements so you can choose the right type of indirect partner - export management company (EMC) and the related variations or piggyback. (Chapter 7 also discussed domestic distributors and gray marketing but these are reactive methods and would not be considered part of a proactive international expansion strategy.) Though these are both indirect export partners, the nature of an ongoing relationship between your company and the indirect partner can be quite different between the two types, and the particular requirements they satisfy will vary.

• EMCS VERSUS PIGGYBACK PARTNERS

To determine which type is suitable for your international expansion strategy, you need to identify the differences between each type. Be aware that the following distinctions are generalizations that will not apply to all EMCs or piggyback partners but will merely highlight the differences you may encounter in your search for an indirect partner.

Future use of the distribution channel. One of the key distinctions between an export management company and a piggyback partner is the nature of the relationship between the partner and its contacts in the foreign markets or the distribution channel. EMCs (including other related forms such as brokers and agents) by their very nature contact foreign distributors and agents on behalf of the manufacturer to represent the manufacturer in the particular market. It is clear from the start that the EMC is simply an extra step in the sales chain and has the full and open support of the manufacturer. It is very much like contracting out your international sales. In fact many times business cards of EMCs will include product logos of the manufacturers they represent to emphasize this support and legitimacy.

A piggyback partner may never make its foreign distribution network aware of the distinction between products it produces and products it distributes on behalf of another manufacturer. Instead, it capitalizes on the fact that outside products enhance or complement its own product offering and leverages the investment in its international channel by representing products other than its own. It is typically not the intention of a piggyback partner to develop an international distribution network specifically for the outside manufacturer. In fact, when you choose a piggyback partner you assume that your product will be sold through the existing international distribution channel of the partner.

This distinction has some important implications. The greatest occurs when you do not renew your contract with your indirect partner. The opportunity to sell through the same channel used during the relationship with your partner may not be a possibility. With an EMC, you often will know the distribution channel the EMC has appointed on your behalf. Eventually, you may attend trade shows or international distributor meetings during which you can meet the distributors or agents. Thus, when you eventually set out on your own and begin selling directly to the foreign market, you'll have a good base upon which to build. (Be aware that the ability to use the existing international distribution network after dissolving the relationship with an EMC varies greatly. An EMC may keep its distribution network hidden from the U.S. manufacturer, which would make it difficult to establish sales into the same network. This is particularly true if the EMC sold directly to end-users during the relationship with the manufacturer.)

With a piggyback partner, it is much less likely you will know who is representing your products. In some cases, it may actually be overseas subsidiaries of your piggyback partner, which could make it impossible to sell to them directly after the contract expires. For example, I worked with a client that manufactured truck parts and wanted to expand into China. The company knew it lacked the experience and resources to deal directly with such a challenging market, so it investigated piggybacking its products with a leading manufacturer of trucks who had an established subsidiary in China with an internal sales and marketing staff. It is an excellent match, but should the partnership ever end, so will any chance of the parts manufacturer selling directly to the Chinese subsidiary of the truck manufacturer. The parts manufacturer would need to establish a new Chinese partner. If it had used an EMC, this replacement may not have been necessary.

With an EMC, your involvement with the foreign distribution channel will be greater than with a piggyback partner. This leads to a greater likelihood that you could use the same foreign distributors (contract permitting) after the EMC representation ends.

Brand awareness. Another implication is that the development of brand awareness of your product in the foreign market may be lower using piggyback partners than EMCs. Again this relates to the nature of the relationship between the manufacturer and the EMC or piggyback. EMCs push the brand strength of the products they represent because they are not manufacturers themselves and have no need to build their own brand awareness with consumers. Piggyback partners have already established brand awareness in foreign markets, which is exactly why you would choose them as your partner. But it is unlikely a piggyback partner would build brand awareness for your products.

Customer service, training, and warranty issues. A manufacturer or service provider chooses a piggyback partner to take advantage of its experience and international strength. If the piggyback partner's experience includes international customer service issues such as training, repairs, parts supply, and documentation, it may be why a piggyback partner is chosen over an EMC. EMCs (and especially brokers and agents) primarily provide sales and marketing support for the companies they represent. Support functions such as training and warranty are often pushed back onto the original manufacturers because they have the knowledge and infrastructure to provide these services. It would be cost prohibitive for an EMC to offer the same customer support function. Thus if your products require a high level of customer support in the foreign market, you may want to choose a piggyback partner who will have the capability to do so. There are of course exceptions and some EMCs may provide significant customer service.

Industry and technical knowledge requirements. If the selling and marketing of your products or services requires extensive industry and technical knowledge, you may be better served by a piggyback firm already in your industry. Though EMCs often specialize by industry, their specialization tends to be quite broad and may be too broad to be able to effectively represent your products. If you require any specific industry or technical experience of your salespeople, you probably need the same experience from your indirect partner.

For example, if your company provides specialized international architectural services and you are searching for representation via an indirect partner, who would be in a better position to represent your company: a U.S. architectural firm not competing with your company or a non-architectural firm? Assuming the quality of the contacts each firm has in foreign markets is equal, the more industry and technical knowledge required to represent your products or services, the greater the need for an indirect partner that understands the issues. This generally means choosing a piggyback partner.

Choosing between an EMC and a piggyback partner for your indirect market entry is influenced by your long-term goals and the requirements you place on your partners in such areas as customer support. Figure 8.1 summarizes differences between EMCs and piggyback partners. Your final plan may include utilizing both types of partners depending on the foreign market.

FINDING PARTNERS FOR INDIRECT EXPORTING.

Figure 8.1 Comparison of Export Management Companies and Piggyback Partners

Issues	Export Management Companies	Piggyback Partners	Issue Generally Favors
Manufacturer Involvement with Foreign Distribution Channel	Generally high, but depends on the openness of the EMC - some keep nearly all overseas customer information unavailable to the manufacturer they represent.	Lower than with EMCs. It will mostly depend on the nature of the piggyback's overseas distribution. If it is mostly corporate owned subsidiaries, involvement by the manufacturer will likely be low.	Favors EMCs
Builds Overseas Brand Awareness	Highly likely because the EMC will have no brand image of its own, and will rely on promoting the brands of the companies they represent.	There may be no brand awareness developed. Partly depends on the strength of the manufacturer's brand versus the piggyback partner's brand.	Favors EMCs
Future Opportunity to Sell through Same Foreign Distribution Channel as Your Indirect Partner	Very likely, especially if contract w EMC contains a Grandfather clause providing for commissions on sales after the contract.	Less likely than with an EMC, especially if piggyback partner has made foreign direct investment in its overseas distribution channel by way of subsidiaries or manufacturing facilities.	Favors EMCs
Customer Service: Training	Depends on the capability of the EMC. Most would probably push training back to the manufacturer, but some have the ability to train overseas customers.	Very likely piggyback partner would have the capability to train, assuming it was agreed during contract negotiations. Because piggyback partners tend to be in the same industry as the manufacturer, training would be fairly easy.	Favors Piggyback Partners
Customer Service: Repair, Warranty Support	Similar to training in that it depends on the capabilities of the EMC.	Difficult to predict. Depends on infrastructure needed to support warranty issues. Piggyback partner should at least have the technical knowledge to support warranty work.	Favors Piggyback Partners

(continued)

Figure 8.1 Continued

Issues	Export Management Companies	Piggyback Partners	Issue Generally Favors
Control Over Foreign Pricing	Moderate control - depends on the openness of the relationship and requirements of the contract	Probably very low. It is likely that the piggyback partner already has very rigid pricing standards that would simply be applied indiscriminately to manufacturer's pricing.	Favors EMCs
Exclusive Contracts	EMC likely to insist on exclusive contracts, especially if EMC will do all sales and marketing in the foreign markets. Agents/brokers are less likely to insist on exclusivity.	Less likely than EMCs to require exclusivity because piggyback firm is probably not going to make significant investments in foreign markets on behalf of manufacturer.	Favors EMCs
Length of Contract	Wants long contract, especially if exclusive.	Less worried about length of contract.	Favors Piggyback Partners
Profit Margin	Depends on industry norms, scale of sales potential, and exclusive or nonexclusive contract. Generally 5-20% with an average of 15%.	Probably higher than EMCs especially if overseas infrastructure is high. But partner may be more effective for manufacturer because of this investment, which would justify a higher margin.	Neutral

• FINDING AN EMC

If an EMC (or broker or agent) is your best partner, there are a number of ways to find a suitable company. Be sure to take your time in the process of selecting your EMC. It is a very important decision because you are effectively turning over your international sales to an outside company. This is particularly true if the territory to be covered by the indirect partner is large, such as the European Union or Latin America. During the process be aware of the tendency of many individuals to select the company that contacted them first. First is not necessarily best. This tendency is discussed in greater detail in Chapter 9.

Finding an EMC is very much like hiring a new employee. You will probably use a combination of methods to find the optimal partner. As with hiring employees, knowing you have found the right one may never be clear. It often comes down to a judgment call between equally qualified companies. This is why networking is a particularly effective technique for finding a partner. Finding an EMC that has been effective for another company may make the difference when choosing one EMC over another. However, networking is only one of five methods you can use to find an EMC partner:

1. *Networking.* A good place to begin is asking peers in your industry if they are aware of any EMCs or indirect export companies. When I worked with an EMC, some of our best customers came from referrals. Because EMCs tend not to do much advertising, especially in the U.S., you probably won't come across EMCs during the course of your domestic business.
2. *International trade centers/local contacts.* Your local, state, or federal trade assistance center frequently receives requests from companies for information about EMCs and brokers. Most ITCs maintain a list of area EMCs, many of which participate in locally sponsored international events.
3. *Internet.* As discussed in Chapter 6, there are a number of online company databases such as Kompass and OneSource. These can be useful resources to find potential partners.
4. *Industry associations.* If you are a member of your national industry or trade association, be sure and contact them to see if they maintain a list.
5. *Trade journals.* Search past issues of trade journals and industry magazines for articles relating to international expansion. Often EMCs are featured as examples of going global without the traditional cost or experience requirement.

• FINDING A PIGGYBACK PARTNER

If you are looking for a piggyback partner, you may already have some in mind. Obvious piggyback partners are manufacturers in your domestic market whose products are enhanced or complemented by your products. You may already be selling to such manufacturers, in which case your relationship just needs expanding. In other cases, your products may be sold with other products combined further down the supply chain - for example, through dealers or retail locations. In this case introductions may be more difficult, but the manufacturers probably are aware of your products.

The challenge in finding a piggyback partner is less in identifying them than qualifying them. Many manufacturers have a policy of only selling their own products, which prohibits them from representing your products. In other cases, manufacturers may be willing to sell your products internationally but only under their brand name. You would private-label your goods under another manufacturer's name. This may be a suitable arrangement if your long-term marketing goal isn't to establish brand awareness.

Piggyback partners may include:
• Current customers
• Current suppliers
• Noncompeting companies in your industry
• Competing companies that don't produce the product you want to export

Many of the same resources listed for EMCs would refer you to piggyback partners. The key difference is your search will emphasize industry-related companies because the attractiveness of a piggyback partner is its success in your industry. Methods such as networking and contacting trade associations are particularly useful for finding piggyback partners.

You can find a piggyback partner through:
- Networking (especially with customers familiar with your products that can identify the synergy between your products and those of another company)
- Trade shows
- Industry press
- Trade associations
- Sales staff

Prior to contacting a potential piggyback company, research their literature and industry news so you are familiar with their products and international activities. This will clarify the opportunities that are available. This research is especially important if the manufacturer you contact is not familiar with piggyback exporting and may not be comfortable with the idea of selling outside products internationally. You need to be prepared to handle such objections. EMCs, on the other hand, would welcome a cold call from a manufacturer.

• WHAT TO EXPECT WHEN NEGOTIATING CONTRACTS WITH INDIRECT PARTNERS

Whether you negotiate your contract with an EMC or piggyback partner, there are some general expectations. Many of the specifics of the following issues are unique to indirect partner contracts. Chapter 12 discusses international legal concerns in general and contains issues not unique to indirect contacts, such as arbitration.

Pricing considerations. An indirect partner generally requires a price equal to or better than your deepest discounted domestic price. Indirect partners are aware of the problem of export price escalation - once all the costs associated with an international transaction are added to the domestic price, the final price paid by the foreign consumer is considerably higher. To mitigate the impact of these costs, indirect partners want to begin with the lowest price possible, sometimes even below your lowest domestic price.

When I worked for an EMC in California, our initial bargaining position was 20 percent below the manufacturer's lowest domestic price, but we would accept 15 percent. We did not go below the 15 percent margin. Quantity was not considered because the EMC purchase price was always the same regardless of the order quantity. (The EMC's export price list may reflect quantity discounts.)

Figure 8.2 Comparison of Net Profit from Domestic versus Indirect Export Sales

Manufacturer's Retail Sales Price:		**$1000.00**	

U.S. Distributor Pricing:

Quantities 1-9	15% discount	850.00
Quantities 10-25	20% discount	800.00
Quantities 26-49	30% discount	700.00
Quantities 50+	40% discount	600.00

Following analysis based on 50+ pricing:

	Domestic Sales		Selling through Indirect Partners
Sell price to domestic distributor	$600.00	Sell price to indirect partner: (15% less than deepest domestic price): 15% of $600	$510.00
Direct costs (material, labor)	(250.00)		(250.00)
Manufacturing overhead (20% of direct costs)	(50.00)		(50.00)
Total direct and indirect manufacturing costs	(300.00)		(300.00)
Manufacturing gross profit	$300.00		$210.00
Corporate overhead (30% direct costs to cover sales, marketing, management)	(75.00)	Corporate overhead not applied as there may be little to no incremental costs associated with indirect sales	0.0
Net profit	$225.00	Net profit	$210.00
		Alternatively, corporate overhead is applied	(75.00)
		Net profit	$135.00

Indirect partners may require as much as a 15-20% discount off your lowest domestic price. This example shows a 15% discount for the indirect partner. Though net profit could be as low as $135, compared to $225 for domestic sales, one argument is that corporate overhead should not be applied because there are little to no incremental costs associated with the indirect export sales. The same argument could be applied to the manufacturing overhead allocation, making the indirect sales even more profitable.

Figure 8.2 is an example of routine indirect pricing. The manufacturer sells a product retailing for $1000 using a discounted schedule from 15 to 40 percent. Its gross profit, based on a 40 percent discount, is $300 when direct and indirect manufacturing costs are deducted. The net profit is $225 after the corporate overhead allowance of 30 percent is deducted.

In this example, can the manufacturer afford to sell at 15 percent off their deepest discounted price for a price of $510? Once both overheads (manufacturing and corporate) are applied, the net profit is only $135, which is probably too low. However, should both overheads be applied? Indirect exporting leads to little or no increase in management resources and probably very little direct cost increases.

The question cannot really be answered but one argument suggests ignoring the corporate overhead because there may be only a marginal impact on nonmanufacturing departments. If the manufacturer's overhead relates to items such as R&D, capital expenditures, and rent, none of these items will be impacted by the export sales. It could even be argued that the analysis should ignore the manufacturing overhead. In either case these issues will be argued during negotiations with your indirect partners in order for them to get the lowest price possible.

Whatever price you negotiate, be sure to discuss the international pricing your indirect partner will employ. For example, with a 15-20 percent discount off your lowest domestic price, your partner will probably be able to offer an ex-works price (pricing without any freight) at or near your domestic pricing. This would mean the international list price will be as close as possible to your domestic list price, though clearly freight and foreign taxes will have an important impact. What you want to avoid is giving your partner an excellent price (known as aggressive pricing) that your partner does not use to offer equally aggressive pricing to the foreign markets instead of achieving inappropriate profits.

Negotiating pricing with an export trading company. As contrasted with EMCs, export trading companies tend to be larger and price negotiations may be more formal. Dustchin Rock is a former employee of a Japanese trading company and makes the following recommendations:
1. Don't offer concessions on pricing too easily. Even if you can lower the price, do not give it all up at once. The pricing will always be negotiated down.
2. It is best to have one person dealing with the trading company. Having too many people involved only encourages miscommunications.
3. If the U.S. trading company intends to sell to another trading company in the foreign market, the U.S. trading company may negotiate a "hidden" commission to be paid by the U.S. manufacturer to the U.S. trading company. This is particularly true if the U.S. trading company has an equity stake in the foreign trading company and cost information is shared. The hidden commission provides the U.S. trading company with a profit buffer to lower prices to the foreign trading company when needed.

4. When the manufacturer provides technical support for in-warranty problems, time and travel expenses are typically paid by the manufacturer. Out-of-warranty support is paid by the trading company.

Exclusive contracts versus nonexclusive contracts. In general, the greater the commitment required by your indirect partner, the higher the chance it will demand an exclusive contract. If your partner will be performing the full spectrum of sales and marketing needs, from distributor appointments and product launches to foreign receivables and order fulfillment, it should receive exclusivity. Otherwise, other companies could bypass your partner and sell directly into the foreign market. Your partner risks not getting its sales and marketing investment back. You want to motivate your indirect partner to invest in the foreign market.

There may be occasions when an exclusive contract is not desired. You may consider the partnership informal and temporary or transaction oriented. This is particularly true if brokers or agents have contacted you for a one-time sales opportunity.

When a company uses indirect market entry as part of its overall international expansion strategy, it requires commitment from the indirect partner. Typically that commitment should be matched with an exclusive contract.

Territory covered by the contract. Be very careful about how much territory you give away in your indirect contracts. Partners will want a global or regional contract. That may be appropriate depending on your company's situation. But if you are using indirect exporting in conjunction with direct exporting, you need to be selective about your negotiations.

An important aspect to consider is the strengths of your indirect partner. For example, if they only sell into one part of Europe, be wary of signing a contract that would also include all of Europe (though they will argue you should!). Your contract should match the experience and depth of your partner. Legally such distinctions are difficult to enforce because many regional trading pacts disallow constraints to trade. But limiting the territory reduces the chance of formal distribution contracts being signed on your behalf by your partner in territories that you designated as outside of the contract.

Be aware that the EMC may attempt to breach the territory. It will be natural for the EMC to want to sell as much as possible, even if a sale goes outside the territory defined in the contract. Depending on the specifics, you may decide not to take action. However, you may decide that the breach is too serious to disregard, especially if the sale is into a territory already represented by another distributor or indirect partner. Such situations are always difficult. I found the most effective technique was to openly discuss the situation with the EMC. It will know it is in the wrong because the contract has stipulated its territory. Often it is just a matter of explaining to the EMC that a breach cannot be tolerated because it disrupts the overall distribution strategy, in the same way the EMC wants its territory protected. If the potential for cross-territory sales is particularly likely, consider developing a formal response plan to be used in particularly serious situations.

Marketing and customer support considerations. Be careful to spell out your expectations in the contract. How should warranty issues be resolved? Who pays for training? Who pays for translations? Who pays for the printing of international brochures? All are reasonable expenses for international success, but which party pays depends on the contact. As a guideline, if you give a 20 percent margin, you should expect good support from your partner. If you only offer 5-10 percent (standard for a broker or agent) you will need to perform more of the sales and support functions.

Length of contract. For an exclusive contract that includes strong sales and marketing support activities by your indirect partner, you can expect to sign at least a one-year contract. Your partner will probably want two to three years. Clearly industry norms will dictate such arrangements, but given that most foreign markets can take at least a year to develop, the one year minimum is traditional. If a shorter contract is required, expect to take on more of the risk and investment.

Grandfather clause. A clause in a contract that provides for a commission on sales after a contract expires is called a grandfather clause. These clauses are common with EMCs if the contract is exclusive and requires significant investment of the EMC in the foreign markets, including marketing, translation costs, and training. The assumption behind a grandfather clause is that the majority of the sales received by a manufacturer for the first few months after a contract expires are the result of actions made by the indirect partner before the contract expired. You don't want to mention such clauses proactively because they are a cost to you, but they help ensure a smooth transition from indirect to direct exporting because it is in the best interest of your EMC to assist you right up until the contract expires.

It is important to remember the perspective of EMCs. They represent more than one manufacturer. On a 10-20 percent margin, profits are tight. EMCs are looking for what the industry calls home runs, or contracts with manufacturers that result in significant volume. By the nature of indirect exporting, once international sales become extremely successful and quantities are significant, the manufacturer will want to pursue a direct strategy. All EMCs understand this and know they won't be able to hold onto the arrangement forever. The grandfather clause gives them further motivation to invest in the market.

EMCs will probably request a one-year grandfather clause. Again, industry norms will dictate the specifics of your contract negotiations, but I would be hesitant to grant more than a six-month clause with the commission gradually declining during those six months on a proportional basis starting no later than the second or third month of the clause period.

Errors and omissions insurance policy. International business has legal risks which are discussed in greater detail in Chapter 12. For the purpose of negotiating a contract with your indirect partner, you should ensure your partner has some type of umbrella policy for errors and omissions and other operational concerns related to the export of your products. Should a liability arise from such export activities, it would be preferable that the partner's insurance covers the action.

CHAPTER 9

Finding Your Partners for Direct Exporting

C hapter 8 discussed the fairly straightforward process of finding indirect export partners. Indirect partners are by definition domestic customers so finding them involves no international travel, no cultural barriers, and little cost.

But finding partners for direct market entry is a different matter. Direct export partners are for the most part located in foreign markets, which makes finding and choosing them more complex, risky, and potentially expensive. The key to finding good overseas partners is to travel to the market, research potential candidates, and choose them carefully. But this is easier said than done because it requires time, money, and resource commitments that not all companies can make. Not that you must travel to the market as some methods of finding partners do not require travel. But to ensure the best partner, you general should visit the foreign market.

• SALES AGENT OR DISTRIBUTOR?

Once you have determined that direct exporting is the best entry mode for your international strategy, you'll need to decide which type of partner is most suitable for your needs. Your options in most markets will be sales agents and distributors. Though the distinctions between these can be blurred, it is important to understand the most commonly accepted role of each. A summary is provided in Figure 9.1

Figure 9.1 Comparison of Agents and Distributors

Issue	Agents	Distributors	Generally Favors
Type of representation	Exclusive or nonexclusive	Exclusive or nonexclusive	Neutral
Size of company	Often a one-person company.	Can also be small operation, but generally larger than agents.	Distributor, depending on the industry
Sale to foreign end-user made by ...	Agent	Distributor	Neutral
Takes title to the goods during the sale	Typically, no	Yes	Distributors because exporter deals with only one company
How does representative earn its profit and does the exporter have strong control over foreign pricing?	Generally, through commissions paid to agent directly by exporter. High control over pricing.	On the margin between their purchase price from the exporter and the selling price to the local end-users (or next level of distribution.) Generally, low control over pricing.	Agents because exporter has more control over foreign pricing.
Marketing activities such as advertising, trade shows, translation of marketing materials	Low compared to distributors	High compared to agents	Distributors, assuming such activities are not to be done by the exporter
Customer support activities such as training, warranty repair, customer inquiries	Low compared to distributors	High compared to agents	Distributors, assuming such activities are not to be done by the exporter

Continued

Figure 9.1 Continued

Issue	Agents	Distributors	Generally Favors
Foreign receivable risk assuming terms not payment in advance	Risk is potentially high because sales can be to different buyers each time	Probably lower because sales are to the same distributor(s).	Distributors
Overseas inventory maintained?	Generally, no	Generally, yes	Assuming maintaining a foreign inventory is of benefit, distributors
Speed of delivery of goods to foreign end-user	Slower compared to distributors if no inventory is maintained	Faster compared to agents if inventory is maintained	Assuming maintaining a foreign inventory is of benefit, distributors
Direct contact with end-user to solve technical issues or other customer support issues	Likely	Unlikely depending on specific role assumed by distributor	Probably neutral as exporter may either prefer or not prefer to deal directly with foreign end-users
Knowledge of importing procedures and local regulations	Perhaps lower than distributor but varies greatly	Generally strong	Distributors
Termination of relationship challenges	Difficult to say. In some countries agents can be legally treated as employees, making termination complicated.	Also difficult to say. In some countries local laws strongly favor distributor making termination complicated.	Varies by country
Ability to effectively represent exporter	Depends on specific background and industry contacts	Depends on specific background and industry contacts	Neutral
Preference of local market	Varies by country, but some markets tends to use agents more than distributors	Varies by country, but some markets tend to use distributors more than agents	Neutral – depends on market

Sales Agents

In international markets, the role of a **sales agent** is very similar to that of a domestic sales agent. They represent your products in the market but never take legal title to the product. With a domestic agent, the manufacturer ships directly to the purchaser, which may be a retail store, the U.S. government, a distributor, or even the final consumer or end-user. The agent makes the sale, but the manufacturer invoices the customer and assumes the accounts receivable risk. Once payment has been received, the manufacturer pays the agent a commission.

It is much the same with an overseas sales agent. The agent locates potential customers, initiates sales calls, and eventually completes the sale. The details of the sale are then communicated to the exporter per the terms of the contract between the exporter and the foreign agent. The manufacturer then ships the product, invoices the customer, and eventually collects the receivable from the overseas buyer. The overseas buyer may be a foreign government, distributor, key account, buying group, or even the final end-user. Depending on the sales terms and the shipping instructions, title of the goods will pass from the manufacturer to the foreign buyer at some point along the way. But the foreign agent never will assume title to the goods. Once payment has been received, the manufacturer pays the foreign agent a commission.

This arrangement has some important implications for exporters contemplating foreign agents. First, the manufacturer is selling to various customers in the foreign market, which implies various foreign receivable risks. Though this is less of a problem if payment terms are cash in advance, competitive pressures will dictate that at some point the exporter offers terms rather than payment in advance. Offering terms in the foreign market to a variety of customers creates a complex accounts receivable management challenge. Using a distributor, the receivable risk is limited to one company - the distributor.

A second implication is that generally no overseas inventory is maintained by the foreign agent. Sales are made by the agent and then fulfilled by the exporter. The buyer has to wait for all the necessary steps to be completed, including shipping and customs clearance, before receiving merchandise. This puts the manufacturer at a competitive disadvantage if other manufacturers offer inventory in the foreign market. This is particularly important when manufacturing related products because companies continue to shrink their input inventories and move toward a just-in-time approach to purchasing.

The third implication is that the agent and the foreign customer may not be familiar with specific import regulations or restrictions because they do not directly import. Distributors, on the other hand, would be very familiar with restrictions, taxes, and the necessary paperwork. They will also have good freight contacts to keep freight costs competitive. When using agents, the exporter will have more of the logistics issues pushed back onto them from the foreign buyer. The foreign purchaser also must be made familiar and comfortable with importing.

A final concern is that the local laws of some countries may recognize your agent as an employee of your company. Canceling your rep agreement may be equal to firing an employee, which means the terms of the cancellation may be dictated by the government to include such actions as payment of commissions after the termination of the contract even though the contract did not specify such a grandfather clause. (This can also apply to distributors as discussed in Chapter 18.)

There are also some important benefits to using agents. One is increased control over the sales process. Because the agent does not accept the order on behalf of the manufacturer, the manufacturer can accept or reject orders. This means the manufacturer can more easily restrict sales of the agent to specific territories or types of customers. With distributors, the manufacturer will ship all orders from the distributor with little or no knowledge of who the end buyer will be. If the shipment is outside the authorized territory of the distributor, local law (such as within the EU) may permit onward shipments limiting the manufacturer's control.

Another benefit is that the manufacturer is much more involved in the sales process, knows who is purchasing its products, and has greater feedback from the foreign markets.

Finally, sales agents or reps may be the most effective way to represent your product. I once visited Mexican Manufacturing Week, a large national convention for buyers and sellers of manufacturing-related technologies and products in Mexico City. I met numerous Mexican agents, each of whom had extremely valuable knowledge and access to some of Mexico's largest manufacturers. Many specialized in particular industries such as automobiles or electronics. It was clear the selection of two or three of these reps by an exporter could result in a nearly overnight introduction of its products into the Mexican market. Distributors with the same depth are less common. (This depth is also typical of the Mexican market compared to the European market. Given its close proximity to the U.S. market, Mexico is characterized by a strong network of agents. In some industries agents are more important than distributors.)

Distributors

Unlike agents, **distributors** order directly from the exporter, take title of the goods per the sales terms, and inventory the merchandize locally in the foreign market. The exporter ships to the distributor in bulk with no knowledge of who the final consumers will be.

Because distributors require a more significant infrastructure than agents, they will generally be larger organizations than agents. In fact, in many respects, a distributor is like an overseas office of the exporter, even though the manufacturer has made no foreign investments. I've been to many offices of distributors where the branding of the manufacturers they represent is so strong, one would have thought they were actually visiting a subsidiary of the manufacturer.

But this strong branding and commitment leads to important distinctions between distributors and agents. Distributors are much more likely to be aggressive in their marketing activities, such as local advertising, printing local brochures, and participating in trade shows. Agents are less likely to participate in such expensive marketing activities and rely more on a strong, direct sales campaign.

Distributors are also more likely to conduct customer support activities such as training and product repairs. Because agents don't inventory product, most do not have the facilities to repair products or conduct training seminars. Distributors, who tend to sell and market related products, have developed their company around the importance of such activities.

Finally, distributors have extensive knowledge of local importing practices and restrictions, especially if their primary activity is representing foreign companies. They also have good transportation experience with local connections to move freight cost effectively. And because distributors import in bulk, the per unit international freight costs will be less than agents' costs. In fact, some distributors consolidate their purchases from a particular market, for example the U.S., so the freight is moved in a whole container, which is substantially less expensive than less-than-container loads.

Pricing Considerations

There is an important distinction between agents and distributors in regard to pricing. With agents, the exporter is more likely to be able to impose a price schedule on the foreign market. The agent sells off this price schedule, and receives a commission on the sale once completed and paid. A distributor, with its larger infrastructure and more significant marketing activities, calculates its landed price (manufacturer selling price plus freight and insurance plus all applicable local taxes) and applies a markup. This markup may be significant, even as much as 50 to 100 percent depending on the product and industry. As a manufacturer, you have no control over the foreign selling price other than your ability to not renew the contract. In fact, you may be prohibited by law from dictating pricing. When you select a distributor, it is important to discuss its pricing policy so you are not surprised when the distributor eventually develops the local price list for your products. Whether a distributor sticks to that price list, however, is another matter, though if you remain involved in the market (trade shows, client sales calls) you'll be able to confirm the pricing policy.

Agent or Distributor - Which Type?

Which method is appropriate for your company? One or two issues may be so important they will dictate your decision. For example, if your product is large or heavy but low in per unit value, shipping costs may be prohibitive unless your products are shipped in full container loads. This may force you to use distributors unless you can find an agent who can consolidate its orders (which may be a competitive disadvantage if orders need to wait until a full container load is ordered).

If the nature of your product requires fast delivery times, the use of distributors may be necessary. Competitive pressures also may dictate your decision. Your concern over foreign receivables risk may also influence you to choose a distributor. On the other hand, your international strategy and industry may be best served by a network of agents and reps. In the end, you may use a combination of the two depending on the needs of the market. If it remains unclear which type would be best, do not make a final decision until you begin to investigate specific potential buyers. The decision may be made for you based on the qualifications of the best company for a particular market - which may be an agent or a distributor.

• TO TRAVEL OR NOT TO TRAVEL? . . . THAT'S THE QUESTION

Once you have determined which type of direct partner best suits your company, you'll need to begin looking for one for each of the markets you have targeted for expansion. Do you have to travel to the market to do so?

That is a difficult question to answer because the answer depends on your product and industry. As a rule of thumb, travel is better than no travel. You are much less likely to appoint the wrong distributor if you have the chance to meet with it and evaluate its strengths and weaknesses and match those to your requirements. The wrong distributor doesn't necessarily mean it's a bad distributor. For a given market, there will probably only be one or two for which the timing is just right for them to really develop the potential for your products in those markets. Others may do a good job, but not the best job.

Visiting a market before appointing representation affords another benefit - the ability to meet with a variety of distributors. Make the most of such visits. Get to know the agents or distributors, their strengths and weakness, their pricing policies, their sales contacts, and their employees. Once you appoint local representation, those same companies will become competitors. You are much less likely then to have such access to their employees. Once you appoint an agent or distributor, the doors will close to most everyone else. It would be unfortunate to lose out on the opportunity to meet with your future competitors while they are still prospects.

But can you only understand the opportunities and challenges of the market through travel? Eventually your customers will provide feedback, but you will have a weaker perspective from which to judge that feedback if you have never traveled to the market. And without travel, you may not know the important issues to research when you select your representation. For example, until I visited Scandinavia, I underestimated the differences between each country. As a naive yank, I lumped Sweden, Norway, Denmark, and Finland together as one market. Without travel, I would have probably appointed one distributor to represent all four countries. Once I visited the markets, I soon learned that none of the prospects adequately covered all four, and the only option to reaching our full potential was to appoint four distributors.

Travel to your foreign markets may be crucial to your success. But I also recognize that travel may be a luxury, especially for smaller firms. The reality is that not all firms will be able to visit all markets. Decisions regarding foreign representation often have to be made without travel.

• FINDING INTERNATIONAL CUSTOMERS WITHOUT TRAVEL

If you must appoint representation in a foreign market without traveling to the market, the key to success will be the research you conduct and the utilization of your resources. Even if you plan to travel to the market, research should be conducted prior to the trip because it will enhance the effectiveness of your foreign travels.

Conducting research for the purpose of appointing representation in a foreign market involves understanding local conditions in the market that will influence the success of your product. You also should develop a list of indicators that will be used to rate the attractiveness of your candidates. Finally, you'll need to learn as much as possible about each candidate so you can make an informed decision without any travel.

Research Requirements

You already have gathered a significant amount of data on the market during the initial stage of selecting foreign markets, as discussed in Section One. Review this data again from the perspective of distributor or agent selection. Often the same reports that provided market and industry data will list potential agents and distributors. This is common practice in many of the data sources discussed in Chapter 6.

Your goal is to develop a list of key indicators that you will use to rank your candidates. For example, if you determine that the market in question is widely scattered geographically, such as Germany with its strong markets in the northern, western, and southern regions, you may need to determine if the candidate has more than one office in the market, or at least good contacts and representation throughout the market. If you have determined that the import restrictions are complex, your foreign partner may need significant import experience. You may have also discovered that only a few key customers make up the majority of the market for your products so your partner should already have access and experience with these customers.

Each of these are examples of factors that will help determine where you will look for potential partners and the questions you'll want them to answer before making a decision. Figure 9.2 summarizes many of these indicators.

Once you have researched the market and developed a list of key indicators to use when choosing your export partner, you need to develop a list of potential candidates. The following are the top ten ways to get contacts for potential agents or distributors. Many of the resources and techniques have been discussed in Chapter 6.

Figure 9.2 Helpful Indicators for Distributor / Agent Selection

Indicator	Issue for the Company
Company Size	Most manufacturers will want to match their own size and scale with that of their partners. The cultures of each company will probably then be a better match. Size is also an indicator of many other factors such as experience, depth, breadth of market experience, etc.
Product Lines Currently represented	One of the best indicators will be the products the candidate already represents. This reveals a great deal about its Rep experience, strengths, and focus. There may be some lines that would be competitive with the manufacturer's product, and preclude any potential for a representation agreement.
Number of Currently Represented	This is particularly important for exclusive representation Lines agreements. Manufacturers want to avoid Line Collectors, which are companies who try to represent as many product lines as possible in hopes that ultimately one or two will be huge successes. Getting the attention of such companies can be difficult and frustrating.
Industry Focus and Technical Knowledge	Most agents and distributors focus on particular industries. Though their focus may not be a perfect match, it can be used as a guide. If particular technical knowledge is required, such capabilities will need to be identified.
Number of Employees	Related to company size.

(continued)

Figure 9.2 Continued

Indicator	Issue for the Company
Years of Experience	A good or bad indicator. Manufacturers are sometimes attracted to younger agents and distributors that may be more aggressive given their relative need to grow and succeed versus other competitors in the market.
Sales Volume	Related to company size. Also, by comparing projected sales of your product in the market to the company's total sales you'll have a better idea of how important your product line will be to the agent or distributor.
Sales Structure	Critical indicator. Describes how the company sells and to whom. For example, does the distributor only sell to retail locations, but never to the end-user? Does the distributor sell to key accounts? U.S. sales experience will provide important experiential information to use for this indicator.
Key Accounts	If research has determined that particular customers are crucial, such as government sales, some clarification by the company needs to be made to ensure such accounts will be contacted.
Professionalism and Attitude	Review literature, company letterhead, and business cards from the company. All are indicators of how the company presents itself, both to suppliers and, most importantly, to its customers. Review any correspondence to evaluate how eager it is to represent or distribute the product.
Customer Support	If training, parts distribution, or product repairs will be necessary, determine what customer support functions the company is able to provide.
Office Locations	The location of the main office and any other offices will indicate its geographical sales focus. It will help determine what part of the territory it can effectively cover.
Product Launch Experience	Some products require more planning and marketing for a successful launch. This is especially true for products that are new to the foreign market. If a company can demonstrate experience in launching new product lines it would be a significant advantage over others in the market.
References	All of the significant aspects of the company must be confirmed. Conversations with U.S. manufacturers already represented by the company would provide very useful input.

Top Ten Methods for Finding Overseas Agents or Distributors

1. Existing distributor and agent lists. The easiest way to find agents and distributors is to let someone else do the work for you. Compile a list of all the agents or distributors of complementary and competitive companies in your industry. You'll soon see trends once you have the list for four or five companies. (Chapter 6 discusses how to find such lists.) Your top candidates will probably be listed more than once. Some may already carry product lines that will be too competitive so you'll have to cross them off your list. But others may be top contenders, especially if you receive positive information from other sources. Though this is a reactive method that relies on the judgment of others, it is a good shortcut when travel is not possible.

2. Networking with industry contacts and trade associations. Nothing is better than getting advice from peers that have already been through the process of selecting overseas buyers. This is particularly useful if your lists of distributors and agents is incomplete. Sometimes a company that has not formalized its distribution in a certain country would be willing to tell who they have worked with. Trade associations can be particularly helpful because they organize trade shows and have access to useful databases. You will find your peers happy to share information as long as you don't compete too greatly. They understand a new (hopefully successful) product line will enhance the product lines of their foreign buyers and increase the profile of the agent or distributor in the market. Eventually you'll be able to give information in return from other markets. Networking is a very powerful research tool. Don't underestimate its importance.

3. U.S. Department of Commerce. The U.S. Department of Commerce (USDOC) has a number of services designed to find agents and distributors. The services have generally been standardized across many countries, but you should contact your nearest USDOC representative for an update of services and costs. Your local trade specialists will also be able to assist you with USDOC services.

An important USDOC service to consider is the **International Partner Search (IPS)**. For around $600 per search, the USDOC will provide up to six foreign prospects. To initiate the service, you complete a questionnaire that describes your company and products and details the type of partner required. You will also include copies of your literature. The briefing package will be sent to USDOC staff working overseas in U.S. embassies or foreign commercial offices of the USDOC. Using databases and industry sources, the staff will contact prospects and discuss with them their interest in representing your product. This results in up to six qualified prospects with comments about each company and any questions that may have been raised. For the relatively low cost, the IPS is a great way to get an initial list of potential partners.

A more tailor-made report is the **Customized Market Analysis Report (CMA)**. It assesses the potential for your specific product in the foreign market and includes details on competitors, distribution channels, pricing of comparable products, potential buyers, marketing venues, quotas, duties and regulations, and licensing or joint venture interest. CMAs are particularly useful if your other secondary research methods have been less than satisfactory or if the market in question is a crucial market in your international business plan. The cost varies, but CMAs that I have seen contained an astonishing wealth of information for a relatively low cost.

Once you find a potential agent or distributor, the USDOC and others can assist with obtaining company background reports and credit ratings. Refer to Chapter 16 for further details.

4. Local and state contacts - State foreign offices, U.S. chambers of commerce. Utilizing local contacts helps save time and money. Ultimately you will be competing for the good agents and distributors with all your industry competitors. Many states operate offices in foreign countries with databases and resources only available to companies located in their state. Such resources are not always commercially available, and therefore not available to others. Foreign state employees also have contacts with other resources.

Your local and state chambers of commerce can also be important resources. Local chambers often sponsor workshops and other trade-related events which may result in links to overseas buyers. State chambers are even more likely to have some type of export support service. Each will also be able to link you to the **American Chambers of Commerce Abroad (AmChams)**, which are resources for locating foreign partners. AmChams are voluntary associations of business executives concerned with U.S. foreign trade and investment. Like a state-operated trade office, they will have a wealth of contacts and databases not readily accessible by nonmembers. Best of all, the cost is considerably less than other options. Also in many U.S. cities representatives from foreign chambers of commerce reside and can be especially helpful in finding overseas partners. For example, Chicago has nearly 100 foreign organizations representing the business interests of companies abroad. These are in addition to the many foreign consulates located there.

Local and state international resources are constantly addressing the need to find good foreign partners for local companies. Take advantage of that experience and decrease the costs and time needed to find good foreign buyers.

5. Online database. As discussed in Chapter 6, the private sector offers a number of online databases to search for overseas partners. Because the primary business of these companies is to sell data, they are able to invest considerable resources in the infrastructure required to keep the data current. Figure 9.3 summarized four of the leading providers.

6. Trade shows. One of the most effective methods to find partners is to attend a industry trade show or conference. Most have extensive exhibition halls with manufacturers, distributors, and agents. Even if a particular distributor is not exhibiting, they may be attending the show and you can meet with them. Chapter 19 has a detailed discussion of trade shows for finding potential partners and supporting existing partners.

Figure 9.3 Online Databases to Find Potential Export Partners

Database	Number of Companies*	Coverage	Search Methods	Available Details	Cost
Kompass	2,525,880	Global but limited U.S. and limited So. America	Excellent by importer, NAICS Hcode + free text	Contact details for free, financial for a fee	Free limited search; fee for full access
OneSource	4,652,334 to 19,460,000 if U.S., Canada, and U.K included	Global	Excellent w/free text +NAICS or SIC	Extensive including analysis	Subscription only
Alibaba	Unknown	Started in China, about 15 others	Good, mostly free text	Limited but easy to link to company's website	Free but need account
Solusource (Thomas Register)	650,000	About 30	Excellent: free text, category, company	Limited but good to get company contacts	Free to search

estimated and subject to change

Website Addresses:
Kompass: www.kompass.com
OneSource: www.onesource.com
Alibaba: www.alibaba.com
Solusource: www.solusource.com

7. Trade missions. Closely related to the use of trade shows are trade missions which are group travel to a country or perhaps a trade show. This has the advantage over solo-travel in that additional resources and connections are provided by the host which is often federal or state government. I went on a trade mission to Eastern Europe that include very high level meetings including the ambassador to Hungary. Though many on the trip were seasoned international travelers, each agreed that the trade mission brought a much higher profile to the visit than any single company could have organized. Chapter 19 discusses trade mission in more detail.

8. Ask the potential customer base for recommendations. Asking your customers or related parties who they recommend as an agent or distributor is a very simple but powerful technique. For example, I was trying to locate a distributor in the U.K. prior to a trip. Our product dramatically enhanced the performance of IBM computers, but the product did not compete with IBM. So I called the IBM's sales and marketing division in the U.K. I eventually reached a very knowledgeable manager who was impressed I had tracked him down and was happy to give me his recommendations. The best part was that I then used his name as an introduction when I called the distributors.

This method works particularly well in industries where the end-user understands the need to purchase from importers (distributors) rather than directly from the U.S. or abroad. They will be accustomed to buying from distributors and will be able to mention the large players in the market. Retail stores can be helpful, though probably shocked to get an overseas phone call. This method can be easy and cheap, though you'll need an interpreter if you don't speak the local language.

9. Advertising. Your advertising options are fairly limited because you won't want to do too much advertising in the foreign market until you have your distribution network in place. Responding to individual sales inquiries from single buyers can be time-consuming and rarely profitable.

There are some other options. The simplest is to include the message "International Distributor Inquiries Welcome" on all domestic trade advertising. You'll want to make it discreet, but be assured, international agents and distributors will see it. They are used to searching for similar announcements. If fact, even without such wording, you will probably receive inquiries from your domestic advertising.

Another advertising option is **Commercial News USA** (CNUSA). This is an international publication specifically geared to finding worldwide agents and distributors for U.S. companies. It is managed and published by ThinkGlobal Incorporate (http://www.thinkglobal.us) on behalf of the U.S. Department of Commerce in a very effective private industry/government partnership. The monthly magazine is essentially a collection of small, four-color ads grouped by industry, similar to product announcements seen in industry trade magazines. CNUSA is distributed to U.S. embassies and consulates worldwide with a readership in over 170 countries. Its electronic version reaches even more. Foreign overseas agents and distributors have learned to use it as a source for new products to represent. I know of clients who have received orders directly from end-users through the CNUSA. It is an excellent, cost-effective way to broadcast your product information to worldwide markets and qualified buyers with interest and experience in dealing with U.S. goods. And because it will reach markets in which you may already have representation, you can pass the leads back to your agent or distributor which will generate goodwill.

10. Other Internet resources. There are a number of other online resources. GlobalEdge at Michigan State University (globaledge.msu.edu) is the best place to start because as shown in Figure 9.4, GlobalEdge links to numerous company directories around the world. (On their website visit the Reference Desk / Global Resource Director / Company Directories.)

Figure 9.4 Sample Listing of Websites Offering Company Information

GENERAL: The Fortune Global 500
GENERAL: WorldOpinion Worldwide Directory of Market Research firms
GENERAL: I-Trade Searchable International Business Directory
GENERAL: COMFIND Global Business Directory
GENERAL: Pronett Business Search Engine
GENERAL: 123Link - 1st Global Directory
GENERAL: Business Seek
GENERAL: East-West Business Link - Emerging Markets of Europe and Central Asia
GENERAL: EC Directory
GENERAL: Export Hotline - ExporTel
GENERAL: WTE Internet Business Tower
Africa: MBendi - Companies of Africa
America (North and South): America's Trade Source Search Engine
Arab Countries: Arab World Online Commercial Directory
Argentina: Companies Directory
Asia: Asia's Premier Business and Leisure On-line Directories
Asia: Netsource Asia - Asia's Premier International Online Trade Directory
Asia: Asia Yellow Web
Asia: Orient Business Express
Australia: Australia on Display
Baltic States: Business in Baltic States
Bolivia: Bolivia Business Online - Company Directory
Canada: Canadian Trade Index
Canada: Canadian Company Capabilities
Canada: Canadian Exporters Catalogue
Central America: IPL Trade Directory
Chile: Chilnet Electronic Yellow Pages
Chile: ProChile Directory of Exporters
China: Directory of Chinese Manufacturers
Costa Rica: Company and Institutions Directory
Czech Republic: Business Directory
(continued)
Denmark: Krak's Export Directory of Denmark
Egypt: Egypt Company Profiles
Estonia: Estonian Export Directory
Europe: Europages - The European Business Directory
Europe: Internet Amadeus
France: France Import Export Companies Search Engine
Guatemala: Quetzalnet Exporters Database
Hong Kong: Hong Kong Shipping Directory
Hong Kong: Online Hong Kong Business Directory

Figure 9.4 Continued

India: Indian Business Directory
India: The Indian Corporate Gateway
Indonesia: Indonesian Yellow Pages
Ireland: Irish Businesses On the Web
Ireland: Irish Trade Board Supplier Directory
Israel: The Interactive Business Directory of Israel
Israel: Israel's Yellow Pages
Italy: Pagine Gialle Online
Japan: Directory of Major Japanese Organizations
Latin America: Latin American Business Connection
Latin America: MERCOSUR Exporters Directory
Malaysia: Malaysia Yellow Pages
Mexico: 1995 Directory of Mexican Exporters
Netherlands: Holland Exports
New Zealand: Yellow Pages
Norway: Norwegian Yellow Pages
Peru: Peruvian Exporters, Importers and Services Directory
Philippines: PhilExport Membership Database (searchable)
Portugal: Portugal Offer Company Search
Russia: Company Directories
Russia: Russian Organizations - Yellow Pages
Singapore: Singapore Company Profiles
Slovenia: Chamber of Commerce and Industry of Slovenia Member
Directory
Slovenia: Import-Export Directory of Slovenia
South Africa: iDex South African Business Directory
Sweden: Swedish Export Directory
Switzerland: Swiss+Directory Worldwide Online
Switzerland: Swisscom Yellow Pages
Taiwan: Taiwan Business Directory Online
Taiwan: Directory of Manufacturers of Products
Thailand: Commercial Directory of Thailand
Thailand: List of Thai Manufacturers/Exporters
Turkey: TurkEx - Turkish Export Center
Ukraine: Business Contacts in Ukraine
United Arab Emirates: UAE Yellow Pages
United Kingdom: UK Business Directory - Millenium Facilities Ltd.
Uruguay: Business Link - Uruguay
Venezuela: Venezuelan Export Directory
Venezuela: Trade Venezuela Company and Product Directory

Source: Michigan State University globalEDGE globaledge.msu.edu

• SELECTING AGENTS OR DISTRIBUTORS WITHOUT TRAVEL

The previous ten methods for finding agents and distributors should be effective in creating a list of potential representatives for your products. If you find that either budget or time considerations prohibit you from visiting the foreign market, you must select your agents or distributors without travel. Though this is not ideal, the reality is that many companies encounter such constraints. Even if this situation does not apply to your company, I urge you to continue reading. Many of these concepts apply to the process of selecting a representative even with travel.

The challenge of selecting the right agent or distributor without travel requires getting as much information as possible without face-to-face contact. A number of techniques may be helpful:

- Email questionnaire. Review the questions and issues in the next section, and those shown in Figure 9.2 and 9.5. These are questions you can include in a written questionnaire.
- Phone or Skype calls. Interview each potential representative via a phone call instead of a direct visit. Though the dynamics of the exchange will be lower than a face-to-face meeting, it will still provide important insight to issues not clarified through written correspondence.
- Financial background checks. Invest in the credit reports available (discussed in Chapter 16). Though some are expensive, they are less expensive than foreign travel.
- Check references. Check references thoroughly because they can indicate potential problems.
- Ask for a written marketing plan. If the stakes are relatively high, such as appointing an exclusive representative in a large, strategically important market, have the potential agent or distributor create a marketing plan describing how it would launch your product and support it, as well as its estimated sales projections. Some may balk at such a request, but others will be eager to accept the challenge as a way to differentiate its ability and highlight its commitment.
- Wait until a domestic trade show. If there is an important domestic trade show with strong international attendance, consider interviewing the foreign agents or distributors at a trade show in your domestic market or one nearby.

Each of these methods can be effective in dealing with the challenge of selecting the right agent or distributor without visiting the foreign market.

• SELECTING AGENTS OR DISTRIBUTORS WITH TRAVEL

The most effective way to qualify your prospects and choose the best candidate is to travel to the foreign market and meet with the prospects. Not only will it put you in a more informed position to make a decision, it will give you invaluable market information and experience to use in the future as you implement your marketing campaign.

Even if you plan to travel to the foreign market, you should consider using some of the previous methods for finding agents or distributors. The research will save you considerable time and reduce the timeframe required to appoint a suitable agent or distributor. Plus, some of contacts identified during the research, such as industry contacts, will be important contacts to include during your visits. Prior to any foreign travel, research the overseas markets and develop a list of potential candidates as if you were not going to visit the market.

When to Go

Deciding when to travel to the foreign market can have an important impact on your success. Generally the following issues should be considered:

- Trade shows. One of the best times to visit a market is during an important trade show or convention. Whether you exhibit or not, you will have the opportunity to meet with potential buyers in one convenient location and see competing products and buyers.
- Holiday and vacation conflicts. Some markets are virtually shut down during specific times of the year. For example, there is little hope of conducting business in Paris during the month of August, when most Parisians take their vacations.
- Combine multiple markets. Obviously, you want to increase the efficiency of foreign travel by combining trips to more than one market. You may want to use a particular trade show as the foundation for the trip, and then add on other surrounding cities.
- Seasonal buying. Many industries are dominated by purchasing cycles or seasons that could impact the effectiveness of your visits. You may find that confirming appointments is more difficult during hectic selling seasons.

There may also be internal or domestic considerations. For example, an upcoming new product release or large domestic marketing initiative may enhance your foreign travels and increase your impact.

Above all, don't wait for the perfect time because it will probably never come. Foreign travel is nearly always disruptive, given the nature of travel times and preparations. Because not all of your prospects may be able to confirm a meeting, you may not be able to schedule your visits as tightly and efficiently as with domestic trips. Just don't let such issues stop you from traveling.

Arranging Meetings

In general, you will find access to potential foreign agents and distributors relatively easy. Most potential foreign buyers keep abreast of industry trends and new products and understand the need to meet new companies. I always found it fairly easy to get through to the top decision maker for foreign buyers, especially after I made it clear I was calling from the U.S. Email and Skype makes the task even easier and reduces language barrier issues because most companies staff some employees with English capabilities.

It helps to have a reference, even if you have to stretch the issue a bit. For example, if you contacted any local experts or customers, be sure to make reference to them. After calling IBM U.K. prior to my visit to England, I was sure to always say, "Mr. John Doe at IBM U.K. suggested I contact you about our products." I was generally able to confirm an appointment with minimal explanation.

Do Not Overbook Your Schedule

There is a tendency to overbook their overseas itineraries. Many of us are accustomed to meetings starting on time and lasting a predetermined length. The culture of many countries is much more relaxed and keeping to a tight schedule can be difficult. Visits to prospective agents and distributors often require at least a half-day visit, especially if the initial discussion is positive. Visits may also include social time, such as lunch or dinner. Allow plenty of time around appointments to allow for expanded discussions and company tours, especially for your top prospects. Try to avoid the tendency to fully book up your schedule just to justify the trip.

The Gold Key Service from the Commercial Service

Imagine having someone else contact potential agents and distributors, arrange all the meetings, provide meeting space, and even provide a translator! That is the idea behind the Gold Key Service provided by the Commercial Service, part of the U.S. Department of Commerce. Commercial Service staff are generally located in U.S. embassies throughout the world. It is a custom-tailored service for U.S. companies planning a visit to a foreign market that combines market research, assistance in developing a marketing strategy, orientation briefings, introductions to potential partners, interpreters, and follow-up planning. The Gold Key Service fee varies by country, but is generally $400-$700 per day. (Some U.S. embassies have their own websites with Gold Key information. For example, visit www.usembassy.org.uk and select Commercial Service.) The easiest way to initiate a Gold Key Service is to contact your closest U.S. Export Assistance Center. It can be an extremely effective service that saves money and time. It is particularly effective if combined with a foreign trade show.

Don't Just Visit Buyers

During your travels you want to take advantage of the opportunity to meet with more than just potential agents and distributors. Also visit industry leaders and customers. For example, I would always schedule a visit with the editor of the local trade magazine for a particular country. Like foreign buyers, editors keep track of trends and products. They can be harder to pin down for a visit, but if you can meet with one you'll get invaluable market information. During the meeting ask for recommendations of agents or distributors. Also grab back copies of their magazines that you can scour for new contacts. If you have trouble meeting with editorial staff, contact the advertising department. They will be eager to meet if they think some future advertising is in the offing. Plus, they will know good contacts within the industry.

Selecting the Right Representative is Like Hiring a New Employee

The process of selecting the right agent or distributor is never easy. Prior to your meetings, you'll have indications of which is the best, but like hiring a new employee, surprises invariably occur along the way.

Like an employee, your foreign representative will be representing your products, company, brand, and ultimately be responsible for the image and reputation that is established in that market. The effectiveness of your foreign representation is even more critical if the contract will be exclusive. You must treat the process of appointing your foreign representative like that of employing a new salesperson. Many would argue it is more important because the process of ending the relationship with a foreign representative is more difficult and complicated than firing an employee. (Hiring versus appointing should only be a psychological comparison. In no way should you ever represent to a foreign buyer that you are "hiring" them. This can lead to legal issues upon termination. Chapter 18 discusses this in greater detail.)

Issues to Discuss during Meetings

During your visits with potential agents and distributors, you'll want to assess their ability and enthusiasm for representing your products. Each will offer particular strengths and weaknesses and your eventual selection will be a compromise from what you considered the perfect representative. The goal during your visit is to get as much information as possible so you can make an informed decision. By the same token, you must also educate your representative about your company and product so he or she can make an informed decision about electing to represent your product. Building excitement with your representative early on will make the contract negotiation process easier.

The questions you ask during a visit will depend on the requirements you have identified for an excellent representative and whether you are selecting an agent or distributor. Figure 9.5 lists areas you should investigate. Some are more important than others depending on your specific situation.

By the end of the trip, you should be able to assess each candidate's capability in the following areas:

- Company strength (history, financial, reputation)
- Market access (reputation, sales network, market share)
- Marketing ability (new product launches, P/R and advertising, brochures)
- Technical ability (training, repairs, ability to market technical products)
- Infrastructure (employees, technical support, building, facilities)
- Sale projections (initial order they would place, sales forecasts)
- Overall match with your goal including complementary products

You should also have a good idea about how each candidate approaches the local market. Do they sell direct? Do they only sell through dealers? These are important questions that may lead to critical distinctions between prospects. By reviewing their projected pricing structure, many of these issues will be even clearer. (Chapter 11 discusses international pricing and shows examples of price exercises.)

Determine the Motivation of the Foreign Agent or Distributor

Perhaps the most difficult task is determining the driving motivation behind why each candidate wants to represent your product. This may be crucial to your decision, but it can be very difficult to really pinpoint a company's motivation.

The reason motivation is so important is because a good partnership between a manufacturer and its foreign representative builds your global business. The partners will enjoy the success but also have to overcome the failures - the true test of a partnership. There will be problems - missed shipments, products that don't work, delays - but working through those problems will depend on the motivation of your partner and how each of you handle problems.

You should search for companies that want to represent you because your products or services fit into the strategy of their company. If the timing is right, even better. Good candidates will want your product because it enhances their current product offerings and will open even more doors. Good candidates will want your product because it utilizes the strength and resources of their company.

There are two types of motivations that you want to avoid. The first is a *line collector*. This is a company that, as the name implies, collects lines just to have them. To be more accurate, it collects lines hoping that one or two of them will become big sellers. Line collectors may support your products, but not with the same investment in time and resources as a top representative. The easiest way to identify a line collector is to compare the number of lines it represents to the size of the company. Another way is to have the company discuss exactly what it has done to market each specific line. A line collector will tend to group sales and marketing activities for all the lines the way a catalog company would. The really bad line collectors are more like order takers than order makers.

The second motivation to avoid is the *block-your-product* buyer. This type is more obvious. Block-your-product companies are interested in your products essentially to keep them off the market. They sign a contract and sit on the product to ensure other competing products they represent succeed. If you don't detect this from the start and you contract such an agent or distributor, you will constantly encounter problems and obstacles such as why the product just doesn't seem to sell well. You want to avoid this motivation entirely.

Once you have met with all your candidates, compiled answers to all your questions, and understand their motivation, you are ready to make a decision. Sometimes I go back to industry leaders, customers, and vendors at this point to get further input. This can be especially important if any of the information gathered from the candidates seems to contradict earlier recommendations. Asking for more input is also helpful if one or two issues seem to dominate your decision and you want specific opinions on those issues. You should also hold internal meetings to fully discuss the decision.

Figure 9.5 Factors to Consider when Choosing Foreign Agents/Distributors

Company Overview

- History, age, structure, sales volumes
- Financial strength: bank references, standard payment terms, ownership, debts
- Personnel: number of employees, management structure, training, expertise
- Cultural considerations: Language capabilities, familiarity with importing products

Market Access

- Reputation: How does the market see the company? Any past problems or disasters?
- Customers: profile of customers, government; key accounts; retail; end user
- Current product: What product lines (especially American) do they currently import?
- Brand: strength of their own company name in the market
- Territory: What areas of the market do they effectively cover?
- Industry focus: Does the company specialize in particular industries, customer types?
- Relations with local resources, trade associations, government

Marketing Ability

- Product launch: examples of products they have launched
- P/R: depth of experience and contacts with newspapers, TV, trade press
- Advertising: experience, past examples
- Your products: How do they see selling and marketing your products?

Distribution/Logistics/Order Fulfillment

- Warehouse capabilities
- Technology support for sales function
- Freight, shipping expertise

Competitive Situation

- Market share of the candidate versus competitors
- Key accounts
- Other products lines already represented

(continued)

Figure 9.4 Continued

Budget/Forecasts

- Marketing: What resources would candidate commit to launch the product?
- Opening order: What would be their opening order?
- Forecasts: What is their short-, medium-, and long-term forecast for your products?
- How would they price your products? Review price structure and profit goals.

Infrastructure

- Web presence and B2B or B2C capabilities
- Capabilities of the main office
- Other offices in the market

Technical Ability

- Technical experience
- Training ability
- Ability to market and sell technical products
- Product related issues: repair, customer support

Motivation/Contract

- Synergy between candidate and manufacturer
- Why do they want to represent the manufacturer?
- Long-term plans of the candidate? Growth goals?
- Any special contract considerations that could be a problem?

Sometimes it will be very difficult to decide. The decision will rarely be easy. You'll wish you could combine two candidates or take a strength from one and add it to another. But like hiring from a pool of equally qualified potential employees, you eventually have to make a decision.

The most difficult decision is when your top two finalists are very different companies. For example, one may be a strong, experienced company with many success stories. The other may be a smaller rising star, with limited success but a very attractive, aggressive attitude. With the larger company, you met senior staff but not the president. With the smaller company, you had dinner with the president and top executives. These choices can lead to sleepless nights.

When I worked for Western Digital/Paradise Systems my most important distributor in Europe was in Germany. It was a small start-up company based in Hamburg with little to no national exposure. Most would consider that a recipe for disaster due to the size of the German market. To make matters worse, this company was essentially a computer dealer turned distributor, which is often a problem. Yet within a year, its average order was over $200,000, and it was soon our number one distributor. On the other hand, the only company that was ever successful with our products in the U.K. was a much larger established company. It was the opposite of the German distributor.

To say there is a model that will work for each decision is fruitless. The more scientific you try and make the process, the greater the chance you'll miss the larger picture. Get as much information as possible and then make the decision. Not making a decision is ultimately the greatest mistake you could make.

It is okay if the size of the opening order ends up being the deciding factor. I'll admit I did it more than once. If you are facing overall sales expectations from management, and see an easy opportunity for a big sale, that may make the difference. At least it means your representative will be under pressure to sell from that point onward. Just don't let the size of the opening order obscure other more important issues, especially if the candidate is financially weak.

Don't Predict the Outcome

One final point. There is a temptation to think an initial contender is the best: the first to be recommended, the first to be visited, the first to be identified as the strongest. While the first may turn out to be the best don't make that determination too early. Many individuals have a tendency to predict the outcome of the search based on their initial research. Before the travel begins, they may have a feeling that one particular agent or distributor is best and all further information gathered during the trip is colored by this prediction. Such assumptions can be dangerous.

Do not be taken in by the first agent or distributor that really makes you feel comfortable or accepts you as a foreigner. This is difficult to explain, but I noticed it more than once, especially when I started out selecting international distributors. I was strongly swayed by distributors that made me feel comfortable. Perhaps there was more socializing or they spoke better English. Whatever the reasons, it is not uncommon if you find you simply like one distributor more than another.

The danger here is twofold. First, never forget that it is a competition. Candidates will probably ask you which other agents or distributors you are visiting. When you mention the others, the candidate may quickly offer his personal opinion and advice about the other candidates. I can remember many occasions when a potential distributor would tell me something confidential about another distributor. More than once I would later find that the information was not true. Did the potential distributor purposely not tell the truth? Who knows, but it is dangerous to be lured into a false sense of security just because you build a bond during an initial meeting with a prospective representative.

Second, the reason you like them may have nothing to do with their ability to get the job done for your company. Perhaps it seems overly simplistic to even say this, but in the end, it should be their commitment to your product and their ability to market and support the product that forms the basis of your decision. Your choice should not be influenced by the distributor that selected the best weekend activities during your visit. And don't laugh as you read this until you find yourself in the difficult position of telling a distributor it was not selected, even though you became best friends during the visit.

I also cannot nevertheless overemphasize the importance of these interpersonal/human issues. Often it will only be the trust that was developed during the initial and subsequent meetings that will support the manufacturer/foreign representative relationship during difficult times, such as product failures or shipping delays. Chapter 10 discusses the culture of international business in detail, so I do not want to imply here that such interpersonal issues are not important. However, when selecting the best agent or distributor, be aware of the natural tendency to go with one you like, rather than the most qualified.

International Business across Cultures

We have all heard of the ugly American. I saw one of the worst while eating at an outdoor café in Paris. He was the husband of a couple on what must have been their first trip to France and he was not happy. The husband was constantly complaining about the food, the service, and the bathrooms. Nothing made him happy and he made sure everyone else in the restaurant knew of his discontent. Very loudly in English, he barked orders to the waiter. I heard it all, including the conversations between him and his wife in which he stated the French don't know how to do anything right. Finally, he said loudly to his wife - and the whole restaurant, "How much of this funny money is this going to cost me?"

It seemed to sum up his view of things. It wasn't real food, real service, or a real restaurant. The money wasn't even real. I left amazed and saddened that one of my countrymen was that insensitive to international culture. To him, the American way was the only way.

Barbara Tuchman must have had a similar encounter with an ugly American when she wrote:

In April 1917 the illusion of isolation was destroyed, America came to the end of innocence, and the exuberant freedom of bachelor independence. That the responsibilities of world power have not made us happier is no surprise. To help ourselves manage them, we have replaced the illusion of isolation with a new illusion of omnipotence.[1]

This describes my encounter in Paris. That man thought he controlled the world, the restaurant, and the waiter. Sad. On the other hand, I've met individuals that seemingly have no home country. They so completely adopt and embrace foreign cultures that they don't seem to have one of their own. I often saw this in Britain where some Americans lost their American accent, their American attitude, and in some cases their respect for America. Some clearly preferred living in the U.K. and made that point of view very clear to all they encountered, especially other Americans. I'm not sure Theodore Roosevelt would have approved. He once wrote something to the effct: "The man who loves other countries as much as his own stands on a level with the man who loves other women as much as he loves his own wife."

Such a dilemma. Do we, as international business professionals, make our own nationality and cultural identity a priority or do we fully embrace cultural differences and disregard national borders? Is one right and the other wrong? Do we consider our culture to be the best or do we respect others as equally valid?

This is the essential issue discussed in this chapter. I will also address the nature of the cultural challenge and issues international business professionals should consider as they interact with other cultures. It is a fascinating topic and one that helps clearly identify one of the most important differences between domestic and international business.

• EXPERIENCING CULTURAL DIFFERENCES

There are certain components of a society's culture that we immediately identify as different from our own. Language is the best example. From the moment you step off the airplane in a foreign country, the language difference becomes apparent. The language of a society permeates a visitor's experience. From signs and advertisements to media and conversations, language differences are always present.

Beyond language, other differences between cultures exist but may not be as obvious, for example, religion. The impact of religion on business may be subtle. Likewise, a country's views on education, social mobility, and economic philosophy will also be harder to determine. The impact of those issues on advertising, public relations, customer support, and other business functions may not be evident, but international businesspeople must be aware of these differences in order to be successful in that society.

To understand a society's culture, it is important to recognize that its culture is derived from more than just history or current events. It goes beyond language differences. A society's culture includes its beliefs about marriage and the role of the family, its view of money, and its respect or disdain for high achievers. Many anthropologists believe that a society's culture is the sum total of its beliefs, rules, techniques, institutions, and artifacts that characterize human populations.[2]

It is also important to recognize that a society's culture does not necessarily follow national borders. Switzerland, for example, is its own country and represents the highest level of political integration - a political union. But Switzerland has three distinct cultures: (1) Swiss French, (2) Swiss German, and (3) Swiss Italian. Each has its own society and each culture speaks its own language. It would also be wrong to think the Swiss German is the same as the German spoken in Germany. I remember telling my German distributor in Hanover in northern Germany that I wanted to study German in Zurich. He was surprised that I considered Swiss German the same as his native tongue. He joked that Swiss German movies have subtitles when shown in Germany!

Cultural differences cannot be defined by country borders nor can you assume they cross borders.

Understanding Cultural Differences: the Hofstede Cultural Dimensions

It is the broad, all-encompassing nature of culture that makes it such a challenge for the international businessperson. One model that is helpful in understanding cultural differences is the work of Geert **Hofstede**, a Danish psychologist. He interviewed thousands of employees worldwide as part of his job with IBM. He isolated four dimensions that he claimed summarized different cultures:[3]

1. Individualism versus collectivism
2. Power distance
3. Uncertainty avoidance
4. Masculinity versus femininity

Figure 10.1 shows a selection of countries and Hofstede's value for each dimension.

Individualism versus collectivism. This aspect of Hofstede's model centers around the relationship between the individual and others in the society. Individuals in individualist cultures are primarily concerned with themselves and their immediate family. Individual freedom and achievement are valued. Individuals in collectivist cultures belong to groups where each member of the group is expected to take care of the other individuals. For example, the U.S. favors individualism and Venezuela favors collectivism. All these aspects are known as Hofstede's **individualism** index.

Power distance - accepting differences in power. Hofstede's **power distance** dimension attempts to quantify the level to which individuals in a culture accept the dif

Figure 10.1 Hofstede's Value Dimensions

Country	Individualism	Power Distance	Uncertainty Avoidance	Masculinity
Mexico	30	81	82	69
Venezuela	12	81	76	73
Colombia	13	64	80	64
Peru	16	90	87	42
Chile	23	63	86	28
Portugal	27	63	104	31
United States	91	50	46	62
Australia	90	49	51	61
South Africa	65	49	49	63
New Zealand	79	45	49	58
Canada	80	39	48	52
Great Britain	89	35	35	66
Ireland	70	28	35	68

ferences in power between individuals. In a large power distance culture, differences in wealth and power are accepted. Low power distance cultures are less inclined to accept these differences. Peru and Mexico are examples of large power distance societies and Ireland is a low power distance culture.

Uncertainty avoidance. This dimension analyzes the extent to which a culture accepts uncertainty and risk. Individuals in high-uncertainty avoidance cultures tend to stay in their jobs for a long time and prefer a stable workplace with clear instruction from management. Individuals in low-uncertainty avoidance cultures, such as the U.S., are mobile and willing to take risks.

Masculinity versus femininity. This index ranks the degree to which a society embraces masculine societal values versus feminine ones. A high masculinity score means the society values aspects such as assertiveness, acquisition of money and status, and organizational awards. A society with a stronger emphasis on feminine societal values places an importance on quality of life issues and concern for others. Feminine cultures also have less differentiation in the roles of each sex. Mexico is an example of a country with a high masculinity value in Hofstede's index.

The Implications of Hofstede's Research

The results of Hofstede's research offer a fascinating insight into cultural differences and help identify business and management practices that may warrant adaptation depending on the culture. For example, individuals in a collectivist culture are more likely to prefer group decision making where the emphasis in an individualist culture is on individual decision making. A large power distance culture, such as Peru and Mexico, is more likely to accept a hierarchical company structure and decision making system. Countries with a high uncertainty avoidance do not easily accept change. A culture with strong femininity prefers a corporate culture that places an emphasis on the welfare of all employees.

Many of these implications directly apply to international companies that have established overseas subsidiaries and must choose company structure and management techniques that are appropriate for the local culture. Insensitivity to these issues will have a detrimental impact on the performance of employees and the subsidiary as a whole.

What about companies without overseas subsidiaries? Are there implications evident in Hofstede's research other than corporate structure and decision making issues? The most important implication for a company in its initial stages of international growth is the recognition that cultural differences are deeper and more subtle than the obvious differences of language and religion. The overt differences are important on a practical level so communication is possible by learning the language and individuals are not offended because you ignore their religious beliefs. However, Hofstede's dimensions help us understand the more emotional and subtle differences. They explain, for example, why a new, revolutionary sales campaign may be more readily accepted in one culture over another. Language and religious differences alone do not offer that same insight.

The second implication is that international businesspeople need to acknowledge that their culture is not better, just different. For example, prior to a foreign visit, a visitor may believe the country he or she is from has the 'best' or most valid beliefs and traditions. This is known as **ethnocentric behavior**: a belief that one's one culture is superior to others. Hofstede's work (along with many others) helps us to see that very few countries are completely isolated in their cultural beliefs and values. The naive traveler may believe that Mexico and Ireland have little in common. Yet Hofstede's research indicates both societies favor masculine values. If the visitor better understood that foreign countries share certain cultural elements with their own country, he or she may be more tolerant.

Understanding Cultural Differences: High Context, Low Context

A alternative model to understanding cultural differences was developed by Edward T. Hall.[4] He categorizes these cultural differences as 'high-context' versus 'low-context' and centers on communication and social norms. A **high-context culture** places most of the importance not on the communication itself but on the relationships. In some respects what it not said is as important as what is said. In a high-context culture long-term relationships are important and form long-lasting business relationships. If you were to visit a high-context culture, imagine it will be something like visiting a family reunion: everyone will know the rules ahead of time so you need to know them as well. This is contrasted with a low-context culture in which the communication style is very direct. The message is clear, logical and specific. One imagine the conflict is someone from a high-context culture visits a low-context culture, such as a Chinese visitor to the U.S. The Chinese visitor may expect meetings to be relaxed, and an opportunity to get to know each other. Whereas the U.S. host may be rushed, keep to an agenda, and expect resolution of the meeting that day.

• PUTTING CULTURAL DIFFERENCES INTO PRACTICE

Beyond the implications of recognizing cultural differences and respecting foreign cultures, other aspects of Hofstede's research are suitable for smaller companies that are exporting into foreign markets. Traveling to a foreign market, signing distribution contracts, and developing marketing campaigns all have cultural implications.

For example, the introduction of a new distribution method or sales campaign may be more difficult in a high uncertainty culture. Similarly, Hofstede's research would indicate that when choosing a gift for a foreign buyer in an individualistic culture, the gift should recognize the individual over the group, such as giving a gift to only the president rather than a gift for the office to share.

Projecting too many generalizations onto individual foreign buyers and contacts is potentially dangerous. In practice, international business is really about business between individuals, and within any culture, individuals vary tremendously. I know some Brits that are more American than many of my American friends. I know some Japanese that seem to contradict all cultural generalizations of their country. Thus it is just as

Tips for Dealing with Cultural Differences

Build Trust

Your primary goal should be to develop trust which will serve your seller/ buyer relationship well. Building trust takes time. It means investing the extra time and a longer travel schedule to ensure quality time with buyers, instead of a whirlwind trip through their city and company. It means professionalism in all aspects of the relationship. Learn how to pronounce names correctly. Take cues from others when addressing individuals, such as when to use first names. Dress appropriately for the locale. Take an interest in them, their company, and their country.

Study Foreign Cultures and Current Events

When first meeting with potential foreign buyers, it is common to discuss non-business issues before any serious business. This could be a long discourse or only a few minutes. It depends on the nature and length of the visit. It would be prudent to study the local culture, history, and current events so your conversation is lively and you avoid embarrassment. I once felt very flustered when I had to ask a potential Irish distributor what the population of Ireland was during a contract negotiation. It was an important fact because it would determine the sales forecast. It was a statistic I should have known. Equally, it is insulting if your foreign partner mentions the president of his country and you respond, "Who is that?"

Never Assume You Know It All

Understanding foreign cultures is not easy. Knowing everything about a foreign culture is impossible because there is simply too much to know and understand. Thus there is a danger that after a few visits or a prolonged stay, you may believe you know all there is to know. This could lead to a false sense of security and eventually mistakes. It is far better to rely on the input of local experts than assume you know everything.

Gestures and Etiquette

Roger Axtell has written a number of enjoyable and informative books on the topic of gestures and international etiquette. They are fun to read and highly informative. One of the most popular is Dos and Taboos Around the World. It contains country-by-country suggestions on everything from gestures and body language to gift giving and general protocol. These can be very useful hints to help you avoid embarrassing cultural faux pas. Axtell relates a number of terrific instances where a little local cultural knowledge can go a long way to enhancing the relationship between buyer and seller.

dangerous to ignore cultural differences as it is to use them as the sole justification for decisions. The issue of cultural differences is fluid. Some foreign buyers and contacts typify the culture of their country. Others display attributes that contradict the cultural norms of their society. The key is to remain flexible and adapt to the differences of the situation.

When expanding internationally, the most important advice is to keep an open mind, embrace the diversity of cultures, and treat each individual as an individual. Avoid projecting generalizations on any one person. Instead show respect for him and his culture, and let his own individuality and cultural identity develop as the relationship develops.

Beyond treating everyone as an individual and accepting differences, there are some important tips for dealing with cultural differences. These are issues, such as building trust and studying cultures, that should be a priority during foreign travels, hosting foreign visitors, or meeting with overseas distributors and agents at a U.S. trade show.

• BACK TO THE DILEMMA AND THE ROLE OF CORPORATE CULTURE

Having discussed cultural differences, their impact on our experiences, and the practical aspects of dealing with cultural differences, how do we solve the dilemma posed at the start of the chapter? Do we, as international business professionals, give priority to our own culture or do we embrace cultural differences and disregard national borders?

The final answer depends on the company, the industry, and most importantly, the corporate culture of the company. At the individual level, there is no question each person should be treated as an individual. As previously discussed, it is too dangerous to project the entire cultural identity onto one person.

There are, however, instances where a company may make its own culture a priority. More accurately, it should make its corporate culture a priority. A company's corporate culture is similar to a society's culture in that it is also a set of beliefs, rules, techniques, institutions, and artifacts. One can easily imagine the different corporate cultures of a large Manhattan-based bank and a small software company in California. Each has its own feel, its own culture. In this way, each should utilize its culture in international business. Some of that corporate culture borrows from the local, regional, and national culture. Other aspects are unique, especially the legends or stories of past company successes, failures, and individuals.

A company's corporate culture can be a very powerful tool. It can help identify individuals that would be most comfortable in that company. It can help mold a marketing campaign. It can help in the decision process because rules such as the need for innovation and creativity are often implied.

Internationally, corporate culture can also play a role. Our final choice for our German distributor was partly based on the perfect match between our corporate culture at Paradise Systems and that of the distributor. We preferred creative and innovative marketing tools. So did our distributor. In fact, it duplicated a number of our U.S. product launch ideas that had not been widely used in Germany. Another German distributor may not have been as comfortable or successful with the same marketing ideas.

No matter what size the company is, its corporate culture will dictate how to solve the dilemma of combining its culture with other cultures. There are occasions where imposing the corporate culture over local culture is suitable. In other cases, the local culture must take precedence. A strong use of the corporate culture may also include a strong use of the home-country culture. An American clothes manufacturer would clearly do well pushing both its corporate culture and that of the U.S. However, there is less benefit in a soap manufacturer closely matching its foreign market identity to that of its home market.

The solution to the dilemma? Respect individuals. Respect other cultures. Adapt as needed based on local culture. But never lose sight of the importance of the company's corporate culture and that of the home country. Creating the right blend can be a powerful competitive tool.

• NOTES

1. Barbara Tuchman (1912-1989), U.S. historian. "How We Entered World War I," New York Times Magazine (May 5, 1967).

2. I. Brady and B. Isaac, A Reader in Cultural Change, Volume 1 (Cambridge, MA.: Schenkman Publishing, 1975).

3. To see the Hofstede dimensions for various countries, visit the official website at www.geert-hofstede.com. Most introductory college textbooks about international business have a detailed discussion of Hofstede's work. For direct writings of Hofstede, try either of these two articles: (1) G. Hofstede, "The Cultural Relativity of Organizational Practices and Theories," Journal of International Business Studies, Fall 1983. (2) G. Hofstede, "Cultural Dimensions in Management and Training," Asia Pacific Journal of Management, January 1984.

4. Edward T. Hall, Beyond Culture(New York, NY: Anchor Books, 1976).

CHAPTER 11

International Product and Pricing Strategies

I n this chapter I address two very important components of a company's overall international marketing mix: its product and pricing policies. In both cases, the domestic strategy cannot simply be duplicated. Companies must make very considered decisions as regards to its product and pricing strategies. These are discussed in this chapter.

We being by looking at a company's product strategy. This mostly revolves around two key questions: can a company keep its current product strategy with little adaptation? And if a company offers a range of products or services, which should be the first to be sold internationally?

• PRODUCT STANDARDIZATION VERSUS ADAPTATION

International expansion would be much easier if foreign markets would accept products and services from a company's home market with no modification. But this is highly unlikely no matter how hard a company tries to establish their product as the standard. Forces as varied as consumer tastes and governmental restrictions force exporters to modify their products in order to reap the benefits of a global market.

The decision to modify your product to fit foreign market needs may be a big one. Frantz Manufacturing, in Sterling, IL, understands this issue all too well. Frantz manufactures ball bearings for commercial applications, primarily in rollers for conveyor belts. The economy of scale of manufacturing ball bearings is significant enough that Frantz has a strong international potential for selling its ball bearings manufactured in the Midwest throughout the world. However, the size of each ball bearing must fit the technical specifications of the product in which it will be incorporated. Sizes of ball bearings are measured using inches in the U.S. so all of Frantz's ball bearings are sized with inch measurements. But because most of the world's product specifications use the metric standard, any market using the metric system was not a potential market for Frantz. The cost of adapting all the tooling and machinery to the metric standard seemed prohibitive, but the company was able to justify the investment when their nonmetric international sales were strong enough to justify expanding into metric markets.

Kevin Taylor, previous Worldwide Director of International Sales, explains their decision: "In the past our only sales were to foreign companies that had engineered to American standards. Adapting our product removed that barrier. When dealing with an engineered product to be used in an engineered system, adaptation is imperative. Sales are otherwise next to impossible!"

Should a company always adapt their products or services? Are there instances when adaptation is not the right strategy? When adaptation is required, how far should a company adapt? These are some of the questions I will address in this section. This issue can most easily be understood by first identifying the pressures on manufacturers and service providers to either adapt or standardize. As you review these pressures, identify the ones that apply to your company.

Pressures to Adapt Your Product or Service

Differences in technical standards. As clearly shown in the example of Frantz Manufacturing, sometimes the requirements for a product are so absolute that no sales are available in certain foreign markets unless you adapt. One of the most common examples is the difference in technical standards between countries and markets. Issues that most often come to mind are the metric versus nonmetric standard and differences in electrical voltage. Other common issues include cell phone standards, electrical plugs, and environmental standards For service providers, differences in management, legal, and accounting standards create challenges. Often the difference in technical standards is in the form of government testing or quality standards such as the CE Mark and ISO 9000 requirements discussed in Chapter 4.

Variations in consumer behavior, needs, and ability to buy. The strongest influence on your decision to adapt your product or service may be from the consumer. Even low prices and high quality won't create a demand for your product if it doesn't address the needs of the consumer. Factors influencing consumer behavior and needs are as varied as differences in climate and geography, and basic behavioral activities such as driving patterns and cooking techniques. Socioeconomic differences will also have a major impact, from religion and education to attitudes towards wealth. Language differences also are a consumer-based force. These factors will exert significant pressure on a exporter to modify its product or service.

The tremendous variations in consumer tastes and socioeconomic demographics would seem to make the job of product adaptation enormous, and for global companies like Procter & Gamble, it has been a major part of their international marketing challenge. However, a convergence of tastes and other factors help mitigate this otherwise overwhelming force.

Government standards and restrictions. Another important driving force behind product and service adaptation is the role of foreign governments. Often local environmental, product safety, or labeling requirements dictate the need for product modification. In some markets, especially those still practicing fairly closed international trade policy, import barriers such as government tariffs on foreign imports necessitate product modification. A manufacturer may need to ship partially built products or assemblies so more locally manufactured content can be added in the foreign market to avoid excessive tariffs. The European CE Mark and requirements for ISO registration are other examples of government-led initiatives that may impose a product modification strategy on the exporter.

Pressures to Standardize Your Product or Service

Pressures to standardize are generally internal issues rather than external pressures. Depending on your industry, these pressures may be significantly stronger than any pressures to adapt.

Economies of scale in R&D and production. Many industries are characterized by having significant entry barriers associated with R&D or production. Pharmaceutical companies have massive R&D budgets for testing and developing various drugs, only a few of which may become commercially viable. Automobile manufacturers make equally massive investments in manufacturing technologies in the never-ending pursuit of achieving highly differentiated products at low cost. Both types of companies represent industries where the upfront and ongoing investments are so large that new start-up companies are the exception rather than the norm.

The key to profitability for firms with massive R&D and production costs is the economy of scale achieved through high volumes of sales. Once the R&D or production-technology costs are spread across the products sold, the cost impact is minimal enough to keep the product competitive. But the benefit from economies of scale isn't available if the products have to be continually modified. It is the very nature of their standardization that makes the high upfront costs possible.

If it weren't for the pressures forced on manufacturers by the foreign marketplace, the goal of all international companies would be to completely standardize their products to achieve maximum economies of scale. Depending on your product or service and the industry, your cost structure may push you to standardize as much as the market will allow.

Product usage dictates standardization. In some industries, customers must have product standardization in order to use the product. A good example would be a microprocessor manufacturer such as Intel. Its customers, computer manufacturers, have established manufacturing facilities throughout the world. A computer manufacturer in France may produce computers in Malaysia and Brazil for shipment to the U.S. Intel may ship the manufactured processors made in the U.S., Ireland, or Israel, among others. The computer manufacturer must be sure that each processor is identical and it relies on the standardization of product. Due to the nature of international manufacturing, industrial goods tend to be more standardized than consumer goods.

Company size forces standardization. In some cases, the cost of adaptation may simply be too high for a company given its size and maturity. This is especially true of companies with products that require large capital expenditures on R&D or manufacturing in order to comply with foreign market needs.

Country of origin effect. The consumers' perception of where a product originates and the impact of that perception on their purchasing behavior is referred to as country of origin effect. For example, Swiss made watches enjoy a worldwide reputation of quality. For some consumers, the label "Swiss Made" is a significant incentive to purchase a watch over a similarly featured non-Swiss watch. In cases where part of the product culture lies with the perceived country of origin (even if the product is actually not produced in the home country of the manufacturer) the manufacturer may pursue a policy of standardization in order to maximize its home-country image. For example, U.S. cigarette manufacturers benefit from the standardized use of U.S. tobacco.

Converging tastes. Emerging markets with less exposure to foreign goods tend to favor locally produced products that reflect their local tastes. But as the market opens up to foreign goods and media and the per capita income of the consumers increases to match that of more developed countries there is a convergence of tastes toward global standards. An example would be a country that goes from only preferring fresh vegetables and meats to eventually using microwave ovens and demanding more frozen products. This results in consumers demanding more products reflecting global standardized tastes, which would be a force to standardize products.

To Adapt or Standardize?

Rarely will a company fully adapt or standardize a product. The cost to adapt is in most cases too expensive and too disruptive of a company's global goals. Likewise, a pursuit of total standardization for the sake of cost control results in a product offering too narrow to be internationally viable. A company will probably follow a path of compromise between both extremes. Like so many business decisions, it becomes one of balancing the risk versus the reward offered by each option. The company's long-term international strategy and goals will also guide a company through these difficult decisions. A very aggressive international expansion plan with a product or service that requires adaptation will no doubt need strong support of an adaptation program.

There is no right or wrong; it depends on the circumstance of the company, its products and services, and the foreign markets. What would be wrong would be to ignore international differences and to strictly impose your U.S. product or service. This disregard for foreign customers will not be productive. A company that embraces a customer-oriented attitude will find it has made the right decision.

Product or Service Selection

What is a company has more than one important product or service it sells? How should the company select which products or services to internationalize?

Generally, a company will first export the product or service that is most linked to its competitive advantage – meaning that product or services which really makes the company unique. This is simply because it will be its most competitive products or services that will first get the attention of foreign buyers. This may be the product with the highest quality or most features. It may be one which offers disruptive technology - technology highly innovative in the industry. The least expensive product may also be the best choice. For a service company, it is likely the key service most identified with the company.

Another consideration is linked back to the topic of standardization versus adaptation. If the costs associated with adapting a product are too high, a company may select a product which requires less adaptation.

Regardless of how a company chooses which products or services to globalize, the key point is that when a company has a wide-range of offerings, it will likely start with a more limited range of products or services when expanding internationally.

• INTERNATIONAL PRICING STRATEGIES

A company must make a number of choices in its marketing strategy, but arguably one of the most important is its pricing structure. Often the pricing strategy employed by a company dominates its marketing message. The familiar price wars in the supply of various consumer goods, such as gasoline, air travel, and food items, are just a few of the many examples of companies using price as their primary competitive differentiation. And even where price is not the key competitive selling point, such as with a luxury automobile, setting the correct price to maintain long-running profitability still presents a formidable pricing challenge.

Your pricing structure may make or break your sales success. Domestically, you already have established your price structure and understand the issues such as price elasticity, discounting, image, and volume pricing specific to your industry and company. But can the same strategy and price structure be implemented internationally?

That is the primary question addressed in this chapter. I will first look at the issues that differentiate domestic and international pricing. Second, I will highlight how to calculate your foreign landed cost, which is the starting point for your international pricing strategy. I will also discuss pricing issues such as variable versus full costing methods. Finally, I will discuss the issue of using pricing as a competitive tool including the question of pricing in domestic versus foreign currency.

International Pricing versus Domestic Pricing

It would be a mistake to simply duplicate your domestic pricing policy when you go global. For one thing, your international pricing strategy must be consistent with your international strategy. For example, an aggressive international strategy in terms of timeframe, market share, and number of markets will dictate an aggressive pricing policy which may be different from your domestic pricing strategy. In other words, for the sake of fast international growth, you may decide on a lower profit margin on your international sales than domestic sales. Independent of your international goals, your international pricing strategy also should factor in foreign market conditions that will impact the final price paid by the consumer.

Establishing an international pricing policy follows the same guidelines as domestic pricing methodology because pressures such as competition, consumers' ability to buy, and corporate costs and profit goals all must be factored into the pricing model. The key difference in formulating an international pricing policy is that additional variables must be incorporated into the model. These include foreign exchange pressures, tariffs, freight and logistics, foreign government legal considerations, and local market conditions.

Foreign exchange pressures. The Asia crisis of the late '90s serves as a good example of how foreign exchange impacts international trade. Devaluation of numerous currencies led to more expensive exports from the U.S. into Asia and cheaper imports into the U.S. from Asia. Yet the price changes had little to do with the cost structure of the manufacturers. Asian consumers had to pay more for American goods not because the U.S. companies had increased their prices but because their home currency was devalued compared to the dollar.

The pressure will not go away by pricing only in U.S. dollars. U.S. companies may pursue a policy of pricing in dollars, believing it best to push the impact of exchange rate fluctuations onto their foreign buyers. But ultimately, someone has to absorb the impact. Though it may be simpler to only offer dollar pricing, it may also mask the issue. Unless some hedging tools are utilized - which also have a cost - foreign exchange fluctuations will impact your global pricing. Even if your export price list remains unchanged, the prices paid by your foreign buyers will increase and decrease as the dollar increases and decreases in value against other currencies.

Tariffs. In the U.S. market, we are accustomed to a variety of city, county, and state sales taxes. Clearly they can have an impact on customer behavior. For example, a car buyer might travel to a nearby city to take advantage of a lower sales tax rate. But local sales taxes are generally not an important factor when a U.S. company develops its pricing strategy. This is because differences in sales taxes among adjacent markets (cities, counties, and states) is generally not much more than 2 to 5 percent, except for heavily taxed items such as tobacco, gasoline, and alcohol. Sales taxes also are applied equally to domestic and imported goods.

This is not the case with import tariffs and duties. Because their specific purpose is to discriminate between foreign and locally produced goods, their impact can be significant. For example, as recently as 1990, Brazil had import duties of over 100 percent. And even though the World Trade Organization (WTO) and other trade negotiations prompted important reductions, countries continue to protect local industries through import tariffs. Such tariffs are not applied to locally produced goods or goods from members of any applicable free-trade agreements. This places exporters at a significant competitive disadvantage and creates an enormous impact on the pricing policy when selling to foreign market. For all international markets, the impact of import tariffs must be factored into your company's pricing strategy.

Freight and logistics. Getting products to foreign markets is generally more expensive than servicing your domestic market. Though international logistics is increasingly more efficient and cheaper compared to past years, it is an important consideration when developing international pricing policies. This is especially true if shipments are small and not in full containers.

Foreign government legal considerations. The local legal environment in each country also influences pricing. Beyond the import tariff impact previously discussed, there are myriad nontariff barriers as discussed in Chapter 4. These barriers, such as contract laws, industry and commerce legislation, and the lack of enforcement of intellectual property rights, all impact your price strategy.

Local market conditions. Though taking local market conditions into account will already be part of your domestic pricing methodology, all the assumptions regarding income, industry structure, brand importance, and cultural considerations must be changed for each foreign market. Not the least of these will be the consumer's ability to buy. Because the vast majority of the world's population lives in countries with per capita income levels below that of developed countries, it is clear many markets may not be able to afford all products and services.

Furthermore, your domestic pricing may rely on buying habits or consumer behavior not found in a particular market. For example, you may consistently command a premium price for your products domestically because you are able to effectively communicate your product's differentiation to consumers who are in the habit of taking the time to research their purchase decisions. However, in some foreign markets, consumers may not rely on research to make their purchase decisions. Cultural behavior regarding sales, coupons, or discounts also could have an impact.

Distribution also can impact pricing. A manufacturer, accustomed to directly selling to the consumer in its home market to keep pricing low, may find it difficult to sell in countries where tradition has created long, multilayered distribution channels, such as Japan.

Another import consideration is the current state of the foreign market's industry vis-à-vis the the exporter's home market. There may be important product life cycle differences that will impact pricing options.

• COMPETITIVE PRICING CALCULATIONS

Establishing your international pricing strategy will probably be a process combining market research with trial and error. Your current domestic pricing structure could be used as an initial base for your international pricing. In other words, you could simply set your international pricing identical to your domestic pricing. However, with so many factors potentially increasing foreign prices you'll need more data before making a pricing decision. You need to know if your product will still be competitive after all the international cost factors are considered.

To determine if a particular export selling price is competitive in a foreign market, you must calculate the various incremental costs. To illustrate these calculations, I will use an example of a product being exported from the U.S. to Brazil. In the following example, it is assumed that the importer (the Brazilian distributor) will pay the ocean freight and all customs costs. However, for the purpose of comparing the U.S. product pricing to other products, it is immaterial which party actually pays the costs because someone has to pay them. The goal is to determine the eventual list price so it can be compared with other products.

A Case Example: Exporting to Brazil

A U.S. manufacturer based in Los Angeles is planning to export a product to Sao Paulo, Brazil. The product will be purchased by a Brazilian distributor who in turn will sell to a retail store. For this product:

Selling Price:	$10,000
Payment:	Letter of Credit
Terms of Sale:	Ex-works Los Angeles

Note: Ex-works is a shipping term meaning the buyer (in this case the Brazilian distributor) pays all freight from Los Angeles. It is part of the Incoterms discussed in Chapter 15.

The company wants to work through the pricing calculation to determine if its product will be competitive. It is specifically concerned whether the $10,000 sell price is going to be low enough to compete with a product produced in Brazil and another that is imported from Argentina. This involves the following three steps:

1. Calculation of the landed price
2. Calculation of the price at which the distributor will sell to the retailer, and the price at which the retailer will sell to the public. This example assumes the distributor marks up the product by 33 percent and the retailer marks up the product by 40 percent.
3. Comparison of these prices to a locally produced product and one imported from Argentina. As Brazil and Argentina are members of Mercosur, there is no import duty on the Argentine product. The comparison assumes the Brazilian and Argentine products are sold through the same distribution channel with the same markups.

Step 1: Calculating the foreign market landed cost. The initial step in developing a local pricing model for a particular foreign market is to calculate the landed cost. Essentially the **landed cost** calculation attempts to identify all costs associated with getting the product from the U.S. manufacturing facility to the door of the foreign buyer including logistics and import duties. It would not typically include local taxes or local distribution costs because these would affect domestic products as well. The goal of the landed cost exercise is to be able to compare the landed cost of product to the price of similar locally produced products or the landed cost of other foreign suppliers to the market. (The following calculations use U.S. dollars to make comparisons easier. Clearly the prices should be converted into local currency.)

Line	Cost Items:	U.S. Product
1	CIF Calculation: Ex-works Price (Los Angeles)	$10,000
2	Freight (LA - Sao Paulo)	1,200
3	Insurance	200
4	CIF Price (cost, insurance, freight)	11,400
	Landing Charges:	
5	Import Duty (20% of CIF)	2,280
6	Post Costs/AFRMM (merchant marine tax - 25% of ocean freight)	300
7	Warehousing and expediter (0.65% of CIF)	74
8	Terminal handling charges (average $315 per container)	315
9	Compulsory contribution to the Custom Broker's Union (2% CIF or minimum of US$140 and maximum of US$280)	228
10	Custom brokerage fee (average)	700
11	Bank costs (1 to 3% of ex-works price)	200
12	Total landing charges:	$4,097
13	Landed Sao Paulo cost (internal taxes not included)	$15,497

This calculation begins by determining the CIF price. The CIF price is calculation of the invoice price (or cost) plus insurance plus freight. It is calculated separately because the CIF will be used later for Brazilian tax calculations. The CIF calculation is shown in line 4.

Next, the landing charges are added. These are all the costs associated with having the product ready for the distributor: the Brazilian import duty, local port-warehouse-terminal costs, custom clearance costs, and bank costs. These costs are itemized in lines 5-11. The total landing charges are $4,097 as shown in line 12. This total is added to the CIF price to calculate the Landed Cost. The landed cost for the U.S. product is $15,497, as shown in line 13.

Step 2: Calculating the distributor and retail price. The landed price is the beginning point for the distributor's calculation of the selling price to the retail store. The distributor pays $10,000 to the U.S. manufacturer, but also pays the landed charges. Thus, the final cost of the product to the distributor is the landed cost, or $15,497. Local taxes and the distributor's markup will be added to this price.

From discussions with industry experts and potential foreign distributors, the U.S. manufacturer has anticipated the markups for its products. In this example, the distributor applies a 33 percent markup and the retailer a 40 percent markup. (These percentages will vary by market, industry, and channel characteristics. The markups used in this example may be low.)

1	Cost to Brazilian distributor	$15,497
2	Markup by distributor (33%)	$5,114
3	Selling price to retailer	20,611
4	Markup by retailer (40%)	$8,244
5	List price for Brazilian consumer before local taxes	$28,855

After the 33 percent markup, the distributor will sell to the retail store at $20,611 as shown in line 3. After the retail store's 40 percent markup, the retail price (before local taxes) is $28,855, as shown in line 5.

Local taxes. The local taxes must next be applied to determine the final amount the end-user will pay for the product. These taxes vary by country and local province or state. In the case of Brazil, there are two local taxes to be added: (1) the manufactured products tax (IPI) and (2) the local state tax (ICMS). These are important taxes to calculate because they have a dramatic impact on the final price and will exacerbate the price comparisons done later. Also, the ICMS is a cascading tax - a tax applied on top of a previous tax - which only makes the situation worse.

1	List price for Brazilian consumer before local taxes	$28,855
2	Local Taxes:	

1) IPI (manufactured products tax) 12% on CIF plus import duty, plus 12% on all profit add-ons in the distribution channel:

CIF:	11,400
Duty:	2,280
Distributor markup:	5,114
Retailer markup:	8,244
Cost for IPI calculation:	27,038

3	IPI: 12%	$3,245

2) ICMS (local state tax)
18% on CIF + duty + IPI, plus 18% on all profit add-ons in the distribution channel:

CIF:	11,400
Duty:	2,280
IPI:	3,245
Distributor markup:	5,114
Retailer markup:	8,244
Cost for ICMS calculation:	30,283

4	ICMS: 18%	$5,457

5	List price to final consumer including local taxes:	$37,551

The IPI is calculated first because it will be used in the ICMS calculation. As shown in line 3, the IPI is $3,245. It is 12 percent of the CIF plus import duty plus distributor and retail markups. The ICMS is calculated next. As shown in line 4, it is $5,451. It is 18 percent of everything used for the IPI plus the IPI itself. These two taxes are then added to the before tax retail price of $28,855 to calculate the list price including local taxes of $37,551, as shown in line 5. The $37,551 needs to be compared with other products (both local and Argentine) to determine if the U.S. product is competitive.

Step 3: Price comparisons. To compare the U.S. product with a Brazilian and Argentine product, the first two steps are repeated for the other products.

	Cost Items:	U.S. Product	Local Brazilian Product	Example if no duty paid on foreign import such as Argentina
1	CIF calculation: Ex-works price (Los Angeles)	$10,000	$10,000	$10,000
2	Freight (LA - Sao Paulo)	1,200	None	1,200
3	Insurance	200	None	200
4	CIF price (cost, insurance, freight)	**11,400**	**$10,000**	**11,400**
5	Landing Charges: import duty (20% of CIF)	2,280	None	- duty free -
6	Port costs/AFRMM (merchant marine tax - 25% of ocean freight)	300	None	300
7	Warehousing and expediter (0.65% of CIF)	74	None	74
8	Terminal handling charges (average $315 per container)	315	None	315
9	Compulsory contribution to the Custom Broker's Union (2% CIF or minimum of US$140 and maximum of US$280)	228	None	228
10	Custom brokerage fee (average)	700	None	700
11	Bank costs (1% to 3% of ex-works price)	200	None	200
12	Total landing charges:	**$4,097**	**None**	1817
13	Landed Sao Paulo cost (internal taxes not included)	**$15,497**	**$10,000**	**$13,217**

Notice the tremendous competitive advantage of the Brazilian product. Because it is already available to the distributor in Sao Paulo, it has no freight, insurance, or landing charges, including no import tax. This demonstrates the impact of freight and taxes on an international export. Assuming a Brazilian manufacturer could produce the same product at $10,000, it would have a $5,497 cost advantage over the U.S. product, as shown in line 13. As you will soon see, this has a tremendous impact on the final price paid by the consumer.

The Argentine product also has an important cost advantage. Even though it has many of the same landing charges, it does not have an import duty due to the Mercosur free-trade agreement. (Note that the freight cost of $1,200 was retained so only the difference of not having to pay an import duty will affect the final price. Obviously, the Argentine product will have an even greater cost advantage assuming freight costs from Argentina to Brazil are less than from the U.S.)

Distributor and retail prices for the Brazilian and Argentine products. Repeat Step 2 to get the distributor and retail prices.

	Cost Items:	U.S. Product	Local Brazilian Product	Example if no duty paid on foreign import such as Argentina
1	Cost to Brazilian customer (distributor/agent)	$15,497	$10,000	$13,217
2	Markup by distributor (33%)	$5,114	$3,300	4,362
3	Selling price to retailer	20,611	13,300	17,579
4	Markup by retailer (40%)	$8,244	$5,320	7,032
5	List price for Brazilian consumer before local taxes	**$28,855**	**$18,620**	**$24,611**

The same margins are applied to the Brazilian and Argentine products that were applied to the U.S. product. Even before local taxes are added, some significant price differences are apparent, especially for the Brazilian products.

Local taxes. Finally, local taxes are added to complete the pricing comparison.

	Cost Items:	U.S. Product	Local Brazilian Product	Example if no duty paid on foreign import such as Argentina
1	List price for Brazilian consumer before local taxes	$28,855	$18,620	$24,611
2	Local taxes: 1) IPI (12%)*	$3,245	$2,234	$2,953
	2) ICMS (18% local state tax)**	$5,451	$3,753	$4,962
3	List price to final consumer including local taxes:	**$37,551**	**$24,607**	**$32,526**

* Basis for calculation: The IPI (manufactured products tax) is calculated as 12% on CIF or distributor/agent price, plus import duty if applicable, plus 12% on all profit add-ons in the distribution channel. In the case of the **U.S. Product**, the 12% was applied to

(11,400 + 2,280 + 5,114 + 8,244) = $27,038 cost base. In the case of the **Local Product**, the 12% was applied to (10,000 + 3,300 + 5,320) = $18,620 cost base. And in the case of the **Argentine Product**, the 12% was applied to (13,217 + 4,362 + 7,032) = $24,611 cost base.

** Basis for calculation: The ICMS (local state tax) is 18% on CIF or distributor/agent price, plus import duty if applicable, plus all profit add-ons in the distribution channel, plus IPI. In the case of the **U.S. Product**, the 18% was applied to (11,400 + 2,280 + 5,114 + 8,244 + 5,114) = $30,283 cost base. In the case of the **Local Product**, the 18% was applied to (10,000 + 3,300 + 5,320 + 2,234) = $20,854 cost base. And in the case of the **Argentine Product**, the 18% was applied to (13,217 + 4,362 + 7,032 + 2,953) = $27,564 cost base.

Analysis of the Price Difference with the Brazilian Competitor

We return to the initial question: Is the $10,000 price offered by the U.S. manufacturer competitive with a Brazilian product? As shown, the list price before taxes for the Brazilian product is $18,620, and $24,607 after taxes. The list price of the U.S. product is $37,551 with taxes - a difference of $12,944! How can the pricing be so different when the U.S. and Brazilian manufacturers are both selling the product for $10,000?

The extraordinary difference is the result of two factors. First, the international freight costs and import duty alone create a $5,497 cost disadvantage for the U.S. product. Second, this cost disadvantage gets worse when the distributor and retail markup are added. Although both markups are equal for the Brazilian product, 33 percent and 40 percent respectively, the higher starting price of the U.S. product widens the gap between the two products. Essentially the distributor and the retailer make a profit not only on the $10,000 cost of the U.S. product, but also on the $5,497 add-on. To make matters worse, the same thing happens with the taxes. Because the ICMS state tax is a cascading tax, the U.S. product's list price keeps going higher.

While the distributor, dealer, and Brazilian federal and state governments will make more money from these costs, will the U.S. product even sell at this significantly higher price? With such a price difference, the U.S. product will need to be significantly better in quality, features, or some other value that warrants such an increased cost to the consumer. Another concern is if the Brazilian manufacturer bypasses the distributor and sells directly to the retail network. This would eliminate a significant markup in the distribution channel, even if the manufacturer adds some markup. The U.S. exporter doesn't have this option because it requires the use of a distributor to represent it locally.

International price escalation. This pricing exercise is a good example of international price escalation - the tendency for products to sell for a higher price in foreign markets than in their domestic markets. What many exporters don't realize is that freight costs are just the beginning. Once duties, local taxes, and markups in the distribution channel are factored into the pricing calculation, the list price increases considerably. When you see these factors in an actual example you can see why global reductions in tariffs is a U.S. trade policy priority.

Analysis of the Price Difference with the Argentine Competitor

The Brazilian product's pricing demonstrated the significant cost disadvantage of a U.S. manufacturer versus a Brazilian manufacturer. But what if there were no local competitors? What if the competition came from Argentina, Japan, or Germany?

This is where the calculations become a bit more complex because the application of each cost factor may not apply equally to all foreign imports. Assuming each foreign country's products will be applied the same import duty as U.S. products, the calculation should be the same - no advantage or disadvantage for the foreign products.

However, as our example illustrates in the final column, if the exporting country has signed a treaty to reduce duties, such as Argentina, the impact can be significant. You may be surprised at the difference the lack of the duty makes on the final prices. As the Argentine pricing shows, though all other costs such as freight and bank charges are the same, the resulting price to the consumer is $5,025 less ($37,551 versus $32,526). As with the U.S.-Brazilian comparison, the difference grows significantly due to the nature of markups and cascading taxes. This helps demonstrate the difference of U.S. products compared to imports from countries that have signed a free-trade agreement with another country.

• DEALING WITH INTERNATIONAL PRICING CONCERNS

As shown in the previous example, exporting can be a difficult proposition if your products are more expensive than local products or don't offer some significant benefits. Furthermore, other foreign imports may have an important advantage if their duty rate is lower than the U.S. rate. So what are some options to deal with international price escalation and competition with local products?

Long-Term Price Problems

There may not be an answer in the short term. The freight, duty, taxes, and related costs may simply make a U.S. product completely noncompetitive in a particular market. You need to analyze specifically what is contributing to the problem, for example, freight, duties, or both, and then plan other options. Your analysis may result in the decision that pure exporting is not a viable option, in which case you can investigate these other options:

- *Partial manufacturing*. Rather then export the final product, freight and duty costs may become more favorable if you export the product partially finished. Sometimes this results in a lower tariff because the commodity may be classified under a different harmonized code. It also could result in significant freight cost savings if the product can be shipped in greater bulk.
- *Local assembly*. Similar to partial manufacturing, you can ship components or assemblies, which are then assembled into a final product in the foreign market. This would probably reduce the duty, especially if some local components are included in the assembly process.
- *Foreign manufacturing*. If import duties have you beat, you can manufacture

the product in the foreign market. The location may be in the specific foreign market under study or a nearby market, particularly if the nearby market has signed a free-trade agreement with the target market.

- *Licensing.* If manufacturing in the foreign market can be done by an outside company and your proprietary technology is required to manufacture the product, licensing may be an option.

Short-Term Price Problems

If your price challenges don't necessitate the expensive and risky options listed above such as foreign manufacturing, you may be able to effectively deal with price escalation by using these short-term solutions:

- *Product differentiation.* A textbook example of dealing with a pricing challenge is to shift the focus from pricing to benefits and features - product differentiation. This may be easier in a foreign market that your U.S. competition has not entered. For example, in many foreign markets U.S. fast food chains have had the entire market to themselves with no competition from their U.S. rivals. This makes product differentiation particularly easy because no other authentic U.S. fast food is offered in the market.
- *Challenge the distribution rules.* Part of the challenge in many foreign markets is the long distribution channel which contributes to the price escalation. You may be able to identify ways to bypass the distribution channel. For example, if using the established channel would be too expensive, consider selling directly to retailers or key accounts. This would eliminate one or two levels in the chain. If some local presence is needed, an agent may be the most appropriate representation. There also may be local distributors who are in the process of changing the distribution rules. For example, when I was searching for a computer distributor in the U.K. in the mid-1980s, some distributors were beginning to sell directly to key accounts. It was considered a rogue act in the market at the time, but if I believed a flatter distribution channel was needed for our products, I could have chosen such a distributor which would have decreased my costs.
- *Choose your representation based on pricing structure.* If you decide to stay with the established distribution structure, consider appointing a distributor that has agreed to offer aggressive pricing. For example, perhaps you could find a distributor who will work with a 20 percent markup rather than a 33 percent markup.
- *Lower your pricing.* An obvious option is to simply lower your pricing. For example, you could argue that for a time, international pricing should be calculated using variable costing, discussed later in this chapter, which would result in a lower target selling price. But be sure to do your calculations carefully. As shown in the Brazilian example, it would take a considerable cost decrease to compete with local products.
- *Pricing structure, discounts, and promotions.* Look into offering discounts tied to promotions, or quantity discounts which are more aggressive than those in

your domestic price structure. For example, I frequently included cooperative advertising money for foreign buyers. For each invoice, a certain percentage (usually 2-4 percent) was accrued in an account. The distributor or agent could then use that money for any marketing activities such as advertising or trade shows. The money had to be matched equally by its own funds. (Cooperative advertising is discussed in Chapter 19.)

• DEVELOPING A PRICING STRUCTURE

Once you have all the pricing research completed, including landed cost and projected end-user pricing (using standard markups), as well as local market issues such as consumer ability to pay and competitive pressures, you are in a position to develop your pricing structure. First you must determine your profit requirements for your international sales which involves choosing full or variable costing.

Variable Costing versus Full Absorption Costing

Variable costing is a product costing method where the only costs allocated to products are those which are directly related to the production or sales of the product. On the other hand, **full absorption costing** allocates all manufacturing costs (variable and fixed) as well as nonmanufacturing costs such as factory overhead, sales and marketing overhead, and even corporate overhead (executive salaries, headquarters costs, and R&D). Variable costing results in a lower cost than full costing, so the selling price of a product using the variable costing method will be less than a product using full costing methods assuming the same profit margin is applied.

The idea behind variable costing is profit maximization in which a firm should increase its output until marginal revenue equals marginal or variable cost. In other words, a company can justify lowering prices to achieve increased sales as long as all direct costs will be covered. In the long run, in order to fund corporate overhead and other nondirect costs, full pricing must be used at some point or the company will lose money and not be able to fund future activities.

In practice, most companies employ variable costing in strategic pricing decisions, such as new product pricing, discontinuing a product, bid pricing, and with private label and joint products. These special pricing instances can justify a variable costing approach if the company believes sales would not be achieved without the lower pricing or that lower pricing is justified for competitive reasons. For routine price decisions, a company would use full absorption costing.[1]

International pricing: Full or variable costing? The question then becomes, should international sales be considered a strategic pricing decision and justify the use of variable pricing? The impact will be significant. If items such as manufacturing overhead, R&D, and other overhead items are not included in the costing calculation, the international pricing will be much lower, and thus more competitive in the international marketplace.

The answer depends on the short- and long-term corporate view of the international expansion effort. A fully involved global player, such as a Fortune 500 company, will probably employ full costing methodology in its international pricing strategy. The view is that its international sales are no less or more important than its domestic sales. They are simply part of the overall mix. Thus, full costing is used to ensure long-term corporate viability.

Small to mid-sized companies, especially in early stages of international expansion, might easily justify variable costing. For example, it is unlikely that an increase of 10-20 percent in sales from the international expansion would have much of an impact on management salaries, the manufacturing facility overhead, or corporate overhead. There will be direct sales and marketing expenses, such as travel, commissions, and advertising, but other overhead items will probably remain constant. You could argue that in the short term it would be important to use a variable costing strategy for international pricing calculations.

Whether full or variable costing is used, the individual developing the international pricing strategy should be aware of the issue so it can be fully discussed during the international planning process. A company should avoid the mistake of taking international sales for granted and placing a higher profit expectation on them than domestic sales. More than once I have seen a company take the view that its international sales are a burden and require more profit. As a strong proponent of international sales, I find such a perspective quite narrow! I would hope a company at least prices its exports at the same level as domestic sales.

Market Conditions and Competitive Position

The discussion of variable versus full absorption costing was intended to raise the issue of accounting costing methods used for developing your international pricing strategy. It was not meant to overshadow the fundamental issue of developing your international pricing and that is to consider the foreign market structure and competitive position of your products. By foreign market conditions, I am referring to issues such as the consumers' ability to buy, distribution options, consumer expectations, regulatory and political environments, and industry structure. By competitive position, I am speaking of the issue of how your product will compete in a particular foreign market: on the basis of product differentiation, lower cost, improved customer service, or quality. Both issues will mirror your domestic pricing philosophy because your domestic market strategy will probably be similar to your method of competing internationally. But because foreign markets can be quite different than the U.S. market, your competitive position may need to be different.

Ultimately, your international pricing strategy must be driven by the fundamentals of the foreign markets and your ability to compete. What makes the challenge greater than that of establishing a domestic pricing policy is the sheer number of variables, both known and unknown. For example, you may know the landed price based on current tariff rates, but you won't know the exchange rate position for the future. That one unknown is significant because local competitors won't face the challenge of exchange rates. International pricing will probably always be a best guess process of trial and error, especially in the early stages of international expansion. Once you have experience with a few international markets, you will be in a much better position to more effectively establish your international pricing.

Consistent Pricing between International Markets?

You want consistent pricing between foreign markets (assuming similar competitive strategies), especially within a given region where trade occurs within adjacent markets. If your pricing varies too greatly within the region, gray marketing will occur, in which a foreign buyer with a lower price will sell around another foreign buyer with a higher price. This can happen even with consistent pricing and the legal framework of the country may prevent you from stopping it. Consistent pricing is the easiest and fairest strategy to implement.

There are, however, occasions where market conditions necessitate different pricing strategies. For example, competitive factors or government restrictions may necessitate that you offer prices lower than your standard international pricing. How much you lower depends on your goals and expectations for the particular market. It also depends on the time frame of how quickly you want to gain brand recognition and market share. But be careful - it is always more difficult to raise prices than to lower them later.

Who Pays What?

Another important issue of developing your international pricing structure is to identify which costs you will pay as the manufacturer and which costs the foreign buyer will pay. Most often this involves establishing your freight terms. For example, you may establish your pricing as FCA Sellers Premises Dallas, which means you will provide the goods for pickup from your facility in Dallas, clear the goods for export, and your buyer will pay all costs onward. On the other hand, you may specify CIF-Hong Kong, which means freight and insurance will be paid by you, but the foreign buyer must pay all customs charges and duties. The specifics of these freight terms are discussed in Chapter 14.

This issue of who pays what is always difficult. Some argue it is best to always price your goods from your location. This is the least work and risk for you and puts the burden on the buyer. The reasoning for this is that foreign buyers are accustomed to importing so it is better if they arrange the logistics. This generally leads to lower costs overall.

The argument also can go the other way. You can arrange a worldwide logistics contract with a local shipping company, reducing the overall freight impact, and offer CIF for the foreign country. This can lower the landed cost in each country. It also creates less work for your buyer, which may make your products more desirable. It also means you are in control of the freight up to the foreign port.

There is no correct answer. The most important consideration is working with a great freight forwarder as discussed in Chapter 14. As you get more experience, you probably will include foreign freight in your price quotes but this also depends on the needs and preferences of your foreign buyers.

Which currency?

A final consideration you need to make early in your global expansion is in what currency to price your products and services. It is easiest to simply price everything in U.S. dollars. However, competitive or foreign buyer pressure may force you to offer pricing in the local currency of the foreign market.

The essence of this decision is the risk. Home currency-based pricing places all foreign currency risk on the foreign buyer such as a U.S. company selling in U.S. Dollars to Europe. Foreign currency-based pricing places the risk on the exporter. Once pricing has been established, and the exchange rate between the two currencies changes, one of the two parties must absorb the difference or pass it on to the consumer. In the case of home currency-based pricing, the foreign buyer absorbs the difference - either the distributor or the consumer or a combination. In the case of foreign currency-based pricing, the exporter absorbs the change, assuming the exporter does not alter prices.

The issue is most serious when the home currency becomes stronger vis-à-vis the foreign currency because a stronger domestic currency means more of the foreign currency is used to purchase the home currency. This effectively increases the cost of the exported product.

In the case of U.S. exporters, it is fair to say most small to mid-sized companies, especially in early stages of international expansion, price in U.S. dollars. They simply do not have the experience to take on the risk of foreign currency pricing. This is not to say that specific transactions, such as bids or particular projects, aren't priced in the foreign currency. The exchange rate risk of such special situations are easily covered by traditional foreign exchange products available from banks.

You should never underestimate the competitive advantage of pursuing foreign currency pricing. Once a company understands that someone has to absorb foreign exchange movements, it becomes easier to justify a more aggressive pricing policy that includes foreign currency pricing. The risk is simply figured into the margin. The competitive advantage of offering stable, foreign currency pricing may outweigh the costs. Seek assistance from a bank with international experience to investigate these options. Chapter 16 offers advice on how to deal with foreign exchange rates.

• NOTES

1. The discussion on variable versus full absorption costing draws generally on information provided in the following book: Thomas M. Brueggelmann, Gaile A. Haessly, Michael Schiff, and Claire P. Wolfangel, The Use of Variable Costing in Pricing Decisions (Montvale, NJ, National Association of Accountants, 1986).

CHAPTER 12

Legal Considerations

I n this chapter, I will discuss the key legal factors likely to impact your international activities. It should be stressed that international law is one of the areas of international business that requires caution; a little knowledge can be dangerous because it may create a false sense of security. When it comes to international law, you are best served by seeking outside legal assistance from a qualified lawyer. The issues are too complex and expensive to ignore outside assistance. Do not let the size of your company keep you from seeking legal assistance. Many legal firms are increasingly addressing the needs of small exporters and offer very affordable services. For example, they may be able to customize an existing contract for the specific requirements of the exporter at a lower cost than you might expect.

It is still important to understand the fundamental issues. There are four key legal issues to consider when expanding globally: (1) types of legal systems, (2) U.S. legal considerations, (3) foreign law, and (4) contract law.

• LEGAL SYSTEMS

One of the first things to understand when expanding globally is that there are three basic forms of legal structures used throughout the world: (1) common, (2) civil, and (3) theocratic law. The **common law system**, practiced in the U.K., federal courts of the U.S., and many of the U.K.'s former colonies, is based on tradition, precedent, and custom. Courts interpret the law based on these characteristics. It is not unusual for a court to overturn a law that it considers unconstitutional. By contrast, laws in a common law system are constantly revised by elected officials and government agencies.

The **civil law system** is based on a detailed set of laws organized into codes. Countries that employ civil law systems include Russia, Japan, and many countries in Europe. Courts are not often required to interpret the law. Laws in a civil law system are rarely revised, and have been developed with a greater consensus than similar laws under a common law system.

A **theocratic law system** bases its legal structure on religious precepts. Familiar theocratic law countries include Saudi Arabia and Iran where the laws of the state are based on Islamic principles.

The impact of each system can be very important to companies operating in foreign markets. You will see this impact later in the chapter, but a good example is contract law. In common law systems, contracts tend to be lengthier to take in various contingencies not already covered by law. Contracts in civil law systems are shorter because many of the issues of concern for a business contract are already incorporated into the civil law system. The first step in evaluating the legal issues of importance for a particular foreign market is to identify its legal structure so you have a better understanding of its implication on your contract and business.

• LEGAL CONSIDERATIONS FOR U.S. COMPANIES

It may seem odd to consider U.S. laws when going global. Why would the U.S. be concerned with what a company does overseas?

The U.S. government believes the foreign business of U.S. companies is their concern and a number of laws have been created that impact U.S. international business activities. Some of the laws, such as the Foreign Corrupt Practices Act, directly impact what a company can and cannot do as part of their international business practices. These laws have cost U.S. businesses billions of dollars in lost sales.[1] Other laws, such as embargoes, completely stop U.S. companies from doing business in specific countries. Familiarity with these laws is crucial if you wish to avoid expensive fines or imprisonment.

Foreign Corrupt Practices Act

One of the U.S. laws that gets the most attention is the U.S. Department of Justice's **Foreign Corrupt Practices Act (FCPA)** passed in 1977. The legislation was developed to address the growing concern about U.S. bribery practices in the 1970s (specifically stemming from a Lockheed overseas bribery scandal). The law prohibits U.S. companies or individuals from making corrupt payments to foreign officials for the purpose of obtaining or keeping business. The Department of Justice is the chief enforcement agency with the Securities and Exchange Commission (SEC) playing a coordinating role. The law not only outlaws bribes directly by U.S. citizens, residents, and any business organized under the laws of the U.S., but also any bribes made by intermediaries. Thus the foreign distributors, agents, and subsidiaries of U.S. companies are also disallowed from making bribes. The law is quite broad:

> The FCPA's basic antibribery prohibition makes it unlawful for a firm (as well as any officer, director, employee, or agent of a firm or any stockholder acting on behalf of the firm) to offer, pay, promise to pay (or even to authorize the payment of money, or anything of value, or to authorize any such promise) to any foreign official for the purpose of obtaining or retaining business for or with, or directing business to, any person.[2]

A similar prohibition applies to payments to a foreign political party, official, or candidate for a foreign political office. Violations can lead to criminal penalties including fines to the company of up to $2 million and fines and imprisonment up to five years for individuals, including employees of a business.

Grease payments? It is generally accepted that the FCPA allows **grease payments**, which are sums paid to a lower-level foreign official to carry out a routine governmental action. This should be an action that the foreign official would normally perform, such as documentation. It should not be an action that would be out of his or her normal routine. For example, it would be illegal to pay a customs officer to waive through contraband or lift an import fee.[3]

Specifically, the law lists the following examples as routine governmental actions eligible for facilitating or expediting payments:

obtaining permits, licenses, or other official documents; processing governmental papers, such as visa protection, mail pick-up and delivery; providing phone service, power and water supply, loading and unloading cargo, or protecting perishable products; and scheduling inspections associated with contract performance or transit of goods across country.[4]

Any company considering paying grease money should consult an attorney to ensure this action is legal. An incorrect interpretation of the law could be expensive.

When the FCPA was first passed into law, the U.S. seemed the lone supporter of anti-bribery practices. Other governments saw the legislation as an attempt by the U.S. to impose their moral code onto foreign countries. However, recent trends indicate other countries are beginning to support the U.S. position. For example, 34 countries of the Organization for Economic Cooperation and Development signed a binding agreement in 1997 outlawing bribery of foreign public officials. Furthermore, some U.S. firms believe the FCPA has helped them because it offered them a legal basis to refuse to pay bribes.

Whether it helps or hurts your global expansion, be aware of the constraints placed on international payments to foreign officials. If you need further clarification, contact your legal counsel or the U.S. Department of Justice, Fraud Section, Criminal Division. The U.S. Department of Commerce also offers general guidance to U.S. exporters.

U.S. Embargoes and Export Controls

As a method of implementing U.S. foreign policy and other objectives, the U.S. often places embargoes and trade sanctions on U.S. businesses. **Embargoes** and **trade sanctions** prohibit all or limited exports and foreign direct investments into targeted countries. The restrictions often are multilateral embargoes in which many countries join in the prohibition of exports (typically led by the United Nations). In other cases, such as the U.S. trade embargo with Cuba, the prohibitions are unilateral; the U.S. acts alone in restricting trade and investment. In either case, the impact is severe. U.S. businesses, by law, are limited or prevented from doing business with the government or other businesses in the affected countries.

Another set of U.S. laws restrictions the exports of particular technologies or products that if imported by the improper companies or individuals, could pose a treat to U.S. national security. These sets of laws are referred to as **exports controls**. These regulations determine if or if no a particular product or technology can be exported. Both embargoes and export controls are discussed further in Chapter 15.

Antitrust Laws

The U.S. and many other countries have developed laws that help develop an economy based on competition. In the U.S., such laws are collectively called **antitrust legislation**. In the European Union, they are often called restrictive trade practices laws. The laws are designed to ensure the efficient allocation of resources by providing consumers with goods and services at the lowest price that efficient business operations can profitably offer.

U.S. companies must comply with both U.S. antitrust law and the foreign country's law. The types of practices targeted by such legislation include price-fixing agreements and conspiracies, divisions of markets by competitors, and certain group boycotts and tying arrangements.

Most U.S. companies are familiar with antitrust laws that impact their domestic business. For example, one of the goals of The Sherman Act was to outlaw any restraint of trade between states. This means a U.S. company cannot legally restrict another company from selling anywhere within the U.S. The act also has important implications on U.S. companies attempting to manipulate markets by forming cartels or limiting industrial output.

But what about the export and overseas activities of U.S. companies? You may not know that the same legislation that impacts domestic business activities, primarily the Sherman Antitrust Act and the Federal Trade Commission Act, also impacts international business activities. Specifically, overseas actions by U.S. companies can be contested if it can be demonstrated that there is a direct, substantial, and reasonably foreseeable effect on the domestic or import commerce of the United States or on the export commerce of a U.S. individual. In other words, if your business practices abroad are demonstrated to impact competitive business in the U.S., antitrust laws may prevent such activities.

In practice, U.S. antitrust laws do not impact most international business activities. The primary areas of concern involve foreign direct investment activities such as overseas joint ventures, mergers, and acquisitions. In some cases these laws can also impact your international distribution agreements. As with export controls, seek professional assistance if you believe U.S. antitrust laws may impact your overseas activities.

Product Liability

Americans do not need any education about the significance of product liability issues. Just say the words "scalding McDonald's coffee" and most everyone will remember the 1994 lawsuit against McDonald's Corporation for serving coffee that was too hot. An 81-year-old woman purchased the coffee at the drive-through window of an Albu-

querque McDonald's and while removing the lid to add cream and sugar spilled it caus-
ing third-degree burns. She was awarded $2.7 million in punitive damages after jurors
found McDonald's had engaged in willful, reckless, malicious, or wanton conduct.[5] The
amount was eventually reduced but the suit shocked consumers and the business community alike.

A similar case involved a doctor who sued BMW of North America for selling
him a new car which he later determined had been repainted prior to delivery. An Ala-
bama jury awarded the doctor $4,000 in actual damages (the amount of depreciation to
the car) and a surprising $4 million (later reduced to $2 million) in punitive damages. It
seems BMW sold 983 such refinished cars in American over a ten-year period.[6]

Both cases received global attention and heightened the image of the U.S. as a
country out-of-sync in its tort laws - laws designed to compensate for personal injury and
damage to property. Though tort reform remains a legislative priority in many states, U.S.
businesses have long known that the primary protection is through liability insurance,
often directly related to specific products.

Such product liability insurance can be expensive. For example, as tort-reform
debates increased in the mid-1990s, it was revealed that the Girl Scout Council in Wash-
ington, D.C. has to sell 87,000 boxes of cookies annually just to pay its liability premi-
ums.[7] In fact, the expense of liability insurance can be so high, it can keep a product from
coming to market. Just ask Axminster Electronics, a small British firm whose devices
help prevent Sudden Infant Death Syndrome (SIDS) by monitoring a baby's breathing.
The company finally decided not to sell its product in the U.S. because it was unable to
secure product liability insurance.[8]

In light of these challenges, does it only get worse when a company decides to go
global? Fortunately, product liability claims are not as common overseas as they are in
the U.S. so the risk is arguably lower. Differences in the other foreign legal systems limit
or even prevent such product liability lawsuits. For example, it is only in the U.S. that
lawyers accept lawsuits on a contingency fee basis in which no legal fees are required to
begin a lawsuit or continue its action. Fees are due only when the outcome of the suit has
been determined. For a successful trial this may result in the client paying a sizable legal
bill representing as much as one-half of the settlement amount, but the damaged party
may never have been able to initiate the case if the contingency fee option had not existed. Another example of legal differences outside the U.S. is that a party not only pays its
own legal costs but also the legal costs of the defendant if it sues and loses the case. Both
of these differences help curtail product liability suits outside the U.S.

Nevertheless, a U.S. company must be aware of its legal exposure as it expands
globally. The potential liability increases as the scope of its global activities expands and
matures. If you are in your initial expansion stage and are only exporting, you have two
primary concerns. The first is to review the warranty terms of your international sales
agreement and/or distribution contract. Unless you limit your liability, you face any and
all potential damages arising from the use of your products in the foreign market. You
probably already have a statement of use or similar product-related statement in your current domestic warranty declaration. However, unless this same statement accompanies
your products internationally, your risk exposure could be very high. You also should be

sure your distribution contract states that your foreign representative or distributor does not add or modify any of your warranty statements.

A second concern is that your foreign distributor or agent carry liability insurance. Generally, a reputable buyer already will have such insurance in place. But it is a standard clause in many international distributor agreements.

The local laws of the particular foreign market may supersede your precautions. For example, even if your warranty states a limitation of your liability, local legislation may hold you responsible.

• FOREIGN LEGAL CONSIDERATIONS

Once you have addressed concerns presented by U.S. legal restrictions on your global expansion, be prepared for an even greater challenge - foreign legal considerations. I've already discussed that differences in legal systems (common, civil, and theocratic) give rise to legal differences when doing business overseas. But what is the day-to-day effect of these differences?

There are two key areas of concern that U.S. companies should address. The first is the protection of intellectual property rights such as patents and trademarks. The second is the use of legal contracts.

Intellectual Property Rights

The protection of intellectual property rights (IPRs) internationally is a somewhat complicated issue and one probably best left to the appropriate legal experts. What makes it complicated is that IPRs in the U.S., such as trademarks and patents, are only legally recognized and protected within the 50 states and U.S. possessions and territories. They are not automatically recognized internationally. Thus a company that receives a U.S. patent does not at the same time receive protection outside of the U.S. IPR laws vary greatly from country to country. Generally, to obtain IPR protection in a particular country you are required to obtain protection in each country, which can be a timely and expensive process. Fortunately, there are a growing number of IPR agreements where filing in one country results in protection for a region (collection of countries). The European Union offers such agreements.

Patents. To obtain overseas protection after receiving a U.S. patent, applications must be made with each foreign country or regional authority (when available) where protection is desired. What will surprise some is that unless the application is made within a prescribed time frame, the foreign patent may not be obtainable.

In 2013 the U.S. joined many other countries in using the **first to file standard** in which an eligible patent is awarded to the first inventor to file or publicly disclose the invention. (Prior to 2013 the U.S. used the **first to invest standard** in which that date the technology was invented determined patentability.) Technically an inventor can disclose their technology and then file for a patent. But in some countries, that public disclosure could then preclude the inventor from obtain a patent in that country.

Fortunately, there are multilateral patent agreements of which the U.S. is a member that help companies avoid this situation. An important component of these treaties is the establishment of a priority date. The priority date establishes a grace period in which the patent holder can still apply for foreign protection. Generally, a company that has filed for a U.S. patent will have one year in which to file the same patent in other countries which are also members of the treaties (which are in excess of 100). Meanwhile, the company may make public disclosure of its technology without fear that it will lose its right to file a foreign patent application.

The Patent Cooperation Treaty (PCT) takes this grace period one step further. A PCT application can be made in the U.S. which will extend the time limit from 12 months to 20-30 months. It also offers a standardized format of the patent application that is recognized by all members of the PCT. This can greatly simplify the searching and filing of international patents. (Do not make the mistake of thinking a PCT application is a patent application. It is only an application to extend the time limit during which foreign patent applications must be made to still be valid.)

Companies generally cannot file foreign applications directly. They must appoint a foreign agent. The filing can also be handled through a U.S. agent or law firm that would in turn use overseas agents or subsidiaries. Regional patents, such as those found in the European Union, can make the process easier for particular regions.

Trademarks. As with patents, there is no automatic international protection offered to holders of U.S. trademarks. Instead, applications must be made individually with each country or region. In the U.S. and some other countries, the first entity (company) to use the trademark in connection with a product is the owner, regardless of whether the trademark is registered or not. This is called *first use*. A registration enhances those rights. In other countries, the first to register the trademark is the owner. This is called *first to file*. This has led to instances of trademark squatters or bandits - companies that register

Distinguishing between Patents, Trademarks, Copyrights, & Trade Secrets

• **Patent**: Protects the invention or product itself. Example: A widget.

• **Trademark**: A word, phrase, symbol, design, or combination of these. Protects the identifier of the source of the widget. It is not the thing or the service. It is the word or phrase that identifies the manufacturer or distributor of the product or the provider of the service. Trademarks are used to distinguish one product from other similar types of products. Example: The Acme Widget.

• **Copyright**: Protects an original artistic or literary work and the expression of an idea. Example: The Acme Widget song.

• **Trade Secrets:** Protects know-how, methods, or recipes otherwise not protected through a patent. Example: KFC secret chicken spices.

trademarks for brands that have been established elsewhere, but not in their country. These trademark bandits then sell the local rights of the trademark to the original manufacturer when it wants to offer its product or services in the country.

Fortunately, as with patents, holders of U.S. trademarks have a time period in which to file for international trademark protection. Unlike patents, if the trademark filing falls beyond this time period, an application can still be made but may not be granted if another company has subsequently filed for use of the trademark in that country. The implication of this is that companies must be proactive in their international trademark planning, especially in first-to-file countries. Fortunately, under the **Madrid Protocol**, U.S. holders of trademarks, for a fee, may apply for foreign trademark protection through the U.S Patent and Trademark Office website (www.uspto.gov/trademarks - search for 'international registration'). This means that a holder of a U.S. trademark does not have to hire a lawyer in the foreign country to register the trademark.

Copyrights. Generally, international copyright protection is easier to obtain than patent or trademark protection. In most countries, the place of first publication of the copyrighted material is an important criterion for determining whether foreign works are eligible for local copyright protection. In the case of works first published in the U.S. on or after March 1, 1989, when the U.S. joined the Berne Convention for the Protection of Literary and Artistic Works, works are automatically protected in more than 80 countries. Nevertheless, holders of U.S. copyrights should seek legal assistance to determine what protection is available or automatic in the foreign countries in which there is a concern of copyright infringement.

Trade Secrets. A final important aspect of intellectual property protection is trade secrets. Companies protect important processes, procedures, techniques, or recipes using trade secrets. They are not filed with governments for protection because their very nature is that they are to be kept secret. Under WTO guidelines, member countries respect the rights of companies to maintain these trade secrets and companies can use the legal system to settles claims that the secrets have been misappropriated. However, companies need to seek professional legal assistance to best understand how to protect their trade secrets internationally.

• INTERNATIONAL CONTRACTS

The topic of international contracts easily lends itself to its own book. It also lends itself to one simple rule: get expert assistance. The investment in appropriate legal advice when developing international contracts will pay off in a number of ways. I remember more than once having to terminate a distributor contract and being thankful that our company had a strong, reliable contract in place.

I address the issue of distributor contracts because they are the most common for companies beginning their international expansion. International law will also impact other contracts, such as joint venture and licensing. In these cases it is imperative to seek legal assistance.

The following are some specific issues to consider when developing an international distributor contract. A sample contract can be found in Appendix A. It should not be used as either an actual contract or the basis of a contract. It is solely intended as an illustration of a completed contract. Also note that each country's local law may have a major impact on the contract. For example, the concept of exclusivity of representation is often highly regulated by local law. Some countries will either prohibit such a contract or not enforce such limitations. The differences between countries regarding agency (representation) laws are critical differences that must be addressed in the contract. (Some specific examples of how local law can impact a contract are given in chapter 18.)

The initial contract and negotiation. Generally, it will be the manufacturer or service provider that will provide the initial contract. I say initial contract because, of the dozens of international distributor contracts I've signed, each had to be individually negotiated. There were always some specific issues that required modifications. This is especially true if the boilerplate (initial) contract offered from the manufacturer to the distributor is especially protective of the manufacturer's interests. For example, the contract in Appendix A is extremely biased toward the manufacturer. I am certain that most distributors would succeed in removing or altering at least some of the provisions in that contract. (They will at least argue for more than the 30 days' notice of price changes as currently shown in the sample contract.)

After your first few distributor contract negotiations, you will have a much better understanding of what is fair in an international contract. Good distributors will recognize the boilerplate contract from the start and quickly remove various provisions. Do not worry. With appropriate legal advice, many of the standard international provisions may not apply to your situation and you can allow them to be eliminated or changed.

Always remember, however, that the negotiation is just that, a negotiation. There will be some provisions that must remain. Others are negotiable. I tended to start with a fairly aggressive contract, one that highly favors our position. I then quickly negotiate away items of little concern and hold tight on those that really are important to our company. I also use the good guy/bad guy routine where I would be accommodating but blame my boss if our company would not give in on a particular item disputed by the distributor. This was done with the full consent of my boss, of course. This is not to say we would take advantage of distributors. Good contracts should respect both parties.

Also remember that contracts should be used in virtually all overseas representation situations, even for nonexclusive distribution. There are too many unexpected events that can occur that can be potentially harmful to the manufacturer if no contract is in place. Avoid the temptation to ignore the need for a contract. They are always important.

Contract/agreement guidelines

- Definitions. Distributor contracts begin with an identification of parties, common terms, and perhaps even a description of products. The product description can be moved to an appendix. I would do this so if not all of the product line is to be included under the contract, the contract can essentially remain the same, and I would simply alter the appendix. The territory should also be defined in an appendix.

- Exclusive versus nonexclusive. The format and content of the contract will vary depending on whether it is exclusive or nonexclusive. If exclusive, be sure to have some performance targets in place or the exclusivity is offered with no condition of performance. This could easily lead to a line collector situation as discussed in Chapter 9. (Chapter 18 also includes a discussion of issues to consider when deciding between exclusive and nonexclusive representation.)

- Term of the agreement. Contracts with automatic extensions should be avoided. It is much better to put the decision into the hands of the manufacturer, in that the manufacturer must provide a notice in writing if the contract will be extended. A one-year initial term is probably the most common, though distributors may argue for a two-year period. Industry norms will also impact this aspect of the contract. Some industries will require substantial initial activities on the part of the distributor that in turn would dictate a need for a longer contract term.

- Technical information. International contracts should contain a stronger emphasis on the protection of technical information than may be in a company's domestic distributor contract. The sample contract in Appendix A illustrates these points in depth.

- Duties of distributor. As illustrated in the sample in Appendix A the contract should expressly state what is expected of the distributor, including such issues as translation, training, installation, and customer support.

- Duties of the manufacturer/service provider. Likewise, the contract should detail the duties of the manufacturer or service company. This will avoid issues such as which party is to pay for training or brochures.

- Termination. A critical portion of the contract is the conditions that allow for termination and the rights of each party upon contract termination. Some local laws allow for considerable benefits for the distributor in the case of termination without just cause, especially in the absence of a contract. The sample contract in Appendix A takes a very strong position in favor of the U.S. company.

- Dispute resolution provision. The use of arbitration is becoming increasingly important for international contract disputes. Consider including an arbitration clause in the contract. In the end, such an arrangement can save considerable time and money.

- Choice of law. It is important that the contract establish what law governs the contract in cases of dispute. In the sample contract in Appendix A Article VIII provides for U.S. law to govern. It is probably most common for a U.S. manufacturer to specify U.S. law. The local law of the distributor should be avoided. A neutral, third country can be a compromise but only under the advice of your attorney.

Reading through the sample contract in Appendix A will help clarify issues that are unique to international distribution contracts. Remember that the sample contract is pro-manufacturer.

• NOTES

1. William M. Daley, "The Battle Against Bribery," Wall Street Journal (17 December 1997): A22.

2. U.S. Department of Justice, "Foreign Corrupt Practices Act" (20 December 1996, National Trade Data Bank).

3. Gali Kronenberg, "In Deals Abroad, Grease Payments a Slippery Business," Los Angeles Times (3 November 1997): D2-19.

4. U.S. Department of Justice, "Foreign Corrupt Practices Act" (20 December 1996, National Trade Data Bank).

5. Andrea Gerlin, "A Matter of Degree: How a Jury Decided That a Coffee Spill Is Worth $2.9 Million," Wall Street Journal (1 September 1994): A1.

6. "No paint, no gain: product liability," The Economist (25 April 1996): 67.

7. "Revenge of the Reptiles," The Wall Street Journal (7 March 1995): A18.

8. "No paint, no gain: product liability," The Economist.

CHAPTER 13

Tax and Accounting Issues

There are a handful of issues related to expanding internationally that tend to be a bit technical - for example, the various calculations required to determine the impact of import duties and cascading taxes detailed in Chapter 11. The financial tools available to hedge foreign currency risk, which will be discussed in Chapter 16, are also technical. But the issues that really make an international manager's eyes blurry and glassy are international tax and accounting issues. Perhaps this is because taxes and accounting are often misunderstood or maybe people just don't like them.

If you are part of the group that shies away from tax and accounting issues, read this chapter. It will not make you an expert. It will not inspire you to switch careers and become a Certified Public Accountant. However, it will identify ways that even small exporters can save money. It will also cover some important terminology so that when you discuss these issues with a qualified international tax and accounting expert, you will have some idea of what they are saying.

At least work through the most important topics of this chapter to determine if they are relevant to your company. I will be discussing the topics most likely to impact a company during the initial years of international expansion: (1) transfer pricing, (2) duty drawback, (3) free trade zones and bonded warehouses, and (4) value-added taxes (VAT). At the end of the chapter I'll also briefly discuss tax credits for exporters.

You do not have to become an expert in these areas. There are many experts who understand this material and can apply it to your company. I encourage you to discuss these issues with an international tax and accounting professional who can determine how to maximize your international success into even greater profit.

• TRANSFER PRICING

You would think that a company exporting to its foreign subsidiary could invoice its product at any price it wanted. For example, if Nike were to export its shoes to its Nike headquarters in Europe, it could put on the invoice as low or high as price as it wanted since essentially it is not 'selling' at all – only transferring the shoes from one office to another. However, the concern of governments is that companies will pick values on these invoices that help to minimize taxes. If taxes are higher in one country versus another, the company will simply set a price to use that minimizes overall taxes. To avoid this situation, most countries have transfer pricing regulations. **Transfer pricing** is the pricing used on an international invoice between two related parties. **Related parties** are companies that have a financial interests in each other, such as Nike and its European subsidiary. Even having a minority ownership in a foreign company would still trigger transfer pricing rules.

What are the transfer pricing rules? Like anything complicated it depends! But an easy answer is that a company should use a price that is defendable and justifiable if the 'sale' was being made to a non-related party. In other words, if the exporter can show it uses the same price with companies with which it does not have any financial interest, that price would be okay. This non-related party pricing is known as the **arm's length price**. Of course nothing in international accounting is so simple an in fact a whole area of international tax assistance is with transfer pricing. And there are other techniques than arm's length pricing. The key is to seek professional assistance.

• DUTY DRAWBACK

If the products you export contain components or raw materials that were originally imported into the U.S., you may be able to obtain a refund on the import duties paid when the components or materials were imported.

U.S. companies have been eligible for relief from such import duties since 1789 when drawback was authorized by the first tariff act of the United States. The goal was simple: to make sure American companies could compete in foreign markets without the handicap of import duties. Though the goal may have been simple, applying and receiving drawback is not, due to the paperwork needed to prove the basis for the drawback.

What Is Eligible for Drawback?

Essentially, any product that was imported into the U.S. and then exported, or incorporated into a product in the U.S. that is later exported, is eligible for duty drawback. As long as a duty was assessed on the product when it was imported and drawback procedures are followed, the duty will be refunded when the product is exported. The exception is Canada and Mexico which do not qualify unless the product exported is same product and not incorporated into a final good.

There are some complicating factors. For example, what if the imported product has been intermingled with a domestic product of the same kind? Let's say you import copper wire from Argentina with a 5 percent import duty and you also use copper wire that has been produced in the U.S. Once the wire is in your manufacturing facility, it may be difficult to track exactly which products used the copper from Argentina and which used the U.S. wire. Further assume that you produced enough exports to have used up all the Argentine wire but you can't be sure only Argentine wire was used in the product. Given a choice, you would want the Argentine wire used because it represents a 5 percent improvement in your profits if the duty is rebated. Should you take the time to implement an inventory system to track the Argentine wire versus the U.S. wire?

Fortunately, you don't need to implement such a system. Under the substitution provision in the U.S. code authorizing drawback, it is immaterial whether the exported products used the imported material or the domestic material. The code gives the exporter the benefit of receiving the full duty available without tracking the material through the manufacturing facility.

How to Obtain Duty Drawback

Because drawback involves the refunding of import duties that directly increase the bottom line of the company, the system can be abused if not properly monitored. Thus, the procedures for claiming drawback are fairly strict, increasing the burden on the exporter and lessening the potential for fraudulent claims.

There are two restrictive requirements that legitimate claims must meet. The first is that prior to exporting the products, the exporter needs to file a drawback proposal with the regional commissioner of customs. Once approved, the exporter receives a copy of the approval letter from customs. The proposal and letter then form the basis for the drawback claims.

The second requirement is that the exporter needs to maintain significant documentation to ensure compliance with the drawback procedure. This includes documentation relating to the initial importation of the goods. For this reason, some exporters find it easiest to have their broker or freight forwarder involved in both the import and export process so the documentation can be coordinated. The documentation requirements were tightened in 1998, so manufacturers need to understand the documentation rules to avoid penalties.

There are other restrictions and documentation requirements, but the essential point is that the manufacturer stands to gain important duty rebates as long the required procedures are followed.

Drawback Rates and Dates

For most drawback claims, the exporter receives the full amount of the duty as a refund, less a 1 percent handling fee to customs. Claims for refunds can be made for up to five years after merchandise is imported, assuming it is used in the manufacturing of another good. For the simple re-exporting of imported goods in the same condition as imported, the time limit is three years.

It is also worth mentioning that products that need to be destroyed also qualify for duty drawback. For example, if a significant portion of your imported inventory has to be destroyed because the product reached an expiration date, you would be entitled to a duty refund even though the goods were not exported. Destruction of the goods must be supervised by customs. An exporter with an interest in pursuing duty drawback should contact its freight forwarder or broker, a local international trade center, or the U.S. Customs Service directly.

• FOREIGN TRADE ZONES AND BONDED WAREHOURES

The use of a foreign trade zone (FTZ) can be a powerful tool to reduce or eliminate import duties. But there is also quite a bit of confusion about FTZs. It is important to understand when the use of a FTZ is a good idea, and when a bonded warehouse might be better.

In the U.S., **foreign trade zones** are specially designed areas (zones) designated by U.S. Customs and Border Protection as FTZs. They are generally managed by a local non-profit entity such as an economic development council. FTZs may be an entire manufacturing facility, or a warehouse. The key to understanding the use of a FTZ is to understand that when a product is imported into the U.S. and placed into an FTZ, it is physically in the United States, but legally it has not be 'imported'. Meaning the goods are in the country, but customs still considers them under their 'control' and not available for local consumption.

Then what is to happen to the goods in the FTZ? Two things typically happen next. If the goods are later exported, then any duty that might otherwise have been due, will not be paid. It essentially eliminates the need for duty drawback because no import duty is paid. And not all the goods have to be exported: some might be 'imported' into the U.S. for consumption and duty would then be paid. The rest can be exported and no duty paid.

The second activity that might happen is the goods may be incorporated into a final product that is 'imported' into the U.S. I put 'imported' in quotes because remember, this all happens physically in the U.S. But why would a company manufacturer in a FTZ? Because if the duty rate on the final product is less than the duty rate on the imported component, the lower duty rate is used and applied to the value of the component. So if a car radio is imported into a FTZ that manufactures cars, and radios carry a lower duty rate than cars, the lower rate will be used for the duty associated with the radio. (The rest of the car would have no duty except for other imported components.) A final activity that could be done is testing or destruction of the imported product which also avoids duties.

Bonded warehouses are somewhat akin to FTZs in that a bonded warehouse is a physically separate space. But rather than a whole facility, it may only be part of a warehouse. But what makes a bonded warehouse different than a FTZ is that the only activity generally allowed in a bonded warehouse is the storing of inventory either for export or local consumption. So it offers the same delayed duty or no duty as an FTZ, but does not offer the ability to manufacture or test products. Bonded warehouses are less expensive and easier to administer. They also can be located anywhere within the U.S (and other countries), not just within a FTZ.

• VALUE ADDED TAX (VAT)

Unlike the U.S., most foreign countries have some form of national sales tax. This may seem peculiar to Americans who are accustomed to paying state and local sales taxes but no federal sales tax. Outside the U.S., from Asia to Europe, South Africa, and Latin America, most industrial countries have some form of national sales tax. They are commonly referred to as **value-added taxes** (VAT) or national consumption taxes.

VAT is generally applied to products and services which is why it is considered a consumer consumption tax. VAT is unlike import duties or industrial taxes which are designed to implement specific economic or political objectives that discriminate against other products. VAT rates can be over 20 percent and may actually represent a larger source of federal tax income than personal or corporate taxes.

The mechanics of a VAT may seem difficult to understand because you may be unfamiliar with national consumption taxes. For most VAT regimes, VAT is collected at each point along the channel of delivering a good or service to the end user (the consumer), as opposed to U.S. state and local taxes which are not collected until the final sale of the product is made to the consumer. Regardless of the role each company plays in the chain (manufacturer, distributor, or dealer), each collects and pays VAT. But because the VAT is rebated as the product is sold down the chain, the final effect is that only the consumer actually pays the VAT.

For example, if we tracked the manufacturing of shirts using a VAT rate of 15 percent, the collection and payments would be as follows:

- *Thread manufacturer*. Sells thread to garment manufacturer for $1,000 (this assumes the thread manufacturer locally grows the cotton and has no purchase of raw materials). The thread manufacturer collects $1,000 for the thread and $150 in VAT. The thread manufacturer pays the government the full $150 of the VAT collected.
- *Garment manufacturer*. Manufacturers shirts from the thread and sells the shirts to a dealer for $2,000. The garment manufacturer collects $2,000 for the shirts and $300 in VAT, of which $150 is paid to the government ($300 minus the $150 already paid to the thread manufacturer).
- *Dealer*. Sells all the shirts to its customers for $3,000. Dealer collects the $3,000 plus $450 in VAT, of which $150 is paid to the government ($450 minus the $300 already paid to the garment manufacturer).

Thus, the final result is the consumers pay $450 in VAT. The thread manufacturer, the garment manufacturer and the dealer do not incur any VAT, though along the process they collect and pay VAT. The government receives the VAT in stages; $150 (thread company) plus $150 (garment company) plus $150 (dealer).

Implication of VAT for U.S. Exporters

U.S. exporters should understand that VAT is applied to a product directly at the point of entry when the goods are cleared through customs. The responsibility of collecting the VAT generally falls on the importer of record - the company that is legally responsible for the importation. Thus for exporters that are selling to distributors in a foreign country, their distributor will pay the VAT.

Certain countries, such as Canada, allow foreign companies to establish a nonresident importer status in which the foreign company prepays all duties and taxes to make its products easier to sell because they have already been cleared through customs. In these cases, the exporter (who also becomes the importer) may be required to pay the VAT up front, though it would eventually receive the money back when the product is sold. In this instance, the U.S. exporter needs to register in the foreign country for the ability to collect VAT and be prepared to meet the collection and reporting procedures.

It is important to remember the distinction between duties and VAT. Duties are typically applied only to imports to adversely discriminate against foreign-produced products. VAT is applied to all products (and perhaps services) regardless of where the goods were produced.

• U.S. TAX INCENTIVES FOR EXPORTERS

The U.S. has offered a series of tax benefits for exporters since the early 1960's. The most common program was the Foreign Sales Corporations (FSC). But FSCs and other replacements have generally been ruled as illegal under WTO law. Ultimately only a tax expert can confirm if your international activities can result in any tax incentives. However, it is worth a quick discussion of one method, the IC-DISC.

Interest Charge Domestic International Sales Corporations (IC-DISC)

The **Interest Charge DISC**, or IC-DISC should not to be confused with a DISC, which used to be a common tax-savings device, but is no longer commonly used. Depending on its structure, it can defer tax savings to a company or offer a permanent tax savings to shareholders. Use of IC-DISCs is normally confined to smaller exporters because the tax benefits of deferral are limited to the first $10 million of qualifying export sales. They also tend to be used by closely held corporations instead of publicly traded corporations because part of the tax benefit is accrued at the shareholder level, which would be difficult to manage outside of a closely held corporation.

An IC-DISC is essentially a paper company created to derive tax benefits. Unlike an FSC, the IC-DISC is a domestic corporation, typically a subsidiary or sister company of the exporting company.

Most IC-DISCs are commission IC-DISCs. They function as follows:

- Each time the U.S. exporter makes a qualifying export sale, the IC-DISC is entitled to earn a commission based on the sale price or profit from the sale. The commission is a fully deductible expense for the exporter.
- The commission is income to the IC-DISC but as long as the commissions are reinvested in qualified export assets the IC-DISC is exempt from paying federal tax on the income.
- Unlike an FSC which pays a dividend of its net commission income back to its shareholders once a year, an IC-DISC has the option of not paying the dividend back to the exporter each year. When the dividend is paid to the exporter

it is treated as income and tax is due. As long as the IC-DISC continues to delay the dividend, the eventual tax event is deferred.

The potential for tax savings from using an IC-DISC can be achieved in two ways. First, if the shareholders of the IC-DISC are paid the dividend directly from the IC-DISC rather than through the exporting corporation, a tax savings will occur because the double tax on the distribution of corporate earnings is avoided. Second, if the personal tax rate of the shareholders has lowered between the time the commissions in the IC-DISC are earned and when the dividends are paid, a tax savings will occur.

There are, of course, a number of complicating factors. The most important is that the shareholders of the IC-DISC must pay the U.S. government interest on the amount of tax that is deferred with respect to the IC-DISC's taxable commission income. Also, as with FSCs, not all products qualify for IC-DISC treatment. In the correct circumstance, however, IC-DISCs can be an important tax savings and deferral mechanism.

A competent advisor should be retained to steer you through these rather complicated tax-saving and tax-deferring mechanisms.

The Mechanics of Going Global

Believe it or not, in many ways the hard work of planning how to go global is done! Yet you may wonder, "What about all the nitty-gritty details such as shipping, insurance, documentation, or getting paid?"

One of the biggest misconceptions in international business is that the greatest challenge is related to the actual movement of goods or the financial aspects of going global. While these may at times be monumental issues, they are less of an obstacle to international growth than many perceive. This is because companies quickly discover that there are excellent resources available to assist them with the detail-oriented, paper-intensive aspects of international trade. In practice, most of the logistics, documentation, and finance challenges can be diminished through the effective use of an experienced freight forwarder or logistics company, a competent bank, and international trade assistance organizations. Each plays an important role in handling what otherwise would be difficult obstacles to international expansion.

Nevertheless, it is still vital that international companies pay close attention to these aspects of international trade. Mistakes are expensive. For example, violation of U.S export laws can result in significant fines and potentially jail. Equally, no company needs educating about the costs of bad debts. Imagine how complicated it would be to collect debts thousands of miles from home.

This section is titled *The Mechanics of Going Global* because these three aspects, logistics, documentation, and financial issues, are the most common day-to-day aspects of international trade. With the proper use of resources and adequate internal training, they can also be the easiest aspects to handle when going global. In fact, when done well and strategically, these 'mechanical' aspects of going global will become significant competitive barriers.

Chapter 14

Logistics

I t is hard to imagine why anyone worries about international logistics today. Break-
throughs in technology, transportation methods, and the ensuing cost reductions have
made products competitive internationally that in the past would have never made it
across their home country's borders.

For example, shipping a can of Heineken beer from Holland to Hong Kong costs
only one cent a bottle despite the rather circuitous route required through the Mediterra-
nean Sea and the Suez Canal.[1] This example always amazes uninformed audiences when
I use it to demonstrate the impact of recent logistics innovations. It quickly destroys the
illusion that high-end import beverage products are expensive because of the international freight costs.

Whether you ship beer, ball bearings, or boats, the timing could not be better to
move your products internationally. With the growing use of containerization and intermodalism, combined with technology, global shipping costs have become increasingly
affordable.

Yet the process remains risky to the unaware exporter. For example, when a vessel is in danger, such as in a storm, the ship's master has the right to sacrifice property
(freight) and/or incur reasonable expenditure. Such an act is called a general average act
and the steamship line has the right to spread the cost of the loss or expense across all
freight onboard. The implication is that shippers need to have the appropriate insurance to
safeguard against such unexpected incidents. Most do. But this highlights one area of international shipping that is different than domestic trade.

In this chapter I will discuss a variety of issues related to the movement of international freight. I begin by discussing why international freight movements have become
increasingly efficient through the use of containerization and intermodalism. This will
acquaint you with the jargon the freight industry uses when moving goods internationally. I also will detail the shipping terms for international freight, or Incoterms. This is a
critical section because the use of Incoterms is tantamount to payment terms: they identify which party is responsible for what. Finally, I will look at the role of freight forwarders
and how they can be used to reduce the costs and challenges of your international freight
movements.

• CONTAINERIZED CARGO AND INTERMODALISM

Two important changes over fifty years ago are impacting how freight is moved internationally. The first is **containerization**: moving freight in standard containers. (See The History of Container.) the second is **intermodalism**: moving containerized freight between different modes of transport such as truck to rail to ocean to rail and then truck. Combining containerized cargo and intermodalism has increased efficiency and lowered the costs of shipping globally. The impact has been particularly significant on door-to-door container service where the shipper packs the container at its shipping warehouse and ships it directly to its customer in the foreign country. Transportation companies handle the container, not the freight, which reduces damage.

For example, it is now possible to have a container brought to your warehouse by truck (essentially a semi-truck's trailer). Your staff loads your products into the container to ensure it is packed properly. Essentially, you decide what to put where in the truck and what products are allowed to be placed on top of other products. The truck then drives the container to the freight rail line where it is placed on a rail-freight carriage. The train takes it to Los Angeles where it is loaded directly onto a ship by crane. The ship takes the container across the Pacific to your foreign market, say Madras on the southern tip of India. The container then goes by rail to Bangalore and eventually by truck to the foreign buyer. Through all these interchanges and modes of shipping, from your warehouse to Bangalore, the goods are never exposed to outside elements or further handled by shipping personnel. The only time the door of the container may be opened is for an inspection by customs.

This containerization of cargo results in a number of benefits to shippers. The first is reduced costs. By utilizing standard shipping containers, ships are able to handle more freight, more efficiently. A single ship can hold the equivalent of 10 or even 15 thousand containers, each 20 feet long, 8 feet high and 8 feet wide. The second benefit is reduced damage to the products because they are only handled twice, at the shipping warehouse and eventually at the customer's site. This also results in a reduction in shipping risk associated with pilferage. Before containerization, more people had access to the goods as they passed through the various shipping stages, resulting in a higher visibility and greater chance for theft. These factors all contribute to the most important benefit: containerized goods are more likely to arrive at their destination faster and on time because many of the potential bottlenecks are removed.

Container Dimensions

Today containers for land transport (truck, rail, and sea) come in a variety of sizes and purposes. Generally, containers are either 20 feet or 40 feet in length, though other lengths are used. The 40-foot containers are the most popular and are the ones with which you will be most familiar. You see them as the rear portion of a semi-truck or stacked two high on a freight train. Near a port, you can often see hundreds of them either waiting to be loaded onto a ship or in storage for later use. Exporters and importers generally don't own containers; they simply use them for a shipment and return them to a pool to be used by other shippers.

The History of Containers

The first widespread use of containers dates back to the post-World War II years. The U.S. military learned that metal boxes worked best to move family goods between the U.S. and its overseas locations. Previously goods were shipped as breakbulk cargo, which is cargo shipped on its own, without containerization. As breakbulk cargo, goods are loaded aboard vessels in a net or by a sling, conveyor, chute, or other method. During loading and unloading, goods are exposed to the elements including rain and snow. During the transit, breakbulk goods may be stacked on top of one another or shift position during movements of the ship or other transport method.

The potential for damage and loss led the U.S. military to adopt metal boxes as a standard which they called conex containers. Though the conex containers were smaller than today's standard containers, you often see news articles referring to containers as conex containers.

While the U.S. military may have been the first to use such metal boxes as standard shipping containers, it was the shipping line Sea-Land that first used containers commercially. During the 1950s, Malcolm McLean of Sea-Land Service Inc. took an old tanker named the Ideal X and converted it to hold containers. The first shipment from New York to Houston carrying 50 containers started what has now become the preferred shipping method.[2] (Use that little bit of trivia on your next long, international flight when you want to impress your seatmate!)

As a rule of thumb, containers are slightly more than 71/2 feet in both width and height. This translates into a freight capacity of 2,376 cubic feet. The shipper packing the container can ship anything it wants and pack it in any way (though keep in mind the ocean tariff will depend on the commodity being shipped). There is a weight limit of 60,350 pounds. The weight limit may be even lower if the container is transported by truck. Be sure to check the highway maximum weight limitations in the export and import markets if surface transport of the container is expected.

If more space is needed for a particularly bulky commodity, there are high cube containers which add an additional foot in height over the standard container. They also tend to be longer with a typical length of 48 feet. Other types of containers for specialized goods include:

- Refrigerated containers that have special refrigeration mechanisms for perishable goods. The freight trade refers to such containers as *reefers* - a shortened expression for refrigeration or refrigerators.
- Side loading containers are equipped with side doors for use where end loading is not easy or possible. For example, containers that will be loaded while on rail cars would normally be side loading.
- Open top containers allow products to be loaded through the top. Open top containers may or may not have a top.

- Ventilated containers offer ventilation through one or both ends and may even include powered air-circulating fans. The typical application is for cargo that generates heat or is susceptible to sweating.
- Insulated containers help prevent fluctuations in temperature either through ventilation or use of a heating system.
- Flat rack containers have two or more sides missing for transporting machinery, vehicles, bulky items, lumber, and mill products.

Door-to-Door versus Port-to-Port (LCL) Container Service

Up to this point, the discussion of containerization has presumed that the exporter is able to fill a 20- or 40-foot container completely. That is, the exporter has sufficient export sales to one foreign location to justify paying the price of a full container. But what happens when a company is just beginning to export? What options are available to smaller exporters?

In general, if you can fill at least one-half of a container your costs will be about the same as contracting for a full container. This is only a rough guide because rates vary considerably by destination and commodity, but if your shipment will fill up at least one-half of the space, it is best to contract for the full container. This would be called door-to-door service because the container will be delivered from your door directly to the door of your foreign buyer. Door-to-door service is the most desirable, not only because it is cost efficient, but because it provides all the other benefits previously discussed, such as lower risk and lower damage potential.

However, not all shippers have enough volume for door-to-door, full container service. In such cases, port-to-port container service is an option. These also are referred to as LCL containers or LCL loads - less than container loads. For LCL shipments, goods from one shipper are combined with goods from other shippers in the same container. This consolidation of freight into one container is done by forwarders, consolidators, or the carrier. LCL service is less cost effective, and does not offer the same product protection against damage and theft. But LCL is still desirable over breakbulk shipping and does have its cost advantages.

If you are planning a door-to-door container shipment and don't have the container filled completely, you should consider doing your own consolidation and combine the goods of a nearby company with your products. Be aware, however, that the tariff (cost) of the ocean portion of the container shipment will depend on the exact commodities (products) being shipped in the container. There may also be some liability concerns, such as shipping insurance, that you will want to address.

Air Cargo Containerization

Containerization of cargo is not limited to land transport options. Increasingly, air cargo is containerized due to the cost savings for both shippers and airlines. Containerization increases the speed of loading and unloading the aircraft, minimizes exposure of cargo to potential damage or theft, and helps ensure efficient use of the limited cargo area in the aircraft.

There are two categories of air cargo containers. You are probably already familiar with lower deck containers if you have ever seen a wide-body plane being loaded prior to departure. Lower deck containers are specially designed to fit the dimensions of the lower deck of a wide body jet and lock directly to the plane's structure. Such containers are typically metal and can be sealed for safety and security. Another version of lower deck containers are box-type containers, which are often made of wood, fiberglass, plywood, fiberboard, metal, or a combination.

A second type is an air cargo pallet. You often see these pallets being used on conveyor systems in terminals and being loaded onto aircraft. Cargo is normally secured to the pallet with plastic, nets, or straps. Though palletized air cargo doesn't offer the security of a sealed container, it is often the only containerized option on smaller aircraft.

As with land containers, if you do not have enough cargo to fill an air cargo container or pallet you can still lower your air freight expense by using the services of a freight forwarder, broker, or carrier who will containerize your cargo with other cargo. For example, I can remember when shipping from Los Angeles to Australia, we would always try to ship on either Thursdays or Saturdays because those days offered containerization service from our freight forwarder – known as 'consols'. We could still ship on other days but the air freight charges were higher.

Noncontainerized Cargo

Clearly not all products can be containerized. Some circumstances dictate that the cargo must be sent breakbulk for sea transport or as individual shipments for air or land transport. Noncontainerized cargo, such as bulk liquids or automobiles, is transported in specialized vessels. Such vessels would typically not be suited for containers, but rather are fitted specifically to accommodate particular products. Though you lose the benefits of containerization, it may be the only option for many industrial goods and bulk commodities. Freight shipped in this manner is sometimes referred to as 'ro-ro' or 'roll on, roll off'.

• UNDERSTANDING INCOTERMS - THE TERMS OF SALE

To avoid costly misunderstandings between sellers and buyers, the international community (including exporters, insurers, bankers, and lawyers) have adopted a set of transportation terms known as **Incoterms**. The International Chamber of Commerce (ICC) has developed this set of international rules for the interpretation of trade terms in foreign trade. The most recent revision was Incoterms 2010 summarized in Figure 14.1

It is critical that each company fully understands Incoterms because they precisely determine who is responsible for what between parties. Incoterms are also part of international law. They establish:

- The geographic location at which the buyer becomes responsible for the goods
- Who arranges for shipping, handling, insurance, and inland freight costs

It is the precision of Incoterms that makes them appear complex. Yet this precision is exactly what is needed in international shipping, where there are a number of complicating factors not found in domestic trade. For example, what happens if a container falls into the water while being loaded onto an international vessel? What if an invoice indicates freight from Shanghai to Mexico City was added, the buyer may have the impression import costs have also been included since Mexico City is an inland city. But is that the case? Or, if the seller intends to pay all costs to get the goods to the door of the foreign buyer, does it also pay the import duty?

These are the gray areas that are eliminated through the use of Incoterms. To accommodate a variety of shipping circumstances, the set of Incoterms is larger than terms generally used in domestic shipping. There are 11 separate Incoterms. They can be grouped in two ways: (1) by the freight cost items that are included in the term and (2) by the appropriate mode of transport for their usage. Grouping the 13 Incoterms by freight cost items is the easiest to understand. Figure 14.1 shows the Incoterms grouped by which freight cost items are included. See also 'Quick Tips for Leaning Incoterms'.

Putting the Incoterms to Use

To better understand the use of Incoterms, I will discuss in-depth five of the Incoterms to make important distinctions: EXW, FCA, FOB, CIP, and DDP. These are some of the commonly used terms. A summary of each term is shown in Figure 14.2

Quick Tips for Learning Incoterms

• **The First Letter Matters**: Incoterms begin with either an E, F, C, D. This order is important because it starts with the least responsibility for the exporter to the greatest.

• **Incoterms Are From the Exporters Perspective**: The specific Incoterm tells you what responsibility is on the exporter not the importer. Meaning the Incoterm prescribes what the exporter must do, and the import does everything else.

• **Must Have a Named Place**: All Incoterms must be followed by a named place. EXW is not complete. EXW Dallas, TX is complete.

• **E/F terms versus C/D terms.** One of the most important distinctions is that all E and F terms do not include the main international freight, such as the ocean freight. C and D terms do.

• **Mode of Transport Matters.** Of the 11 terms, four are for ocean and inland waterway: FAS, FOB, CFR, and CIF. These four a also best used with non-containerized freight.

• **Incoterms and Title Transfer.** Often misunderstood is that Incoterms do no determine when ownership (title) passes from seller to buyer. Title transfer is determined by the contract or terms of sales in combination with local laws.

Figure 14.1 Incoterms 2010 Grouped by Which Cost Items Are Included

Incoterm Groups	Incoterm	Description
Group E / Departure Group E contains the only term whereby the seller makes the goods available to the buyer at their premises	ExW	Ex Works (... named place)
Group F / Main carriage unpaid Group F includes terms whereby the seller delivers the goods to a carrier appointed by the buyer. Thus the buyer pays the bulks of the freight costs.	FCA	Free Carrier (... named place)
	FAS	Free Alongside Ship (... named port of shipment)
	FOB	Free on Board (... named port of shipment)
Group C / Main carriage paid Group C includes terms whereby the seller contracts for the freight, but without assuming the risk of loss or damage to the goods or additional costs due to events occurring after shipment and dispatch. Thus the seller pays the bulk of the freight costs.	CFR	Cost and Freight (... named port of destination)
	CIF	Cost, Insurance, and Freight (... named port of destination)
	CPT	Carriage Paid to (... named place of destination)
	CIP	Carriage and Insurance Paid to (named place of destination)
Group D / Arrival Group D includes terms whereby the seller has to bear all costs and risks needed to bring the goods to the country of destination.	DAT	Delivered at terminal (...named terminal at destination)
	DAP	Delivered at place (...named place of destination)
	DDP	Delivered Duty Paid (... named place of destination)
Indicates only used for sea and inland waterway transport, and preferably non containerized freight		

Figure 14.2 Incoterms Comparison

Ocean Freight	EX-WORKS	FCA PLACE	FOB VESSEL	CIP PLACE	DDP PLACE
Cost of goods	S	S	S	S	S
Export packing	S/B	S	S	S	S
Loading charges/warehouse	S/B	S	S	S	S
Export documentation	S/B	S	S	S	S
Banking fees	S/B	S	S	S	S
Freight forwarder's fees	S/B	S/B	S	S	S
Insurance to port (optional)	S/B	S/B	S	S	S
Inland freight	B	S/B	S	S	S
Terminal handling charges	B	B	S	S	S
Forklift charges	B	B	S	S	S
Loading onto vessel	B	B	S	S	S
Harbor maintenance fees	B	B	B	S	S
Ocean freight	B	B	B	S	S
Fuel adjustment factor	B	B	B	S	S
Currency adjustment factor	B	B	B	S	S
Destination delivery charge	B	B	B	S	S
Insurance to destination	B	B	B	S	S
Import duties	B	B	B	B	S
Customs fees	B	B	B	B	S
Inland freight to buyers	B	B	B	B	S

S = Seller B = Buyer S/B = Negotiable
Shaded area: responsibilities of the buyer

It is important to clarify that each Incoterm is always followed by a physical location. If the location is omitted, the buyer could select a costly or infeasible location. Also, terms of sale build upon and naturally follow each other. For the five common Incoterms, EXW represents the terms of sale in which the seller has the least responsibilities and the EXW price quoted only includes the costs of the goods and making the goods available at the name place (generally the shipping dock of the exporter). On the other hand the DDP Incoterm represents to most responsibilities for the seller who arranges essentially for everything: the freight to the port or airport; the international freight, clearing through foreign customs and duties, all insurance, and final freight to the name place. The terms in between EXW and DDP represent stages of increased responsibility for the seller. Figure 14.2 shows this progression of responsibilities to the seller. Note as as the Incoterms move from the E to the F to the C and finally to the D terms there is increasing responsibilities for the seller (and decreasing for the buyer).

It is also worth stressing that the use of Incoterms clarifies which costs items have been included in the price quote from the buyer to the seller. Once the terms of sale are accepted, it is the seller's obligation to pay its costs, and likewise for the buyer. Thus, the exporter should take care when preparing its sales quotation so the appropriate costs are factored into the cost estimate so that no profit is lost because of a mistake, such as forgetting insurance if it is to be paid by the seller. This is discussed in greater detail in Chapter 15. (Some companies may treat various items, such as packaging, as overhead costs. In these cases they would not be part of the sales quotation.)

Ex-Works (EXW). This represents the least responsibilities for the exporter. When offering an EXW quotation, stated Ex-Works Town, State/Province/Country, the price includes only those costs involved up to an agreed point of origin, usually the seller's factory or premises. The seller places the product at the control of the buyer at a concurred place, date, and time. Prior to Incoterms 2010, EXW was very common and for U.S. shippers it is most akin to FOB factory. However, under EXW, it is the responsibility of the foreign buyer not the seller to clear the goods for export. This of course would not be best practice in export compliance. And in fact legally it is the responsibility of the exporter to ensure the export documentation is done correctly. Though many exporters using EXW likely do the export documentation, often they rely instead on the importer's local agent in the exporting country. Given this conflict, the guidance provided when Incoterms 2010 was released is that when an exporter wants the least responsibilities, rather than EXW Seller's Premises, use FCA Seller's Premises. The only difference is the FCA terms includes the responsibility of the exporter to clear the goods for export.

EXW costs can include:
- Raw or processed products
- Standard packaging
- Pallets, banding, shrink wrap, slip sheets, slings, one-ton big bags
- Special labeling
- Translation and printing
- Inspection certificates (phytosanitary, health, quality, or export license)
- Bracing or inspecting a container
- Export packaging

Additionally, if the buyer wants the seller to coordinate the shipping, the freight forwarder fees and documentation fees can also be included by the seller. Banking fees may also be included in an EXW quote.

Free Carrier (FCA). FCA, stated FCA named place State/Province/Country, is used in two instances. The first, as discussed above, is the preferred term when the exporter wants the least responsibilities (though FCA Seller's Premises does put the responsibility on the exporter to clear the goods for export). The second use is if the goods are loaded on board an inland carrier at a location beyond the factory. FCA terms of sale can include delivery of the goods to a freight forwarder, a railway terminal, or a container yard in a city beyond the exporter. For example, FCA O'Connor Freight Forwarders, Anothertown, Anotherstate. FCA signifies a precise location where the product is turned over to a carrier or person who will ensure carriage (freight). When offering an FCA quotation, the price will include those costs involved up to that agreed point, including transportation and loading, if required. Another example would be to the nearest port such as FCA Baltimore, MD or FCA Hamburg, Germany.

FCA costs can include EXW plus:
- Inland transportation to the port of exit
- Insurance cost for inland transportation
- Additional freight forwarder's and documentation fees

Free on board (FOB). FOB, stated FOB ship's rail Ocean Port of Exit, State/Province/Country, signifies a precise ship and ocean port location where the product is loaded on board an ocean carrier, and the goods are cleared for export. When offering an FOB quotation, the seller places the product over the ship's rail (side). FOB only applies to sea or water transportation. Furthermore, FOB should only be used with Roll-On/Roll-Off (Ro-Ro) freight or non-containerized freight. If the freight is containerized, FCA is more appropriate.

FOB costs can include EXW plus FCA plus:
- Port charges (including terminal handling or receiving charges, or stevedore, wharfage, forklift, off-load, etc.)
- Cost of loading goods on board ship
- Heavy lifting charges

Carriage & Insurance Paid to (CIP). CIP, stated CIP named place, State/Province/Country, signifies that the seller clears the goods for export, and arranges and pays the ocean or air freight and other freight charges to a named place in the foreign country. The seller insures the shipment to the named place. However the seller is not responsible for any import customs fees or duties.

CIP costs can include EXW plus FCA plus FOB plus:
- Ocean freight or air freight
- War risk (ocean)
- Harbor maintenance fee
- Fuel adjustment factor (FAF), bunker surcharge, or bunker adjustment factor (BAF)
- Currency adjustment factor (CAF)
- Destination delivery charges (DDC) or container service charges (CSC)
- Cargo insurance

Delivered Duty Paid (DDP). DDP, stated CIP named place, Country, is the Incoterm with the most responsibilities for the seller. DDP signifies that the seller clears the goods for export, and arranges and pays the ocean or air freight and other freight charges to a named place in the foreign country. The seller insures the shipment to the named place. Seller is responsible for all import customs fees and duties in the foreign country.

DDP should be used cautiously because when a price quote is given using DDP, the exporter needs to have all foreign country importation costs accurate since they are responsible for them. DDP is most commonly used for samples or warranty repairs.

DDP costs can include EXW plus FCA plus FOB plus CIP plus:
- All import costs including customs fees and duties

Some Concerns When Using Incoterms

Interpretations of trade definitions, such as terms of sale, can and do vary from buyer to seller and from country to country. Furthermore, the courts of various countries have interpreted these definitions differently. It is important to have a firm understanding and agreement of the terms of sale between the buyer and the seller. JuDee Benton summarizes these concerns in her rules of thumb shown below.[3]

Though the use of Incoterms is an important step toward preparing for potential disputes, there are still other considerations that must be taken into account for a shipment to be successful. The best advice is to be sure that you work with a skilled freight forwarder and attend training programs so you understand these terms.

Rules of Thumb When Using Incoterms

Rule 1: The seller must clearly define the terms and conditions for shipment, payment, which port, time frame, and all other issues.

Rule 2: The farther the geographical place is from the warehouse (EXW), the higher the costs of getting the product to the site.

Rule 3: The seller must determine what charges are included in the quotation, as based upon the terms of sale and the geographical location.

Rule 4: Charges omitted in the quotation come out of the seller's pocket. Otherwise the seller must re-invoice (assuming shipment has occurred), which would probably not be accepted by buyer. Seller will appear inexperienced.

Rule 5: Do not assume that the buyer knows all the regulations.

Rule 6: The seller is ultimately responsible for ensuring the inclusion of costs, timely shipping, compliance, documentation, and payment. Freight forwarders provide an important linkage and service, but it is the seller's company and order. The buck stops with the seller.

Rule 7: Do not assume anything!

• THE ROLE OF FREIGHT FORWARDERS

If you are growing concerned about how to learn everything regarding export logistics, don't worry. There is an important resource that can reduce your global logistics anxiety - a **freight forwarder**. Though its role is often seen as a travel agent for freight, freight forwarders can become important trade partners that fulfill a role beyond simply booking your freight onto a ship or airplane.

Essentially freight forwarders are trained and equipped to handle the entire process from the initial freight cost quotation and shipping arrangements to related documentation and customs clearance. As shown in Figure 14.3, their portfolio of services can be extensive. For many of these activities, the forwarder will be completing documents on your behalf so you will be required to sign a limited power of attorney appointing the forwarder as your agent in matters dealing with the movement of freight.

With such extensive services, it's no wonder even large companies with significant internal logistics staffs still utilize the services of freight forwarders. Virtually all shippers use freight forwarders at some point in the shipping process. It simply makes sense to outsource some or all of the export logistics process to experts that offer important knowledge and economies of scale.

Your Reliance on Freight Forwarders

As your company develops its international business plan, you will need to decide how much your company will depend on the services of a freight forwarder. Smaller and less experienced firms will be well served by a high reliance on freight forwarders.

Figure 14.3 Services Provided by Freight Forwarders

- International freight quotations
- Booking inland and international freight movements
- Containerization and consolidation of freight
- Providing scheduling of carriers
- Transshipments
- Export and import documentation
- Applying for export licenses
- Overseas documentation and foreign government requirements
- Preshipment inspections
- Marine and air insurance
- Warehousing
- Export packing
- Supervising freight movements (such as the loading of goods onto carriers)
- Assisting with insurance claims
- Overseas logistics strategies such as free trade zones and warehousing
- Computerized tracking of international freight movements
- Import customs clearance / brokerage

The expertise and relatively low cost of freight forwarders is difficult to duplicate internally in the early stages of a company's international growth. But as exports grow and a company's international business matures, particular portions of the logistics challenge may be brought into the company. This also is true if your company is seeking greater control over its international logistics. For example, it is not unusual for a mature exporter to handle its international documentation requirements internally.

One of the more important functions of freight forwarders is the containerization and booking of freight. Depending on its size, a freight forwarder will develop its own containerized service on particular shipping routes and modes. It may also have negotiated significantly reduced tariffs (especially in the air cargo industry) with specific carriers. Its strength and connections can translate into important cost savings to you or your foreign buyers. This also may mean that you will need to deal with more than one freight forwarder. You may find one freight forwarder that is very competitive on European routes, and another for Asian routes. This is not uncommon. Each forwarder's expertise may also be focused on a particular region of the world. For example, with the challenges of shipping into Russia, some freight forwarders have established a niche of just servicing trade with Russia.

Choosing a Freight Forwarder

Given the important role of a freight forwarder in your international shipping, choosing a good one can be crucial to your export success. Freight forwarders in the U.S. are regulated and certified by the Federal Maritime Commission, which issues a license to the freight forwarder and also audits its activities. Many freight forwarders are members of the National Customs Brokers & Forwarders Association of America, Inc. (www.ncbfaa.org).

It has already been discussed that you may want to work with more than one freight forwarder so that you can benefit from a freight forwarder's specialization. It is also important to not depend on one freight forwarder for competitive reasons. Though most freight forwarders understand they must remain competitive to keep their client's business, it is not a good idea to assume they are competitive. Equally, you should not spread your international freight business among so many freight forwarders that you don't have the attention of any of them. The relationship between seller and freight forwarder can be one of the most important partnerships for your company. It is important to keep enough freight with a forwarder to make the business significant for it. A successful relationship with your freight forwarder is a two-way street.

Because freight forwarders come in all sizes, backgrounds, specialties, and experiences, you will find it helpful to ask freight forwarders for company details and references. Their initial response will give you a good idea about each company. Once you select one or more freight forwarders, keep the lines of communication strong. Nurture the relationship so you can utilize their strengths whenever possible. Develop a realistic understanding of what your forwarder can and cannot do. And as mentioned earlier, develop internal expertise of international freight movement and documentation by having staff trained. This also helps ensure compliance with trade regulations.

What to Look For in Your Freight Forwarder

Your freight forward is a critical partner for your international strategy. Choosing a reliable freight forwarder is an important process. Get suggestions from local resources such as trade assistance centers or bankers.

Here are some considerations when choosing a freight forwarder:

Forwarder background, history, ownership. Some companies tend to be large, multinational companies with foreign subsidiaries. Other forwarders are single location operations. One is not necessarily better than another but such differences can impact the strengths and priorities of one forwarder versus another.

Customer references. Ask for customer references to substantiate their customer service claims.

Specific areas of expertise and service offered. Forwarders tend to either specialize or generalize in their freight forwarding services. Such distinctions may indicate a preference for one forwarder over another depending on the requirements of the seller/shipper. Equally, not all freight forwarders offer the same services. It is important that the services of the forwarder match the needs of the seller/shipper.

Foreign market strengths. Forwarders often have foreign offices indicating their emphasis on that country or region. Often these are affiliates or company owned. Access to such offices can be critical for high risk or problematic countries.

Surface, air, ocean strengths. Forwarders sometimes focus on one particular mode of transport. For example, a forwarder with extensive air experience and containerization contracts would match well with a seller that relies heavily on air shipments for its exports.

Import services. Manufacturers may want to consolidate both export and import service with the same forwarder.

Technology support. More and more forwarders offer some form of electronic interface with the seller/shipper. For high volume exporters, such a service may be critical to the selection of a forwarder.

Third Party Logistics (3PL). 3PL services include warehousing, pick and pack, inspection, and perhaps light assembly. These may be important services for the exporter.

• OBTAINING AN INTERNATIONAL FREIGHT QUOTE

Even if you have not yet shipped internationally, it is fairly easy to get quotes for your international freight. The key is to have the right information before you contact a freight forwarder. During your initial international business planning and foreign market research, you needed freight quotes to determine the landed cost of your goods and to estimate the selling price for the product. These will be used for the competitive analysis. As you receive specific order inquiries, the buyer also may request a freight quote. You will need the following details when contacting the freight forwarder:

- Description of the goods to be shipped
- Packaging details (dimensions, weight)
- Value of the shipment
- Destination
- Shipping terms

Work with your freight forwarder to offer more than one option to the foreign buyer. Generally a forwarder will encourage you to ship under a Incoterm C term because it keeps the exporter more in control. Will payment terms of Letter of Credit or Collections, C terms should be used. However, the foreign buyer, especially if large, may simply want a EXW price and they will arrange all freight. Generally you want to avoid quoting a D Incoterm because of the risks associated with not having accurate important costs prior to export.

You will also want to ask the freight forwarder how the freight is calculated. Did it use a containerized rate? Did it assume a full container? A good freight forwarder will help identify ways to save money and clarify your options. For example, I always suggest exporters also get a 20- and 40-foot container quote so they can see how far they have to go before they can justify a full container, which is the most efficient and safest shipping method. (As a general rule, if you can fill half a container, the price will be similar to a full container which is preferable because only your freight will be in the container.

You may want to get more than one quote, especially during your planning stage, because the freight component will be an important part of your global planning. However, realize that getting quotes can involve quite a bit of time and effort on behalf of a freight forwarder. It will likely need to contact its overseas office or affiliates to get the overseas inland freight costs, plus customs costs, if required. Don't be surprised if the quote process involves a number of days. On the other hand, if the freight forwarder is not responsive, it may be a sign of potential problems.

• INTERNATIONAL LOGISTICS SOLUTIONS – 3PLS

A growing industry, related to freight forwarding, is international logistics and the use of **third-part-logistics (3PL)**. 3PL offers the ability to outsource parts of the logistics to another company. 3PLs provide complete global solutions, including product shipping, warehousing, sales fulfillment, and customer support functions. 3PLs offer the ability to outsource (contract-out) many of the time-consuming, expensive functions associated with global expansion. For example, a logistics company might provide warehouse space, packing and testing of products, and delivery of the product to the customer - all without any fixed overhead costs to the manufacturer. It provides an excellent method of solving international logistics problems without investing in overseas facilities, technology, and staff.

For an example, visit the site of Neovia (www.neovialogistics.com) which was founded as part of Caterpillar Logistics. Another is the logistics division of UPS (United Parcel Service) at www.ups.com, and, following links to business solutions, to UPS Logistics Group or FedEx Supply Chain Services (www.fedex.com).

3PLs have turned what was simply a problem and a challenge (getting freight moved around the world) into a competitive advantage. Companies that understand how to leverage the strength of these 3PLs can beat out competitors that lag behind. And must of the 3PL services would not be obvious to the foreign sales channel – meaning even if your 3PL warehouse is outsourced, it looks like your own warehouse to your buyers. A great resource for understanding the whole supply chain industry and use of 3PLs is a free website offered by Supply Chain Brain at www.supplychain.com.

• C-TPAT AND CSI

One final note relating to logistics. The U.S. government and foreign governments are addressing the increased security concerns after 9/11 with two programs. The **Customs-Trade Partnership against Terrorism** known as C-TPAC is a voluntary program available to U.S. manufacturers to certify their commitment to best practices in supply chain security. The primary benefit to participating in C-TPAC is to lower the number of cargo inspections when importing goods. Less inspections means faster cargo movements which reduces inventory costs. The second program is the **Container Security Initiative (CSI)** which seeks to identify potentially high-risk freight in foreign ports prior to arriving to the U.S. It also is researching ways to make freight containers 'tamper proof' so that once in the supply chain, dangerous good such as 'dirty bombs' cannot be put into the containers. Both programs are managed by the U.S. Customs and Border Protection (www.cbp.gov).

• NOTES

1. Ho Swee Lin, "Asian Cargo Shippers Batten Down Hatches . . .", The Seattle Times (12 March 1998): C4.

2. The following article has a good detailed discussion of the use of containers in global trade: Al Gibbs, "Very Simply Revolutionary," The News Tribune (Tacoma, WA, 13 October 1996): D1.

3. JuDee Benton is a past president of Nasbite and long-time friend. She helped greatly with this chapter!

Chapter 15

Documentation and Export Compliance

I t will probably come as no surprise that the greatest number of phone calls we receive at our Illinois SBDC International Trade Center are regarding documentation issues. Other export assistance centers relate similar stories. Though documentation questions represent the highest number of calls, they do not represent the majority of the research or assistance time; that tends to be spent on international market research tasks. Documentation issues are not the greatest barriers to export growth, but the very nature of international documentation - that it is unique for each country of destination - makes the task often complicated and confusing. Complying with export regulations can also be confusing.

Fortunately, companies facing international documentation and compliance challenges can utilize numerous outside resources to assist in both understanding the requirements and completing related documents. Outside assistance may be crucial to avoiding delays. However, the key to successfully handling your international documentation and compliance issues, even with outside assistance, is to first understand the basic issues so you are in a better position to manage the process with accurate and timely results.

In this chapter, I will discuss the issue of international documentation and export compliance as it relates to exporting U.S. products. However, in practice, most all of the documents discussed are international documents that are recognized and used by contries worldwide. Figure 15.1 identifies those documents specific to the U.S. I will detail the most common export documents including the NAFTA certificate of origin.

This should provide you with a good working knowledge of the terminology and procedures associated with export documentation. However, export documents can become quite complicated and you are well advised to seek outside assistance in their preparation. From freight forwarders to local trade assistance centers, there are a number of resources available to help you complete export documentation.

Having said that, the exporter, not outside companies, is in the best position to determine the accuracy of these documents. I have seen numerous instances where assumptions were made by outside companies leading to inaccurate export documents. At times this results in minor problems such as using the wrong harmonized code on the shippers export declaration. Other errors, however, such as an inaccurate NAFTA certificate of origin, can be much greater, resulting in severe penalties.

All exporters should learn as much as possible about preparing export documents. To fine tune your export documentation skills, attend documentation workshops offered by local, state, or federal export centers. These workshops are affordable and offer the opportunity to network with local exporters. The U.S Department of Commerce website (www.export.gov) lists links to training events, including webinars and local events. Other resources discussed in Chapter 6 would also be helpful such as GlobleEdge.

• STANDARD DOCUMENTS FOR INTERNATIONAL TRADE

International documentation refers to the paperwork that is required for an international sales transaction. Such documents provide important information that will be used by various interested parties along the path of the shipment from seller to freight companies, import country government, and finally, the buyer. The key information contained in these documents includes:

- Description of the goods
- Mode of transport
- Terms of sale (which party pays for what)
- Value of the goods
- Country of origin for the goods
- Identity of the seller/shipper
- Identity of the buyer
- Terms of payment
- Shipping instructions
- Evidence of shipment
- Compliance with related trade controls

Each international shipment has a certain number of minimum documents. These include: the commercial invoice; a truck, rail, or ocean bill of lading, or air waybill; and in most cases a packing list. Certain countries require a certificate of origin. Some buyers also require an inspection certificate.

The products in the shipment may also dictate any additional documents that may be needed. A phytosanitary or health certificate attests to the good health of agricultural products or animals. If the product is deemed sensitive to security, political, and related concerns of the U.S. government, a validated export license may be required. The buyer also may require additional documents, depending on the country and product, such as a customs invoice or certificate of free sale. In the case of U.S. exports, the Electronic Export Information record should be filed, and any related export license obtained if needed.

A summary of the most common trade documents and their purposes is found in Figure 15.1. The flag shows the two documents unique to U.S. exports.

Figure 15.1 Standard Documents for International Trade

Document	Issued By	Required By	Purpose
Buyer's Request for a Quotation	Buyer	Seller and Buyer	First Step
Pro Forma Invoice	Seller	Buyer	Determines Terms of Sales
Import License	Buyer's Government	Buyer's Government	Export or Import Requirements
Shipper's Letter of Instruction	Seller	Freight forwarder	Establishes shipping terms
Letter of Credit	Buyer's Bank	Seller, Buyer	Payment Terms and Conditions
Commercial Invoice	Seller	Banks, Buyer and Government	Main Document for Entry/Exit (Duties)
Certificate of Origin	Seller	Buyer's Government	Establishes Origin of Goods
Packing List	Seller	Buyer, Buyer's Government	Customs and Inventory Control
Ocean Bill of Lading or Air waybill	Carrier	Buyer, Seller, Government, Bank	Contract of Carriage
Phytosanitary Certificate	Government Agency	Buyer, Buyer's Government	Certified Purity of Ag Products
Health Certificate	Government Agency	Buyer, Buyer's Government	Certifies Health of Animals
Inland Bill of Lading	Carrier	Seller and Trucker	Movement of Goods
Electronic Export Information - EEI	Seller or Freight Forwarder	U.S. Government	Export Control and Data
Insurance and Endorsements	Seller or Freight Forwarder or Insurance Company	Buyer, Seller, Bank	Insures Goods in Carriage
Validated Export License	U.S. Government	U.S. Government	Required for some U.S. Exports
Restricted Article Statement	Seller		Safety in Carriage

How to Prepare Documents

Before discussing specific documents, it is worth mentioning some general issues associated with preparing documents.

Other than preprinted document forms, such as bills of lading, insurance certificates, and certificates of origin, there is no set format for international trade documents. The layout of each document is not important as long as it has some structure and the information is easy to locate. The information contained in the document is critical.

Much of the same information is contained on each document, which often confuses a first-time exporter. This occurs because each document serves a different purpose for a different entity or agency along the chain of the shipment. There are some exceptions. For example, the insurance policy and certificate numbers only appear on insurance documents. Consistency and accuracy is essential. Care needs to be taken to thoroughly complete the documents to reduce the chance of error. In some cases, errors can result in delays and additional costs, especially when a letter of credit is used for payment. Also be aware of the increased documentation requirements when working with letters of credit. These are discussed in the Tips box in this section. Some companies have abandoned the use of abbreviations on their export documents to avoid misunderstandings by the buyer. If you do use abbreviations, such as Incoterms, it is best to spell them out.

Remember that you and your company are accountable for your export documents. You should know how to prepare these documents even if you utilize the guidance and assistance of outside resources. The more knowledge you possess, the less chance for loss. Also be sure you fully understand harmonized codes, discussed in Chapter 3, and Incoterms, highlighted in Chapter 14.

Working with Letters of Credit and Export Documents

When the payment method for a shipment is a letter of credit, it is extremely important to read the letter of credit immediately upon receipt. (Letters of credit will be discussed in more detail in Chapter 16, but they are a very secure method of payment highly favored by international sellers and buyers.) A letter of credit will specify the documents required by the bank in order to receive payment. It will also specify what information needs to be on each document. For example, it is not unusual for a letter of credit to specify that all documents contain the letter-of-credit number.

A letter of credit may only specify a minimum number of required documents, but other documents required by the seller, buyer, or governments should not be ignored. The buyer trusts that the seller will provide the documents required by the letter of credit and any others required. A letter of credit can help you determine what documents are required and what information must be included on the documents.

• BASIC INTERNATIONAL TRADE DOCUMENTS

There are nine documents that form the essential group of documents used in trade as shown in Figure 15.2. As every export is another country's import, these doucments are essentially used by exporters and importers. Each of the nine export documents are discussed in detail in the next section along with the EEI which is required for most U.S. exports. Examples of each document and specific instructions for their completion can be found in Appendix B.

Quotations

The start of the export document process may be a request from a potential buyer for a quotation from the seller. There is no standard format for a quotation.

The purpose of a **quotation** is twofold. First, it confirms the selling price of the goods to the buyer. Second, it clarifies the various costs that the buyer will have to pay in addition to the product costs, such as export packaging, freight, insurance, and special documentation charges. Even if the buyer has a price list from the seller, it still needs to know all the additional costs. Price lists tend to include ex-works terms, meaning the buyer pays all the costs of getting the goods from the seller to the buyer. A quotation completes the pricing exercise so the buyer can determine its landed costs as shown in Chapter 11.

There are instances where a buyer may not request a quotation, especially if the buyer already has experience with the seller and can estimate its own freight, documentation, and related costs. The buyer may have already ordered similar products in the past. The buyer also may request a pro forma invoice instead of a quotation as discussed in the next section. If the request for a quotation comes from a company not known to the seller, the seller may request that the buyer clarify its intentions and company background. In

---

Figure 15.2 The Nine Essential International Trade Documents

Document	Issued by:
1) Quotation	Issued by seller before
2) Pro forma invoice	sale is confirmed
3) Commercial invoice	All generally issued by seller and
4) Packing list	accompany shipment
5) Electronic Export Information (U.S. exports only)	
6) Bill of lading or air waybill	Issued by freight company
7) Certificate of origin	Issued by seller but not always required
8) Insurance certificate	Issued by various parties
9) Draft	Issued by seller's bank but not always required

most cases, a company's international (export) pricing is confidential and should only be disclosed to serious, qualified buyers. If the inquiry originated from an email, it can be extremely difficult to determine its validity. It may be a foreign competitor seeking pricing information.

Format of an international quotation. The challenge of preparing a quotation is ensuring all the required cost items are included. Many of the cost items are readily available to the seller. Other cost items will have to come from outside companies, such as a freight forwarder or banker. It can sometimes be difficult to get all the details together and respond to the buyer within a reasonable time frame.

As a seller, you will need to provide the following information:

- Cost of the goods (such as the sale price to the foreign buyer excluding all other charges; also known as the ex-works price)
- Cost of export packaging in cases where special packaging or pallets is required
- Cost of special labeling, translation, or printing, if required
- Inland freight if the freight forwarder is not arranging the transportation to the port of exit
- Handling charges, inspection or other certificates, or any specific charges important to your quotation

Also, remember to include the bank charges if appropriate, especially if the payment terms are letter of credit.

In addition to those initial cost elements, the freight forwarder will provide a breakdown of its charges, such as freight and the fuel adjustment factor. These specific charges need to be detailed on the quotation. Ask the freight forwarder to put the prices in writing and ask for a validity date for charges so you do not get caught in a freight rate increase.

A sample quotation checklist is included in Appendix B. The sample includes a range of cost elements, many of which will not be applicable for all shipments. However, it presents a complete picture of all the charges that should be factored into preparing a quotation. Some other considerations include:

- *Taxes.* Though Incoterms typically clarify the responsibility for foreign taxes and import duties, not all foreign buyers will be completely aware of the specifics of the particular Incoterm used. Assuming it is not your intention to pay foreign taxes, you may want to add a note such as, "All foreign taxes and import duties shall be paid by buyer."
- *Warranty.* If product warranty is a significant issue for your products, you may want to list the specific warranty offered by your company.
- *Expiration.* If the sales quote is considered a binding offer, it is particularly important to specify how long the pricing is valid.
- *Other limitations.* If your sales quotes tend to be complicated in terms of prod-

uct specifications, technical issues, or other issues that may confuse your buyer and lead to order inaccuracies, consider using wording that limits your liability in terms of accepting any future orders. For example, you may want to clarify the quotation as a nonbinding offer and state that any subsequent purchase order will be subject to acceptance by the seller.

If your company foresees issuing sales quotations frequently, you should seek the assistance of a lawyer to draft a boilerplate sales quotation that meets the specific requirements of your company and its products or services. This is particularly useful if sales orders represent sizeable sums of money.

Pro Forma Invoice

A **pro forma invoice** serves many of the same functions as a quotation. It confirms to the interested buyer the cost of the goods and all other related cost items. Importers will frequently request a pro forma invoice in order to open a letter of credit. Another use of pro formas is to help foreign buyers obtain the necessary import documents, such as import licenses. Pro formas also may take the place of a quotation. The information is similar to that of a quotation, and for some companies will be identical. The format, however, will be different. The distinction between a quotation and a pro forma may only be the fact that a pro forma is a document, whereas the quotation can be a letter, an email, or a fax. Also, because a pro forma has the words *pro forma* affixed to the top of the document, it will be recognized by other users, such as foreign governments, as a specific document.

Accuracy and comprehensive data are the crux of a pro forma invoice. If the pro forma is done correctly, many problems can be avoided, including needless communications, confusion, annoyance, expense, and possibly the loss of the sale.

The following section lists many pertinent items generally included on a pro forma. Detailed instructions for completing a pro forma are shown in Appendix B.

Elements of a pro forma invoice

- The goods. An accurate description of the products should include the specifications, quantity, item, price, extended price, and total.
- Terms of sale. The shipper/seller must determine what terms of sale will be offered. This not only includes the payment terms discussed next, but what costs are included. The terms of sale would also include the Incoterm to identify which freight costs are included in the pricing.
- Terms of payment. The seller determines what type of payment will be required and the terms of that payment. This decision evaluates the risk, competition, cash flow, standards, and client history. Specify all aspects of the terms. For example, if payment is to be a letter of credit, it is important to include: the bank, including the preferred international advising and confirming branch; and the type of letter of credit (advised, confirmed, at sight, etc.) It is also advisable to request a letter of credit validity date. Chapter 16 discusses letters of credit, including suggested wording to use when requesting a letter of credit.

- Validity date. All pro formas must contain a statement which specifies the length of time for which the quote will remain valid. The inclusion of a validity date can prevent losses due to increases in labor prices, materials, and shipping costs.
- Shipping date. It is important for the seller to formally advise the buyer at what point the product can be shipped. This date can be based on the production or processing time or the mode of payment (e.g., shipment 30 days after receipt of an acceptable letter of credit). The buyer of the opening bank may specify this as "last date of sail," "shipment no later than," "shipment by," or "last date of arrival or delivery to."
- Documentation. The pro forma should include the types of supporting documentation that the seller will provide. This also can include any supporting documentation that is required by the buyer, primarily import certificates or licenses.
- Weight/dimensions. This information can be of value to the buyer if the importing country requires this type of data for the issuance of permits.
- Mode of transportation. The pro forma must specify the type of transportation, such as air, ocean, truck, rail, or courier.
- Banking charges or information. This information is applicable to letters of credit or drafts. It is customary to request that the buyer pay these charges.
  Note: This does not always occur, so banking charges should be figured into the original quotation.
- Country of origin. The origin of the goods should be shown in the pro forma. (See this topic under 'commercial invoice'.)
- Other terms.
- The seller's correct name and address
- The seller's pro forma reference number and any buyer references
- Any specific inclusions, such as a specific insurance coverage
- The type of packaging, and/or special packing
- The request for partial shipments and/or transshipments
  Note: If partial shipments or transshipments are required, explain the situation thoroughly to the buyer. Otherwise, partial shipments or transshipments will generally not be allowed.

Commercial Invoice

Once an order is received and you are ready to ship the goods it is time to prepare a **commercial invoice** – which is essentially the sales document. As discussed in the pro forma section, you do not have to use preprinted commercial invoices. As long as you can add notes or extra fields to your existing domestic invoice, you can use it for international orders.

Be aware that there are many additional fields on an international commercial invoice than a domestic one. A quick look at the instructions for a commercial invoice in Appendix B will highlight this point. There are also a number of elements to the invoice that will list information supplied from outside the company, such as the bill of lading number or air waybill number. Attention to detail is important because the commercial invoice is more than just a document between the seller and buyer. It also forms the basis for various decisions along the way, the most important of which is the import duty applied by the customs of the foreign government.

There are a couple of important considerations when preparing a commercial invoice. If the terms of payment are a letter of credit (L/C), be sure to thoroughly read the L/C to highlight any specific requirements of the invoice. For example, it is common that the invoice must show the L/C number and packing marks. The description of goods may need to exactly match those in the L/C. If it does not, the documents can be sent back for modification, which leads to costs and time delays.

Also, research should be done to determine if the destination country has any specific requirements. For example, Latin American countries often require the commercial invoice be completed in Spanish. They also have very specific declarations that must be placed on the invoice. Jordan requires that commercial invoices be legalized by a Jordanian consular official, the cost of which depends on the value of the invoice. The higher the invoice price, the higher the legalization fees! BNA's Export Reference Guide on the Web highlights these issues at www.bna.com.

Commercial invoices for U.S. exports should have an export control statement at the bottom such as, "These commodities licensed by U.S. for ultimate destination _____ (fill in country of destination). Diversion contrary to U.S. law prohibited." The control statement is essentially saying that the shipment is under the control of U.S. law regarding export license requirements. This is true even if the specific shipment did not require an export license, as will be discussed later in this chapter. For example, even if the shipment does not require an export license, it cannot go to an embargoed country - a country that is prohibited from receiving U.S. products. This statement helps protect the exporter should the foreign buyer redirect the shipment to an embargoed country.

There also may be a requirement, either of the destination government or the letter of credit, to place marks on the invoice. Though often misunderstood, marks are simply any labeling that has been applied to each carton. For example, if the address, purchase order, and package number is on each carton, the marks would be listed as:

MARKS:/ AS ADDRESSED
P.O. 1294SWTA
NO. 1/9

Finally, a commercial invoice may also act as a certificate of origin. Often a separate certificate of origin is note required. Instead, all that would be needed is to state the origin of the goods. An example would be: "All the above products are entirely of U.S. origin". More is discussed in the certificate of origin section.

Appendix B contains specific instructions on preparing a commercial invoice.

Packing List

Many international shipments require a packing list, especially those using a letter of credit. It is a good practice to always include one with all shipments. Though you can use the same format you use for your domestic packing list, it will probably have to be adapted to include some extra items. For example, your **packaging list** should include weights and measures and type of package. Foreign government regulations sometimes also require information on the packing list. Ensure that all references to the packing list in other export documents, such as the commercial invoice, are in agreement, including the marks, weights, and especially number of packages. If a packing list is required due to foreign law or a letter of credit, it is a good idea to affix a signature on the packing list. See Appendix B for detailed instructions and a sample form.

The Electronic Export Information (EEI) Filing through AES Direct

The freight forwarder often completes the **Electronic Export Information (EEI)** so you may not be familiar with it. The EEI is a mandatory electronic filing of all U.S. exports (except to Canada) if the shipment value of a single commodity is at least $2,500. (Previously this was known as the Shipper's Export Declaration or SED.) You should be aware that the exporter is legally responsible for the accuracy of the EEI, not the forwarder who prepares it. Since the exporter is liable for the accurate filing of the EEI, it is probably best you learn how to file them. It can also save you money because forwarders charge a fee whereas the U.S. government allows the EEI to be filed at no charge.

A common mistake on the EEI is using an incorrect harmonized code. Exporters are often asked by their foreign buyers to use a different harmonized code for the invoice than the exporters would normally use and then the exporter uses that incorrect classification on the EEI. For example, I work with an exporter of artwork that was asked by one of its buyers to classify the product as educational materials because the import duty would be significantly reduced. This would be wrong. And in either case the EEI does not leave the U.S. so the foreign buyer need not see the classification. Nor is the Schedule B number have to be included on the commercial invoice.

To better understand the EEI and it use, be sure and visit the training videos available on the U.S. Census website at http://www.census.gov/foreign-trade/aes/exporttraining/videos/. They are quick and very information and cover a range of topics beyond the EEI.

When is the EEI required? A declaration is not required for shipments in which the total value of each single harmonized code product category does not exceed $2500. In other words, if you shipped three different types of products, as defined by having different ten-digit harmonized codes, and the value of each product is equal to or less than $2500, the EEI filing is not required. This is true even if the total value of the export invoice is greater than $2500. Similarly, if a shipment contains multiple products (harmonized codes), some of which are valued over $2500 and others less than or equal to $2500, only those items over $2500 need to be listed on the EEI. If an export license is required for the shipment, then the EEI is required regardless of the value of the commodities. Exports for ultimate destination of Canada also do not need the EEI filing unless an export license is required.

Filing the EEI. Exporters (or forwarders working on their behalf) may file the EEI through an online portal called **AES Direct** (aesdirect.gov). The portal is a administered by U.S. Census and in cooperation with U.S. Customs and Border Protection. There is no cost to file EEIs through AESDirect. However, you must be registered user and to become registered requires taking a short quiz after you have completed the online training.

Appendix B contains more information on what is required on the EEI, however the primary information is:

1) Shipment Information: includes a variety of required fields such as:
Origin State
Country of Destination
Departure Date
Conveyance Name (vessel or carrier name)
2) USPPI – U.S. Principal Party in Interest: the person in the U.S. that receives the primary benefit, monetary or otherwise, of the export transaction.
3) Ultimate Consignee - the company receiving the shipment in the foreign country
4) Commodity line: the Schedule B (or in most cases U.S. HTS is also allowed)

When all the information has been entered on a shipment through AES Direct, the system will generate an Internal Transaction Number (ITN). This is your proof that the EEI was filed. The ITN should be obtained before the export occurs. If your forwarder or other entity is filing the EEI, be sure and request they provide you with the ITN for your shipment as the exporter is legally responsible for the filing.

Certificate of Origin

This is one of the most misunderstood international documents which is even more complicated by the enactment of NAFTA and other FTA's – Free Trade Agreements. There are a number of reasons why a certificate of origin is required with the shipment, but the most common is to determine import tariff treatment. The applicable duties applied to imports vary by trade agreements. In some cases, such as trade between NAFTA countries, particular products may be duty-free. However, the same products produced outside of a NAFTA country would incur a duty. For example, a table produced in the U.S. can be shipped to Canada duty-free. A table shipped from China to Canada, however, would have a duty applied.

But what if the same table is shipped first to the U.S. and then shipped to Canada? Does the duty still apply? In fact, if nothing is done to the table other than warehousing it before shipping it to Canada, the duty would apply. But if the table from China was made of unfinished wood, and was given a hand-applied finish in the U.S., can it qualify for duty-free status? Certificates of origin help customs officials determine duties in these situations.

A **certificate of origin** is used to establish the country of origin so when the good reaches its foreign destination, local customs officials can determine the appropriate import duty or other applicable taxes. Some certificates of origin are quite complicated, such as the one for NAFTA. Others are very easy. In fact, in its simplest form, all that is required for a certificate of origin is the country of origin for each good on the commercial invoice (meaning no separate country of origin document). Other countries require that a separate certificate of origin accompany the shipment.

Generic certificate of origin and the chamber of commerce. Depending on the country, a generic certificate of origin is generally acceptable. In exporting guides you will find the statement to the effect, 'No special form of origin certificate is necessary; the general form, as sold by commercial stationers, is acceptable.' This means that the country with this designation does not require that a specific form be used. A manufacturer can purchase blank certificates from any number of suppliers, such as Rapid-Forms or Unz and Co., or desktop publish its own certificate. A sample generic certificate including instructions can be found in Appendix B.

In other cases the certificate must be certified by a chamber of commerce, which can be a complicated. When chamber certification is required, you should contact your local chamber of commerce to determine its procedure. Some require that you provide proof that the goods are indeed of U.S. origin. In other cases, the chamber performs more of a notary function essentially stating that to the best of its knowledge the certificate is accurate based on what it has been told by the shipper. A certificate of origin is not the only document of which a foreign country may require certification. You may find that some countries also request a chamber certify other documents such as a pro forma.)

Differences in the required specifics of a certificate of origin are common and vary by country. Determine what is required by the importing country through a reference guide, your freight forwarder, or a local assistance office. If needed, consult your local chamber of commerce for further assistance.

Specific certificates of origin and consular legalization. In some cases, very specific formats for the certificate must be used. For example, the NAFTA countries, South Africa, and Israel all have unique certificate formats. The NAFTA certificate of origin can be duplicated on a photocopy machine or desktop published by the exporter. For other countries such as Israel, the forms must comply with specific color and size specifications, so it is probably easiest to purchase blank certificate forms from a stationer.

Also be aware that countries sometimes require that their embassy or consulate in the U.S. legalizes certificates of origin. This may also be true of a commercial invoice. This can be expensive if many documents require legalization because the cost not only includes fees but also time lost while attaining the legalization. Expensive handling fees may also be involved if expediter services are required.

Reliable, specific information regarding a certificate of origin is always required. Utilize your export resources, such as your freight forwarder or local assistance centers. They can save you time, trouble, and potentially expensive mistakes. The export.gov website and BNA discussed in Chapter 6 contain guides on each country's requirements.

The NAFTA Certificate of Origin

The NAFTA certificate of origin is probably the certificate to beat all other certificates in terms of complications, difficulty, and potential liability. I have reviewed numerous NAFTA certificate of origin documents and the majority of them had at least one potential problem. And the liability associated with inaccurate certificates is quite high for both the company and the individual that signed the certificates. Penalties for knowingly providing false information can range from $10,000 to $100,000. Companies that consistently make mistakes on the certificates can be eliminated from participating in the NAFTA program. And if a certificate is found not to be valid, the reduced duty would not apply and the local customs authority can impose a higher tariff plus interest and fees.

Despite the potential penalties, companies continue to issue inaccurate certificates, mostly because they don't know better. Fortunately, instances of companies or employees being hit with fines seem to be rare. Nevertheless, it makes sense for companies to be as vigilant as possible in accurately completing the NAFTA certificate of origin. Given the importance of the document and the potential impact on exporters and their NAFTA customers, this section is dedicated to the specifics of this document.

Why all the fuss? When so many countries accept origin certificates that are quite simple, why is the NAFTA certificate so complicated? The answer is part history, part politics. The NAFTA agreement was an outgrowth of the Canadian Free Trade Agreement (FTA) which had its own certificate of origin that served as the basis for the NAFTA certificate. At the time the FTA certificate was developed, no one envisioned it would eventually become one of the most important shipping documents used by U.S. companies. That is the history behind the document.

As for the politics, consider the goal of NAFTA: to eliminate all tariffs between the U.S., Mexico, and Canada. This is quite a political feat considering the fears that existed in the early 1990s regarding potential job losses due to manufacturers moving away from the U.S. once tariffs didn't hamper product flows. One of the most important considerations is the fact that only products manufactured within the NAFTA countries qualify for the zero tariff benefit. As was the case in an earlier example, the negotiators of this agreement did not want Chinese tables to simply enter one NAFTA country and with little to no additional work on the table be exported to another NAFTA country with no tariffs applied. The fundamental purpose of the NAFTA certificate of origin is to ensure that products shipped between NAFTA countries only receive the lower tariff treatment if the products are indeed manufactured in the U.S., Canada, or Mexico.

Defining exactly what is meant by manufactured or produced in a NAFTA country is sometimes difficult. In the Chinese table example, the table was unfinished. Further work was needed to make it into a usable table, but is that enough to qualify it as a NAFTA product so it is entitled to the lower tariffs?

The NAFTA agreement helps answer these types of questions. Once you become familiar with how the agreement works, it actually makes a lot of sense, and as a tax payer you may even be impressed with how the system protects non-NAFTA products from wrongly taking advantage of the agreement.

The basics of how a product qualifies for NAFTA treatment. The NAFTA agreement uses some peculiar terminology that can be somewhat confusing. Because the terminology is used throughout the process of qualifying a product, it must be understood.

The important terminology used in the NAFTA certificate of origin is:

- Preferential treatment. This refers to allowing a product to be imported into a NAFTA country at a lower tariff than would otherwise be assessed. For example, U.S. products into Canada enter with a zero tariff whereas products from Europe into Canada are assessed an import duty. In this respect, the U.S. products receive preferential treatment. The term is used as a substitute for lower or zero tariffs. For example, you could say a U.S.-made table qualifies for preferential treatment which means the U.S.-made table will not incur any import duty when going to Canada.
- Originating materials. This refers to parts, raw materials, components, or finished products that have been determined to be from a NAFTA country. For example, steel manufactured in the U.S., wheat from Canada, or leather from Mexico would be considered originating materials.
- Nonoriginating materials. This refers to parts, raw materials, components, or finished products that are not from a NAFTA country. They are foreign parts and materials such as steel from Japan, wheat from Brazil, or leather from China.
- Transformation. This is the concept that a final product is actually made up of other products which are turned into a final product. A table is actually wood, glue, and some metal hardware that is transformed into a table. The term refers to the fact that products can be classified as manufactured in a particular country if the transformation occurred in that country.
- Regional value content. In simple terms, this is a calculation used to determine in dollars the percentage of originating materials in a product compared to nonoriginating materials. There are two methods used to calculate regional value content: (1) transaction value and (2) net cost.
- Annex 401. This is the part of the NAFTA agreement that describes all the rules that determine how products qualify for NAFTA preferential treatment in the form of no import duties.
- Qualify for preferential treatment. When a product has met the requirements of the rules in Annex 401 it is considered to be produced or manufactured in a NAFTA country and said to qualify for preferential treatment. It can then benefit from reduced import duties.

- Parties. Countries that signed the NAFTA agreement - Canada, Mexico, and the U.S.
- Territory. The geographic boundaries of the parties to the agreement.

Using this terminology, I can now explain how products qualify for preferential treatment. Products basically qualify for one of three reasons:

1. The product itself originates within the territory; for example, corn grown in the U.S., salmon from Alaska, or deer from Canada. Many products have their origin in the territory because they were born, planted, or grown within a NAFTA country. This does not apply to products manufactured in the territory.
2. The product was transformed within the territory; for example, a table manufactured in the U.S. even if the wood was from China. The powerful part of transformation is that the materials don't have to be originating materials. As long as the product is created in the territory, it doesn't matter where the raw materials originate. Sufficient manufacturing occurs in the territory to satisfy the requirements for it to become a qualifying product.
3. The product was assembled using only originating materials; for example, a clock assembled in Mexico using clock parts manufactured in the U.S. Sometimes the parts used in a product are essentially the same as the final product so transformation does not occur.

These three rules are simplified, but they convey the essence of how products qualify under NAFTA for preferential treatment. To understand these three rules, think about your own product and ask the following questions:

- Is it grown in the territory such as a vegetable? Was it born and raised in the territory such as cattle or fish? If so, it will probably qualify under Rule 1.
- If your product is manufactured from other products, are the inputs (bill of materials) primarily made up of products that are not the same as the final product? For example, a table is made from slabs of wood which could also be used for walls, floors, and toys. Clearly a table is transformed from materials that are not a table. These types of products qualify under Rule 2.
- If your product is manufactured from products that are essentially the same as the product itself but all of the input materials come from the territory, then the product will qualify under Rule 3.

If you can see how your products would qualify for NAFTA treatment, then hopefully your products will benefit from the lower tariff rates. You should complete the NAFTA certificate of origin and make it available to your freight forwarders and NAFTA buyers so they can benefit from the lower tariffs. I use the words hopefully qualify because the actual application of these rules is quite complicated and often requires mathematical computations. Detailed work, described in Appendix C, is required. On the other hand, if it appears that your product will not qualify even though it is manufactured in a

NAFTA country, you may not be able to use the NAFTA certificate and your products will have a higher tariff applied to them when imported into a NAFTA country.

Preference criterion. These rules help clarify how products qualify for NAFTA treatment. However, these exact rules are not specifically used. Instead, the NAFTA agreement uses preference criteria - six specific methods to qualify products for preferential treatment. The six criteria are lettered A through E. The first three, A, B, and C, roughly equate to the three rules already discussed. Criteria D, E, and F are not commonly used but were established to accommodate some very specific issues related to particular products. A summary of each criterion is presented in Figure 15.3.

Figure 15.3 Summary of NAFTA Preference Criteria

Criterion	Summary	Example
A	Goods wholly obtained or produced entirely in the territory of one or more of the parties (i.e., goods extracted, harvested, born and raised, hunted, fished, etc.)	Fish, Corn, Deer, Cattle, Sea Coral
B	Transformation - any nonoriginating materials used in the manufacturing process undergo an applicable change in tariff classification set out in Annex 401 as a result of production occurring entirely in the territory of one or more of the parties. This criterion qualifies products that are manufactured from raw materials that clearly are different than the final product. Clarification of what constitutes transformation is detailed in Annex 401.	Table made from planks of wood
C	The good is produced entirely in the territory of one or more of the parties exclusively from originating materials. This criterion is well suited for products that are assembled using parts that were all manufactured in NAFTA countries.	Clock assembled from clock parts manufactured in the territory
D	Used in special circumstances where transformation does not occur because of the harmonized codes of the final product and its relationship with the harmonized code of the raw materials. Application is very limited.	Very uncommon
E	Certain automatic data processing goods and their parts that do not originate in the territory are considered originating upon importation into the territory of a NAFTA country from the territory of another NAFTA country when the most-favored-nation tariff rate of the good conforms to the rate established in Annex 308.1 and is common to all NAFTA countries.	Computer industry products
F	Used in special circumstances in the agricultural industry	Agricultural products

When you look at the summary of the six criteria, it may be obvious which criterion applies to your product. For example, if your product is not grown or hunted, it does not fit Criterion A (though there are some exceptions, of course!). If you manufacture a product that clearly becomes something very different than its raw materials, there is a good chance Criterion B will apply. Once you determine which one of the criteria fits your product, you will use it on the NAFTA certificate of origin to indicate how the product qualified. In order for your goods to receive preferential treatment, they must fully qualify as determined by the specific rules associated with the preference criterion used.

A more detailed analysis of each preference criterion is provided in Appendix C along with specific instructions to complete the NAFTA certificate of origin. There are a number of aspects of the certificate that many find difficult to understand. Area workshops discussing the certificate are valuable opportunities to fine-tune your NAFTA certificate skills and avoid the potential liabilities associated with the improper use of the document.

Insurance Certificate

As discussed in Chapter 15, international shipments should have adequate insurance to insure against product damage or loss and potential liability. It is important that the seller ensures that insurance has been arranged, even if the costs are going to be paid by the buyer. Often the buyer will expect the seller to arrange for the insurance and simply add the costs to the invoice. The insurance certificate may be issued by the seller, the freight forwarder, or an insurance company. Sellers and freight forwarders can issue insurance as part of an open-cargo policy issued by an insurance company. The insurance amount is usually established at CIF value (product invoice value plus insurance plus freight) plus an additional 10 percent.

A sample insurance certificate and its instructions are provided in Appendix B.

Bills of Lading

Bills of lading are issued by the carrier and serve three purposes: (1) as a receipt for the cargo, (2) as a contract for the transportation of the goods, and (3) as a document of title (possession). They are issued by trucking, railroad, and shipping lines (when issued by airlines, the bill of lading is called an air waybill).

In respect to a bill of lading acting as a document of title, there are two types: (1) negotiable and (2) nonnegotiable. A **negotiable order bill of lading** can be bought, sold, or traded while the goods are in transit. Though this may seem dangerous, the flexibility is critical to make international payments methods, such as letters of credit, work properly. The negotiability of the bill of lading means the exporter can endorse the bill over to its bank (who the exporter trusts). This means right of possession passes from the exporter to the domestic bank. The U.S. bank in turn will endorse the bill onward to the foreign buyer's bank, but only when it has the confidence payment will be made. Because the letter of credit will give it that confidence, it endorses the bill over to the foreign bank, which eventually endorses it to the foreign buyer, who finally gets possession of the goods. Each entity in the chain has trust in the next link (which is established through a mechanism such as a letter of credit). With a nonnegotiable bill of lading, the carrier can only deliver the goods to the consignee.

With **order (negotiable) bills of lading**, foreign buyers are typically unable to obtain possession of the goods before payment has been made and the buyer presents the appropriate documents. This gives the exporter some extra protection against the release of the goods prior to payment or the wrong party taking delivery of the goods. Some further clarifications:

- Bills of lading that are nonnegotiable are called **straight bills**. These bills are normally made out to the consignee. Nonnegotiable bills are used when order (negotiable) bills are either not allowed by the foreign government or when the safeguards afforded by order bills are not followed.
- A **clean bill of lading** is issued when the shipment is received by the carrier with no indications of damage or shortages. If damage or shortages are discovered by the carrier, it will be noted on the bill of lading. Such a bill would then be called a **foul bill of lading**.
- An **ocean bill of lading** is a bill of lading issued by an ocean carrier for sea freight.
- An on **board bill of lading** certifies that the cargo has been placed aboard a certain vessel and is signed by the master of the vessel or his representative. Such bills are normally required when a letter of credit is involved.

An example of an ocean bill of lading is provided in Appendix B.

Drafts

A **draft** is an unconditional order (instruction) in writing from one party to another party. In an export, the seller (drawer) orders the buyer (drawee) to pay a fixed amount of money as specified in the draft. The draft is the instrument used to effect the payment when certain payment methods are used, most commonly when the payment method is a letter of credit. Each letter of credit gives specific instructions as to how the draft is to be drawn (created). Appendix B includes a sample draft form and instructions.

Miscellaneous Documents

Beyond the basic nine documents, there are other documents that may be required depending on the product and destination country, for example, health certificates and phytosanitary certificates. Reference guides from BNA or Export.gov, mentioned at the beginning of this chapter are a good source of further details on miscellaneous documents. Two discussed next are inspection certificates and Shipper's Letter of Instruction.

Inspection certificates. Some international shipments require **inspection** of the goods before they leave the manufacturer's or exporter's facility. The requirement for such inspections can depend on the product, the regulations of the foreign government, or even the foreign buyer. In some cases, it may be a condition of the seller and buyer in order to mitigate potential product-related warranty claims.

A number of companies offer inspection services. Some have been mandated as the official inspection company of a foreign government. One such company, Inspectorate is part of Bureau Veritas Commodities (www.bureauveritas.com).

Shipper's Letter of Instruction. If you have your forwarder complete the EEI, you will likely be asked to complete the **Shipper's Letter of Instruction**. It is used to convey key information about the shipment including all the fields required on the EEI. Even if your forwarder is not completing the EEI, they may still request you complete this document in order to have a written understanding of the shipment.

• U.S. EXPORT CONTROLS

Compliance with U.S. export controls has changed dramatically over the past years. Export controls were imposed under the Export Control Act of 1949 during the start of the Cold War. The principal targets of export controls were the former Soviet Union, China, and countries such as North Korea and Vietnam. Products under control of the legislation were primarily high-technology products in an effort to preserve technical superiority of the West in the event of military conflict with its Cold War foes.

Many other countries joined with the U.S. in prohibiting such high-tech products. Essentially, all of the West plus Japan coordinated national export controls through the Paris-based multilateral regime known as the Coordinating Committee (COCOM), now disbanded.

Since the fall of the Berlin Wall and the dismantling of the Warsaw Pact, many of the controls have been removed. I can remember in the mid-1980s, our company needed an export license for all of shipments of computer graphic cards, interface cards used in personal computers to control the display monitor. Getting such licenses was a tremendous barrier, because the paperwork could take weeks. More than once a sale was lost simply because the export license could not be attained fast enough to meet competitive pressure. Today, the same product can be shipped freely with no export license required.

Even though the end of the Cold War has seen the removal of many export controls, the U.S. prohibition of particular products remains, though the emphasis of the controls has changed. Concerns of Cold War differences have changed to concerns about the proliferation of weapons of mass destruction, terrorism, and the disruption of regional stability. This includes a heightened control of any products used in chemical and biological weapons manufacturing.

What is the impact on a U.S. business? Essentially if your products have the potential for use as weapons of mass destruction, tools of terrorism, or products that can disrupt regional stability, you may find that your products will require an export license. In some cases, your product may not receive approval for export. The emphasis now is less on products and more on end-uses of exported items and technology. Your products do not have to feature state-of-the-art technology to require a license. Controls may also apply to medium- and low-level technology. It is the potential use of the technology that is questioned.

What Is Controlled by U.S. Export Controls?

The U.S. government essentially has three main concerns relating to the regulation of exports:

1) **Who Imports**: there are individuals and companies that either may not purchase goods or services from the U.S., or to do so requires prior-approval as in a valid export license.
2) **What is exported**: there are technologies, products, and defense/military articles that if improperly exported pose a risk to U.S. national security interest.
3) **Where exports are going**: regardless of the 'who' or the 'what', the U.S. also restricts exports to particular countries or regimes.

So as you think about U.S. export controls, they essentially control the who, what, and where of the export process. For many companies, it is only the 'who' part that affects them as the vast majority of U.S. exporters do not have products that are controlled, nor do they want to export to the 'countries of concern' such as North Korea.

The other important think to know about U.S. export controls is that they really are 'controls', not an absolute stopping of exports. Meaning even if your products do fall under export controls, you very well may be able to export them – you just need permission by way of a valid export license.

The Four Key U.S. Agencies for Export Controls

There are four U.S. government agencies that play the most significant role in export controls. Following is a short summary. Note that these roles are not absolute and other agencies have roles in controlling exports. However, in trying to understand at a big-picture level, the summary in Figure 15.4 may be helpful.

Figure 15.4. Four Key U.S. Agencies for Export Controls

Government Agency	Bureau or Program	What They Do
U.S. Department of Commerce	Bureau of Industry and Security (BIS)	Controls exports of products/technology and lists of individuals and companies controlled.
U.S. Department of the Treasury	Office of Foreign Assets Control (OFAC)	Enforce trade sanctions to countries and individuals
U.S. Department of State	The Directorate of Defense Trade Controls (DDTC)	Controls defense / military articles through the The International Traffic in Arms Regulations (ITAR)
U.S. Customs and Border Protection (CBP)	No specific program – whole agency	Imports (border security) & Exports (AES Direct)

1) U.S. Department of Commerce
Bureau of Industry and Security (BIS) www.bis.doc.gov.

BIS has two primary roles: 1) to control the export of technology and non-military products that if improperly exported could pose a threat to U.S. national security; and 2) to control the exports to specific individuals or companies for which BIS has a concern. Of all the U.S. export controls, it is those controlled by BIS that affects everyone. That is because all exporters must comply with the requirement to ensure their products or services are not sold (without approval) to the individuals and companies controlled by BIS.

To understand how to comply with BIS regulation, we must first discuss some important terminology:

Export Administration Regulations (EAR): The **EAR** is the set of authorizing regulations under which BIS operates. You will sometimes hear the question: Does your product fall under the EAR? The question is trying to determine if a company's products are such that they are controlled by BIS.

Export Control Classification Number (ECCN): Those products that are controlled under the EAR are given an **ECCN**. The ECCN is not the same as the harmonized code. ECCNs are strictly used within the context of U.S. export controls and are structured differently. Note that defense article, guns, munitions, etc. are not covered by the BIS but by the State Department. All ECCNs have 5 characters all starting with a number. For example, the ECCN for handcuffs is 0A982:

0A982 Restraint devices, including leg irons, shackles, and handcuffs; straight jackets, plastic handcuffs; and parts and accessories, n.e.s. Reason for control: CC.

Commerce Control List (CCL): This is where you find if an ECCN exists for your product. The CCL includes an alphabetical index which is probably the best place to start. Don't be surprised if your product is not on the list as the majority of U.S. exports are not. If your product is not on the CCL than your default ECCN is **EAR99** and you do not need an export license. The CCL may be found at www.ecfr.gov and select Title 15: Commerce and Foreign Trade, then Part 774. Or the link is off the BIS website.

Commerce Country Chart: Once you have your ECCN you have to determine if an export license is required in order to export. The **Commerce Country Chart** lists each country and then indicates when an export license is required. If an 'X' appears under the column relating for the 'reason for control' for your ECCN, then a license is required.

But what is the 'reason for control'? Refer back to the 0A982 ECCN above and you will see following the description is the 'the reason for' CC which stands for crime control. There are a number of 'reason for control' including CB: Chemical and Biological Weapons; NS: National Security; NP: Nuclear Nonproliferation; and AT: Antiterrorism. Within each category is most often a 'column number' such as CC1 or CC1 for Crime Control column 1 and 2. When you find your ECCN it will also show your reason for control and column number. Using that you can determine if an export license is required for the importing country. Not all countries have the same restrictions. So if an export license is needed to say Argentina, it may not be needed when exporting to Australia.

Simplified Network Application Process Redesign (SNAP-R): If you need a valid export license, you request it through **SNAP-R**. This is a secure website which allows you to upload not only the license request but any related documents. SNAP-R can also be used to request BIS confirm if an ECCN classification is correct.

Lists to Check: As funny as it may sound, the official site to search for individuals or companies (parties) that are of concern to BIS, is to review the 'lists to check' website at BIS. The **Lists to Check** is actually a number of separate lists including the Denied Persons List, Unverified List, and the Debarred List. BIS combines these into one single file to make finding companies, individuals, and addresses easier.

To making search the Lists to Check even more accurate and faster, private companies offer subscription services that can even interface with your order software. An example is Visual Compliance (www.ecustoms.com). This process is known as **denied parties screening** or **restricted parties screening**. The service is not as expensive as you may think and even allows for batch screening by uploading your current customer list.

Complying with BIS Regulations

Essentially the process of complying with BIS regulations is two-fold: First, confirm your product is not on the CCL. If it is you must use the Commerce Country Chart to determine on a country-by-country basis when an export license will be required. Secondly, for all exports, you must confirm that the buyer in not on the Lists to Check. If they are, you need a license to sell to that buyer. The license may or may not be approved.

One other issue to consider is **deemed exports**: this is when technology otherwise covered by the EAR is released to foreign nationals while in the U.S. – meaning foreign visitors or students. An example would be a company hosting visitors from overseas in their facility and showing technical specification, blueprints, or even publically discussing technology otherwise control. This 'release' of the technology is deemed an export and would require a license before allowing its release. For this reason some company have a policy of no non-U.S. visitors beyond a certain part of their facility. Similarly U.S. colleges and universities have to be very careful about research activities of foreign students that may violate EAR regulations.

Export Management System (EMS): Companies seeking to be aligned with best practices in complying with export controls are advised to develop an **export management system (EMS)**. Though the name implies some type of technology system it is not.

It is simply taking the time to document policies and procedures a company takes to remain compliant with export controls. As stated by the BIS website (www.bis.doc.gov); "An Export Management System (EMS) is an optional compliance program that companies may implement, in order to ensure compliance with the EAR and to prevent sales to end-users of concern. Establishing an EMS can greatly reduce the risk of inadvertently exporting to a prohibited end-use/user." The website goes to offer examples of steps a company would take to develop their EMS including staff training, assessment of the company's knowledge relating to export controls, and writing down their policies and procedures in an export compliance manual.

Red Flags: Related to the issue of best practices in export compliance is the issue of **red flags**. These are circumstances an exporter may discover as they export. As summarized in the box 'Red Flag Indicators' examples are: an unusual freight route requested by the importer; vague responses to questions about how the product will be used; and buyer seems very unfamiliar with industry or products. The idea behind red flag indicators is U.S. companies need to have staff trained to recognize these flags which may indicate the buyer is attempting to circumvent U.S. export controls.

2) U.S. Department of the Treasury
Office of Foreign Assets Control (OFAC) - www.treasury.gov

It is the role of OFAC within the U.S. Treasury to enforce U.S. trade sanctions. By the way, it is worth pointing out the at first glance one might think the U.S. State Department enforces sanctions. But no; U.S Treasury does. As we'll see next, the U.S. State Department handles exports relating to defense and military products. Yet you'd think that would be the U.S. Department of Defense! It can all be a bit confusing. The OFAC website summarizes their primary goals and activities:

"The Office of Foreign Assets Control (OFAC) of the US Department of the Treasury administers and enforces economic and trade sanctions based on US foreign policy and national security goals against targeted foreign countries and regimes, terrorists, international narcotics traffickers, those engaged in activities related to the proliferation of weapons of mass destruction, and other threats to the national security, foreign policy or economy of the United States. OFAC acts under Presidential national emergency powers, as well as authority granted by specific legislation, to impose controls on transactions and freeze assets under US jurisdiction. Many of the sanctions are based on United Nations and other international mandates, are multilateral in scope, and involve close cooperation with allied governments." *(http://www.treasury.gov/about/organizational-structure/offices/Pages/Office-of-Foreign-Assets-Control.aspx accessed July 20, 2013.)*

The U.S. embargo against Cuba is a well-known example of a sanction enforced by OFAC. Notice in the excerpt above, sanctions are against both countries and regimes (such as a military dictator). Sanctions are not necessarily an absolute embargo against trade with a country or regime. It just means that trade restrictions are in place. For example some medical and food products may be exported to Cuba if approved by OFAC.

Red Flag Indicators www.bis.doc.gov

**The U.S. Department of Commerce Bureau of Industry and Security
Red Flag Indicators of Potentially Inappropriate End-Use, End-User,
or Destination**

- The customer or its address is similar to one of the parties found on the Commerce Department's [BIS] list of denied persons.

- The customer or purchasing agent is reluctant to offer information about the end-use of the item.

- The product's capabilities do not fit the buyer's line of business, such as an order for sophisticated computers for a small bakery.

- The item ordered is incompatible with the technical level of the country to which it is being shipped, such as semiconductor manufacturing equipment being shipped to a country that has no electronics industry.

- The customer is willing to pay cash for a very expensive item when the terms of sale would normally call for financing.

- The customer has little or no business background.

- The customer is unfamiliar with the product's performance characteristics but still wants the product.

- Routine installation, training, or maintenance services are declined by the customer.

- Delivery dates are vague or deliveries are planned for out-of-the-way destinations.

- A freight forwarding firm is listed as the product's final destination.

- The shipping route is abnormal for the product and destination.

- Packaging is inconsistent with the stated method of shipment or destination.

- When questioned, the buyer is evasive and especially unclear about whether the purchased product is for domestic use, for export, or for re-export.

The key issue to know about OFAC controls is that they apply to not only the U.S. exporter, but to agents and distributors as well. Meaning if you have any indication the ultimate destination is not your agent or distributor's country, you must make every effort to ensure they are not attempting to circumvent OFAC controls. If you are in any doubt, always seek assistance either by contacting OFAC directly, or work with your nearest U.S. Export Assistance Center as U.S. Commercial Service specialists are cross-trained on export control issues.

3) U.S. State Department of State
The Directorate of Defense Trade Controls (DDTC) – www.pmddtc.state.gov

The U.S. State Department, through the DDTC, controls the exports of defense, military, and munitions articles. If it happens you manufacture such products, you will likely already be familiar with their role. As these products are also regulated within the U.S., it will be no surprise they are also controlled when exported.

However, more products are controlled by the DDTC than may be obvious. The regulations that control these products is known as **ITAR – International Traffic in in Arms Regulations**. When a product is controlled by ITAR we say it is 'subject to ITAR'. What may be surprising to some is that products otherwise not seen as 'defense' articles, say a motor, but that has been modified specifically for defense use, is likely subject to be subject to ITAR. Meaning in the case of the motor, if as requested by the U.S. Army is modified for their use, will probably be controlled. This is because products otherwise not subject to ITAR controls, but modified for defense use, then becomes subject to ITAR. Any company that is not sure if their products are subject to ITAR may request a formal decision from the DDTC – known as a **commodity jurisdiction**.

It is critical to know if your products are subject to ITAR not only because you must obtain a valid license in order to export them, but also because if you manufacture product subject to ITAR controls, you must register with the DDTC. This is the case even if you do not export those products. So in the motor example, even if the company was only selling to the U.S. Army within the U.S. and not exporting, it would still have to register.

As with OFAC, being compliant with ITAR regulations can be somewhat difficult. Seek advice if you believe you are in any way associated with ITAR regulated products or services.

4) U.S. Customs and Border Protection – www.cbp.gov

Though U.S. Customs and Border Protection is best known for protecting U.S. borders and collecting import duties, they also play a role in exports. The CPB helps maintain the AES Direct system along with U.S. Census and other federal agencies. But another important role somewhat related, is they help protect you from the illegal import of your goods, meaning if someone has violated your trademark or patent within a product and attempts to export those products to the U.S., you can have CPB prevent them from entering the U.S. This program is known as recordation.

Chapter 16

Financial Risk, Payment Methods, and Trade Finance

Nothing worries an exporter more than the prospect of shipping an export order, not receiving payment from the foreign buyer, and facing the prospect of collecting a bad accounts receivable from thousands of miles away. Whether it's a natural dislike for collecting bad debts or the confusing nature of the process, the issue of international financial risk can be an ongoing challenge.

Financial matters are often at the forefront of exporters' concerns. At the International Trade Center at Bradley University, I hear all their concerns. How will I get paid? What security is there for me? How can I fund the working capital? Will the bank loan money against the letter of credit?

Once I worked with a local manufacturer on a bid for a large infrastructure project in the Middle East. Its portion of the bid was nearly $1 million which was quite a large order for the firm. It knew its product and pricing was competitive and it was very excited about the opportunity to bid. However, issues regarding the payment terms generated the most emailing back and forth between the manufacturer and its overseas representative. I also acquired assistance from local resources including an international bank (advising on terms), the Small Business Administration (advising on working capital opportunities), and ExIm (advising on the potential for foreign receivables insurance). It's no wonder a small exporter can get confused in this process.

Sometimes international finance takes creativity. For example, I remember my shock when my German distributor suggested purchasing its $250,000 orders on a credit card! I later found this practice was not uncommon. At the time, I could only envision what our company's controller would say regarding paying the commission to the credit card company or bank. Fortunately, the credit card company offered an attractive rate to process each payment of $250,000 and we in turn offered a discount to the German distributor for what was effectively cash payment. The situation worked out perfectly and our company avoided the nagging problem of trying to accommodate the distributor's rapid sales growth and our somewhat conservative credit policy.

Like any good sales and marketing representative, I hate conservative credit policies. "Why can't we offer open accounts?" I repeatedly asked more than one controller. With time and experience, I have begun to appreciate the real issue behind these policies - risk. The financial risk associated with a company that expands internationally is different from that of a company with only domestic business. I begin this chapter with a discussion about international financial risk and its components because it is important to understand the basis for the risk before the tools used to solve risk, such as payment methods, can be discussed. After defining the risks, I will address specific tools and solutions for each risk. I will detail various international payment methods including a letter of credit. This chapter ends with the topic of other international financial issues such as foreign receivable insurance and long-term financing.

International finance is not overly difficult if you utilize resources. There are three critical partners: (1) your bank, (2) your local trade resources, and (3) the federal government. They, in turn, can lead you to other resources. Your bank ultimately will do most of the work. If your local bank lacks the international experience to fully support your international growth, you may need to push them or farm out some of the business. Your local trade resources are important because they can train and assist you through the initial steps. Finally, the federal government is important because it has the financial strength to offer products such as foreign credit insurance.

• INTERNATIONAL FINANCIAL RISK

All business has some financial risk. Domestic business contains financial risk, as evidenced by the numerous support services designed to assist companies reduce that risk. The U.S. has a tremendous infrastructure that helps reduce financial risk, including a developed financial institution network, services that report on a company's risk and operations, a common currency, and a legal system that protects the rights of injured parties.

However, internationally the landscape changes dramatically. No longer is a reliable infrastructure in place for all markets. Credit reporting can be slow, incomplete, and expensive. There is no common currency. And legal systems vary as greatly as the currencies, at least in terms of jurisdictions. With all these considerations, international finance can easily worry an exporter!

Incomplete International Data

One of the main reasons companies face greater risk when they go global is that decisions often must be made using incomplete information. Unlike the wealth of information available about U.S. companies, company background information abroad is not readily available. This is changing as companies such as Dun & Bradstreet (www.dnb.com) and Coface (www.coface-us.com) offer credit information on international buyers. And there is no question that these services are faster, cheaper, and more reliable than a few years ago. But these services are only as good as the infrastructure and local business and government protocols allow them to be. For example, U.S. financial disclosures and filings are available almost immediately electronically. This is not always the case in other countries. Even when data is available, comparability is always an issue. If foreign financial statements are denominated in local currency (the currency of the foreign buyer), some translation must be made. But at what rate? Today's rate, or the rate when the company made its sales, or the rate when the company acquired its assets?[1]

However, if you focus on the lack of company data you miss an even larger issue involving the financial strength (and risk) of the foreign buyer's country. In the U.S., we generally do not worry that a customer will not pay because of problems with the economy. Yet overnight currency devaluation, government imposed currency controls, and hyperinflation can all have an immense impact on a foreign buyer's ability to pay. And none of these factors can reliably be predicted. Even armed with the best indicators, companies have to make decisions facing some important unknowns.

Greater Likelihood of Procedural Errors

International transactions are more complicated than domestic transactions no matter how experienced the seller is. The fact that international trade involves trade between two countries means the involvement of two legal systems, two governments, and two cultures and ensures the potential for error. For example, I remember assisting a manufacturer with an order to Australia. The container had already left the U.S. when the manufacturer wanted to review its documentation. I asked about insurance and the client replied, "I don't worry. I assume the Australian buyer is liable so I tell the freight forwarder to price the sea freight without insurance." Due to the client's misconception about insurance, the goods were en-route uninsured. I explained that the situation can be financially disastrous. Should the ship encounter weather problems and dump some freight containers overboard in an attempt to save the ship, the exporter would incur the costs. Under the little known precept of general average, if a ship's crew takes steps to save the ship resulting in the damage of goods, the cost of the loss is shared by the owners of all goods on board. The ship's owner is not liable. With that uninsured container out on the seas between the U.S. and Australia, the manufacturer was risking not only loss of its goods, but the potential cost of the loss of other exporter's goods. Not a comforting thought.

Events Outside the Company's Control

Even with foreign buyer creditworthiness and perfect export documentation, exporters still face financial risk. Unless steps are taken to protect that risk, exporters can encounter obstacles resulting in a monetary loss. One of these risks is currency devaluation. If a sale was denominated in the foreign currency, profits may be lost or a loss incurred if the foreign currency is devalued and the manufacturer receives fewer dollars than expected. If the sale is denominated in dollars to avoid foreign exchange risk there still may be a problem if the foreign currency is devalued. After the devaluation, the foreign buyer will have to pay more in local currency to buy the same number of dollars and if the devaluation is significant it could lead to the buyer's inability to pay.

Company Financials Contain Risk

A final contributor to a company's financial risk is the issue of actually accessing that financial risk. Companies may find that when they present their financial statements to U.S. banks to obtain a loan, the banks may treat the foreign receivables as such high risks that they are effectively worthless. This would reduce the amount of the loan because the bank will reduce the value of the accounts receivable on the balance sheet by the amount of foreign receivables. Reducing the receivables lowers the collateral available to the bank. The bank does not want to accept as collateral something that could be impossible to convert to cash if the loan is liquidated.

A company may be successful in expanding its international sales, but unsuccessful in converting those sales into greater financial strength. Clearly this depends on the terms offered by the company and the profile of its international sales. Companies offering unsecured open accounts to foreign buyers clearly have more financial risk than those that offer only cash-in-advance. Likewise, a company that is overly reliant on one international country or region, or has a sporadic international sales pattern, will have higher risk. Financiers are still reluctant to rely on any financial stability offered by international sales, even for companies with strong patterns of international success. This is especially true for small or mid-size companies. Banks would rather rely on domestic success.

What can small to mid-size global companies do? Facing the valid concerns of banks, companies must mitigate these concerns by seeking tools and solutions available to improve their financial strength. This is why federal programs such as the U.S. Small Business Administration and ExIm Bank's Export Working Capital Program are so important to U.S. companies trading internationally. These programs provide government-backed guarantees to banks to counter their international financial risk concerns. The first step in addressing these concerns is to define the specific financial risks companies face when going global.

• INTERNATIONAL TRANSACTIONS: THREE RISKS

When companies begin to expand internationally, their initial entry is typically via export sales. If those sales are generated using indirect export methods such as an export management company or broker, the company faces little to no international financial risk. Though the level of risk depends on the specifics of the contract between the manufacturer and its indirect partner, generally the EMC absorbs all international risk as part of its contractual obligation. This is one of the advantages of using indirect exporting as a method of growing internationally.

However, as companies grow, they invariably move to direct exporting. This is when international financial risk increases. In exchange for greater control and feedback, the company must prepare for increased risk. Despite the increased risk, companies successfully expand internationally using techniques to mitigate that risk. In fact, many companies eventually increase their international involvement to include foreign direct investment, giving them even more control and feedback and additional financial risk. The risks of foreign investment are offset by the advantages as discussed in Chapter 23.

Figure 16.1 Summary of International Financial Risk Types, Sources to Assess Each Risk, and Techniques to Lower Risk

	Commercial Risk	Political Risk	Foreign Exchange Risk		
			Transaction	Economic	Translation
Source of Risk	Foreign buyer's inability to pay invoices due to internal problems	Foreign buyer's inability to pay invoices due to government action	Change in exchange rate between seller and buyer resulting in loss on a particular transaction for one of the parties	Over time, seller may become non-competitive due to movements in the exchange rate	Loss resulting from restating the values of assets and liabilities on foreign denominated balance sheets
Sources of Data to Assess Risk	Public sources: U.S. Dept.of Commerce International Company Profile Report Private sources: Dun & Bradstreet, Coface, etc.	Public sources: National Trade Data Bank / Export.gov (Country Commercial Guides, Country Background Reports, etc.) Private sources: Dun & Bradstreet International Risk and Payment Review	Risk tied specifically to the two currencies involved in the sale for a specific period of time. Company must develop an internal view of the potential exchange rate movement between the two currencies using a variety of public and private sources including the federal governments, private research services, and banks.	Company must develop a long-term internal view of the potential exchange rater movements of the currencies for all international markets using a variety of public and private sources including the federal governments, private research services, and banks.	Total exposure must be quantified by first analyzing balance sheet to identify specific exposures and then comparing to internal forecasts of future exchange rate movements. (continued)

Figure 16.1 Continued

	Credit Risk	Political Risk	Foreign Exchange Risk		
			Transaction	Economic	Translation
Techniques to Lower Risk	Match payment terms with identified risk: the higher the risk, the greater the use of secured terms. Foreign receivables insurance from ExIm.	Match payment terms with identified risk: the higher the risk, the greater the use of secured terms. Foreign receivables insurance from ExIm.	Hedging techniques such as netting and forward contracts	Company's international strategy must be flexible enough to deal with long-term foreign exchange movements. Company can diversify sales markets and potential through sourcing and manufacturing locations.	Nettings, swaps

What are the international financial risks associated with international transactions tions? There are three that should concern companies going global: (1) commercial risk, (2) political risk, and (3) foreign exchange risk. Details of each risk are summarized in Figure 16.1.

Commercial Risk

The risk most often recognized with any transaction is **commercial risk** - the ability or inability of your customer to pay the receivable in full and on-time. It is also known as credit risk. A foreign buyer may be unable to pay its supplier for any number of reasons including lack of sales, poor profitability, cash flow challenges, or delays with the receivables from its own sales.

There is no credit risk associated with a transaction if no credit is extended. For example, if the payment terms are cash in advance or a credit card is used, the invoice is paid prior to shipping and no risk is created. (Commercial risk is also the risk that a foreign partner breaks a contract.)

Political Risk

Unlike domestic sales, international transactions always contain some element of **political risk** - the inability of your customer to pay the receivable in full and on time due to government action. Political risk is also known as **country risk**. The level of political risk is generally associated with the political stability and outlook of the government of the foreign buyer. Examples include the risk of war, kidnapping, or significant economic shocks that could affect exporters such as a delay of payment. Political risk also includes the risk of **expropriation** (government takes over the assets of a private company). Political risk is related to **sovereign risk** – the risk of a foreign government breaking a contract or not paying a receivable.

Foreign Exchange Risk (FX Risk)

Probably the best known risk specifically associated with international sales is **foreign exchange (FX) risk** - a change in the foreign exchange rate from the time the sales price was established and accepted to when payment is made. Whenever the exchange rate changes, it impacts either the seller or the buyer. From the standpoint of a U.S. export sale, if the sales price is denominated in U.S. dollars, the risk is placed on the foreign buyer. If the sales price is denominated in the local currency of the foreign buyer, the risk is placed on the U.S. seller. This type of FX risk is called **transaction risk**.

It is a common misunderstanding that if a U.S. exporter prices its products in U.S. dollars there is no foreign exchange risk. From the perspective of the U.S. exporter, this is technically true. However, there is always foreign exchange risk with any transaction involving two currencies (unless the currencies are pegged to each other and effectively become the same currency, such as the Bermuda dollar, but even then some low level risk is still implied). What many U.S. companies fail to recognize when they price their products in U.S. dollars is that they are simply pushing the FX risk onto their foreign buyers or foreign consumers. Unless the risk is removed through hedging techniques, someone has the risk associated with movement in exchange rates.

The decision as to which party, the seller or the buyer, absorbs this risk is a significant strategic decision and must be made as a part of the whole international pricing strategy that was detailed in Chapter 11. Always understand that unless steps are taken to remove the risk, one party to the transaction has FX risk. This may result in a profit or a loss depending on the movement. It can also lead to higher prices and potentially decreased export sales.

Though each international transaction contains an element of foreign exchange risk, there are two other FX risks that develop over time: (1) economic risk and (2) translation risk.

Economic risk. This FX risk results from the potential for an international company to become noncompetitive due to changes in the exchange rate between its base of operations and that of its customers. For example, a company that manufactures product in the U.S. consisting mostly of U.S.-sourced materials may initially be very successful internationally if foreign buyers find that the products are priced competitively in their local market. However, if the value of the dollar increases (appreciates), this would make the company's product more expensive to foreign customers. When the dollar's strength increases, it takes more of a foreign currency to purchase the same amount of dollars.

Thus, **economic risk** is associated with a company's ability to be competitive in the face of changes in the exchange rate between its home currency and that of its buyers. This is particularly significant if the exchange rate movement is not equal for all competitors in a specific foreign market. For example, a U.S. manufacturer selling into the U.K.

during times of a strengthening dollar will face competitive pressure because their products will be more expensive than those produced locally. However, sales may remain strong if the U.S. manufacturer's only competition is from another U.S company. If its primary competition comes from Japan and the yen was depreciating against the British pound, the U.S. manufacturer may experience a dramatic reduction in export sales to the U.K. The depreciating yen makes the Japanese competitor's products cheaper while the strengthening dollar makes the U.S. products more expensive. Any analysis of the impact of economic risk must take into account the exchange rate movements between the currencies of all exporters in the foreign market.

A final concern of economic risk is the prospect that a company will become so dependent on one particular region or country that long-run exchange rate movements have a disproportionately strong impact on the company. For example, if a U.S. company's international sales were primarily targeted to one country, and the FX rate changed over time to the disadvantage of the U.S. company, it may find the all of its international sales are affected. This could impact the viability of the international department, if not the entire company. Thus, companies must remain diversified in their international market mix to help alleviate the potential of such economic risk.

Translation risk. When a company makes a foreign sale or a purchase from a foreign supplier, the specific sale or purchase contains transaction risk. Over time, as the company continues to conduct international business, its balance sheet may reflect a considerable level of foreign denominated assets and liabilities. When the financial statements are prepared, these assets and liabilities must be translated into U.S. dollars to make the financial statements readable. The losses or gains that can result from restating the values of these assets and liabilities is called **translation risk**. Unlike transaction risk, translation risk encompasses all of the company's foreign exchange risk exposure - both assets and liabilities. Translation risk is significant to outside users of the financial statements such as lenders and shareholders.

• MINIMIZING INTERNATIONAL FINANCIAL RISK

Having discussed the types of financial risks facing companies as they expand globally, international expansion may seem too risky. Fortunately, there is plenty of help to minimize each specific risk - commercial, political, and foreign exchange. The key is to first identify the risk and then take steps to minimize that risk. Successful companies can actually turn their effective management of financial risk into a competitive advantage over competitors who shy away from risk. Rather than backing away from the risk, investigate the following techniques to see which may be useful for your company. Discuss these with your bank and other international resources so you are aware of any specific programs of support that may be unique to your location. (Some states offer specific financing options tied to export development.) Above all, do not ignore these risks or make the mistake of thinking they cannot affect your company.

Minimizing Commercial Risk

The financial risk associated with a particular transaction is by far the most straightforward risk to minimize because the risk can be clearly identified - an exact amount for an exact period between two parties. Foreign exchange economic risk assessments are never straightforward because they require assessing the future economic outlook for one or more countries. By comparison, commercial risk is relatively easy to identify. The U.S. seller knows how much money is involved, when it is to be paid, the identity of the foreign buyer, and the currencies involved.

Perhaps it is the relatively simple nature of commercial risk that leads many companies to believe the answer is to push the risk onto their buyers by requiring payment in advance or letters of credit. (Letters of credit are payment contracts between two banks and are considered low-risk payment options.) Evidence from my work at the International Trade Center indicates that the majority of companies conduct all their international sales via these two secure methods. Such a strategy is understandable: payment in advance or L/Cs eliminate commercial risk. Both are secure methods of payments that guarantee payment to the seller.

However, is this the best way to eliminate commercial risk? For first-time exporters and companies in their initial stage of global expansion, it probably is the best method. Requiring payment in advance or the use of L/Cs is an accepted way to do business internationally. However, a more aggressive strategy that utilizes other payment methods may provide a competitive edge and lead to increased sales. If a company continues to insist on prepayment or L/Cs it risks losing sales and market share to a more aggressive competitor who may be offering open accounts.

Moving beyond payment in advance and L/Cs - open account. How does a company decide when to be more aggressive and move beyond requiring payment in advance or L/Cs? It will probably first happen because foreign buyers will continually press for other options. Prepayment is the most restrictive because it offers no protection to the buyer and creates a cash flow burden. When payment is required in advance, the buyer has to have the cash available weeks before it receives the product. L/Cs are slightly better because the buyer has greater security against paying without receiving the product. However, the buyer still has to effectively prepay for the shipment because the bank will require a deposit of the money in order to open an L/C, or attach to a line of credit if the buyer has such a line in place. In both cases, the buyer is at a significant disadvantage. An aggressive exporter will understand this and explore other options.

Moving beyond payment in advance and L/Cs requires the ability to assess the specific risk associated with a transaction. Even with strong pressure from foreign buyers, an exporter would be foolish to loosen its credit policy without some protection or confidence that the foreign buyer is creditworthy.

As shown in Figure 16.2, there are both public and private sources of data to determine the credit background of a foreign buyer. These sources can be used to determine if you should offer open account - shipments with no guarantee in place other than stopping future shipments if payment is not paid.

If you are already using credit reporting services to determine the credit policies

---

Figure 16.2 Sources of Data to Assess Commercial Risk

Public/International Company Profile (ICP)
This report is available from the U.S. Department of Commerce Foreign Commercial Service and comprises information compiled by staff located in foreign embassies and consulates. At a reasonable cost, the ICP provides details on foreign companies including bank and trade references, personnel, product lines, financial data, sales volume, local reputation, and market outlook. Beyond background details, the report also may include recent news items, the company's U.S. relationships, activities of prominent owners, and operational problems. Because the ICP is specifically developed for the use of U.S. companies seeking to establish closer links with a foreign buyer, the commercial specialist who develops the report will offer his or her recommendation on whether you should extend credit and on what basis. The advantages of ICP are its custom format and relatively low cost, though this service can take between 30 and 45 days. For more information, contact your local trade assistance center or your closest U.S. export assistance center.

Private Credit Reporting
Many companies offer credit reporting services on foreign companies though the information is not as well developed as that on U.S. companies. For example, Dun & Bradstreet (www.dnb.com) offers a number of international products. The advantage of private credit reporting is its speed and convenience - reports are available over the Internet or by fax. They also can be expensive if purchased individually. Most suppliers offer quantity discount options, which can make the reports much more affordable, though it can be argued the data is so important that price shouldn't be a concern. Other companies offering international credit reports include Coface (www.coface-us.com) and GraydonAmerica (www.graydonamerica.com). Your bank or accounting firm also may be a source of foreign buyer credit information.

for domestic customers, you will probably find their international counterparts quite similar. Establishing the credit policy for an international buyer is a similar process involving an analysis of its financial history, current financial status including bank references, and a review of the credit levels offered by other suppliers. You can then set a credit limit. The supplier of the credit information, such as Dun & Bradstreet, also can offer assistance in evaluating credit reports. Assistance also should be sought from the international department of your banking institution.

Obtaining foreign receivables insurance. One of the most powerful techniques to minimize credit risk while moving beyond payment in advance and L/Cs is to obtain foreign receivables insurance. Policies are available from both the public and private sector, but the program offered by the Export-Import Bank (ExIm) is the best known. Its small business policy allows exporters to offer open account payment terms to foreign buyers and ExIm insures the sales against nonpayment. The insurance provides 100 percent coverage for political risk (nonpayment due to action of the foreign government), and generally 95 percent coverage for all other risks (commercial risks) that could lead to nonpayment by the buyer. This means the exporter is allowed to offer an open account to a qualified foreign buyer with the assurance that if something should happen and the foreign buyer does not pay, the exporter will still receive nearly all the value of the invoice.

As more companies are discovering the competitive advantage of offering open account, they are turning to programs such as ExIm's foreign receivables insurance. Best of all, this can actually save the exporter money. If previous transactions were primarily using L/Cs, the exporter paid considerable L/C fees. The cost of the ExIm insurance may be less than the L/C fees, even though the program requires all sales to be covered. Best of all, it also saves money for the foreign buyer who also saves on L/C costs and frees up cash flow. For further details, visit ExIm's website at www.exim.gov or contact your local trade assistance center or ExIm directly at a U.S. Export Assistance Center.

ExIm requires that products sold under its insurance be at least 50% U.S. origin. So the private sector also offers insurance that does not have a U.S. content requirement. Examples are listed in Figure 16.3.

Minimizing Political Risk

Political risk is similar to credit risk in that the risk is associated with a specific transaction. But unlike credit risk, even a strong foreign buyer with an excellent credit rating still may be unable to pay an invoice due to government action. Assessing political risk should be done through research on the government and political environment of the foreign buyer. Export.gov and GlobalEdge both offer political risk information on countries. Euler Hermes (www.eulerhermes.us) offers country specific reports and a global report on political (and economic) risk.

There are really only two ways to minimize political risk. If the risk is high enough, the payment method should be adjusted accordingly. For example, if the creditworthiness of the foreign buyer justifies open account, but the political risk is too high, the payment terms should be changed to payment in advance. Prepayment is the best way to avoid political risk. Other methods, such as L/C or documentary collection, still contain an element of political risk.

If prepayment is not acceptable, a second option is export credit insurance. ExIm offers programs other than its small business policy that can be applied to a specific transaction. For example, its short-term single buyer program applies to a single sale or repetitive sales over a one-year period to a single buyer. This means an exporter can use a mix of open account, prepayment, and L/Cs for most foreign buyers, and ExIm insurance for only those transactions with significant political risk.

Figure 16.3 A Selection of Companies Offering Export Credit Insurance

- American International Group
- Euler Hermes
- Fidelity & Deposit
- Lloyd's of London

- Coface
- Exporters Insurance
- Foreign Credit Insurance Agency
- Trade Underwriters Agency

Minimizing Foreign Exchange Risk

Before you can decide how to lower your foreign exchange risk, you must determine how much risk you are willing to face. This involves creating a corporate risk management policy. Even if the policy remains informal and basic, there should be consensus between the international staff and financial staff as to how the foreign exchange risk will be managed. Given the somewhat technical nature of foreign exchange management tools, be sure to involve your bank because it will be a crucial resource in developing an effective policy.

To illustrate the process of developing a strategy, Clifford Vadnais of American National Bank/Bank One has developed the international lifecycle model. This model is helpful in identifying how different companies approach their foreign exchange management. The model is detailed in Figure 16.4. It implies that as companies develop internationally, and their international business becomes more significant to their overall business, they can justify a more in-depth FX management policy that commits more internal resources. This development happens in three phases:

- Phase 1. This phase represents companies during their initial global expansion, when they are only involved in exporting. These companies rely heavily on outside expertise and assistance, probably from their banks. Because they are averse to foreign exchange risk, all pricing is in U.S. dollars and payment terms are limited to only secure methods such as L/Cs or credit insurance.

Figure 16.4 Clifford Vadnais' International Life Cycle Model – Three Phases

Risk Tolerance Approach	Phase 1 Adverse	Phase 2 Tolerant	Phase 3 Strategists
International Business	Small percent of total business	Significant percent of total business	Fully global, integrated company with overseas investments and operations
Pricing	Dollar-based pricing	Dollar and foreign currency pricing as determined by competitive needs and opportunities	Dollar and foreign currency pricing as determined by competitive needs and opportunities
Payment Terms	Prepayment, Letters of Credit, credit insurance	Full range of payment terms including open account	Full range of payment terms including open account
Internal Resources for FX Management	Heavy reliance on banks and consultants	Growing independence and internal capability	Risk management division developed using specialized staff

Find the Right Bank – Solving Your International Finance Needs

A company may find that as it expands globally it may not have a bank that can meet its international requirements. Changing banks and establishing a new business relationship with such a crucial resource is not easy. However, because many companies began their banking business at a time when international business was only a distant thought, the bank's international expertise was generally not part of the decision. But what do you do in this situation?

Above all, take your time. Talk to your current bank about your international needs. It may have the experience and capacity to satisfy your international needs through another branch or office. It may also have a relationship with another bank that can provide the support while working through your existing bank.

If you do decide you need a new bank, to either supplement or replace your existing bank, shop around as you would for any other supplier. Ask for references from other companies you trust. Get a referral list from your local trade assistance office. See what banks are involved locally in international trade activities, even if their international activities are based in another city. Insist on meeting directly with international staff, especially specialized staff that may be handling your more challenging requirements such as FX management. When shopping for a new bank:

• Determine the bank's overall international expertise and structure including staff profiles, client profiles, and overseas operations.

• Ask it to offer its advice on how it believes it can make you more competitive through its international products and services. What FX products does it recommend? What paperwork would be involved? Costs?

• Assess how personalized its service is. What happens with problems? Where are international staff located and will they ever visit your facility?

• Determine its experience with state or federal finance programs such as those offered by the Small Business Administration or ExIm Bank.

• Investigate non-international issues that may also improve your overall business such as financing, paperwork, electronic services, and research support.

- Phase 2. As companies begin to expand in their global activities, their international business justifies a more aggressive FX policy that can be developed into a competitive advantage. Phase 2 companies begin to offer foreign currency pricing and less restrictive payment terms such as open account. Their increased international business justifies developing internal expertise to manage their FX risk.
- Phase 3. A fully involved global company approaches FX management as a strategic process, internalizing expertise of the process with specialized staff. The FX management is fully integrated into all business aspects including tax,

accounting, and finance.

There are some important implications behind this model. The most important is the understanding of FX management as a competitive tool. Companies in their initial stage of global expansion probably are too occupied with sales and marketing issues to become distracted by FX concerns. The international sales volume may not justify much involvement beyond a Phase 1-type of approach.

However, as the international business increases, a company can justify taking a more proactive approach. Notice that this does not mean taking on greater risk! It means that a Phase 2 company sees the competitive advantage of investing time and resources, such as employee training, to be more creative in its mix of pricing and payment terms. If the company is able to outsmart its competitors, perhaps by being the first to offer foreign currency pricing, it could create an advantage internationally. Understanding this source of competitive advantage, Phase 3 companies embrace these concepts and establish FX management as its core international strength.

The second implication is that FX management, as a strategic tool, is not limited to Fortune 500 companies. Notice that none of the characteristics of a Phase 3 company indicate that the company has to be huge, only that the international sales must be significant enough to justify the investment in time and resources. This is especially true if a small to mid-size company utilizes the strength of outside resources, such as its bank. With international financial services remaining extremely competitive, even small companies can afford FX management tools that increase their competitiveness in the international market. However, as you will see later, not all FX tools fit all companies or all sales levels.

The final implication is that FX management must always be linked to other aspects of a company's operation, including marketing, logistics, tax, and finance. To view FX management as only a sales tool, one misses the larger perspective that until a company fully embraces the reality of a world with hundreds of currencies, it may miss opportunities to become more competitive. FX management is not just removing the foreign exchange risk associated with one transaction. It should also be considered an issue when the company expands its international sales markets, overseas investments, foreign sourcing, and other aspects of international expansion. The typical applications of an FX risk management strategy occur when:

- Exporting products or services and the established sales price is in foreign currency
- Importing equipment or materials and the established purchase price is in foreign currency
- Receiving dividends or royalties from overseas subsidiaries or investments that are denominated in foreign currencies
- Funding an overseas investment, acquisition, or expansion

Financial Tools for Managing Foreign Exchange Risk

Never before have so many options been available to help companies manage their FX risk. From traditional devices such as netting, to the sophisticated realm of foreign exchange derivatives, the FX solutions and their applications are as varied as the companies using them. As products become more varied, so do the users of these products. From small to large, urban to rural, international companies today enjoy unprecedented choices to satisfy their FX management needs.

Does this sound like a recipe for more sales, improved competitiveness, and a simpler life? Not quite. The range of solutions also creates a jungle of terms, conditions, paperwork, and decisions, not to mention the need for an understanding of how it all works. I urge any company to seek outside assistance prior to embarking on the path of implementing a foreign exchange management program. Make at least two phone calls: one to your local trade assistance center (city, state, or federal) to find out what workshops or training programs are available, and the second to your bank. If you are not comfortable with the international capability of your bank, consider supplementing your current banking relationship with that of a second bank with a strong international capability. You could change your bank altogether, though such a decision is normally dictated by needs beyond only your international requirements.

FX Tools

I need to define a few terms prior to detailing various FX tools:

- **Hedging** - The process of protecting against the potential of foreign exchange loss due to currency exchange rate fluctuations.
- **Spot rate** - The foreign exchange rate quoted between two currencies for transactions that require either immediate delivery or delivery within two days. Spot rates found in publications such as The Wall Street Journal are typically rates for interbank transactions.
- **Forward rate** - The foreign exchange rate quoted between two currencies for delivery in the future. These rates are typically quoted for 30, 60, and 90 days delivery and for some currencies even further out. It is often misunderstood that the forward rate is a prediction of what the spot rate will be in the future. It is actually a function of interest rate differences between the two countries/currencies. It is a calculation based on known factors mostly using bond rates. Because bond rates do factor in the future outlook of the market on any given day, the forward rate does reflect some of the market's perspective.

Netting:

- Has low cost,
- Fits Phase 1, 2, and 3 companies, and
- Fits all transaction sizes.

Imagine if a company wanted to cover its foreign exchange risk associated with a 90 day export sale to Mexico using foreign currency pricing. Assume the U.S. export price is $5,000 and the spot rate for the peso/$ is ten pesos to the dollar. Because the company has agreed to offer foreign currency pricing, the company issues an invoice to the Mexican buyer for 50,000 pesos, due in 90 days. Let's further assume the U.S. company wants to eliminate the risk that the exchange rate will change and it will receive less than $5,000 when it converts the 50,000 pesos to dollars in 90 days. For example, if the peso weakens to 12 peso/$, the company would only receive $4,167. (50,000 / 12)

Using netting, the company would arrange an intracompany hedge through its own network. This requires that the U.S. company has some relationship with a company in Mexico such as a subsidiary, affiliated company, or even a parent. The Mexican affiliate would investigate opportunities for an offsetting transaction - for example, the purchase in the U.S. of goods for $5,000, 90 days out. Because the two exposures are opposite each other, they net out and remove risk. The attraction of netting is that the FX market is removed completely. However, netting is only an option if the company has a structure in place to create the hedge. If a Mexican subsidiary does not exist or has no dollar obligations, the hedge couldn't be created.

Forward contract :

- Has low cost,
- Fits Phase 1, 2, and 3 companies, and
- Fits all transaction sizes.

One of the most common hedging tools is a **forward contract** - a contract with another party (typically a bank) to deliver a fixed amount of one currency in return for a fixed amount of another currency at an agreed future date (the value date). It is a binding agreement that sets the exchange rate for a future date so you know today what the value of the exchanged currency will be in the future. No funds are exchanged until the value date.

Forwards are routinely available in the major trading currencies for 30, 60, 90, and 180 day deliveries. For some currencies even longer forwards are available, as are forwards for lengths other than the standard lengths. The greatest benefit of forward contracts is their flexibility compared to futures contracts. They also vary in specific features. For example, an option-dated forward gives you a span of time during which the exchange transaction(s) can be conducted rather than only on the value date.

In our Mexican trade example, if the U.S. company wanted to cover its risk on the $5,000 sale, it would enter into a forward contract for 50,000 pesos for delivery in 90 days (using today's 90-day forward rate). Why 50,000 pesos? Because we have already established that the invoice amount will be 50,000 pesos, payable in 90 days. When the Mexican buyer pays the invoice in 90 days, the U.S. buyer will take the 50,000 pesos and exchange into dollars. But at what rate?

This is where the forward rate in effect at the time of the original transaction comes into play. Let's assume that on the date of the shipment the 90-day forward rate for the peso is 10.5. This means the forward contract would be to exchange 50,000 pesos into $4,761.90 in 90 days (50,000/10.5 = 4,761.90). In effect, by entering into a forward contract the U.S. seller is guaranteed to receive $4,761.90 in exchange for 50,000 pesos in 90 days.

The cost of the FX hedge to the seller is $238.10 ($5,000 - $4,761.90). Does this seem too high? The answer depends on the company's perspective of risk. By using the forward contract, its risk is limited to a cost of $238. If in 90 days, the peso moves beyond 10.5, the company will have made a very good decision. On the other hand, if the peso strengthens to 9 pesos to the dollar, the decision does not look so good.

The decision must be made at the time of shipment, not in 90 days when hindsight is perfect. For a company that wants to offer foreign currency pricing, yet not be exposed to foreign exchange risk, the cost of $238 may be acceptable.

Futures contract:

- Has low to moderate cost,
- Fits Phase 2 and 3 companies, and
- Fits transactions over $1 million.

If a company enters into a forward contract and partway through the contract (say 45 days in the above example) decides to get out of its obligation to conduct the future exchange, what are its options? Could it sell the contract to another party that needed the exchange in 45 days?

This is the idea behind **futures contracts** - forward contracts traded on financial exchanges. Because futures contracts are traded daily, their price constantly changes as the market factors in the data and opinions of the market. Thus, on any given day, a futures contract may be more attractive than a forward contract. However, futures contracts are highly inflexible because they come in fixed amounts with standard delivery dates. Their use is effectively limited to transactions above $1 million. Nevertheless, they are an important component for many companies in their management of FX risk.

Currency options:

- Have moderate to high cost,
- Fits Phase 2 and 3 companies, and
- Fits transactions over $1 million.

Start with the concept of a tradable forward contract and add the feature that when the contract comes due the holder has the choice of either buying the currency at the agreed price or not buying the currency. This is the idea behind a **currency option** - the right, but not the obligation, to deliver a fixed amount of one currency in return for a fixed amount of another currency by an agreed future date. It differs from forward and futures contracts in that the contract does not have to be exercised.

Assume, in our example, an option to purchase dollars from pesos at 11 pesos to the dollar. If the spot rate is 10 pesos to the dollar when the company holding the option needs the dollars, the company would not exercise its option. It would get more dollars

Figure 16.5 Comparison of Various Hedging Tools in Regard to Cost, Suitability of Transaction Size, and Fit for Companies

FX Hedg-ing Tool	Cost	Suitability for Transactions <$1 million	Suitability for Transactions <$1 million	Suitability for Phase 1 Companies	Suitability for Phase 2 Companies	Suitability for Phase 3 companies
Netting	Low	X	X	X	X	X
Forward Contract	Low	X	X	X	X	X
Futures Contract	Low to Moderate		X		X	X
Currency Options	Moderate to High		X		X	X

by converting at the spot rate of 10 rather than option rate of 11. On the other hand, if the peso has weakened to 12 pesos/dollar, the company would exercise the option. It would get more dollars for its peso using the option rate of 11 rather than the spot rate of 12. This ability to make the decision to convert or not convert based on the option exchange rate is the fundamental benefit of options.

The downside is that the brokerage fee and premium must be paid whether the option is exercised or not. Thus, options tend to have a moderate to high cost versus other tools, and, like futures, they are limited to large transactions.

Comparison of FX Tools

Not all tools to manage FX risk are suitable for all companies or situations. Nor can generalizations be easily made as to when and why a company should use a particular tool. The nature of foreign exchange risk, the particular currencies involved, and the overall strategy of the company must all be considered in determining the appropriate tools.

Some generalizations can be made, however, as summarized in Figure 16.5. The chart shows that all companies can consider using netting and forward contracts. It also indicates that the use of futures and options will probably be limited to larger companies pursuing a more aggressive risk strategy. Whichever tool you choose, be sure to learn all that you can about your internal requirements and the solutions offered by banks. It is a worthwhile investment resulting in an increased ability to control your foreign exchange risk that will give you a strong competitive position.

• INTERNATIONAL PAYMENT METHODS

It may seem to you that we put the cart before the horse by discussing financial risk before payment methods. However, a company must first determine its overall approach to risk before choosing payment methods. It would be easiest for a new company going global to insist on prepayment or letters of credit, but it would miss the opportunity to create a competitive opportunity through other options. Most companies start by only offering prepayment and L/Cs as their accepted payment methods. They are the most secure options for the seller, hence their popularity with exporters. For the same reason, they are less popular with foreign buyers. The company to first offer more creative solutions, such as open account backed by export credit insurance, may be the company that gains the greatest market share.

In this section, I will discuss the four main payment methods and highlight how they can be used competitively to create an advantage over other companies less strategic in their accounts receivable. The risk of each method will be identified because the payment method must match the level of risk. No company can afford significant losses due to international bad debt or other financial risk. But to rely solely on prepayment or L/Cs is equally risky, competitively speaking.

One caveat before detailing the payment methods: as with foreign exchange management, you should utilize the many resources available to you to create an effective portfolio of payment methods for your global transactions. Letters of credit, for example, can be surprisingly confusing. You only can learn by doing. Seek out local workshops and training programs on international payment methods and finance to fully acquaint yourself with the appropriate procedures and safeguards. Your bank will be a critical resource as well.

Cash in Advance

- Risk to seller: none
- Risk to buyer: very high; relies solely on good faith of seller to ship
- Buyer receives goods: after payment
- Cost: low, not related to value of transaction

The most common international payment method is **cash in advance**. This is unfortunate because it is wholly unbalanced in that all the risk is taken by the foreign buyer. This is not intrinsically bad, it is just not a competitive policy.

The low cost and ease of this method makes cash in advance the most popular payment method used by companies during their initial international sales growth. Payment by the foreign buyer is frequently sent by wire, which a bank calls **SWIFT** transfer (Society of Worldwide Interbank Financial Telecommunications). This is a secure method banks use to electronically transfer funds between banks. The cost of this transfer is low - around $50 each for the sender and the receiver. Swift transfers are fast, and in some cases even same day. Other methods of cash in advance include credit card and checks.

One caution about wire transfers: work with your bank to ensure transfers are credited to your account expeditiously. Be sure the sender has complete and accurate U.S. bank details, including the routing number (which generally is the number before your account number on a check). Also find out what the route of the transfer will be and if a correspondent bank will be used. More than once I've had an inbound wire take a number of days to clear the U.S. account due to delays along the way. By working with your bank you can sometimes avoid these delays.

Letters of Credit (Irrevocable)

- Risk to seller: little to none if an advised L/C
- Risk to buyer: little: no shipment . . . no payment, buyer relies on seller to ship goods as specified in order
- Buyer receives goods: after payment for a L/C sight draft; before payment for a L/C time draft
- Cost: can be high, related to value of transaction

Letters of credit have become fundamental payment methods for international transactions. Though the cost can be high compared to other methods, the attraction is the protection L/Cs afford both buyer and seller. Though an irrevocable L/C slightly favors the seller, it is generally seen as the fairest method, which is why it is so popular. It can also be quite complicated and potentially expensive.

Types of L/Cs. L/Cs used issued either as irrevocable or revocable. A revocable L/C can be amended or cancelled at any time without the permission of the seller. Clearly this is unacceptable to an exporter because it removes the protection for the seller. After the adoption of **UCP 600** (the governing rules over letters of credit) L/Cs are all irrevocable and cannot be changed unless both the buyer and the seller agree to make the change.

L/Cs are also issued sight draft or time draft. A **sight draft** means payment will be made to the seller as soon as the documents verifying shipments are presented to the bank. If a longer payment period is negotiated between seller and buyer, the L/C is a **time draft letter of credit**. (Time draft L/Cs are also known as usance L/Cs.) With a time draft, payment is made at some time after the documents are presented for payment. For example, a time draft starting "at sight-90 days" would mean payment is expected 90 days after presentation. The delayed-payment period can also begin with the date on the bill of lading. Time L/Cs are an effective marketing tool for sellers because they offer secure payment to the seller and provide a delayed payment option for the buyer. (Though as you'll see later, the buyer may still have to give money up front to the bank before an L/C can be opened.)

Why L/Cs are secure. The key to understanding why L/Cs are secure is to understand that an L/C is a commitment by a bank to pay the amount of the L/C if certain conditions are met by the seller. The foreign buyer (the applicant) goes to its bank to open the L/C. The seller is the beneficiary listed on the L/C. The role of the foreign bank is to act as an intermediary between the beneficiary and the applicant. In other words, in cases where the seller is uncomfortable offering open account and the buyer is uncomfortable with prepayment, an L/C is a compromise. The bank that opens the L/C (the issuing bank) is giving its guarantee that as long as the seller ships the goods and provides the required documents, the bank will pay the invoice. An L/C is more like a contract between a bank and the seller. This removes the risk for the seller because the only way the seller will not get paid is if it doesn't ship or provide the required documents or if the bank defaults. Because none of these are likely, the L/C is considered a secure method of payment.

It also important to realize that foreign buyers will only be able to open an L/C if they deposit the invoice amount as collateral or access an existing credit line with the bank. Because the foreign bank is putting its full faith behind the L/C, it only does so with cash or good credit from its customer (your buyer). This means the foreign buyer may still have to come up with the cash weeks before it receives the product.

The use of a letter of credit may be clearer if you review the typical steps involved in an L/C, shown in Figure 16.6.

The advising bank. Because L/Cs are issued by foreign banks, the seller probably will have no way of verifying its authenticity or the financial strength of the foreign bank. This is why a second bank located in the country of the exporter is involved. It receives the L/C directly from the foreign bank and verifies its authenticity. Through the use of similar codes, as with Swift wire transfers, the domestic bank can verify that the foreign bank actually did issue the L/C. This process is called **advising** and the domestic bank is called the **advising bank**. You specify to your foreign buyer that your bank will be the advising bank before the L/C is opened.

A confirmed L/C. Once you receive an L/C that has been advised by a local bank, you have an L/C that you can trust to be genuine. The only remaining risk is if the foreign bank refuses or is unable to pay after the shipment and documents are sent. If this is a concern, you can ask the advising bank, for a fee, to add its guarantee to pay the L/C as long as the goods are shipped and the appropriate documents provided. When a the local bank makes this guarantee, it is called a **confirmed letter of credit**. Now all international risk is removed because the agreement to pay is given by a domestic bank. (In practice, if a confirmed L/C is required, it must be part of the instructions to the foreign buyer. The foreign buyer will instruct its bank, the issuing bank, to ask the domestic bank to both advise and confirm the L/C.)

You would think that most foreign banks that issue L/Cs pay them. And in fact, most L/Cs are only advised, not confirmed, so the exporter is comfortable with the creditworthiness of the foreign bank. However, there are times when an exporter will not want to take this risk, such as when dealing with emerging markets that don't have a well developed or secure financial system. In these cases, the exporter requests both advising and confirming services of the U.S. bank.

Why don't exporters have all L/Cs advised and confirmed because they clearly are the most secure? The simple answer is that banks charge a fee for advising and confirming L/Cs. Advising fees are quite low, but confirming fees can be expensive. This is understandable because the confirming bank is taking on the risk if the foreign bank doesn't pay. Once confirmed, the U.S. bank will pay the L/C when presented for payment, assuming all documents are in order. If the issuing bank does not pay the confirming bank, the exporter still keeps the money, and the confirming bank takes the loss. The

Figure 16.6 Typical Flow of a Letter of Credit

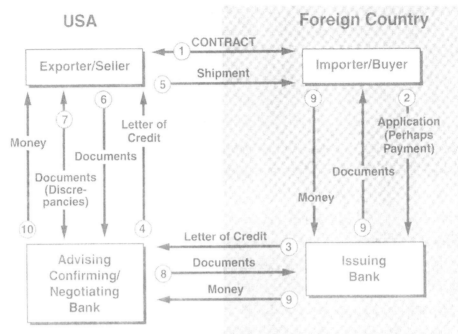

By following the flow of a standard letter of credit, you will better understand how it works:

1. The seller and buyer agree on the conditions of the sale including which party will pay the costs of the L/C and if the L/C will be at sight or payable a certain number of days after the shipment.
2. The buyer opens the L/C with its local bank, the issuing bank. Buyer may have to make payment to secure credit to open L/C.
3. The issuing bank sends the L/C to the U.S. bank.
4. The U.S. bank verifies the authenticity of the L/C and advises the beneficiary, the seller. A copy of the L/C is sent to the seller. If requested, the U.S. bank also adds its confirmation.
5. The seller ships the goods.
6. The seller presents the required documents as specified in the L/C to the U.S. bank.
7. The U.S. bank checks that all the documents are in order and match the requirements of the L/C. If there are discrepancies in the documents, the seller is informed of the problem. The seller corrects the deficiencies and resends documents.
8. Once the documents are accepted by the U.S. bank, the bank claims reimbursement and presents the documents to the issuing bank.
9. The issuing bank makes payment to the U.S. bank. (If the buyer has not yet paid, the buyer pays the issuing bank.) Documents are sent to the buyer.
10. The U.S. bank makes payment to the seller.

fee charged by the confirming bank is based on the size of the transaction, the risk associated with the issuing bank, and the economic and political risk associated with the foreign country.

Problems with letters of credit. Despite their low risk, there are some problems with the use of L/Cs. These issues can be frustrating as you eagerly try to get all the paperwork in order:

- **Discrepancies**. One of the most frustrating aspects of an L/C is making sure the documents are completely in order so you can receive payment. This may seem like a simple task until you try it. It is not as easy as you may think. For example, the L/C may require that all documents, including the packing list and insurance certificate, list the L/C number. If the number is not listed, the bank will reject the L/C for payment due to a discrepancy. Worse, you have to pay a fee for each discrepancy, and they are not cheap! Be very careful to follow the instructions on the L/C to the letter.
- Date of shipment. Another classic problem is when the buyer opens the L/C with an unrealistic shipment date deadline. Obviously, it is eager for the shipment as soon as possible, but if unrealistic shipment dates are used and you miss the shipment date, you will not get paid. Instead, the L/C must be amended to extend the shipment date, which takes time and money. Similarly, the seller must be sure to present the documents to the bank before the L/C expires.
- Partial shipments. The L/C may stipulate that partial shipments are not allowed, which would include backorders. Be sure that all of the order will be available for shipment within the time allowed by the L/C.
- Costs. The freight terms may include prepayment of some freight costs. The L/C will stipulate the allowable cost maximum. If your costs exceed this, you will not receive more money unless the L/C is amended. Thus, be sure that adequate estimates for such non-product-related expenses are included when the L/C is issued.

One of the ways to reduce problems is to be sure your foreign buyer has the L/C issued with all the appropriate protection and instructions. Figure 16.7 provides some standard wording you should consider using. Notice that it includes a reference to the URR525, which is an international agreement covering how international reimbursements (payments) are to be made. It also lists the clause stating that the L/C must be subject to the **Uniform Customs and Practice for Documentary Credit Number 600** (UCP600). The UCP600 lists a number of rules and understandings that apply in cases of misunderstandings, disputes, or mistakes. For example, under UCP600 all L/Cs are irrevocable. UCP600 also governs how fast certain actions should occur, such as payment.

Figure 16.7 Standard Instructions to Foreign Buyers for Opening L/Cs

> **Place the following wording in your instructions to your foreign buyer:**
>
> • Please issue an irrevocable letter of credit by full cable/tested telex/SWIFT to be advised directly through (list your bank). (If the L/C is to be confirmed state "to be advised through and confirmed by.")
> • The credit must be available with and expire at the counters of the advising bank. (If the L/C is to be confirmed state "advising and confirming bank.")
> • Drafts are to be drawn at sight, allowing for reimbursement by telex from a bank in the United States. Reimbursement must be subject to URR525.
> • All original documents are to be forwarded to the issuing bank and none to the applicant.
> • Ocean bills of lading are to be issued to "shipper's order blank endorsed," or to the order of the issuing bank. Air waybills are to be consigned to the issuing bank.
> • Documents must be presented within 21 days from date of transport document.
> • The credit must be subject to The Uniform Customs and Practice for Documentary Credits, ICC Publication No. 600.

Collections (At Sight, or Against Acceptance)

- Risk to seller: potentially high if foreign bank or forwarder is unreliable
- Risk to buyer: similar to L/C; even lower if buyer is allowed to inspect goods prior to payment
- Buyer receives goods: after fulfilling payment terms
- Cost: low

This payment term is known by a number of names including **documentary collection**, **cash against documents**, and **payment against documents**. When the product is shipped, the seller forwards the documents to the foreign buyer's bank which holds the documents until the payment term is met. The payment term may be at **sight**, which means the buyer must pay prior to taking possession of the goods, known as *documents against payment*. The payment term also may be *documents against acceptance* of a time draft payable a predetermined number of days from the date of shipment. The typical wording of an against acceptance 90-day payment term would be "Documents against acceptance of draft 90 days from the date of shipment." The words *against acceptance* refer to the fact that the buyer must accept the agreement to pay the invoice within the specified time frame.

Companies often use collections because of their low cost. However, be aware of the risks. I remember shipping an expensive order with payment terms cash against documents. Though payment had not yet been made, I received questions from the technical manager of the buyer regarding installation procedures. I asked how it got the equipment because payment had not yet been made. The technical manager simply replied he had no knowledge of the financial side of things. Frustrated, I contacted my freight forwarder who indicated the foreign freight forwarder must have released the goods even though the buyer did not have the documents. Though clearly not legal, depending on the country, it can happen.

I still use collections, but with the knowledge that in some countries they are only slightly more secure than open account. Nevertheless, they do offer more protection than open account and serve as a good bridge between L/Cs and open account.

Open Account

- Risk to seller: potentially very high
- Risk to buyer: little to none
- Buyer receives goods: immediately
- Cost: low

Open account means shipping 'on credit' to the importer so they do not pre-pay. It is surprisingly common given its high risk to the seller. Many exporters eventually move their foreign buyers from cash in advance or letters of credit to open account after gaining experience with the buyer. The reason is easy to understand: this method is simple and relatively inexpensive for both seller and buyer. Open account essentially places all the risk that the buyer will pay on the seller. The seller can release the shipment as soon as it is ready without having to wait for an L/C to be opened or a wire transfer to be received. Likewise, the buyer receives the order as soon as it is released from its local customs without waiting for other steps to be completed, such as the bank releasing the shipment.

Some sellers, however, are still reluctant to use open account under any circumstances because the risk is too great. I suspect the majority of sellers eventually settle on a compromise - their experienced buyers receive open account up to a specified credit limit and all others must pay in advance or use an L/C.

There is no right or wrong method. The decision depends on the company, the buyer, and the risk outlook. The key is to obtain good financial information on the international buyer and to consider the use of foreign receivables insurance.

Matching risk with payment method. When selecting payment method, the goal is to minimize risk while remaining competitive. As with domestic business, these two forces will always be pulling you in different directions. Your accounting department will want secure payments methods, such as prepayment or L/Cs. Meanwhile, your foreign buyers will constantly press for open account. You may wonder, what is standard practice? This is a difficult question to answer without knowing the specific risk. As previously explained, risk involves both credit risk and political and economic risk. (If foreign currency pricing is used, it also involves FX risk.)

For a single purchase such as a direct sale where no ongoing relationship is expected, prepayment is probably the norm, or an L/C in the case of a large transaction. This also would be the case for the first few orders to a newly appointed distributor. Ultimately you will be under pressure from buyers to move to open account or documentary collection.

For sales to a large, established company that offers strong financials and excellent credit references, you may persuaded to offer open account from the onset. However, always be aware that beyond credit risk there may be political or economic risk depending on the country. Always work with your banker to identify all risks.

Whatever your strategy, remember that the more conservative the payment method, the greater the costs and cash flow pressures are on your foreign buyers. For example, many foreign banks require the buyer to come up with the cash before opening an L/C. If it is a growing company, cash flow will be an important consideration. A competitor that shows up offering open account just might get its attention. Also do not make payment decisions without information about support programs such as Export Credit Insurance from ExIm bank.

• OBTAINING LONG-TERM FINANCING

Export working capital program. As a company expands, both domestically and internationally, its working capital requirements often place considerable constraints on its cash flow. It is a common problem: how to finance growth. Numerous magazines and books discuss the variety of options available to companies. Options such as vendor financing (obtaining credit from suppliers), traditional bank lending, and even equity financing (investment in exchange for some percentage of ownership) are all well reported. But you may be wondering if there is any option specific to international expansion that is available to companies.

In fact there is. The export working capital program was created exclusively to assist exporters with cash flow constraints due to international growth or orders. It is offered by both the Small Business Administration and ExIm Bank. The SBA is used for financing deals less than a million dollars, and ExIm for greater amounts. The program is not a loan program but a loan guarantee program. The SBA or ExIm makes a guarantee to the lending bank that should the company default on the loan, the SBA or ExIm will reimburse the bank for up 90 percent of the loan. Be aware, though, that you remain accountable to the SBA or ExIm - the loan is not forgiven. The benefit, however, is that a bank unlikely to lend working capital for international purposes may do so with a loan guarantee. The extra guarantee from SBA or ExIm provides the needed security for the bank to make the loan.

If you are familiar with other SBA loan guarantee programs, such as the 7A, you may see some similarities. However, an important distinction is the level of guarantee to the bank. With a domestic loan guarantee, the SBA covers 70-75 percent of the risk and the bank assumes the rest. With the export working capital program, the SBA covers 90 percent, which is obviously a strong selling point for the bank. In either case, work with your bank to solve cash flow problems and be aware that there are specific programs to help. For more information, visit www.sba.gov.

Sustaining Global Success

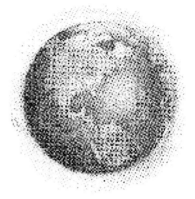

Congratulations! If you have made it this far, you have achieved a great deal. You have identified your global potential, developed a plan, targeted markets, and entered a few of those markets. You have probably appointed some type of representation in those foreign markets and made some sales. What is the next step?

Many companies stop at this point. Their success in a handful of countries provides an extra 5 or 10 percent sales revenue, perhaps even better net profits, a bit of international travel, and good market feedback. The goal to achieve some initial international sales has been fulfilled. No complaints, life is good!

I want to encourage you to go beyond your initial global success. Take your experiences and knowledge from the initial foreign market entries to make the next markets even more successful, creating greater sales and profit opportunities. This is where you will truly begin to set your sights on the real global opportunities for your company - not just a niche player in a few countries, but a fully participating international company with real global impact in your industry.

Too difficult, too expensive, too time consuming? Perhaps, but you will never know if you stop at this point. And plenty of companies do stop here, satisfied with a generally reactive international strategy. More aggressive international tactics such as foreign currency pricing, foreign trade show participation, overseas offices, and true global customer support remain nice goals, but never happen. I understand why. For many firms their domestic market always remains the number one priority. This focus on domestic success and dominance will always impede international growth, at least until the day management realizes its real potential will never be achieved until the company is a global player or it is forced to go international due to depressed conditions in the domestic market. Then it may be too late because your competitors could be way ahead of you. I saw this personally with a number of our clients during the 2008-2009 recession. Yes, everyone was affected. But those that had already achieved strong international sales did much better than others. One was able to avoid any layoffs.

This final section will give you ideas and strategies to increase your international business beyond your initial success. In these remaining chapters, try to identify five to ten ideas or strategies that you could put into place in your company. Then hold a brainstorming session with other management, peers, team members, and perhaps even share-holders, to critique and amplify those ideas. Think (and dream!) about how much stronger your company will be when your international sales are ten times greater. Think about all the new marketing campaigns, brand building opportunities, R&D improvements, and other enhancements that are possible. And think about the impact international activities will have on your company when its success increases tenfold.

The good thing about international success is it feeds itself, creating new sales and profit opportunities that can be turned into more sales and profit opportunities. I know this all sounds very idealistic, and it may be. Ten times international sales growth is a huge feat. But you begin one market at a time. That is the great thing about international business - until you are selling to all markets that have the potential to buy your product, there is still another market to add to your global success. Getting increased sales from that market will probably be easier and cheaper than getting the equivalent sales from your domestic market.

I think a number of readers of this book stop here. This is particularly true for readers preparing for the NASBITE CGBP exam because most of the CGBP topics in this book are in earlier chapters. Still, do come back eventually!

Section Four is all about achieving greater global success, adding more markets at the right pace so you don't risk initial success, enhancing your international tactics, and continuing to push your organization even further. It also contains a great deal of information that can be used even before you appoint your first overseas representative. So even if you haven't appointed your first agent or distributor, read on!

CHAPTER 17

Setting a Pace for Your Export Growth - Assessing Your Export Progress and Success

Once you have entered your first two or three foreign markets, you should begin to adapt your international business plan to reflect the new knowledge and market feedback received during the initial expansion. This is an important step in sustaining global success. If you wait too long to adapt your international business plan, you may be repeating mistakes that will be costly to fix later. This chapter looks at the initial issues you should address after entering your first few markets. These issues will lead to ways to modify and improve your international business plan.

I will use a model that details the three analyses that need to be completed: (1) internal analysis, (2) foreign market analysis, and (3) product analysis. These three analyses have three common issues: (1) resources, (2) time frame, and (3) market selection model. All of these issues will lead to ways to adapt your international business plan.

• A MODEL FOR ASSESSING YOUR INITIAL GLOBAL SUCCESS

Figure 17.1 details a framework for assessing your initial global progress and successes. The model breaks the issues into three key groups: (1) internal, (2) foreign market (or external), and (3) product specific. Your analysis of these three groups should then be extended to include three themes common across all three groups: (A) resources, (B) time frame, and (C) the market selection model (discussed in Chapter 5). The purpose of this analysis is to identify issues and factors that have either contributed to or hindered

1) INTERNAL	2) EXTERNAL	3) PRODUCT
Financial: Impact from international activities – profit/loss **Staff**: Responsibilities, Training Requirements **Organizational Commitment**: Is management committed? Support departments? **Organizational Structure**: changes needed? Reporting, decision making regarding international issues?	**Foreign Buyers**: SWOT / strengths, weaknesses, opportunities, Treats **Entry Mode**: Should a different mode have been used? More overseas involvement? Foreign Direct Investment? **Feedback**: Are we getting enough feedback from foreign buyers & customers? **Channel Management**: Do we have good control of the distribution network? Can improvements be made?	**Sales Achieved**: Market by market analysis: dollar volumes? Quantities? Trends? **Competitive Situation**: Market Share, Brand Awareness – Strength, is product competing differently than in domestic market? **Marketing Activities**: Product launch, marketing materials & translations, support materials, training, translations. **Product Modifications**: Would we achieve greater success with product modifications or standards compliance?

(A) R E S O U R C E S

What resources have been helpful in our international expansion? What new resources do we need? How can we leverage our resources? Which will be the most important for future expansion?

• Bankers • Accouting Firms • Local international resources: City, State, Federal	• Overseas resources • Freight Forwarders • Carriers • Resources for finding foreign buyers	• Statistics to determine competitive situation • Testing Laboratories • Industry experts, journalists

(B) T I M E F R A M E

Based on our experience thusfar, what expectations can we have as regards to the timeframe required to execute our international business plan?

• International Training Requirements • Changes to the organization to optimize international performance	• How long did it take to identify, select, negotiate, and training our foreign representation? • How fast can we repeat the process in other markets?	• How long would it take to make required product changes? • Timeframe for change in marketing materials?

(C) M A R K E T   S E L E C T I O N   M O D E L

Based on the feedback from market already entered, how should we change our Market Selection Model? Which of the following indicators should be added, deleted, increased in emphasis, decreased in emphasis?

• Cultural Similarities • Risk Considerations • Financial Concerns – risks • Match with internal resources	• Macro Economic Indicators • Demographic Indicators • Market Growth Indicators	• Industry Indicators • Export & Import statistics • Tariff and Non-Tariff barriers

IMPACT ON YOUR INTERNATIONAL BUSINESS PLAN

your international progress and success. Ultimately your goal is to modify your international business plan to incorporate what you have learned from your initial international expansion. We now turn to these issues individually.

Internal Considerations

In some respects, all roads lead back home so perhaps the best place to begin your analysis of your international progress and success is to look internally at the impact of your international activities. This part of the analysis is particularly important because without an honest appraisal of the internal impact and progress, future international success and growth may be doomed. For example, it is never too early to judge how much support the international activities received from other departments in the company. Internally, you should consider four issues: (1) financial, (2) staff, (3) organizational structure, and (4) organizational commitment.

Financial. If all roads lead back home, they are probably littered with income, cash flow, and balance sheet statements. As much as I hated all the financial reporting requirements during my initial tenure in international sales and marketing, I soon learned that close attention to the numbers is critical to keeping your company on a successful path. Without them, you really don't know what is happening. This is just as true for international business as it is for domestic trade.

The first area to consider is the *income statement*. As discussed in Chapter 1, you need to decide how far down the income statement to track expenses related to your international activities. For example, how will you allocate overhead such as R&D expenses, fixed overhead, and management? Clearly, the less overhead applied to the international activities, the greater the profit attributed to the international activities. From an accounting standpoint, the issue is variable costing versus full absorption costing, which was discussed in Chapter 11. In your early international expansion stages, you may want to adopt variable costing, which more directly tracks the direct costs related to your international activities rather than taking into account the whole company's efforts. Though this does result in greater profits attributed to your international activities, it can be argued that the other costs, such as management and R&D, would be incurred anyway, so variable costing during the initial stages is probably the most appropriate.

In either case, you must determine your profit or loss impact because future growth and investments in international expansion will depend on profit projections, which in turn depend on previous income statements. If your initial international activities have resulted in a profit, you can make a stronger case for increasing the international expansion. If the company has incurred a loss, it will be critical to determine why the loss occurred, what will turn the loss into a profit, and how long the company can afford to incur losses. This also is a good point to question the structure and format of the income statement. You may find that the reporting is inadequate for your international planning. Perhaps the departmentalization or hierarchy of the statement may need to be changed.

Next, you should look at your *cash flow statements*. These are particularly important in your initial international expansion because they capture many of the uses of cash that have not yet reached the income statement. For example, you may find that you've incurred considerable marketing expenses for printing, packaging, or training materials that have yet to be amortized. Though these items will be captured in the balance sheet, the details may not be specific enough to your international activities to highlight or isolate the cash usage directly attributable to international business. In fact, many consider cash flow statements so important that they review the cash flow and cash flow forecast before other financial statements.

Finally, the impact of your international activities on your *balance sheet* should be addressed. You should look at any international receivables and determine if your international receivables risk is too high or too low. Is the balance sheet exposed in any way to potential foreign exchange movements? Is there a way to favorably restructure any debt in light of your international expansion? For example, if your working capital requirements are being stressed because of the increase in international sales, you may want to consider the SBA export working capital program (discussed in Chapter 16).

Having looked at your financials, you should finish by addressing the issue of your accounting system. Be sure it supports timely and accurate reporting of your international expansion. As you expand internationally, you must be able to depend on the information from your financials to support future decisions. It will be much easier to address these concerns now than later in the expansion process. Brainstorm on what the impact will be if your international sales increase two or three times (or more).

Staff Commitment

A junior accountant in a mid-sized company recently commented to me that he hoped our International Trade Center would come to his company to tell the international department what to do. I was taken aback by the comment because the company has a strong international reputation and I was confident it already knew what it was doing internationally. Upon further discussion, it seemed that communication between the international sales staff and his department was surprisingly limited. All the accountant saw was the expenses related to particular international markets, with seemingly no income. "They spend and spend, we lose money, and the whole company is hurt." I soon realized the issue was one of communication and isolation. The accountant felt completely outside the loop regarding which activities were necessary and saw them only as a cash drain on the company's otherwise successful domestic activities. The answer was not to tell the international department what to do, but to start a training program that helps the accounting department (and other departments) better understand the opportunities of the company's international expansion. I created a training session for the company specifically designed to educate staff about the overall goals and benefits of going global and how each person's role and responsibilities toward those goals have an impact.

Organizational commitment. A second consideration, just as important as the first, is organizational commitment. The importance of organization commitment to the success of your international expansion cannot be overstated. Unless the international plan has the full backing of the company, both management and non-management, the expansion efforts will be delayed, fraught with problems, and potentially fail. Placing this emphasis on organization commitment may seem a bit sensational, but to discount the issue is too risky. A company's international business plan depends on too many departments and their employees to not address the issue of support. In fact, it can be argued that every department is impacted, including domestic sales, which might help train or aid in developing international strategies.

The issue of top management commitment was first addressed in Chapter 2 as a prerequisite for a company's readiness to go global. Again, it should be addressed after your initial expansion. If top management (including owners, shareholders, and boards) does not seem to fully support the international expansion, investigate ways to strengthen its support. For example, perhaps key individuals can be involved in some of the international travel opportunities. They should at least be involved in corporate tours or hospitality events during visits of foreign buyers. These seem like obvious solutions, yet they can be easily overlooked.

Employees/staff. Staff commitment is also critical, and perhaps more difficult because there are fewer opportunities to directly involve staff members. Educating staff about the significance of international expansion will be important. (See sidebox.) However, it will probably take more than education. Staff members also should be involved. As with top management, consider involving staff in international travel or foreign buyer visits to your company. For example, during the next trade show or product launch, perhaps someone from R&D or customer support can attend, along with the international sales and marketing representatives. Your overseas agents or distributors probably already know many of these staff members via phone or fax, never having the chance to meet them in person. Not only will it strengthen the bond between the U.S. company and foreign buyer, but you'll probably find that new information and suggestions arise from the encounters. For example, on more than one occasion when I traveled with R&D staff, they would pick up on product enhancement issues that I missed. A sales and marketing representative will have a different perspective than a full time R&D employee. To involve such staff involves increased expenditure, which at times may be difficult to justify, but I think you will find that these investments pay off in the long term.

A second issue regarding the impact of staff on your international activities is to review the procedures in place to support the international efforts. For example, are shipments delayed due to problems in particular areas such as accounting, warehouse, or customer support? Are those bottlenecks unique to the international sales that need to be addressed? These situations may be obvious to others in the company, and when those responsible for the international expansion ask other staff for input, the problems can be corrected before they become worse. The time to address these issues is during the initial stages of your international growth before problems begin to impact the success and viability of the international business plan.

Internationalize staff. The transition from a company with few international activities to one with significant international business will be smoother if existing staff are given the international tools rather than bringing in new staff who already have the knowledge. This will depend on the speed of your international expansion and the motivation and interests of your existing staff, but as a general rule, try to internationalize staff impacted by the international expansion instead of setting up separate departments. The establishment of a separate international department early in a company's international growth tends to lead to isolation and negative relations between the domestic and international staff. It is preferable to work with existing staff (when practical) by upgrading their skills to handle the international challenge.

Organizational structure. After looking at the financial, staff, and organizational commitment issues, the last issue to address is organizational structure, especially as it relates to staff involved in the international expansion. Nothing highlights weaknesses (or opportunities) in a company's structure more than adding international sales into the mix. If your company has already entered two or three foreign markets, you understand what I mean. It seems that entering foreign markets and handling the ongoing sales and support seems to test a company's ability to respond to change. It is probably because international activities impact so many departments. Whatever the reason, now is a good time to address your organizational structure in terms of who reports to whom, how decisions are made, and how and when reporting is done.

It is beyond the scope of this text to address the different types of organizational structures. If you feel your company could benefit from restructuring, I encourage you to research current literature on the topic and seek outside assistance. Some issues to consider when deciding where to place international staff include:

Healthy Skepticism?

Regardless of your level of initial international success, some individuals will be skeptical about the company's international activities. Likewise, individuals that otherwise wholly support the international expansion may at times be at odds with it. Can this skepticism be good?

Actually, yes. The international marketplace is extremely unpredictable. It is very different from the comfort of the domestic market and customers. As such, it is always fair (and right) to ask questions. As trade experts say, it is not if something will go wrong, but when. A bit of caution, even if it seems to go against the goals of and commitment to global expansion, can help minimize problems.

- *Separate department*. International staff are isolated and function separate from the company. The department has its own sales and marketing functions, and probably separate customer support and logistics. International staff handle all products going to all foreign markets.
- *Functional division*. Company maintains functionally separate departments (sales, marketing, R&D, accounting, and logistics) with one or more individuals in each department responsible for handling international activities.
- *Product division*. International (and probably domestic) activities are separated by product groupings. This division shares non-product-related functions with other divisions, such as accounting.
- *Foreign market division*. International staff are grouped by the foreign markets or regions they support, for example Europe or Latin America. Staff within each grouping would include sales staff, and perhaps other functional areas such as marketing and logistics.
- *Matrix*. Though international staff may be functionally separated via function, product, or market as above, responsibility and reporting is across all departments. A matrix structure is unique because of its many informal lines of communication between staff/departments.

The above distinctions are simply generalizations about how the international staff can be placed within a company. Clearly the advantages and disadvantages of each depend on the size and scope of your company's international activities. One is not better than any other and many share characteristics. You should treat these as ideas or frameworks from which to judge your current structure. For example, it is common for companies in an early stage of international expansion to adopt the separate department approach, especially for sales and marketing functions. If this is the case for your company, you may want to challenge this assumption if you find it leads to communication problems and delays. You may want to consider implementing a matrix reporting structure so communication between departments is enhanced.

The main issue of organizational structure is to be aware of the overall impact international expansion has on your company, and how your company responds to the changes needed to support the international activities. It is easy to overlook these issues in the early stages of international growth, but to do so can lead to bigger problems in the future that are more difficult to change because resistance to international growth becomes institutionalized in various departments. It is better to deal with these issues now rather than later.

Foreign Market Considerations

Did you find the best agent or distributor? How effective has it been? Were you satisfied with the launch of your products in a particular market? What type of feedback are you receiving from the foreign market?

These are the types of questions you should address during the second part of a review of your international progress and success. These issues will probably arise more naturally than those of the internal review because the very nature of going global is looking outward. Four aspects should be considered: (1) foreign buyers, (2) entry mode, (3) feedback, and (4) channel management.

Foreign buyers. You should begin your market review with a SWOT analysis of your foreign buyers, on a market-by-market basis. This involves evaluating the strengths, weaknesses, opportunities, and threats. You have already done a similar analysis prior to appointing an agent or distributor. However, now that you have worked with the specific buyer, you'll have a better idea how accurate your original SWOT analysis was. You may have focused on the agent or distributor's good side prior to its appointment. Now that you have had a chance to spend more time with the agent or distributor, and perhaps its staff beyond top management, you are in a much better position to really evaluate these issues. Figure 17.2 summarizes issues that you should consider when completing a SWOT analysis of your foreign buyers.

Figure 17.2 Issues to Consider during Foreign Buyer SWOT Analysis

Strengths   **Local market reputation**
Industry contacts and Strength of distribution channel
Product launch coordination
Technical ability
Time and attention placed specifically on U.S. manufacturer's products
Sales success with U.S. manufacturer's products
Local marketing efforts (translations, public relations, dealer
    communication)
Customer support
Financial commitment, ability

Weakness   Essentially a review of the same items as "Strengths"

Opportunities
Could their success be enhanced with more support from U.S.?
What is holding them back from more success?
Should the buyer pursue other lines to represent that will enhance U.S.
    manufacturer's products?
Are there other events, opportunities for the foreign buyer/agent that will
    enhance their performance?
Would a change in payment terms increase sales? Lower price? Improve
    training?

Threats   Is the company overall successful? Financially secure?
Any events on the horizon that could negatively impact performance?
Are they giving U.S. manufacturer enough attention versus
    other products represented?
Do other product lines represented by buyer threaten future for U.S.
    manufacturer?

There are two goals of your SWOT analysis. First, you want to identify issues that need to be addressed with your foreign buyers in order to improve their performance. Subsequent chapters will discuss many of these issues in greater detail, but anything you can do to improve their sales and marketing potential clearly improves your sales potential. These issues include pricing, marketing support, training, and customer support. You will be in a better position to make these changes once you fully understand each buyer's strengths, weaknesses, opportunities, and threats.

Second, by completing a SWOT analysis of the foreign buyers you used during your initial global expansion, you'll be in a much more informed position when looking for new representatives for future markets. For example, your star performer may do extremely well simply because it represents another manufacturer that has a product line that complements your product line. Many companies have piggybacked on the international success of another product, but this fact may not be clear during your initial search for representation. Likewise, the importance of other characteristics such as size, financial strength, sales methodology, and industry focus will be much clearer after you have some experience with various types of agents or distributors. The sooner you can identify the characteristics that impact the success or failure of a representative for your products, the sooner you can appoint better agents or distributors. Each market will have its own unique circumstances, but once your global distribution network is in place, you may be surprised how your successful foreign buyers all share certain characteristics.

Entry mode. Having entered only a handful of markets, now would be a good time to evaluate your choice of entry mode. Most companies in the early stage of international expansion pursue a mix of direct and indirect exporting. Companies use direct entry for markets that represent the best combination of market potential without significant risk. Indirect entry method may be used for higher risk markets requiring a great level of

Outside Assistance with Internal Considerations

The very nature of reviewing your own company's initial international success creates the risk of not truthfully addressing the issues and problems because it is hard to step outside your own company thinking. A review must be objective or its impact will not be as significant and the opportunity to improve may be weaker. Your company should consider outside assistance to attain a fresh view. Most companies do not seek outside advice, not to mention consultants! But to believe an unbiased internal review can be conducted without external input is unrealistic.

A variety of public and private assistance options are available, some even at no cost. For example, many of the resources initially used to plan your global expansion would be appropriate. So would a paid consultant that you may not have previously considered. Some states have experimented with an international executive loan program where an individual with the appropriate background is placed in a growing international company on a part-time basis, perhaps one day a week. These innovative new programs and traditional methods such as consultants should all be considered.

international experience, contacts, and investment. (Review Chapter 7 for more details of indirect versus direct market entry.)

Before you enter any more markets, review the results of your international expansion entry mode decisions. Do they still seem like the right choices? If you used indirect exporting, have you given up too much control and feedback? If you used direct exporting, does the potential of the market still justify the increased risk in terms of resources and time? This analysis must be made within the overall context of the results of your international expansion up to this point.

Internal and product issues must also be considered. It is misleading to only consider the performance of your export partner (whether direct or indirect) without factoring in internal and product issues. For example, the real problem may not be your export method, but instead product-related issues such as quality, standards, or features. Also you do not want to make any changes in your entry mode strategy too quickly, even if results are disappointing. If your experience in a particular foreign market is still less than one year, it is too early to make a change.

Assuming results are lower than expected and you believe greater success can be achieved by changing your entry mode, begin by establishing a time frame to make the change. For example, if you are going to change from indirect to direct and the contract with your indirect partner has six months remaining, there is a great deal you can do now to prepare for the change later. You can take an unofficial trip to the foreign market. You also can begin attending trade shows. (Chapter 18 discusses termination of representation.)

Feedback from the foreign market. One of the keys to success in international sales and marketing is developing a strong channel for feedback from the international marketplace (how to accomplish this is one of the topics of Chapter 21). No assessment of your international progress and success can be made without complete and reliable feedback from the marketplace. This is true regardless of the export method, but it is perhaps the most critical when using indirect exporting because feedback tends to be poor.

Feedback from your channel (foreign buyers) and your foreign customers helps put all of the other factors into perspective. Your foreign buyer, for example, should be able to give you some indication of how your sales success compares to similar products launched in the market. Feedback also provides crucial information about how your product competes, why consumers/industry purchase your product, and what changes can be made to make it more competitive.

An evaluation of the progress and success of your global growth will help you determine if you need to increase your international feedback. (If so, consider some of the options discussed in Chapter 21.)

Channel management. The issue of motivating, controlling, and receiving feedback from your foreign buyers (agents or distributors) is collectively referred to as channel management. The notion is that to be successful, you must work in partnership with your agent or distributor rather than just using them to sell your product. Success is a two-way street that depends on your performance and that of your foreign buyers in each market. To ensure maximum success, you must ensure that all the factors that influence the success of your foreign buyers are in place, such as training, communication, marketing support materials, pricing, and the framework of the relationship (exclusive versus nonexclusive). As you evaluate your channel management, ask questions such as: Do we have good control of the distribution network? Are we providing the right tools to motivate our foreign buyers? Are we utilizing our exclusive relationships properly?

Clearly the issue of channel management is interrelated to other issues involved in international expansion. But by highlighting the issues directly relating to management of the sales/distribution network, new ideas for improvement are developed that might otherwise have been overlooked.

Product Considerations

The final segment of the framework for assessing your international progress and success is to analyze performance at the product level. This is the most important analysis because ultimately success is defined by sales. However, be wary of placing too much emphasis on the sales side of the analysis. The sales statistics are critical to understanding your export progress and success, but always understand that sales are the result of a myriad of activities combining internal, market, and product-related issues. To only use sales as an indicator of success may lead to a false conclusion. All analyses of your export/international activities must be done within a framework that looks at all aspects of going global, which is why I highlighted internal and market issues before addressing the product issues. If your international activities are less than a year old, it also may be premature to place too much emphasis on your initial sales levels. More than once, I had a foreign market's sales take off after more than a year of seemingly no progress.

Nevertheless, it is difficult not to ponder your initial foreign market sales results. It's natural. Americans are driven by numbers, and your initial export sales levels are numbers that will be scrutinized by everyone, internally and externally.

Presumably, if you are reading this text, you are responsible in some way for the numbers, so your task is to learn how to put the export sales figures into perspective within all the other factors.

Sales achieved. The first place to start is with an analysis of your international sales on a product-by-product, market-by-market basis. Beyond simply looking at sales levels, be sure to try and develop any trends you identify. For example:

- Did your second market follow a pattern similar to the first market you entered or did the sales levels vary considerably? How about other markets?
- Were there any seasonal differences that can be identified in these early stages?
- Did one product do considerably better than another? Did this hold true for the other markets?
- Are there inconsistencies between sales and market size? For example, did a smaller market do considerably better than a larger market? If so, how can this be explained?

- Did you have any pricing differences in your international pricing strategy? If so, can you attribute this result in sales differences to the price differential? The goal is to try and identify how price elastic (how much demand is sensitive to price) your products are in the international marketplace compared to the domestic marketplace.
- Can you make any predictions on how long it takes your products to take hold in a particular foreign market?
- If there is one market with exceptionally high or low results, to what would you attribute the results?

These are some of the issues you may want to investigate as you evaluate your sales results. Again, beyond simply looking at specific results, always try to develop themes or rationales for particular results. Though it can be dangerous to generalize, especially when it comes to international markets which can vary greatly, the more you can learn about the behavior of your products in a market, the better you will be at predicting results in future markets.

Competitive situation. After a thorough analysis of your sales you should compare the results to those of your competitors. This will be a difficult exercise because the sales figures for your competitors may be impossible to attain. But you may be surprised how much information regarding sales figures is available for both your industry and individual companies. Review Chapter 6 for ways to assess your competitor activities.

Once you have gathered as much information as possible about your competitors, compare it with your sales results. Try to develop a sense of your market share in each foreign market or region. This will be very difficult in the early stages of your international expansion when your sales may only be a fraction of the sales for the industry. Nevertheless, this exercise helps you identify challenges and perfect your techniques for estimating your market share.

You should also review your competitive position in the light of market considerations. For example, your sales levels may be low, but your market share high. Are you able to attribute this to any of the marketing decisions such as choice of distributor or channel management? Is there something a specific foreign buyer is doing that is impacting market share? Did your sales come at the expense of a competitor or are they displacing other products not directly competing with your products?

Finally, you should address the issue of brand strength compared to the competition. Perhaps you are not yet achieving the sales levels you anticipated, but is your brand growing in awareness? Is your product beginning to set the standard for the industry regarding features, benefits, usability, or technology? These are important issues to track as you continue your expansion because they provide some insight into the future direction of your international marketing efforts.

Marketing activities. The issue of brand strength leads into a third product-related issue: international marketing activities by your company and your foreign buyers. Some of the issues to review would be:

- *Product launch.* Compare product launch activities on a market-by-market basis. How did each foreign agent or distributor launch your products in its market? How did they differ and how were they the same? Were there any unique aspects that worked particularly well in one market? Could they be adapted for future international markets? How involved was your company in the product launch? Did your involvement have an impact? What sort of timetable was involved in each product launch?

- *Marketing materials and translations.* This aspect of marketing varies greatly between markets. Some foreign agents and distributors will place a great emphasis on developing local product literature. Others may rely solely on U.S. literature. Differences also vary by industry in that the buyers (end-users) in some industries such as technical products may be accustomed to receiving brochures in English. Foreign representatives may feel less pressure to translate marketing materials for these types of products. Other industries may demand brochures translated into the local language. You will often have to negotiate with the foreign buyer to determine which party will be responsible for localization of literature, training, materials, packaging, and advertising. Assuming the foreign buyer made all translations, you need to determine how much was done and its impact. If you determine that localization of marketing materials helped the success of your products, you may want to consider fostering such activity in the future. You can do this through cooperative marketing (discussed in Chapter 19). Or you can bring the function in-house and manage the process directly. In either case, the goal is to assess the effectiveness of your marketing materials in terms of their usability and effectiveness in the foreign markets.

- *Support materials.* Similarly, you need to determine the effectiveness of the supporting materials used by agents or distributors as they represent you in the market. These include training manuals, technical reference documents, competitive analyses, industry information, logo sheets, corporate information, and software - essentially, everything that is needed to keep your foreign buyer up to date on how to sell your products. The importance of this issue is often overlooked by manufacturers who are concerned about releasing too much marketing information to third parties. It also is important to understand the situation of the foreign agent or distributor. It may feel isolated from the U.S. domestic market and be less able to communicate on a regular basis than domestic customers. Thus, your agents and distributors require a higher level of support materials to make them self-sufficient, especially during the hours of the day when the U.S. sleeps. Your foreign representative needs to be able to answer technical questions or competitive issues that need to be clarified for a customer.

- *Training.* You should review the training procedures that are in place for each of your foreign agents or distributors. Did you or someone else spend time with them conducting the proper training? Did they send employees to the U.S. for training? How thorough were the training materials? As with support materials, your foreign buyers must be fully trained on all aspects of your products to adequately represent your company. If your foreign representatives are required to conduct warranty repair, you should also review if adequate training was in place. You also want to compare how effective the training has been in each market. If some agents or distributors seem to be better trained, you want to see if the differences can also be explained by differences in the background of the particular agents or distributors. These are important observations to use when selecting future foreign representation.

- *Product modifications*. You should address the nagging issue of product modifications. I say nagging because you will find international buyers almost always insist on product modifications. I remember questioning more than once if there was ever going to be an international sales call that didn't result in the potential customer asking if the product could be changed!

   It is wrong to ignore requests for product modifications because more often than not, it is in the best interest of the manufacturer and the foreign representative to try to accommodate such requests. But if your experience is similar to mine, the reasonable requests are far fewer than the unreasonable ones. Nevertheless, you always need to determine if your company is doing all it can to accommodate product modifications.

   In some cases modifications will be necessary before your product can even enter a market. The more difficult modifications are the ones that seem to only benefit a few markets. This is when difficult decisions must be made regarding whether to invest in the modification or delay the request until the costs can be justified. These are never easy situations because you want to support your foreign buyers, but ultimately such decisions must be made within the context of the whole company and its strategy and priorities. Whether you make the product modifications or not, include a review of the requests as part of your ongoing assessment of your international expansion.

• THREE CROSS-THEMES: RESOURCES, TIME FRAME, AND MARKET SELECTION MODEL

Having completed the internal, foreign market, and product assessments of the progress in your international expansion, you should turn to three aspects that cross each of these groups. First you should look at what resources have been particularly important in your international expansion. Was a particular database useful when selecting markets? Was an outside resource helpful in solving international problems? Second, what does the experience from your initial market entries indicate about the future time frame expectations? Can you enter markets more quickly or should the process be slowed to be more effective? Finally, how can the market selection model, developed in Chapter 5, be improved based on the results of your initial market entries?

These three issues should be addressed using a team approach. Gather the staff most impacted by your international expansion and conduct a brainstorming session to discuss these issues. For example, if you come from a sales and marketing perspective, it is important to hear from other departments in the company. There may be resources or issues related to time frame that involve departments other than sales and marketing. Without this input, you risk developing a model for improving your international business that is incomplete and lacks the support of others in the company.

Resources

If you have already entered a few international markets and made various shipments, you will realize the importance of using outside resources to make the task of going global easier. From bankers and freight forwarders to private and public agencies, utilizing resources can be the link to going global quickly and profitably. Before expanding into too many more markets, take time to determine which resources have proved invaluable, which were less helpful, and where you still need help.

The good, the bad, and the ugly. Outside resources come in all shapes and sizes. Some are extraordinarily helpful at little to no cost. Some are a waste of time. And others are dangerous because their information is wrong and leads to mistakes. When beginning your international expansion you need to learn how to tell each apart from the others. A brainstorming session within your company will help highlight which resources are the good ones, which did not help, and which led to problems.

For the good ones, nurture the relationship. Now that you have some international experience, contact these resources, update them on your activities, and thank them for their support. You will probably find they rarely receive such feedback, which will encourage their assistance in the future. Speaking on behalf of a state-funded export assistance center, there is nothing quite as uplifting as knowing our assistance really made a difference. It spurs us on to think of new ways to help the company.

You may want to give the bad resources the benefit of the doubt and try them again, especially if you are short on options. For example, you may be tied to a particular private company due to a relationship it has with your domestic sales operations. I recommend you contact the company and indicate that its information didn't support your efforts.

Finally, avoid the resources that gave you wrong information. During your analysis, don't forget that you need resources for all aspects of your international activities: internal, foreign market, and product. For example, you may be able to use a college or university to assist in training your staff. Externally, you may find a particular government or state agency that is effective in assisting you to locate overseas buyers. And regarding products, you may find a testing laboratory that is extremely effective in assisting with your product testing or standards compliance.

Time Frame

Early in the planning process when you set a timetable for entering your initial foreign markets, I suspect you were a bit more optimistic than realistic. It is natural to hope you will be able to expand internationally faster than perhaps you really can. The excitement of adding international markets can lead to some unrealistic expectations.

Now that you have entered a few markets, you have a much better idea of what time frame is realistic for adding new markets - one that is suitable for your products, your company, and your industry. Some companies, due to the nature of their industry or internal resources, will be able to enter foreign markets more quickly than others. The key is to understand what is suitable for your company. Making that judgement before you entered foreign markets was difficult, but now, you should try to institutionalize your experience by reworking your expansion model to include lessons and new aspects of the process that will more accurately predict the time it takes to add new markets.

Your analysis of your international time frame should include internal, foreign market, and product aspects. The model shown in Figure 17.1 details some questions you should consider during this analysis.

Market Selection Model

One of the most important goals when analyzing your international progress and success is to review the market selection model developed in Chapter 5. After entering only a few markets, you will have a much better idea about how the model can be improved and expanded. You now have a basis to determine how accurate some of your assumptions were. For example, you may have originally thought that a strong indicator of foreign market potential was the level of imports of competing products. Now you can test that assumption by seeing if your sales did better in a country that has strong imports of competing products. You also may have emphasized particular macro and demographic indicators such as population, GDP, GDP growth, and per capita income. Now that you have some sales results, go back and see if there really is a correlation between such indicators and sales success.

In reality, with data from only a few markets and sales results from less than two years, it will probably be too early to validate your model. Most of the other issues outside the model (internal, foreign market, and product) will probably have had an even greater impact on the sales success than any macro or demographic indicators. Thus, any attempt to correlate sales results with indicators may be impossible because there are so many uncontrollable factors.

Nevertheless, the process of continually reviewing and updating your model is a valuable one. You still need some type of model to help determine what markets you enter next. As long as you remember that the market selection model is simply a tool and not a definite predictor of market potential, then its use will be kept in perspective. The process also will help keep you focused on the market-based indicators which, though they are outside of your control, still have an impact on your sales potential in that market.

I recommend you start playing the forecasting game using your market selection model as the forecasting tool. By this I mean go back to the statistical model you developed to rank foreign markets and enhance the spreadsheet to actually try to predict sales volumes in a way that matches your actual results. For example, assume you sell a product that is purchased by companies and each company only buys one. You know that you sold 1,000 in France during the first year. Rework your spreadsheet using the various indicators so that it results in 1,000 pieces sold. Clearly, you are forcing the model to fit the data, but use this new model to see what it predicts for another one of your markets and compare this prediction to the actual results. If the prediction is close to the actual results, your model is becoming more accurate.

This is not an exact science and it will probably drive statisticians crazy, but it can be fun to manipulate the model to get it to work better as a predictor of market success and eventually as a sales forecasting tool. At the least, it will help you to really understand your model!

• ADDING NEW MARKETS

Now that you have completed your analysis you are ready to consider adding more foreign markets. Too many companies fail to properly analyze their past foreign market successes or failures before expanding. Not conducting a thorough review results in repeated mistakes and missed opportunities.

It is easy to understand why you should wait to add new markets until you fully understand the lessons from the first few. There are simply too many issues involved in developing an international business plan that cannot be truly understood until they are experienced in real life market applications. For example, the time frame you initially created was based on assumptions about training, translations, product shipments, marketing campaigns, and other issues. These were your best guesses as to how long market entry would take. Now, you know how long it will take and you can create a more realistic timetable.

Chapter 18

Managing International Channels of Distribution

How a company manages its international distribution channels is often a company's greatest challenge. It knows it has a good product, good marketing materials and international support, and what seems to be a good distributor. But after months of trying, the relationship never really seems to get going, sales results are disappointing, and before long the company looks to end the relationship.

Sound familiar? If not, you are lucky. Most everyone I know in international sales and marketing has at one time or another had to deal with an agent or distributor that turned sour. It is unfortunate because turning around a bad situation is very time consuming and getting out of contracts can be expensive.

The goal is to prevent the situation, which is the subject of this chapter. Through proactive management of your international agents and distributors, you can minimize the chance of having a nonperforming foreign buyer.

These ideas will not work in all cases. There is always the possibility that for reasons out of your control or that of your buyer, the relationship simply does not function as hoped. In this case, you are faced with termination of your agreement (or nonrenewal). I will also be addressing the concerns of ending international contractual relationships.

• EXPECTATIONS OF YOUR CUSTOMERS

Perhaps the best place to begin is by highlighting the expectations of foreign buyers. These points may seem obvious, but many companies lose sight of the fact that their foreign buyers also want to be successful. If the buyer wins, the exporter wins. But the nature of international business creates obstacles that lead to delays, frustrations, and poor results. Many of these obstacles are unique to international transactions, such as exchange rate fluctuations, tariff and nontariff barriers, and international logistics. While these expectations are not unique to international buyers, they are particularly significant because of the international environment.

Appreciating the Unique Role of Foreign Representatives

The first rule to remember is that the customers of your foreign agent or distributor essentially view the agent or distributor as the manufacturer. Of course, your company is the manufacturer (or service provider). But for the end-user of your products in a foreign country, all communication is with the agent or distributor. The buyer (a retail store, key account, government, or end-user) deals exclusively with the importer. This includes ordering, logistics, training, customer support, warranty issues, and repairs. In some cases, if the brand of the importer is particularly strong, the distinction between manufacturer and importer becomes extremely blurred. This contrasts with your sales in your home market where you may conduct some of these functions without dealing with domestic sales channels.

For example, let's say a company manufactures components used in manufacturing medical equipment. For its domestic sales, the component manufacturer utilizes independent sales reps that make sales calls on medical product manufacturers. Because there are often substantial technical support functions before and after the sale, the manufacturer handles all technical inquiries directly from the market. The rep may coordinate the technical interchange to make sure all questions are answered, but the component manufacturer fulfills the need for technical support.

Now change the scenario to international sales. The company appoints a distributor to represent its products in the foreign market. When technical issues arise, it is less likely that the importer will refer its customers to the manufacturer. Instead, its customers will expect the importer to solve their problems. Due to time differences and communication costs, the importer will probably want to solve as many technical questions as possible without relying on the manufacturer. In this respect, the importer will act very much like the manufacturer.

In practice, importers have to conduct many functions that are normally the domain of manufacturers due to differences in time zones, geographic distances, language, and cultural differences. This puts more responsibility on the manufacturer to provide adequate materials and tools to empower the importer so it can duplicate many of the functions conducted by the manufacturer in its domestic market. You must learn to appreciate this unique role of your international distribution channel.

A Product that Works and a Service that Meets Needs

It probably sounds obvious to write this, but I assure you it will be a "hot button" for your foreign buyers. Above all else, foreign importers need products that work and are reliable. You will understand this if you have already made some foreign trips and something did not work, and everyone in your home office was asleep!

Obviously, all products have glitches and quirks, and with business under pressure to bring products out faster and with more bells and whistles, products are released that are not yet 100 percent market-ready. The international impact is that your foreign buyers expect to know the truth about such glitches and quirks, and want the tools to deal with the problems at no cost. They will need extra training to ensure they can troubleshoot problems on the spot. And good communication will have to be established between you and your foreign buyers. Foreign buyers expect product-related problems. Just be sure to give your buyers 100 percent support in resolving them.

Good Communication and Service

Due to time, language, and distance differences, you will probably find your international buyers are very sensitive to your level of communication. When I worked with an export management company, it had a rule that paid big dividends: all communication was to be answered the day they were received, even if only to acknowledge receiving the communication and indicate when an answer can be expected. More than once a foreign buyer would comment on good communication. I don't know that the communication itself was good, but we were attentive.

As long as you treat your foreign buyers like an extension of your domestic office, the communication requirements will be clear. Obviously, you will want to communicate price changes, product changes, and technical information as soon as possible. Remember that the impact of price and product changes is greater on your foreign agents and buyers because they have whole marketing campaigns and materials in place. The time needed to accommodate change is greater for international buyers than domestic buyers. This puts a greater pressure on the U.S. exporter to maintain good, timely communication.

Lack of Discrimination

Another hot button is the issue of fairness between domestic and international markets, as well as between individual international markets. In the early stages of international expansion, an exporting company may attempt to establish different sales and marketing policies for their domestic and international businesses. This discrimination is understandable because there are significant industry and market structures in some foreign markets that justify pricing and other marketing differences. However, if you significantly alter your international marketing in a way that favors the domestic market, be prepared to explain your actions if the international customers learn of the differences. It happened to me more than once. You quickly learn that your international customers will keep you honest. Most industries are too small for significant marketing differences to go unnoticed. If anything, your marketing may need to favor the foreign market.

Discriminating is even more obvious if you use different pricing policies in each foreign market. After your first international distributor/agent meeting, the word will naturally get out as each importer meets the other. It will happen even faster if you appoint a distributor in one market that already knows your distributor in another market. This is particularly likely when you add additional markets because distribution networks often track leading manufacturers. There may only be a limited number of really good distributors in a given market for a particular product. For this reason, it is difficult to maintain significant differences in your marketing policies between different agents and distributors.

Great Prices

Everyone wants the lowest price possible. Why should your international customers be any different? Due to international price escalation, as described in Chapter 11, you may need to lower international pricing compared to domestic pricing. Obviously, it depends on the competitive position of your products in the foreign market. Stronger competition, especially from locally produced products not subject to import taxes, will put even greater pressure on low prices. But be wary of importers that say they have to have the lowest price possible to stay competitive. You may find that they keep the margin and do not pass on the savings to the end-user. The key is to find the right balance.

• MOTIVATING YOUR CHANNELS OF DISTRIBUTION

You probably feel that your foreign buyers want it all. However, there are a variety of ways to keep them in control! The key is knowing what to do, and when. You must analyze the aspects of sales and marketing to help achieve your goals and those of your foreign representatives.

Playing the Exclusivity Game

The single most powerful motivational tool is the exclusive contract. As an exporter, you may prefer nonexclusive contracts, but your customers want exclusive contracts. An importer wants full exclusivity to represent a product line. After the cost of translations, product launch, P/R activities, sales calls, and training staff, the importer wants protection against another company simply coming in and reaping all the benefits.

Exclusive contracts also may be to your benefit. The rationale is simple: exclusive contracts put you in a better position to motivate and manage your agents and distributors. With an exclusive contract, you have the ability to cancel or not renew the contract, which may represent significant business for the importer. Without an exclusive contract, you have less control. Moreover, it is probably the only effective way to ensure your agent or distributor makes the required investment in the market.

The decision is essentially a question of assigning the responsibilities for sales, marketing, customer support, and logistics. The more that is expected of the foreign importer, the greater the need for an exclusive contract. The more that will be done by the exporter, the less the need for an exclusive contract. If you expect your foreign agent or distributor to make a significant investment in the market (on your behalf) in order to successfully sell the product, an exclusive contract will probably be required.

Another consideration when choosing the type of contract is the agent/distributor law for the particular country. Some countries have local laws that have strong provisions against termination of an agent or distributor contract without just cause. These laws can discourage the use of exclusive representation contracts.

When to Move to Nonexclusive Contracts

Exclusive contracts are critical if you expect your foreign representative to invest in the market. But when are nonexclusive contracts suitable? This is a complex issue because the decision to go nonexclusive after entering a market with an exclusive contract can ruin the market for your products if not properly handled. Imagine telling a distributor who has worked for years to build up a market for your product on an exclusive basis that you would like to add a few more distributors in the market. It is rarely an enjoyable task.

Moving to nonexclusive contracts is primarily an issue of market maturity. In the early stages of developing a foreign market, especially if the exporter has no physical presence (sales office) in that market, it is highly likely that representation will be exclusive. As the market grows, both in terms of sales of the exporter's products and sales of competing products, there will be competitive demands to go nonexclusive. These pressures will start as soon as the exporter's profits are significant enough to warrant closer attention and control in the foreign market.

My experience in the U.K. and Europe in the computer industry serves as a good example. When I first began selling computer components in Europe, none of my company's direct competitors had any physical presence in Europe. They were all selling into Europe via exclusive representation contracts - generally, one per country. Though I cannot speak for all of the competitors, most companies had less than $1 million in total European sales during the first year or two. As the European market for computer components grew, sales grew.

Soon there was growing pressure to be more directly involved in the market. My company began by placing a European manager in the U.K. - which was me! Because I was able to more closely follow the activities of our distributors, I soon saw where opportunities were being missed, such as a trade show that our distributor didn't participate in or media advertising that was not as significant as I would have liked. I also saw that multiple distributors would better serve particular markets. For example, Germany has three different markets: north, middle, and south. Our German distributor did a good job of covering all three markets, but had it not I would have been under strong pressure to appoint at least one more distributor in Germany.

Soon, I was placing advertising directly into the media and making direct sales calls for particular products (which were already outside of our regular distribution contracts). My company was taking on more of the sales and marketing responsibilities. Eventually, as our company merged with a larger company which had sales offices in Paris and Munich, we began dismantling our exclusive distribution contracts. The newly formed company had the European infrastructure to handle more of the sales and marketing responsibilities and could sell directly to dealers and OEM accounts.

I use this as an example of how a manufacturer begins with exclusive contracts and eventually moves to nonexclusive contracts. However, the situation will be different for each company. Some will always pursue exclusive contracts, even with significant involvement in the foreign markets. It depends on the long-term strategy and philosophy of the manufacturer. Be aware, however, that the decision to go nonexclusive after a history of exclusive contracts can backfire and it may be difficult to return to exclusive contracts. Your previous distributors will no longer trust you, and you will need to find new distributors. These changes are rarely good for the product and its potential in the foreign market.

Other Methods to Manage the Distribution Channel

Beyond the exclusive/nonexclusive contract issue, there are a number of other methods and techniques you can use to get the most out of your distributors. You should begin by reviewing all the issues raised in the previous section discussing the expectations of international agents and distributors. By brainstorming you can develop ways that your company can meet those expectations. Some ways to meet expectations include:

- *Appreciating the unique role of foreign representatives.* To help support the notion that your customers are essentially an extension of your company, think of your foreign agents and distributors as partners, or perhaps even employees. (Be careful, though, not to refer to them as employees. Ending contracts in some countries may require protection for agents and distributors as if they really had been employees. You want to avoid contributing to that misperception.) When you visit your foreign buyers, spend considerable time with them, just as you would a subsidiary. Do not drop by for a quick visit. Spend at least a day or two so you will have quality time together, including social time. I regularly spent weekends with my foreign distributors participating in tourist activities. In some cases, I would be invited to spend time in their homes, which I always took as a high compliment. The point is to view your foreign customers as an extension of your company overseas.
- *A product that works.* Given that all products and services will have some problems relating to quality or features, the issue isn't so much about delivering a product that is 100 percent reliable. It is more one of attitude - keep good lines of communication with your foreign buyers regarding product-related issues. Consider giving them diagnostic tools or schematics that you would not normally give to domestic representatives. Empower them as much as possible to handle product quality and repair issues.
- *Good communication.* Do all you can to communicate with your foreign customers frequently and thoroughly. Consider an international newsletter. Send essential staff members to overseas trade shows and on distributor visits. Invite your foreign buyers to the U.S. for plant visits. Utilize technology such as the Internet, satellite, compressed video, and multimedia options to increase and improve communication.
- *Lack of discrimination.* If your international pricing is higher than your domestic pricing, be prepared to defend your position. Offer tangible benefits to your international buyers not available to the domestic market to compensate for the increased pricing. If your international pricing varies between regions or foreign markets, be prepared to deal with inevitable questions when the word gets out. The Internet has greatly shrunk the world, increasing networking between buyers. Maintaining separate international pricing may become increasingly difficult.
- *Great prices.* Not all companies can offer great prices to their international customers. For any number of reasons, from internal politics to financial pressures, companies may actually price their products much higher international-

ly. If your pricing is not great internationally, brainstorm ways to make comparing prices difficult. For example, you might add features to your international products not available domestically. Perhaps you can package your products differently. If you can't offer great prices, compensate in other ways such as co-op advertising to minimize the impact of noncompetitive pricing.

• MEETING WITH YOUR FOREIGN BUYERS

No single technique contributes more to a strong relationship between the manufacturer and foreign representation than frequent and purposeful visits. I cannot overstate the importance of making the investment in your distribution channel by taking the time to visit your representatives. One of the most powerful features of direct market entry (versus using export management companies or piggyback partners) is the wealth of market feedback available from your agents and distributors. This feedback can be used to improve your competitive position via changes in product, marketing, and pricing. But the level of quality feedback will be minimal if you rely solely on email, Skype, or phone contact.

During visits, try to accomplish more than just checking up on your agent or distributor. You might want to investigate some of the following activities:

- *Key account visits.* Go with your agent or distributor to visit key accounts, such as retailers, corporate buyers, or government buyers. Observe how the representative sells your products. How well does he or she understand the product and its benefits and features? Does he or she represent your company effectively? Do you observe the need for improved marketing materials that would make the selling task more effective? More training?
- *Blind sales calls.* Visit a retail shop or customer of your agent or distributor to see if it is truly carrying your product. If you do so anonymously, be careful because you risk annoying your agent or distributor if it thinks you are sidestepping it. For example, our computer components were sold through retail computer dealers, so I would often visit dealers to see if our products were prominently displayed on the shelf, and to check on the retail price. After such a visit, I would normally tell my distributor in case the word got back from the dealer. It was a courtesy to the distributor to keep it informed and it helped the distributor understand that it needed to be up-front with me as well.
- *Media visits.* If you are traveling with a key executive, plan a visit to an industry magazine or local business press. When I would travel with our company's president, I would always have at least one or two breakfast meetings with journalists. It impressed the president and often resulted in helpful press. You can also get some good competitive information depending on how talkative the journalist is. If editorial staff is not available, meet with advertising staff. Sometimes they can provide even better competitive information than editorial staff.
- *Training events.* Take advantage of every visit with your foreign agents or distributors to keep training them so they are increasingly effective in represent-

ing your company. When technical or customer support staff from the exporter are traveling abroad, schedule training events to increase their exposure to as many employees as possible. Do not hesitate to commit to a heavy schedule. International travel is expensive and it is often necessary to pack the schedule with a number of events. Likewise, do not reduce visits to all show and no substance.

International trade shows. An effective use of international travel is to plan it so that it coincides with industry trade shows. They are extremely efficient opportunities to meet with important industry contacts such as key accounts, media, or opinion leaders. It is also a great opportunity to assess competitors. You can also walk into the booth of a competitor to view competing products or judge their level of internationalization such as translated marketing materials or adapted products. Trade shows can also be an effective product launching mechanism.

International agent/distributor meetings. As your international sales increase and you add more markets, plan to have an annual international meeting for all of your distributors or agents. Your first reaction may be alarm - a room full of customers are complaining and comparing notes! This can be a concern, but I always found the benefits outweighed the risks. In fact, your foreign buyers will respect you for giving them the chance to meet each other, share their own experiences, and increase their communication with you. It also creates the chance for the best practices of distributors to be cross-pollinated. It is much more effective for new distributors to learn from their peers how to launch a product or deal with a sales challenge than for you to tell them directly.

The computer component company I worked for would hold an international distributor meeting once a year overseas, and meet again as a group during the fall at an international trade show held in the U.S. That provided two annual opportunities for everyone to get together. Each company divides costs differently, but it is not unusual for the U.S. manufacturer to pick up all food costs, and perhaps even lodging. In most cases, airfare is always the responsibility of the distributor but that is an industry/company issue. Regardless of how the costs are shared, consider coordinating such an event if you do not currently do so.

• CONSIDERATIONS WHEN TERMINATING AN AGENT OR DISTRIBUTOR

No matter how effective an exporter is at managing its distribution channel, changes will need to be made at some point. This is often the case when the first distributor or agent appointed in a particular foreign market is not able to step up to the challenge of increasing sales. I saw this more than once: a distributor is very good at getting the product out in the market but eventually hits a ceiling beyond which sales stagnate. This is particularly true for products that begin with limited sales but have the potential to be huge players in the market. Some agents or distributors simply do not have the experience or infrastructure to take sales beyond a certain level.

Regardless of the reason, when a change needs to occur it is rarely easy. Unless both parties are in full agreement that it is best to part ways, issues will arise that complicate the separation.

Contract. The first place to start when you are thinking about making a change is the agent or distributor contract. You may want to seek legal advice even if the contract allows for an easy exit such as a clause that provides for a certain days notice to cancel. Be aware even if the contract allows for dissolution by either party, local law may not. For example, contract law in Puerto Rico has the potentially expensive Rule 75. Adopted in 1964, the law was designed to protect local agents and distributors from withdrawal of distribution rights if just cause cannot be demonstrated. You may not be able to refuse to renew the contract after its initial term unless just cause can be shown. The U.S. manufacturer may be obligated, under Rule 75, to renew the contract. Penalties are expensive: the supplier is required to compensate the distributor for a number of expenses including set-up costs, value of the distributor's inventory, value of goodwill, and past profits. Ecuador had a similar law called the Dealer's Act which was repealed in 1997. However, companies that signed representation agreements prior to 1997 remain bound by the law. Similarly, legislation remains in place in Honduras that discourages the use of exclusive contracts. The use of agents can also be a complicated process in countries where the agent may be treated as an employee, making termination tantamount to firing an employee.

The legal issues associated with terminating an agent or distributor vary greatly from country to country. It cannot be assumed that the laws in any way mirror those of the home market. The most effective way to deal with these uncertainties is to proactively address them during contract negotiations with the assistance of a competent attorney. Likewise, legal advice should be sought before terminating an agent or distributor contract. To learn more about the general nature of agent/distributor laws regarding representation and termination, read the Country Commercial Guides or industry reports available through Export.gov or GlobalEdge, as mentioned in Chapter 6.

Nonlegal issues. Assuming the legal issues have been resolved, you can move on to other business issues related to ending a relationship with a foreign agent or distributor. Again, review your contract to see how it deals with issues such as inventory, proprietary information, and existing orders. Below are ways to deal with some of these nonlegal issues:

- *Inventory considerations.* The issue of inventory would primarily affect distributors because agents do not typically carry inventory. If your distributor has quite a bit of inventory of your products at the time it receives notification that the relationship is going to end, it is not a great situation for either you or the distributor. It will depend on the nature of the relationship and the value of the goods. If the breakup is expected and the marketability of the goods is high, there will probably be no problem. However, if the breakup is unexpected, resulting in bad feelings from the distributor, and the inventory is old and not marketable, there may be a problem. You may want to consider some accommodation for the distributor to keep the breakup smooth. You want to avoid having an old distributor continuing to sell products in the market after you appoint the new distributor.

- *Public relations.* It is always difficult to know exactly what the marketplace will think of a change in distribution. If the old distributor is well respected, with strong links to the market, the public relations fallout can be severe. Therefore, be proactive in managing the information released to the press. What you do not want is confusion in the market. Consider running an ad campaign listing the new distributor in the ad. Contact editorial staff to run a story about the change. Put a positive spin on the situation, such as "with the increased success of Company ABC's products in France, ABC is pleased to announce Paris Plus as its new exclusive distributor for the French market." Insiders will know what is going on so the ad does not need to be too specific. Avoid releasing anything negative about the old distributor just to ease the transition.

- *Choosing the new distributor.* During the process of choosing the new distributor, you will need to be careful about confidentiality if you have not yet notified the old distributor. This can be a delicate situation requiring significant trust on behalf of any potential new distributor that you contact. Before you notify the existing distributor, you probably have a good idea of who would be an appropriate replacement. Whether you contact the new distributor before or after notification of the old distributor is matter of judgment based on the specific situation.

• DIRECT MARKETING VERSUS DIRECT SELLING

One of the most powerful management tools you can use to increase international sales is direct marketing. As your international activities grow, you will find a growing need to begin direct marketing activities especially if you have established an overseas presence.

It is important to maintain the distinction between direct marketing and direct sales. The goal of direct marketing is not to make the sale but to create an environment that generates sales for your agents or distributors. Your goal is to do all you can so that your company's products are preferred and distinguished from those of your competitors.

Direct marketing requires much less infrastructure than direct selling. A company seeking to have greater control and impact on its international growth will be able to initiate direct marketing much earlier in its international expansion than direct selling. For example, a small staff in a European office can do a great deal to assist in the marketing efforts of an exporter. Activities would include pan-European advertising, increased travel, greater participation in trade shows, and direct public relations efforts. Direct marketing can also include participation in sales calls with distributors to key accounts.

Clearly, such a program of direct marketing is only justified if the market has proven itself viable for the manufacturer. Even a one-person marketing office in Paris will not be cheap. However, it is cheaper than replacing your international distribution network with direct selling. It would probably be wise to begin first with direct marketing. Plus, many direct marketing activities can be done from the home market with no overseas presence. For example, foreign industry press may maintain representatives in your home country to coordinate the placement of advertising in their publications or websites. This will greatly assist in your direct marketing activities with little to no overseas presence.

Direct marketing is also a powerful tool you can use to manage your distribution network. Because the direct result of your marketing activities will increase the sales for your overseas agents or distributors, it puts you in a stronger position. For example, when my company would pay for advertising in a given market, we would make sure the sale leads were directed to our European office. We would then send the leads to the distributor. That way we could later follow up with the distributor to see what had been done with the leads.

Chapter 19

International Advertising, Public Relations, and Trade Missions/Shows

Most manufacturers and service companies understand the importance of using advertising, public relations, and social media to build and sustain their domestic marketing program. They also understand the importance of brand equity (strength, asset) and the significant competitive advantage offered by a strong brand.   Effective advertising, public relations, and social media programs require an investment in time and money.

Given the relatively high stakes, companies often turn to outside experts in the form of advertising and public relations agencies. The payoff from a strong advertising and public relations effort that builds brand equity can lead to increased market share, improved profits, and, perhaps most importantly, significant competitive barriers. Depending on the industry, a brand can become so strong that it virtually shuts out new competition.

But are these activities equally important for a company expanding globally? Should a company invest in international advertising and public relations efforts? If so, how early in the global expansion process should such expenditures be made? Can the domestic materials simply be translated with no significant adaptation?

These are the questions that will be addressed in this chapter and you will learn that these issues are perhaps even more important internationally. Building an effective global brand (within the context of a specific industry) can be one of the most important sustainable competitive advantages a company can develop. Just reflect for a moment on the power of some of the truly global brands, such as Coke, McDonald's, Sony, Guinness, or Boeing. Each company has invested millions of dollars to establish, build, and defend brand awareness that has led to a strong competitive barrier both domestically and internationally. For example, in the war between Coke and Pepsi internationally, there is tremendous advantage to being the first to enter a market and establish brand recognition. So within hours of President Clinton lifting the U.S. trade embargo against Vietnam, PepsiCo Inc. began soft drink production in Ho Chi Minh City and had also already prepared a TV commercial aimed at the Vietnamese market.[1]

Of course, the benefit of a strong brand is self-evident for these large multinational corporations, but does the same apply to small companies as they enter the international marketplace? This is difficult to answer without discussing a specific industry, product, or service, but based on my personal experience, I believe it does apply. The difference is simply in the scale and scope of the marketing effort.

When I began to establish European distribution of computer components from Paradise Systems, a U.S. manufacturer, one of my biggest obstacles was the brand awareness of our main competitor, Hercules. It had entered Europe first, and had gained significant brand awareness with distributors, retailers, and even some consumers. Fortunately, Paradise Systems had significant technological advantages over Hercules so it was somewhat easy to get the attention of potential distributors. Eventually, it became the number one brand in many European markets. But this success was not simply due to technological superiority. It also resulted from the emphasis Paradise Systems placed on advertising and public relations to build brand awareness in the U.S. When I brought the brand over to Europe, I tried to duplicate the approach as best I could within my budget. The effort to build Paradise Systems brand awareness in Europe was not on the same scale as the soft drinks war, but the goal was the same - to be recognized within our industry as the number one brand, especially at the retail/dealer level, where the purchase decision was most often made (as opposed to the consumer level, such as in the soft drinks industry). Eventually our brand became recognized as an important player in the components industry among distributors and retailers. After a couple of years, the strength of the brand opened new doors in other countries and consolidated our position in our original markets. Had we neglected the importance of advertising and PR in the European market, I believe our sales would never have become so successful.

For your company and industry, you need to acknowledge the critical role marketing and social media activities can play in building brand awareness and that such brand awareness can lead to significant advantages internationally. Though this is obvious for large, Fortune 500 players such as Nike and Coke, it is often just as applicable to small and mid-sized firms. The difference is in the size of the task. But before getting distracted by the task of building an international brand, let's first discuss the basics of international advertising and public relations. Later in the chapter I will look at how trade missions and trade shows can be used to support your advertising and public relations activities.

• INTERNATIONAL ADVERTISING

Assuming you have only entered a few international markets, the advertising challenge has probably been limited. However, when expanding internationally, there are advertising activities important to all companies, no matter how small. Many of these actions are surprisingly inexpensive, if not free. The key is to include your international activities in your company's entire advertising strategy so international and domestic activities are in sync.

Modifications to Domestic Advertising

One of easiest ways is to modify your domestic advertising to acknowledge your international activities. If you currently are running advertisements in domestic industry press, consider adding the phrase "International Distributor Inquiries Welcomed." Some issues of the magazine will make their way to foreign markets, and if they land in the hands of a suitable importer, the ad could encourage them to contact you when they otherwise may have assumed you already had representation in their country.

If readership of a particular magazine in strong internationally, you may want to go one step further and put the address of your foreign representatives in your advertising for that magazine. I have even seen this done for distributors in Europe and Asia if the overseas readership of a particular publication is significant. In fact, once a company establishes its international distribution, it is common to see its international distributors listed after the domestic dealers/distributors. Even if international readership only represents a small fraction of overall readership, it is a subtle way to communicate to the U.S. market that your company has matured enough to have international distribution and representation. Think of it as a badge of honor - your company has joined the ranks of the international community.

A final consideration for your domestic advertising is to highlight any modifications or technical considerations that are an outcome of your international activities. For example, if your company is now ISO9000 registered to make international sales easier, you should add the ISO9000 logo to your domestic advertising. The same is true of international markings such as the European CE Mark. In the case of technical specifications such as power supply, you may want to add the international options to your technical descriptions. The objective is to make sure that a potential reader seeing the ad, whether an importer or end-user, will quickly realize your company is international-friendly and welcomes international sales.

The goal of all these modifications is twofold. In markets where you have yet to establish distribution, these subtle changes will begin to build brand awareness leading to a stronger position when you decide to enter the market. In markets where representation is established, it supports the activities of your agents or distributors by acknowledging their existence. Plus, any leads generated by the advertising can be fed back to your distribution channel. Your agents and distributors will appreciate the support, and you may gain a better sense of which foreign markets should be strong.

Modifications to Marketing Materials

Your foreign buyers will probably use your domestic marketing materials initially for their sales activities. These include product brochures, corporate profiles, and technical specifications. Depending on the industry, some buyers prefer materials created by the manufacturer because they see them as more dependable. This is particularly true in highly technical industries where their products are used by academic or scientific staff who are comfortable with English. However, consider modifying your domestic marketing materials to reflect your international exporting.

In some cases, the modifications to marketing materials will be minor and are best done by the manufacturer. But for most companies and industries, product specification sheets, warranty statements, and competitive comparisons are best modified or produced by your foreign buyer, especially if the changes are exclusive to a particular market. This is especially true of language translations. Your foreign buyer can probably do the translation faster and more accurately than you. The key is to provide as many tools and support materials as possible to make the job easier. For example, you may want to provide logos and artwork. With most marketing materials done on computers, you can simply send your electronic publishing files.

I recommend working with your foreign buyers when adapting marketing materials in order to maximize their participation to make it as cost effective and as timely as possible. However, as a company matures, more of its international marketing materials may be produced in-house to have greater control and uniformity across all materials. This is more expensive than passing the responsibility on to the foreign buyers, but as the international business grows, the increased control may justify the increased costs.

If you choose not to modify your existing materials, at least create a marketing piece in the market's local language that can be inserted or combined with the U.S./English materials. When a translator is used for such projects, have the translation double-checked for accuracy. An easy way is to use contacts in the foreign market. They can double check the work of your professional translator for issues such as local industry jargon.

You also want to modify your corporate website to reflect your international activities. This is discussed in detail in Chapter 22.

Direct International Advertising

At some point in your international expansion, you may want to begin directly placing international advertising, rather than relying solely on your foreign representatives. The point at which this is justified will vary by company and industry. I do not know of any studies that support this assumption, but I suspect most companies in their early stages of international expansion leave the responsibility for international advertising to their foreign buyers. Because each foreign distributor best knows the most suitable publications in which to advertise and may already have some advertising contracts in place that could lower the cost, they are in the best position to place effective foreign market advertising.

There may be instances where a company will want to begin directly advertising in its international markets. The most common instance would be if a publication is either too broad or too expensive for the foreign buyer. For example, a pan-European or pan-Asian magazine would cover more than one market, and therefore be less attractive to just one distributor. Another instance would be preconference journals or exhibition guides that can be particularly expensive and of benefit to more than one distributor. In these cases, the exporter could directly advertise to support its distribution network and ensure its brand is promoted. Such international advertisements have the added benefit that international buyers tend to hold on to these magazines and journals for a longer time. Thus the life of an advertisement may be much longer internationally than domestically.

If a particular publication has established an office in your home market, it may make economic sense to directly place the advertising through their local advertising representatives. This not only helps decrease the per-insertion costs, but also puts the manufacturer directly in control of both the advertising frequency and content.

Advertising is one of the more expensive promotional activities, so the decision to directly advertise must always be placed within the context of the overall international promotion budget and priorities. Companies, especially in an early stage of international expansion, may find it more cost effective to move marketing dollars directly to their foreign buyers via cooperative arrangements rather than directly placing advertising. However, even small companies may find that some very targeted direct advertising will significantly enhance their international growth.

Placing International Advertising

If you do decide to place advertising directly into particular foreign markets, you should follow some guidelines:

- *Maximize purchase power*. Within particular industries, one publisher may own more than one publication, and some of these publications may be in your target foreign markets. To ensure maximum purchasing power, your international ads can be coordinated to take advantage of any potential discounts through advertising in multiple publications. Often, discounts are available even across magazines not commonly owned. For example, foreign magazines often have local ad representatives that coordinate the placement of international advertising. These reps may be able to offer quantity discounts for magazines in various countries. Coordinating such purchasing can result in tremendous savings in your advertising costs.
- *Negotiate the price!* If you have never purchased advertising space, be aware that the first price quoted may be negotiable. This depends on the industry norms and magazine practices, but you may be surprised at just how soft the advertising rates are. Never assume the prices quoted off the rate card are fixed. Many times ad reps will view foreign-originated advertising as additional business and be open to negotiating. Never give the impression that your advertising budget is too large or they may keep prices high.
- *Last minute placement*. Another great way to save on your international advertising is to mention to your advertising representatives that you are willing to consider placing advertising at the last minute as long as the price is attractive. It is a bit like flying standby - deep discounts for those who wait till the very end. But like flying, there is no guarantee you will get placed, and normally such offers are limited to regular advertisers. You will also have to run an existing ad that the magazine already has possession of because these offers are made typically one or two days (if not hours) before the press run and there is no time to send them a new ad.
- *Use your foreign buyers*. If the foreign market is completely unfamiliar to you and there are no local representatives, you may want to have your foreign buy-

er coordinate the advertising. The magazine will either directly bill your company or you will have to reimburse your foreign buyer. This can be less expensive if your foreign buyer already has significant business with the magazine and has a quantity discount contract in place.

International Ad Copy

Whether you initiate the advertising or it is done by your foreign representatives, the content of the advertisement will almost always be an issue. If you or your distributors plan to use advertising copy or creative ideas originally created for your home market, there may be some translation issues beyond simply changing the language. For example, the use of color can greatly vary between countries. Some cultures prefer colors that are less bright than those readily accepted by Americans.

This issue haunted me when I hoped to transfer a particularly successful U.S. campaign for Paradise Systems to Europe. The headline of the ad in the U.S. read "Customers Go Hog-Wild for Paradise EGA Cards!" and the artwork showed crazy pigs enjoying Paradise products. To appreciate the ad, you have to realize the mood of the computer components industry back in the mid-1980s was one of excitement about the growing boom. So though the ad may have seemed a bit off the wall, it worked.

However, when I showed the artwork to people at our British distributor, the first thing they said was, "What does 'hog-wild' mean?" I knew then that the ad would not work. I did explain the meaning, but because there is no equivalent British expression, the headline would have to be changed and the artwork then wouldn't fit. Deflated, I took the artwork to Paris to show people at our French distributor. They did not even have to ask a question. The look on their faces when I showed them the ad clearly signaled that the ad would never run in France!

Because the advertisement was not usable, I had to commission a new ad from the ad agency back in the states. The new ad showed a computer with international flags coming out of the computer terminal. The headline read "International Customers Go Wild For Paradise Video Cards." In my opinion it was not nearly as effective, but at least it was usable.

The lesson was important. I never again made the mistake of assuming a concept that was successful in the U.S. would be suitable for the international marketplace. You could argue that the advertising agency should have known better, but they were not commissioned to create an international ad. They were asked to create a campaign that would work well in the U.S., which is exactly what they did. Because the U.S. market was our largest market, this was a reasonable strategy. I was simply glad we had the budget to commission a new ad.

Creating truly global advertising concepts can be extremely difficult. Taking into account all the various cultural differences and local regulations effectively reduces the creative opportunities to only the most basic concepts, which may prove to be worthless. Nevertheless, even after years of making mistakes, companies continue to try to create truly global advertising concepts. For example, Levi Strauss used to create separate advertisements for each of its markets, resulting in highly localized advertisements that were not cohesive. By the 1990s, Levi's began shooting semi-annual global jeans commercials which essentially sell a subtle message of American culture. The results worked well for the company. Other companies such as Procter and Gamble and Seagram Company have created successful global campaigns.[2] However, such a strategy may prove extremely difficult for particular industries and is no doubt expensive. This may not even be a viable option for small companies. Should such a strategy seem attractive for your products and international goals, utilize the services of a professional advertising agency with the international experience to meet the challenge.

Cooperative Advertising

One of the most powerful concepts to jump-start your international advertising is to implement a cooperative advertising program with your foreign buyers. Some industries, such as the automobile and computer industries, have used co-op advertising methods for years. It can be an effective way to motivate your customers to invest in local marketing.

The specifics of co-op ad programs vary by industry and manufacturer, but the general idea is that for every dollar of product purchased by your foreign agent or distributor, it earns co-op ad dollars that can be applied toward marketing expenses. The rate is typically a few percentage points, such as 1 to 5 percent. Assuming a rate of 2 percent, if during a particular period a distributor purchased $100,000 of product, it would earn $2,000 in co-op advertising dollars. The manufacturer would then reimburse the $2,000 to the foreign distributor upon submission of the required paperwork. Normally, the buyer is required to match the co-op dollars at some level. In this case, if the match requirement was 100 percent, the distributor would have to spend $4,000 on marketing expenses to receive the rebate of $2,000.

The benefits of co-op advertising within an international context are numerous. The first is that it motivates your foreign buyers to localize marketing efforts for your products. Without such an incentive, the cost of locally printing new marketing materials may be prohibitive. Second, because most co-op programs have some guidelines in place as to reimbursable expenses, it allows the manufacturer to prioritize the particular expenses it prefers. For example, if local brochures are a higher priority than local trade shows, the match requirement could be higher for trade shows than brochures, which would reduce the cost to the foreign buyer of brochures relative to trade shows. The distributor is then more likely to put its efforts into brochures. Finally, and perhaps most importantly, it forces a partnership between the manufacturer and the foreign buyer while empowering the foreign buyer to act locally in making marketing decisions.

Guidelines. There are some general guidelines you should consider when implementing an international cooperative advertising program:

- *Co-op rate.* The rate at which your foreign buyers accrue advertising co-op dollars clearly depends on your pricing structure and profit margins. On one hand, it is important to remember that with the right control, each dollar of co-op represents true marketing investments that should enhance the international success of your products. In this respect, one could imagine a scenario in which the international co-op rate approaches the percentage of domestic advertising expenditures to domestic sales. So if the company has a domestic advertising budget of 5 to 10 percent of anticipated domestic sales, the same percentage could be used as the co-op rate (assuming no other significant international advertising expenditures exist).

On the other hand, in practice, claims from overseas buyers are often combined with other products (such as trade shows) and the direct benefit to your products may be difficult to track. Even if the dollars are reimbursed as credit toward future purchases, they still represent reduced cash flow back to the manufacturer and reduce profits. Setting a co-op level too high could be a risk to expansion of the international program. Thus, the level must be carefully established to enhance the effectiveness of the co-op program, and make it meaningful to the foreign buyer without risking profitability.

The final co-op rate should be determined by a thorough analysis of your international sales forecast and profit projections. Work through different scenarios to see the impact of a co-op rate at 2 percent, 6, percent, etc. Each company has its own attitude about the importance of advertising and marketing expenditures - the more aggressive the attitude, the easier it is to justify a higher co-op rate.

- *Match requirement*. To increase the effectiveness of the co-op program, be sure to require some local match for each co-op dollar accrued. A typical match requirement is 100 percent, meaning for each dollar accrued, the foreign distributor must match it with a dollar. If $10,000 of co-op advertising were accrued, the local marketing expenses by the foreign distributor would need to reach $20,000 for the distributor to receive the full rebate of $10,000. Upon submitting evidence of the $20,000 in expenditures, the manufacturer would issue a credit of $10,000 toward existing or future invoices.

  If the manufacturer believes that particular marketing expenditures are of a higher priority than others, the match requirement could be lowered for priority expenditures and raised for nonpriority items. For example, if the manufacturer wants localized brochures to be printed above all other items, the match requirement could be zero. This effectively means the manufacturer pays the full cost of the brochures, assuming the sales are significant enough to accrue the required co-op dollars. Meanwhile, the co-op requirement for all other marketing expenses may be 100 percent.

- *Allowable expenses*. Another area of control is the issue of allowable expenses. Be sure to spell out exactly which marketing expenses are allowable and which are not. This avoids conflict in the future if questionable claims are submitted. Generally, manufacturers exclude all overhead expenses, such as salaries or travel costs. Trade shows can be another contentious issue because distributors will likely exhibit more than one imported product and it becomes difficult to split the exhibition costs. It is also common for foreign distributors to advertise more than one product per advertisement and submit claims to more than one manufacturer. The most common solution in this case is to split the cost based on the percentage of space devoted to each manufacturer's product.

Because the co-op advertising dollars are not meant to fully reimburse the foreign representative's marketing costs, the best method is to begin with a fairly restrictive list and leave room for future negotiation.

- *Claim process.* If the claims process is not documented, the system is likely to be abused. Have a clearly written procedure, including what evidence of marketing expense must be submitted. The procedure should also clarify how reimbursement is to be made - as a credit toward existing or future invoices or as a check.

• INTERNATIONAL PUBLIC RELATIONS

If advertising sells products, public relations sells companies. If you ignore the issue (and opportunity) of a coordinated international public relations effort you miss out on free advertising and it could eventually ruin your global expansion. Public relations issues for American firms entering foreign markets range from ethics issues such as animal testing to international sourcing questions such as using child labor in manufacturing. Depending on the product and industry, a company's public relations efforts can be as important as its advertising.

Just ask McDonald's, who sued two U.K. activists for libel after the activists began distributing pamphlets outside McDonald's restaurants. The pamphlets accused the fast food restaurant of damaging Brazilian rain forests, contributing to Britain's litter problem, and exploiting underpaid workers, among other criticisms. Three years later, in what was to become Britain's longest trial, McDonald's won the libel suit and $136,000 in damages. But it was a mixed victory because the judge agreed that McDonald's had engaged in some questionable practices, such as exploiting children by encouraging them to pester their parents to eat at McDonald's. Worse, no allowance was made for the estimated $20 million McDonald's spent on the legal costs of the libel suit.[3] It was an expensive public relations exercise, though evidently seen as necessary by the company. Their troubles have not been limited to the U.K. McDonald's has also been the victim of arson and some fairly bizarre incidents in Belgium by animal rights activists.[4]

Hopefully your international public relations challenges will not be as formidable as McDonald's. However, do not underestimate their importance either. Effective international public relations can be an important tool to successfully expand globally, even for small companies. As you increase your international activities, proactively plan your public relations program. Seek outside guidance on how to create and implement your PR program. Above all, be aware that as you enter more markets, you increase the number of competitors and critics as well as the potential for public relations challenges.

PR Activities for the Small to Midsize Company

So what can companies without the budget of a McDonald's do to have an effective international public relations campaign? Quite a lot. Remember that only advertising costs dollars - editorials and press are free. They just require an investment in time, relationships, and professionalism.

Meeting with international editorial staff. One of the first things to realize is that while you may be a small fish in a big pond in your home market, you may be a big fish in a small pond in an international market! Everything is relative.

In most instances I was able to get an interview with the editor of a national computer magazine during my international travels. It helped that the U.S. was leading the way in computer technology and overseas editorial staff knew that Americans were a good source of up-to-date industry information. You will find through your international travels that certain courtesies are afforded to international visitors that are less common domestically. For example, you are less likely to get an appointment with an important editor in the U.S. without working through the appropriate channels. But in other countries, especially where publishing companies may be smaller, it is not out of the ordinary to call an editor directly.

You will have more access to international press than domestic press. When you visit a new country, meet with leading journalists and editorial staff. Simply contact them prior to your departure, explain you are visiting their country to establish representation, and suggest a short meeting. Not only will you establish important relationships for the future, but you can ask them for their input about which agent or distributor would be suitable for your products. You may even get some important competitive information. (Be sure to leave with copies of their magazine/journal in hand. They will be invaluable in learning the competitive position and activities of local competitors, agents, and distributors.)

Once representation has been established, continue to meet with editorial staff, perhaps with your local representative along. This can be especially important if traveling with key staff from the U.S. By keeping your company in the forefront of the minds of the editorial staff, there is a greater likelihood they will feature your product announcements and news in their writings. The ultimate goal is to develop such a good rapport that you become a resource for them. For example, if they were writing an important review of your industry niche, you would want to be included as a resource for the article so you have the opportunity to influence the perspective. You also want them to discuss any negative comments to get your reaction.

Planning public relations events. Always take advantage of any newsworthy event to hold a press conference. This will vary by industry, as will the magnitude of event, but you should attempt to get as much free press as possible. One of the most important opportunities is during the initial appointment of your agent or distributor. Such events should be planned and coordinated by your representative. The representative will already know the critical contacts. You may offer an exclusive to a particularly strong publication. This can be risky, however, because you do not want to alienate editors from competing publications. It can also be an extremely effective way to ensure strong coverage of your new representation or product announcement.

Above all participate in events. Even if you do not speak the local language, ask your representative to plan the event when you will be in town. I have sat through many press conferences with a simple smile, completely oblivious to what was being said. However, the press appreciated my commitment to both the event and their market. Generally, in such situations, the American would be asked to make a few comments in English. You'll probably find that the editorial staff understands more than you expect so be careful! If you can read prepared comments in their language, do so; if not, at least have a few simple phrases worked into the presentation. Regarding the cost of such events, I always had my distributors pay and surprisingly, they always did!

Press releases. Be sure to keep your domestic public relations staff or outside firm up to date with your international activities. All press releases for your firm probably end with a statutory paragraph offering background information on the company. As you add distributors or international offices, be sure to reflect this in your domestic press releases. It is common to have something to the effect of: "ABC Inc.'s products are sold internationally through a network of distributors. The company maintains overseas sales offices in London and Singapore."

Whenever the company has a new press release, be sure to coordinate with your international network. You may want to send a copy to all international agents and distributors concurrent with the U.S. release so they are prepared. Prereleases may even be appropriate so local versions can be prepared and released at the same time as the domestic version, though considerable control must be taken to ensure that information is not released prematurely. When in doubt, coordinate your activities under the guidance of a PR firm.

Global consistency. Remember that your PR activities should always support the ongoing strategy and positioning of your company. If you have established yourself as a leader in a particular industry, emphasize this in all press releases. This is probably already done domestically. Be sure the same message is conveyed in any international press releases that are sent by your foreign representatives. The goal is to maintain global consistency in the message and image. As your international activities grow, you should consider appointing a professional public relations firm to coordinate both your domestic and international PR.

Dealing with problems. Most companies receive unfavorable press from time to time. Whether it is a bad product review or simply a statement that does not quite reflect well on the company, bad press happens. The key is to respond quickly and appropriately. This can be difficult internationally when the manufacturer may not even be aware of the original press. Thus, it is important that your foreign representatives know they can call on your support to respond to articles or editorials that are not positive or accurate. You may want to respond with a letter to the editor written by the company president and translated by your local representative. Clearly each instance requires its own judgement call, but do not hesitate to respond to particularly grievous statements. You may even want to personally contact the editorial staff.

Editorial versus advertising staff. As discussed in previous chapters, advertising staffs for foreign publications can be tremendous resources for competitive information and insider knowledge. However always be sure to maintain a distinction between advertising and editorial staff. Theoretically, there should be an iron curtain between the two. For example, if you arrange a breakfast meeting with the editor of a magazine, do not invite the advertising manager. It would be considered poor taste. The subtle rule is that advertising expenditure should not influence editorial decisions. Obviously it's a gray area: if you are a major advertiser and the editor sees your ads in each issue, how likely is it that you'll receive unfavorable press? Clearly, it depends on how independent the editorial staff views itself. In some publications, the separation is sacrosanct. For others, the editor may be the sales rep! Just be aware of the potential conflict of interest when meeting with either.

Having said that, I did use advertising contacts within publications to get inside information about the editorial staff. For example, if I was considering an exclusive for a particular magazine but didn't have a good editorial contact, I would call the ad rep to get his or her suggestion.

• ONE VOICE, ONE IMAGE . . . ONE BRAND

Your international advertising and public relations activities must form a unified message. Advertising may be directed at products and public relations at the company, but they have to work together to create a unified voice and image and build toward a strong brand. This is known as **integrated marketing communication**: ensuring your sales, marketing, public relations, social media, brand, staff, and corporate culture are all unified and consistent to support your corporate strategies and goals.

Never underestimate the power of building a strong brand through a combined advertising, public relations, and social media effort. The role of your brand may be considerably smaller than that of McDonald's or Nike, but this is an important global tool and one that will increase over time. Truly global brands within industries can become powerful marketing tools. They speed up product introductions, improve customer loyalty, open doors to increased distribution, utilize resources, and create vertical and horizontal expansion opportunities. And most importantly, they create substantial competitive barriers for existing and future competitors.

But achieving global brands takes time, investment, and persistence. Your efforts must be coordinated so the message and image of the brand is consistent globally. Without coordination, you leave the global opportunity up to chance. To achieve one voice, one image . . . one brand, consider some of the following guidelines.

Establish Global Brand Guidelines

Consistency will never be achieved without a system of guidelines. Begin by creating advertising kits of support materials to give to foreign agents and distributors. The kit should include electronic clip art of your brand, logo, and artwork. It should also include paper versions for companies without access to desktop publishing.

Next, establish rules for how these images can be used. I've seen guidelines that go into such detail as to specify the minimum size at which the brand can be printed and color restrictions. Guidelines may also clarify the use of trademark phrases such as "ABC Trucks - Built to Go the Distance" so that any advertisement that uses the brand (ABC

Trucks) will also include the tag line (Built to Go the Distance). Obviously, language differences hinder such specific guidelines, but remember that your foreign representative is effectively your voice in that market and should be consistent with your voice in the domestic market. If these advertising messages are an important part of your long-term brand positioning, establish guidelines.

Help Foreign Representatives Achieve Advertising and PR Goals

Often, your foreign agents and distributors are eager to adopt a common voice and image; they just need help. Be sure your marketing staff has a good relationship with your overseas buyers so issues such as brand usage and advertising themes are more easily coordinated. Sometimes the most important thing you can do is provide complete tools, such as product photography, videos, and competitive information. Your foreign buyer may only achieve your desired goals if given the proper guidance and tools. They may even teach you a thing or two! More than once my distributors would come to me with an idea or theme that was particularly effective. Rather than dismiss such ideas, encourage them. Just be sure to implement guidelines to keep new ideas in line with overall corporate goals.

• SOCIAL MEDIA

Just as with your home market, a strong international social media presence is an important strategic tool to support your marketing goals. It takes work and constant updating, but the relatively low cost (versus other media such as TV) makes it an attractive tool. And as seen with Twitter during the Arab Spring, in some cases social media is the most widely used communication medium within a country or social demographic.

But where to start to internationalize your social media? It depends on your sales channels and foreign markets. Begin by assessing the reach of your domestic social media campaigns. If you use Facebook and LinkedIn, how well do they reach your foreign markets? If you have consumer forums do you offer forums based in foreign languages? If you use Twitter, do you hold accounts for languages beyond English?

Your international social media campaign will also depend on your foreign market entry modes. If you are direct exporting with no overseas foreign direct investment, you may be able to leverage the social media platforms of your foreign representatives. However, be careful because as with all social media, there is little control of the otherside – meaning posts or comments made by users of your partner's platforms. They may be slow to react to issues that directly affects your reputation.

That is why long term, you should control your global social media tools. This of course is difficult if you don't have foreign offices. But that is where outside resources can help. By its very nature the Internet has no borders, and nor do your resources to support your social media campaigns internationally. For example, if you have passionate international users, coop them to support your social media. Find out which platforms of search engines are used beyond the global players. Maybe even have them moderate a discussion board such as a local user forum. Have them watch for local problems which require your attention.

• TRADE MISSIONS AND TRADE SHOWS

Closely aligned to international advertising is the topic of trade missions and trade shows. U.S. companies are no strangers to trade shows: they form the second-largest category of marketing expenditure in the U.S., second only to advertising.[5] However, there is an impression that international trade shows and trade missions are the domain of only large multinational companies. Such a view is understandable because the trade missions that get the most press attention are those led by dignitaries such as the president, a member of the cabinet, or a prominent state official, and the participants' list always reads like a who's who of American industry. In reality, for every high profile trade mission, there are many other trade missions with participation from small and mid-size businesses. These trade-building activities are extremely cost-effective tools for small and mid-sized firms. Some trade missions are even limited to smaller firms because they are subsidized by government grants. If large companies were permitted to participate, the grant money could be seen as corporate welfare.

One point of caution. Americans tend to expect results overnight. These expectations both help us and hurt us. In the context of a trade show or trade mission, it probably hurts us because we expect to take orders during the exhibition or mission. It is more realistic to judge the success of a trade show or mission based on the increased market knowledge received, the competitive information uncovered, and the relationships developed with potential buyers. And in some cases sales will be made. Nevertheless, it is important to ensure that top management has realistic expectations of the outcome of these activities since they often do not include sales.

Trade Shows versus Trade Missions

Given their prominence in U.S. marketing budgets, most executives are familiar with trade shows. So what is their connection to trade missions? A trade mission is essentially any coordinated international travel where individuals from various companies make joint visits to foreign markets. Normally, trade missions are coordinated and sponsored by an outside party, typically a nonprofit organization such as the federal, state, or local government. Trade associations and civic organizations also organize trade missions. Often nonprivate industry individuals accompany trade missions, such as a legislator or government official. These individuals increase the profile of the trade mission which leads to overseas briefings and gatherings with foreign officials and industry experts that might otherwise have been difficult to arrange.

Trade shows and trade missions are linked because many trade missions are planned around a foreign trade show, but they don't need to be. It tends to depend on the nature of the trade mission and its participants. If the participants all come from a common industry and they do not yet have significant distribution in the target foreign market, the trade mission will likely be organized around a trade show. The obvious benefit of a trade show is that hundreds, if not thousands, of potential buyers all come under one roof and visit with the trade mission participant. This increases the efficiency of foreign travel and gives the participant important information about other foreign and local competitors.

However, a trade mission linked to a foreign trade show may limit participants to only meeting those companies who can benefit from the particular trade show. If the country is a good match but the trade show is not, the trade mission is probably not a good idea. For this reason, many trade missions are not planned around a specific trade show. Rather their focus is on one or more countries or sub-markets within a country.

Basics of a Trade Mission

There are probably as many different types of trade missions as there are foreign countries to visit. However, trade missions are generally categorized as either vertical or horizontal.

Vertical trade mission. If the trade mission is focused on one particular industry or related industries, it is referred to as a vertical trade mission. For example, the federal government organizes trade missions for industries in which the U.S. has a particularly strong competitive advantage, such as medical or environmental products.

A tremendous benefit of a vertical trade mission is that all of the foreign events, visits, and dignitaries are related to the common theme of the target industry. For instance, an environmental trade mission to a particular country is likely to meet with top foreign environmental agency officials. The interaction between participants of these trade missions is also relevant because all the participants share common perspectives and goals.

Horizontal trade mission. Horizontal trade missions are also popular. A horizontal trade mission brings together participants from many industries with a common desire to increase trade with the target foreign market. Do not assume a horizontal trade mission will be any less effective without a common industry focus. Some participants are attracted to horizontal trade missions specifically because of the lack of industry focus - they know competitors won't be on the trip with them! They also appreciate the chance to share and learn from other international executives outside their industry, which presents a greater chance to learn new ideas and creative solutions to international challenges. Plus, horizontal trade missions are more likely to be headed by prominent dignitaries such as government officials because the opportunities and political paybacks are greater if the list is not constrained by an industry focus.

Why Participate in a Trade Mission?

The essential motivation to participate in a trade mission is the power of numbers: often a group can accomplish more together than an individual can alone. It is not an issue of experience on the part of participants. Experts and newcomers alike participate in trade missions and reap the benefits from the events, meetings, and appointments that are all a part of the trade mission. Sometimes trade missions are considered to be a way to save money on the travel expenses of the trip, but this is generally not the purpose of the mission. In fact, for many trade missions, participants make their own travel arrangements.

The main benefit of a trade mission is increased exposure to government, industry, and country experts. Each mission has its own characteristics, but most include economic, cultural, and political briefings. Often these briefings are conducted by government officials. Similar meetings can be arranged by an individual traveling alone, but in a trade mission, these meetings are automatically included with no extra effort of the participant.

A second benefit is potential cost savings of nontravel expenses, especially if the mission includes a trade show. These savings occur in a number of ways, but the most significant is from federal or state grants designed to increase exports. Many of these grants are not given directly to companies, but instead go to economic development entities such as state agencies that administer the grant. (Be sure to develop a close relationship with your local, state, and federal export promotion organizations so your company is made aware of these opportunities when they occur.) The grants probably won't cover direct travel expenses but will assist with the cost of booths at a trade show and may keep ancillary costs of the trade mission (such as receptions and meetings) to a minimum. Other cost savings can occur through group discounts, corporate sponsorships of meetings and workshops, and reduced costs for access to government services such as searching for potential distributors and translator costs.

Another important benefit of a trade mission is peer-to-peer learning. International business is by nature a hands-on activity. Despite workshops, videos, and even books like this one, one learns international business mostly by doing. Thus, some of the best teachers are individuals from other companies currently involved in international trade. All too often busy schedules or limited international travel minimizes these opportunities, but a trade mission forces you to meet others and discuss tricks of the international trade. It can be a powerful learning opportunity.

When to Participate in a Trade Mission

The decision to participate in a trade mission is usually dictated by the focus and timing of the particular trade mission. Cost is obviously another consideration, but probably takes a back seat to issues such as the appropriateness of the target market and the fit of the mission to your company's international strategy. I know of a number of instances when an exporter decided not to participate in a trade mission because the focus of the mission and target countries didn't match its strategy, despite the availability of federal grants that would have significantly reduced the cost. Trade missions only make sense when the focus of the mission and/or trade show fits the company. There are three times when a trade mission can be particularly effective:

1. *New market entry.* A trade mission is an ideal mechanism for gathering information about new markets. Because the focus of a trade mission is to educate participants on the local economic, political, and industry information, trade missions are well suited for a company's first visit to a country or region. This is particularly important for emerging markets such as China where a novice traveler may be overwhelmed by the differences and complexities of local market issues.

2. *Support existing marketing activities.* Even after a company has established representation in a particular market, it may still be appropriate to participate in a trade mission to that country. The company may want to enhance its understanding of the market including current market conditions. It may also want to support the marketing efforts of its local distributor or agent by participating in a trade show that may be a part of the mission. (If the agent or distributor has an exclusive contract, it should be made clear to the representative that the intention is to enhance, not replace, its efforts.) Trade missions can also be used when a company is considering a change in representation and needs improved market information.

3. *Networking.* The very nature of a trade mission involves meeting and traveling with other international trade professionals. As such, trade missions offer excellent networking opportunities. Compared to individual travel, interaction with trade mission participants is on an extended basis, professionally and socially, which improves the opportunities to exchange information and build lasting business relationships. For example, if the trade mission includes a local elected official, you have the opportunity to spend days with the official rather than a hurried meeting with other domestic distractions. Vertical trade missions create opportunities to spend considerable time with industry leaders and officials that could lead to improved access to their offices and information in the future.

Considerations When Selecting a Trade Mission

As previously discussed, the key to a successful trade mission is choosing the correct trade mission at the correct time. This involves staying informed of local, state, and federal missions so when the perfect mission is formed you are aware of its existence. You should always maintain a close relationship with all levels of available export assistance: local, state, and government. Your local assistance center, such as the international trade centers affiliated with the Small Business Development Center network in your area, often act as a one-stop location for information related to trade missions. Depending on their connections to state and federal assistance, it also may serve you well to establish state and federal ties with organizations such as your nearest U.S. Export Assistance Center. Other issues to consider include:

- *Cost.* Remember that participation in a trade mission may mean cost savings over independent travel. If the mission involves a foreign trade show, it is likely the mission offers a discounted booth rate. Also, if the mission is supported by a grant, whether state or federal, cost savings will be achieved. However, remember that the main reason to choose a trade mission is not cost savings but increased access to market information, support services, and peer learning.

- *The right trade show?* If the trade mission includes participation in a trade show, the decision to participate may revolve around the appropriateness of the specific trade show. However, remember that even when a trade mission includes a trade show, the real focus of the trade mission is not only the show. Meetings, briefings, and tours are potentially more important. The trade show may simply be an additional forum at which you can learn more about the market even if it is not the ideal trade show for your product.

The right show may simply be the show with the right buyers, even if the industry match is not perfect. In this way, a profile of the buyers that will attend the show may be more important than the industry focus of the show.

- *Last minute opportunities*. Because most trade missions are organized by not-for-profit organizations, the promotional campaigns may be significantly limited by budget constraints. Do not be surprised if you learn of a trade mission opportunity a few months before the event. One of the main reasons companies do not participate in a mission (or foreign trade show opportunity) is because they receive the information too late to prepare for the event. Because their overseas travel budgets and planning are already fixed, management doesn't give them the flexibility to go on the mission. Be aware that some very good opportunities may be presented with only a few weeks' notice. If the opportunity strongly fits your company, consider participating despite the late notice.

Most of all, just try one! I think you will find the networking opportunities and profile of a trade mission a nice change from the independent travel approach most companies use exclusively. Trade missions shouldn't form the basis for all your foreign travel, but they can become an important source of new market perspectives and future resources.

• FOREIGN TRADE SHOWS

While a trade mission may include participation in a foreign trade show, most companies participate in foreign trade shows on their own. In either case, trade shows can be powerful marketing tools in combination with your advertising and public relations efforts. If you think the U.S. is the only country that knows how to put on a big trade fair, wait until you travel abroad. Many foreign trade shows are much larger than their U.S. counterparts.

For example, the Hannover Messe (Fair) in Germany is billed as the largest trade fair in the world. The annual event regularly draws over 300,000 attendees and 6,500 exhibitors, dwarfing U.S. trade shows such as the Consumer Electronics Show with 150,000 attendees. The Hannover Fair can be daunting to a first time visitor or exhibitor. Hotel rooms are virtually impossible to obtain, so most visitors rent homes or apartments vacated by the locals, who earn a good portion of their annual mortgage in rental income from the show each spring. Americans, accustomed to the U.S. format of a trade show that is held in one large exhibition complex, may be surprised by the format of the Hannover Messe. It is essentially its own city, complete with banks, restaurants, and a train station, all open exclusively for events held at the fair site. It even has its own American Express office and, of course, the requisite German Beer Hall! (www.hannovermesse.de)

As with domestic trade shows, international trade shows are ideal mechanisms for finding new customers. Foreign trade shows offer the unique opportunity to meet with potential representatives and visit competitors all in one location. Even after representation in a foreign market has been established, trade shows can be effective ways to support existing agents and distributors when launching new products. (If you already have local representation, you need to coordinate your activities with your agent or distributor. It may be concerned that your direct involvement in the trade show indicates a desire to begin selling directly to the market rather than through it.)

But you do not have to exhibit at a trade show to attend. There are a number of benefits you can gain strictly as a visitor. You can gain insight into the local competitors, foreign competitors, and the product offerings of each. It is an excellent opportunity to collect literature and compare representation lists. You also can attend seminars and workshops that are offered as part of the trade show, though the local language may be used without translators. These workshops may include very valuable local industry information including product or service standards, industry trends, and even competitor details. You will even have the opportunity to meet with potential buyers through either visits with exhibitors or meetings held away from the exhibition area. I have held numerous meetings with foreign buyers in the small coffee and snack areas adjoining trade shows when our company was not officially exhibiting at the show.

Domestic trade shows. It is also worth stressing that some of the most important international trade shows are held here in the U.S. Prior to expanding internationally, participation in some of the larger international trade shows in the U.S. may be more difficult to justify, but when you begin to add foreign buyers you should consider participating in these U.S. trade shows as well as foreign trade shows. The U.S. Commercial Services offer pre-arranged meeting with foreign buyers attending significant U.S. trade shows. Called the International Buyers Program, this no-cost service is a great way to meet potential agents and distributors.

Vertical and horizontal trade shows. In the same way that trade missions are either vertical or horizontal, so are trade shows. If the trade show focuses on one or a group of related industries, it is a **vertical trade show**. If the trade show crosses industries, it is a **horizontal trade show**. Vertical trade shows are the type most familiar to U.S. companies because the U.S. tends to be the mecca for some of the most important industry trade shows such as COMDEX for the computer industry and the National Restaurant Association Show.

Internationally, horizontal trade shows are more frequent than in the U.S. This is particularly true for markets smaller than the U.S. that have a significant metropolitan city such as Santiago in Chile and Caracas in Venezuela. For example, the SAITEX Exhibition in South Africa is the country's largest international multi-industry trade exhibition. Held in Johannesburg, it accounts for 60 percent of all economic activity in the region. SAITEX has grown in reputation as an excellent launching ground for U.S. companies that want to test the South African market for their products. And the fact that the show is horizontal makes it an ideal show for U.S. companies new to the region. A wide range of U.S. companies that have participated in the past includes AT&T, General Motors, Microsoft, Coca-Cola, American Airlines, John Deere and many small and mid-sized U.S. companies. In all, over 1,000 companies from 58 countries exhibit their products and services at the show each year (400 exhibitors from China!). The show draws a strong attendance invited business leaders, the majority of whom are owners, directors, or partners. They represent manufacturers, technology development, service companies, wholesalers, agents, and importers/exporters from every sector of the local economy.[6]

When investigating the relevance of a trade show, it is important to remember that while the trade show may be the focal point of your foreign visit, it is not necessarily the only opportunity for prospecting. It is very common for some of the most important meetings to occur outside the formal hours of the exhibition with companies that may not be intending to go to the exhibition. For example, I have attended the Mexican Manufacturing Week trade show for manufacturing products and technologies held each year in Mexico City. The exhibition doesn't open until after lunch and continues until 8 pm. Thus, exhibitors routinely visit area customers or prospects before the exhibition opens. It makes for a long day, but the targeted visits enhance the chances for success.

Tips for Success in Foreign Trade Shows

Poor planning and coordination of domestic trade shows can lead to frustration and wasted efforts and resources. These are magnified internationally when the issues of language, travel, customs, logistics, and cultural differences are introduced. For example, it is not uncommon for alcoholic drinks to be served during exhibition hours at many international trade shows. I remember my surprise at an exhibition in Denmark when the staff gathered for a shot of Aquavit, a potent type of schnapps, at the start of the show. Another international challenge is foreign import customs procedures. Without proper planning, you could face significant import tariffs on your exhibition products payable upon entry into the market. Though refunds may be due, without adequate paperwork, the effort will prove fruitless. (One option is to use ATA Carnets which are discussed later in this chapter.)

Adequate planning is crucial to ensure success at a foreign trade show. Depending on the country, you may want to consider a trade mission in conjunction with your first exhibit at a trade show because this will considerably reduce the learning curve and potential mistakes.

USA and state pavilions. Most significant foreign trade shows offer a USA pavilion, which is a dedicated group of booths coordinated by the U.S. Department of Commerce or by a state government agency. You have your own booth but it is adjoined by other U.S. firms. These pavilions are great equalizers because booths tend to be the same size for both small and larger firms. Not only can these pavilions save money, they can increase the profile and credibility of your firm at the show because the pavilion is normally located in a prominent part of the show. USA pavilions are particularly good for companies seeking new agents or distributors because foreign buyers know to visit the pavilion in hopes of being one of the first to find a new product to represent. Sponsors of pavilions can also assist with the logistics such as shipping, customs, and translators.

Language issues. Though English may be the universal business language, consider translating at least a few essential marketing materials into the local language. This should include any major signage indicating the nature of your business. Remember that the key to a successful booth is to convey to potential buyers why they should be interested in your product and company. This message will be most effectively conveyed in the local language rather than English even if your other marketing materials have not been translated.

If possible, contract the services of a local translator. Not only will a translator greatly assist in bridging the language barrier, but a good business translator will also offer cultural, economic, and business assistance such as industry and corporate information. For example, a translator I worked with in Mexico had extensive experience with Pemex, the public/private oil company. She was able to offer valuable insight into its history and organizational structure.

Visual aids. Bring visual devices that communicate product features and benefits, especially if the product itself is not easily transportable. For example, during a trade show in Mexico I was representing a company that manufactures chemicals to remove grease and oils. The best selling tool was a jar with asphalt in the bottom that was filled with the chemical. All the oil and grit from the asphalt floated to the top, clearly demonstrating the benefit of the solvent. It was an effective and easily transportable sales aid.

Marketing materials. As any previous trade show experience will have already demonstrated, companies always need at least one inexpensive marketing handout to give visitors, especially those that seem to only be window shopping. It is always a bit awkward if you only have expensive product brochures and attempt to hold them back for only serious visitors to the booth. This is especially difficult in a foreign country where due to cultural and language differences it can be difficult to quickly assess a visitor's potential as a future customer. Rather than having to make such a decision, always have a marketing piece that is low-cost, yet provides a basic description of your company and product or services in the local language. Be sure to include your email address, fax number, and other contact details.

Other marketing materials, such as full product literature, videos (be aware of differences in international video standards), and corporate brochures can be reserved for strong prospects.

Develop a potential buyer database. If this is your first visit to the market or a follow-up, be sure to market to all potential buyers. Maintain a database of contacts developed during the months leading up to the exhibition and send pre-exhibition materials to them before the show. Contact your local international assistance center and inquire if it offers a trade lead service. Many of the resources discussed in Chapter 9 also can be used to add more contacts to the list.

Figure 19.1 Sample International Business Card

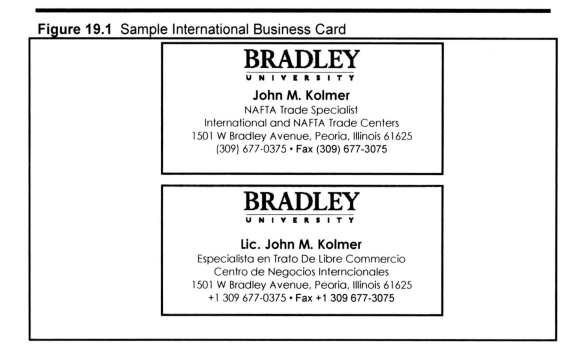

Business cards. One simple rule: always bring plenty! Consider translating your business cards into the local language, putting English on one side and the translation on the other. Seek professional assistance on matters such as titles and technical terms. Do not hesitate to put short local-language product descriptions on the card such as "Manufacturers of quality steel and aluminum nuts and bolts." Prepare your foreign business cards well in advance of the trip. They will probably take longer to be printed than your U.S. cards. As a last resort, hotels often offer overnight business card services.

It is customary in many countries to acknowledge education achievements. As seen in Figure 19.1, rather than write Señor John M. Kolmer, our NAFTA Trade Specialist at Bradley University used Lic. John M. Komer. The Lic. stands for *licenciado*, which means "with licensed business degree." In England, many business cards include a full list of the person's education degrees, including undergraduate and graduate. In the U.S. this practice is limited to Ph.D.s and professional certifications.

Also, note in the example in Figure 19.1 that it is customary to put a +1 in front of the telephone number. This indicates that when dialing the phone number internationally, you first need to dial the international access code followed by the 1 (the international country code for the United States) and then the phone number. Sometimes you will also see parentheses and dashes changed to periods. For example, (309) 677-3075 would be written as 309.677.3075. This decision is more a matter of style than correctness. Finally, you may want to put your photo on your business cards to assist visitors in remembering you and your conversation.

Making the Most of a Trade Show

Trade shows tend to be hectic events, especially for exhibitors. To make the limited time as effective as possible consider the following tips:

For exhibitors:

• Press release. Announce your participation before the show via a press release. If the exhibition has an official magazine sponsor, the magazine will often feature such announcements in any preexhibition articles. Also send the press release to potential clients (agents, distributors) if no representation has yet been established. If you already have an agent or distributor, the press release could be sent to dealers, key accounts, or other potential buyers. Coordinate this press release with your agent or distributor so the marketing activities are coordinated. Be sure to list the booth number on all exhibition announcements. Also have the release translated into local languages.

• Press conference. It is not uncommon to hold a press conference during an exhibition if a new product is being released or some other newsworthy event will be taking place. However, there are two views on the effectiveness of press conferences. One is that unless the company is quite large and can attract the attention of the press, these events will get lost in the overall flurry of the exhibition. Thus, press events are best left to the large players in the industry. The other view is that if the product announcement is significant enough, the press will attend, providing an excellent opportunity for you to get some free press. Having worked for small to mid-size companies, my personal feeling is to leave such press events to the larger companies during exhibitions and instead hold them when press people are less distracted and more likely to attend.

• Booth staffing. If only one representative from the U.S. company is traveling to the foreign trade show, it may be wise to find someone local to assist at the booth. This would allow the U.S. representative to have individual meetings while still keeping someone in the booth. This may seem like a minor point, but nothing is more frustrating to a potential buyer than to visit a booth and find it empty! (The local person also can act as a translator if necessary.)

For exhibitors and visitors alike:

• Trade show directory. Get a copy of the exhibition directory as soon as possible. Carefully review the directory to find competitors and potential buyers. Prioritize your list and set out to visit each booth. Trade shows tend to be so large that it is difficult to walk the entire show. Preplanning which booths to visit can eliminate wasted time and frustration. After the show, keep the directory as a reference.

• Get publications. Visit the booth of every media company, such as industry magazines. Normally, the current issue of their magazine is available for free. If they have media kits (packages describing why you should consider advertising in their publication) get them as well. They often include important industry data. The magazines will help you learn about the local industry, including which companies are advertising and which agents and distributors are your competitors.

• Prearrange meetings. If possible, prearrange meetings with potential buyers for the first day of the show. Appointments made during the show are unlikely to be scheduled on the first day. Expect to have meetings outside of the exhibition, including a lunch or dinner. Consider scheduling meetings before the exhibition opens so you can visit potential buyers at their facilities before they visit your booth.

• International Partner Search and Gold Key Service. The Commercial Service within the U.S. Department of Commerce offers assistance in finding potential buyers and arranging meetings. The Agent Distributor Service is used to find potential buyers and the Gold Key Service is used to schedule meetings. Both are discussed in greater detail in Chapter 9. These services can be particularly effective when combined with trade shows.

• Networking. During the show, maximize your interaction with everyone. It can be particularly helpful to find another exhibitor that does not directly compete with your products but has a strong presence in the local market. If you are new to the market, these individuals can become mentors during the show. Avoid the temptation to go back to the hotel room and collapse. Instead, have dinner with other exhibitors to get a better sense of the local market and industry.

Pricing. I recommend not handing out price lists during international trade shows. It is too easy to give confidential pricing information to the wrong visitor. Even your domestic pricing list is dangerous to distribute if local representation has not yet been established. It could create local pricing expectations that cannot be met due to international pricing escalation, as discussed in Chapter 11. If pressed, provide general pricing verbally so visitors have an idea of how your products or services compete. Releasing pricing details is more appropriate during serious meetings with prospective agents or distributors.

Before you attend a show, make sure you have at least estimated the landed cost for your products, as detailed in Chapter 11. Nothing is more frustrating for potential buyers than to be quoted U.S. pricing with no allowance for freight or import duties. Even if the buyer is ultimately responsible for these charges, the seller should be able to offer an estimated local market price during the initial meetings.

Follow-up forms. You have probably already developed a visitor profile or follow-up form that you use at domestic trade shows. These forms are useful to classify visitors as end-users, distributors, or agents, as well as indicate future action or questions to be answered. Internationally, these forms need to be modified so you can record the differences between potential representatives. You may want to review Chapter 9 and the discussion on selecting the right representatives. It gives clues on the types of information you will want to gather from prospective representatives. Figure 9.4 lists factors to consider when selecting an agent or distributor. Many of these items can be incorporated into a follow-up form.

ATA carnets. If you are planning to exhibit product samples, you need to research the potential for import customs duties, which can be very high if the samples have considerable value. If you are only going to visit one country, most countries offer temporary import bonds or a similar document that allows the product to temporarily enter the country. The product is then re-exported when you leave. A bond will need to be posted to guarantee that the product is not sold or left in the foreign country.

If your travels include a number of countries, it may be easier to get an ATA carnet, which is sort of like a passport for products. ATA is an acronym of the French and English words admission temporaire/temporary admission. Carnets (pronounced "car-nay") are issued and guaranteed by various U.S. companies and agencies under a set of guidelines and conditions established by the International Bureau of Chambers of Commerce (IBCC). Carnets allow for the free passage of goods between over 50 countries without paying import duties or completing new customs forms. Though they are expensive (between $100 and $300 depending on the value of the goods and other issues) they will save you money in the end, and speed up the transit of the goods, especially if you are personally carrying the items. The last thing you want after a long international flight is countless customs delays. (Companies are now offering ATA carnet applications on the Internet. See www.atacarnet.com for one example.)

Above all, thoroughly plan your foreign trade shows. Be sure to clarify your goals and expectations. Familiarize yourself with local customs and business practices, including distribution structures and marketing practices. And investigate the option of participating in U.S./state pavilions and trade missions, especially if you are a first-time exhibitor. They can both reduce costs and increase your effectiveness.

• MACHINE TRANSLATION

One final note about translating your marketing and P/R materials. Traditionally, companies have outsourced content to professional translators to deliver websites, applications, and content to global audiences. Though professional translation will suit most requirements, these services may be out of reach for budget-conscious businesses. Professional translation rates can range from 20 to 35 cents a word. As an alternative, many businesses, large and small, have deployed Machine Translation.

Since the dawn of the computer age, researchers and computer scientists have sought methods to translate one language into another. After a few decades of research and development, Machine Translation has finally become a viable alternative to professional translation services for the delivery of multilingual content.

Machine Translation has been adopted by numerous corporations to address multilingual demands using tools from leading companies. Numerous small businesses are using Machine Translation to address everything from websites, online catalogs, product support information to document and email translation. Overall, Machine Translation has grown in industry acceptance and the quality of Machine Translation has improved to a point where the software has a proven track record to improve relationships with global customers and to help increase revenue.

The company Systran is a leading example of leveraging the use of machine translation for day-to-day activities such as on-demand website translations or emails. One of the keys to its growing acceptance is the ability to have key words and phrases used in your company and industry professionally translated first, and then loaded into a translation library Systran then uses during the machine translation process. See www.systransoft.com for more details.

- ## NOTES

1. "PepsiCo, Coke Move Fast On Vietnam Production," The Wall Street Journal (7 February 1994): B3.

2. Ken Wells, "As the International Media Proliferates, More Firms Use Unified Sales Pitches," The Wall Street Journal (27 August 1992): A1.

3. Donald Macgillivray, "Hard to Swallow: McDonald's Wins a Hollow Victory in Britain," Maclean's (1 July 1997): 96.

4. Stephen Castle, "Eco-terrorists Declare War on Belgium's Burger Bars," The Independent - London (15 November 1998): 16.

5. Letters, Puget Sound Business Journal (2 February 1998): 39.

6.   http://www.exhibitionsafrica.com/ems/press-stories/341-saitex-africa-s-biggest-and-best-business-opportunities-expo.html

CHAPTER 20

Key to Success: A Customer Orientation

If customer service is a challenge to firms operating domestically, imagine the impact of going global. Differences in language, culture, and technology, combined with the factors of time and distance, create a difficult environment for a successful customer service strategy. In fact, obstacles to creating an effective international customer support program (language, culture, technology) make the issue of customer service even more important internationally. The fact that international customers do differ from the U.S. manufacturer in language, culture, and their technological environment means the role of the manufacturer's international customer support program is even more important for its long-term success.

For example, Eger Manufacturing in northeast Hungary produces electrical components for a number of area manufacturers. Its primary production line uses an automated manufacturing process that relies on a machine produced by a U.S. company that was recently installed by a British distributor. Though the machine operated without problems for a number of weeks, it broke during a particularly important job for Eger's number one customer.

The documentation supplied with the machine was in English because the American manufacturer had not supplied many machines internationally and the British distributor mostly sells in the U.K. Under pressure to get the production line back up and running, the Hungarian engineers attempted to fix the problem, but a misinterpretation of a particular instruction in the U.S. technical manual resulted in their breaking a key component of the machine.

On the third day of the production stoppage, the British distributor confirmed Eger's greatest fear - it didn't stock the particular component because it had never broken in the past. Worse, they are unable to understand the original problem. The distributor contacted the U.S. manufacturer but didn't receive an answer until the following day due to time differences. On the fourth day of the stoppage, using technical information e-mailed by the U.S. manufacturer, the British distributor was able to solve the original problem. However, it requested that Eger Manufacturing pay for the replacement part because both the Americans and Brits believed Eger should not have attempted the repair that led to breaking the part. This greatly upset Eger. They felt both the U.S. manufacturer and British distributor were responsible for the problem because their poor documentation and training created the misunderstanding which led to Eger breaking the part. Worse, after express delivery and customs charges, the $500 part cost $750.

Frustrated but fearing it will lose the job from its important customer, Eger agreed to the costs. The next day, the U.S. company sent the part, which arrived two days later, on a Friday, and didn't clear Hungarian customs until the following Monday, the tenth day of the stoppage. With so many days lost, Eger lost the order. For the next year, Eger did all it could to ruin the reputations of both the British distributor and American manufacturer. Sales for the U.S. company never seemed to go anywhere in Hungary for a number of years!

While this example is fictional, it is not far-fetched. This illustration combines a number of very real situations, including misunderstandings about which party should pay for the cost of "unusual" mistakes, international express shipping, poor technical documentation, and time differences that led to seemingly endless delays while the parties waited for answers. Had the problem occurred in the U.S., the production line may have been up and running immediately using English documentation for assistance. Yet due to various challenges unique to the international environment, the problem continued to get worse.

• BENEFITS OF EFFECTIVE CUSTOMER SERVICE

There are considerable benefits of effective customer service. Most importantly, it strengthens and supports a company's sales and marketing efforts. According to the White House Office of Consumer Affairs, the average business never hears from 96 percent of its unhappy customers - for every complaint received, a business will have 26 others that are unreported. Each of those 26 customers that do not directly complain to the company do complain to up to ten other people. Thus, for every complaint received, as many as 260 people hear about a problem with the company or product. Imagine the impact of all those people learning about such problems!

An effective customer service program is the key to building and sustaining your global success. It can assist in a number of ways beyond the general benefit of supporting sales and marketing. It builds customer loyalty. If a customer feels the company has done all it can to assist him or her in using the product easily and reliably, the customer is more likely to purchase the manufacturer's products in the future. It also enhances patience when trouble occurs. An effective customer support structure will give the customer a feeling that though the solution to a problem is taking some time, it is being handled. When customers understand the delay, they are less likely to complain. As with quality, good customer service also prevents problems. For example, in the previous example of the Hungarian manufacturer, had the manufacturer translated its documentation or trained its distributor, the extreme delays may have never occurred. Finally, effective customer service creates product champions - companies and individuals so satisfied with a particular product that they become salespeople for the manufacturer.

International benefits. The above benefits are magnified for global companies. For example, given the sizeable task of global advertising and marketing, nothing works better than happy international customers spreading good word of mouth. Likewise, good international customer support that engenders loyalty and patience is particularly important internationally where time and distance naturally increase the response time.

• CREATING EFFECTIVE INTERNATIONAL CUSTOMER SERVICE - THE ROLE OF THE COMPANY

The Initial Baseline: Domestic Customer Service

Creating a strong international customer service program should begin with a review of your company's domestic customer service program. Any problems and weaknesses in the domestic effort will only be exacerbated internationally. One of the easiest and fastest ways to assess your current customer support program is to hold an internal meeting and critique your efforts. Play the role of customer at each level of the distribution chain - distributor, agent, retailer, and customer - and ask questions that will highlight what your company does or does not do well. Be sure to focus on both pre- and post-sales issues. For example, if your products require considerable technical specifications prior to confirming a sale, investigate how effective your company is in responding to these questions. Can the process be improved through the use of better standardized documentation or technology such as databases or websites?

Your goal is to document your existing customer support program, as well as its strengths and weaknesses. This will help you identify issues that are important internationally and highlight opportunities for improvement. You may want to consider outside assistance in assessing your program. You also can attend any number of national and local workshops designed to develop effective customer support programs. As a start, check out the International Customer Service Association or The Dartnell Corporation.

Meeting the Needs of Your International Buyers

As you develop your international customer support strategy, it is important to remember the expectations of your foreign buyers, both your international distributors and agents and the final end-users of your products or services. As summarized in Chapter 18, the five expectations are:

1. Appreciating the unique role of foreign representatives
2. A product that works and a service that meets needs
3. Good communication
4. Lack of discrimination (between the U.S. and foreign market)
5. Great prices

Your international customer service program must address these issues to be effective. Each expectation of your foreign buyer should play a role in developing your customer service program. For example, the first expectation implies that an effective international customer support program must empower foreign agents and distributors to be able to fully act on behalf of the manufacturer. The impact of international time and distance differences means foreign representatives must be able to solve customer support challenges immediately, without relying on the manufacturer to provide technical information or spare parts. Such routine actions, such as overnight delivery of spare parts, are much more expensive and prone to delays if conducted by the manufacturer. From the start, companies must recognize these challenges and incorporate them into an effective international customer service program.

Figure 20.1 summarizes the impact of these five expectations on a company's international customer support function. The essential issue is that international companies must always strive to be extra responsive to international buyers due to language, culture, and technology differences, as well as time and distance challenges. An excellent international customer service program requires components and services not found in the domestic program.

Specific Issues in International Customer Service Programs

Some issues related to creating effective international customer service are particularly unique to the international environment and probably require individual attention.

Language. Americans are increasingly aware of the impact of language differences on such items as product instructions or warranty statements. Just refer to the literature accompanying today's consumer goods, such as toys, electronics items, or even clothing labels, and you will find several translations. Previously, only the domain of international travel items, such as airline safety placards and hotel welcome messages, multilanguage customer support literature is increasingly becoming the norm for all consumer goods. Translating customer support literature simply makes good sense. As shown in the Eger Manufacturing example, prevention is the best medicine for solving customer support issues. Better to solve a simple problem immediately before it grows into a much larger challenge. Often this means providing at least basic (or critical) instructions translated into local languages.

Local regulations may already dictate some translations, such as labeling requirements in Canada. But rather than only do language issues as required by law, companies should proactively translate customer support literature, from labels and packaging to instructions and warranty statements. Depending on the relationship between the exporter and importer, the cost of the translations can often be shared with the importer.

In the case of exclusive representation, the importer may bear the entire cost of translations. Having the importer involved in the translations offers a number of benefits, not the least of which means you have access to people with native language ability. When companies first expand into a market, they will often rely on the importer for translations simply because this is the least expensive way to ensure some level of quality.

Figure 20.1 Foreign Buyer Expectations and Their Impact on International Customer Support Functions

Expectations	Impact on International Customer Support Function
Expectation: Appreciating the unique role of foreign representatives **Importance Internationally:** Foreign representations often have to act as the manufacturer.	International representatives often have to solve problems and customer support functions as if they were the original equipment manufacturer. Thus international training programs for foreign distributors/agents need to be more complete than their domestic counterparts so the foreign representative can operate more independently. Spare parts inventories, technical documentation, support software, and diagnostic tools need to be complete and empower the foreign representatives to deal with most if not all product inquiries and problems. The manufacturer should consider creating regional "super distributors/agents" that have large inventories of spare parts to supply surrounding countries/markets. Such parts should probably be consigned rather than purchased by the distributor. This function also can be outsourced to a third-party parts-house.
Expectation: A product that works and a service that meets needs **Importance Internationally:** International time and distance differences mean the dependability of the product and service is even more critical for international users.	Above all else, produce good quality products. Establish fast and effective repair policies and procedures. Include complete documentation, preferably translated into the local languages. If selling a service, ensure service agreements are complete and detail how to deal with problems and disputes.
Expectation: Good Communication **Importance Internationally:** Time and distance differences mean effective international communication is particularly critical for foreign buyers.	Strive for fast response time to technical/product inquiries. Employ staff with foreign language capabilities. Create international newsletters, emails, and websites targeted to the unique challenges facing international buyers. Send non-sales employees such as technical and customer support managers and employees on foreign market visits.

(continued)

Figure 20.1 Continued

Expectations	Impact on International Customer Support Function
Expectation: Lack of discrimination (between the U.S. and foreign market) **Importance Internationally:** Foreign buyers are particularly sensitive to policies that ignore their unique international challenges and don't empower them to be locally responsive and effective.	Avoid any policies that appear to favor domestic customers over foreign ones. Put procedures and policies into place that empower foreign buyers to be locally responsive such as releasing technical information that would be considered sensitive domestically.
Expectation: Great prices **Importance Internationally:** International price escalation means the cost to foreign buyers for parts and repair services can easily become exorbitant.	Parts and repair services that are fairly priced. Consider international parts pricing at an even deeper discount than domestic pricing.

You also should investigate using professional translators, which is often the best solution. Though professional translators may appear expensive, their long-term value lies in their ability to create accurate, effective, and locally sensitive translations that mirror the manufacturer's professionalism. How often have you seen a poorly translated instruction accompanying an imported consumer good and thought, "Well, this is a cheap or inexperienced company." Global companies strive to avoid such impressions and a professional translator can play an important role in this process.

International training and documentation. Given that foreign representatives and users of imported products are more separated from the U.S. manufacturer than domestic counterparts, the requirement for effective training and documentation is even more critical. Problems overseas often occur when direct communication with the exporter is not possible. With global time differences, some international businesses are never at work during domestic business hours. Email becomes the communication norm, resulting in slower exchanges while each party responds to the correspondence. Without the ability to coordinate direct communication, a simple problem may grow into a multiday issue as each party exchanges details and potential solutions. (Clearly, the Internet and company websites that include technical information and troubleshooting tips play a great role in reducing these communications challenges as discussed in Chapter 22.)

Manufacturers need to avoid the situation where their foreign representatives can only solve problems by going back to the manufacturer. Though this may seem obvious, many companies have never faced the issue because their domestic customers simply pick up the phone to solve a problem quickly and cheaply. Thus, gaps in a company's technical documentation or training procedures may not be revealed until a company begins its international expansion.

When creating your international customer service program, review all your product literature, technical documentation, and training materials. Are they complete enough to solve at least routine problems? Are there some existing internal documents that should be released to international representatives? Should your training course be expanded to include activities and procedures normally conducted by in-house technicians and customer service personnel? For example, I often received requests from international distributors for the schematics of our computer products. They needed the information in order to repair minor problems. As a company, we had never received such requests from domestic distributors because we handled all repairs at our U.S. headquarters. Though management was reluctant to release the schematics, eventually we understood the need and released them. (Distributors had to sign nondisclosure agreements.)

Cultural considerations. As with sales and marketing, cultural differences between countries and markets will influence your international customer service functions. For example, business decisions in Venezuela often go beyond a simple profit and loss analysis to involve emotional aspects. Venezuelan executives establish business relationships with the individuals more than the companies, so how a warranty or product dispute is resolved may greatly depend on who resolves the dispute. Rather than involving customer service staff, it is prudent to have the executive most involved with the foreign buyer handle the communication. Though sales staff is commonly involved in customer service related functions domestically, it is not seen as an insult if the sales staff was not involved. But this could be the case internationally.

The key is to remain sensitive to international cultural differences, as you would when traveling or selling. In some respects the customer support function is even more exposed to cultural differences because it is a role often associated with problems, mistakes, and malfunctions. In such situations, emotions run high and are tied to cultural attitudes and beliefs.

Logistics. Manufacturers may take for granted a fast and efficient transportation system as an important component of their customer service department. In a domestic market, we have accepted as the norm that we can easily get a replacement part from one side of the country to the other cheaply and quickly. Same-day delivery and weekend delivery options are now standard services. These options make the job of supporting U.S. customers easier and cheaper than in years past.

However, internationally such options may not be widely available. The issue of time and distance virtually eliminates many of the logistics options U.S. manufacturers take for granted. Air carriers and freight companies continue to enhance their international logistic offerings, yet international markets will always be more difficult to service than the domestic market. Thus, when developing your international customer service program, considerations should be made for the logistical challenges presented by an international marketplace.

One solution is to establish regional customer support functions, either through direct investment in the market or through joint ventures with foreign representatives. The direct investment approach, such as opening a customer support center in Europe or Asia, may be justified even before a sales and marketing office. It all depends on the nature and depth of the customer service requirement. It also depends on the relationship with your foreign buyers. If a company sells to more than one representative in a market, it may be awkward to establish a customer support function with one foreign buyer that would be in competition with other representatives. Other foreign distributors may be insulted or reluctant to use the customer support function if it is provided directly by another distributor. However you do it, your goal is to shrink the globe by distributing expertise, repair functions, and parts supply throughout the world so all markets do not have to be serviced strictly by the home market.

Product warranties. The issue of product warranty should be dealt with during contract negotiations between the manufacturer and the overseas representative. Unless the contract limits the manufacturer's obligations, under international law, the seller is responsible and liable for foreseeable consequential damages to the buyer resulting from defective products.[3] This means the exporter could be fully liable for any future claims arising from product disputes. Depending on the product, the country, and the court, damages can be considerable.

Also, even if there are stated warranty limitations in the contract, local law may prohibit particular warranty disclaimers or exclusions. Thus, attempts to limit your exposure beyond that allowed by foreign law may be fruitless. It may simply be illegal to place certain limitations on your obligations as seller. We have similar restrictions in the U.S. The Magnuson-Moss Act, passed in 1975, contains a number of provisions regarding written warranty statements for any consumer products sold in the U.S. For example, the act prohibits a written warranty from disclaiming or modifying implied warranties.

Given these challenges, companies should seek professional guidance about limiting their product warranty exposure and complying with applicable international and foreign laws.

Are they crazy? One final issue worth mentioning is that international customers find the most obscure problems with a product. This happened to me more often than I can count, and led our technical staff to often question, "Are your international customers crazy? That's not a problem we're aware of." The problems would turn out to be real, and eventually we were grateful for the information. It must be the nature of international business that as the customer base grows, new problems arise. Whatever the reason, be prepared for new and unusual problems when you go global. More importantly, do not dismiss such inquiries simply because you have never encountered the problem in the domestic market.

A company's customer service program can always be improved. It is mostly an issue of time and cost versus return on the investment. However, when evaluating your international customer support functions, remember that some of the unique issues, such as time and distance, may justify a more significant investment.

• THE ROLE OF THE FOREIGN BUYERS

The task of building an effective international customer service program involves responsibilities on the part of both the manufacturer and the foreign distribution channel. The manufacturer's strong customer service effort must be backed by an equally effective overseas effort by your representatives.

Repairs and Product-Related Problems

If your products require considerable postsales support, such as product maintenance or repairs, your foreign representatives should have the capability to fulfill that need. This should have been one of the important criteria used when choosing your foreign distributors. Given the logistics of shipping goods internationally, it is unlikely a U.S. manufacturer can fully support its global product warranty policy without local assistance from its foreign representatives.

The specific role your foreign representative plays in the customer support function will vary depending on the industry. In some cases, foreign distributors may handle virtually all customer service functions, from technical support to warranty repair. In this case, the foreign distributor needs to be fully trained and given all necessary technical support tools and documentation. The distributor will probably maintain a significant parts depot depending on the requirements of the specific product line. The significant benefit of this full service approach is the empowerment of the foreign distributor to fully act on behalf of the manufacturer, improving the overall customer service and decreasing the time required to assist an end-user. The disadvantage is less control by the manufacturer.

Another approach would be for the manufacturer to retain considerable control over the customer support function and use the foreign distributors as an interface with the end-user. This keeps more control in the hands of the manufacturer, but clearly comes at the cost of increased inconvenience to both the end-user and foreign distributor. This method is only appropriate for products that require sophisticated support and repair methodologies and equipment. In this case, such functions are best kept centralized to reduce the cost of duplicating equipment and personnel training.

Using Foreign Representatives to Consolidate Shipments

As much as international freight companies continue to improve their international delivery options, time and distance differences, combined with custom clearance issues, will always make shipping internationally more of a challenge. Thus, supporting an international customer base with parts and repair functions is more of a challenge.

Your foreign distributor can help you reduce the number of single shipments between the home and the foreign market by increasing the number of combined shipments.

For example, it is simpler to send monthly shipments of defective parts back to the U.S. Meanwhile, the foreign distributor can work from a consignment of replacement parts so its customers receive immediate repairs rather than waiting for the goods to go back to the U.S.

The specifics of such an arrangement will vary by company, industry, and product depending on the nature of the repair and support challenge. However, the concept is to use your overseas representatives as an extension of your U.S. customer support service. Outside logistics companies can assist you in developing a logistics plan to coordinate such an effort.

Customer Training and Support

Beyond making your training and technical support materials as internationally friendly as possible, you also should ensure that your foreign distributors are actively involved in training and supporting your foreign customer base. With their local involvement and cultural and language ability, they are in the best position to train and support the end-users of your products.

You may find that you'll have to push to make this a reality. The U.S. tends to be a leader regarding customer training and support. With our numerous 800 customer support lines, websites, and good product documentation, U.S. consumers find that they are well supported by U.S. manufacturers and their representatives. However, internationally this may not always be the case. Many countries do not share our "customer is first" perspective, so your international distributor may not understand the need for good customer support.

You need to document the customer support expectations of your international importers. Clarify exactly what is done by the manufacturer and which functions are expected of them in their local markets. Provide them with all the training and support materials needed to ensure they are equally effective in solving customer inquiries and problems. To assist in a coordinated global customer support function, manufacturers often hold regular training sessions attended by employees of international distributors. Though the travel costs can be expensive, these sessions help keep training consistent throughout all your markets. They also give the overseas representatives an opportunity to see the manufacturer's operation and learn firsthand how the customer support function is handled.

Chapter 21

Sustaining Success through Clear Communication and Managing Change

O ne of the most exciting things about business is planning a global expansion strategy, implementing it, and seeing it succeed. Your first successful international distributor meeting, seeing advertisements translated into various languages, and hitting the million dollar mark in international sales are all indications that the planning and work has paid off and your company is on its way to international success.

But sustaining that success has its challenges. Sometimes the challenge is external, such as competitors beginning their own international expansions in your markets. Other times the challenge comes from within the organization, such as the international department becoming isolated and despised by other supporting departments, leading to frustrations, mistakes, and potentially, failure. The challenge also can be strategic if companies lose sight of their overall international strategic plans and become overly dependent on one market or region or fail to invest in their international expansion.

These challenges to international growth are what I will discuss in this chapter. Specifically, I will look at the three keys to sustaining your international success: (1) communication, (2) feedback, and (3) change. Three simple concepts. Perhaps deceptively so, because none of them are easy to accomplish without work and investment. Yet each on its own can significantly impact the future growth of your international expansion.

• CLEAR COMMUNICATION TO YOUR INTERNATIONAL SALES

There is a twofold need for ongoing, clear communication with your international buyers and partners. First, it ensures that you control the image and information related to your company and products internationally. Secondly, it helps to establish your brand and corporate image and create an international competitive advantage over your competitors.

To sustain your international expansion, consider using some of the following communication tools.

Direct Communication. Ongoing regular communication with your international distributors and agents (and even end-users) can be effectively accomplished through emails, newsletters, and social media. Remember that your foreign partners need ongoing communication to adequately represent you.

Market visits. One of the most effective ways to develop strong ongoing communication with your international customers is to visit to their offices and markets on a regular basis. If budget is a consideration, try to consolidate visits to include as many customers as possible, even perhaps an around-the-world ticket which can be extremely affordable considering how many stops you can include.

Advertising, public relations, social media, and trade shows. As discussed in Chapter 19, the traditional methods of communicating with customers and your distribution channel are through advertising, public relations, social media, and trade shows. Each can be an important component of an overall strategy to continue to push your company's brand. Remember, it is important that you develop an international policy that relates to your brand and image presentations. Building a strong, recognizable brand within your industry is one of the most effective competitive tools available.

Internet. Finally, the Internet has revolutionized the ability of a company to communicate to its customers in the global market. Its relatively low cost and immediate access make it the perfect international communication tool. Chapter 22 discusses the Internet in detail.

• ESTABLISHING A FEEDBACK MECHANISM

Good communication from the exporter to its foreign buyers is an important part of sustaining success. However, market feedback is also needed for any sales and market strategy to be successful. It is particularly important internationally because of the geographic and cultural differences. American firms based in the U.S. are naturally up-to-date with current political and economic events in the U.S. as well as important events in their own industries. They will unlikely need their U.S. distributors to provide input about current events and economic outlooks. This is not true for foreign markets. While the media offers updates and insights about international current events, such reporting is normally not industry specific and it would be difficult to keep up with all world markets.

Benefits of an International Feedback Mechanism

There is a strong need for consistent, reliable feedback from your international markets. Ideally the feedback will include input from both your foreign representatives and their customers - the final end-users of your products or services. The primary purposes of such a mechanism would be to:

- *Track problems.* Customers often find problems before the manufacturer because they typically test the product beyond its limits. Just think about how many consumer products have been recalled for safety concerns after the manufacturer had already conducted its own safety tests. Beyond simply testing a product's limits, the international marketplace, with its myriad of cultures and economies, serves as an ideal laboratory to fine tune products. Competitive pressures are different depending on the particular international market and consumer expectations of a product will vary by market. Each of these differences contributes to feedback from the international marketplace that is particularly important to tracking a product's success.
- *Gather local industry and market data.* This can be a very important function of a feedback mechanism because your distributor can act as a filter and provide analysis and data relevant to your industry and product. Your distributor can be a vital source of competitive information such as new companies in the market, product launches, pricing information, and marketing data. This can also be an important method to get the people's perspective on economic and political events in the market - especially those that might affect your international business such as inflation outlooks and currency fluctuations. International market feedback can be used to identify industry trends, especially ones that have not yet gotten the attention of domestic consumers.
- *Suggest product enhancements.* It has become a cliché, but a company must never lose sight of the fact that the consumer drives the company's product strategy. If products and services do not meet real needs, they will likely fail. While this is true internationally, it takes on a slightly different twist. Not only will international market feedback be important for future product development, it can also assist in identifying why particular products are not selling. There may be some hidden cultural issues or local market conditions that are significantly influencing a product's performance. Without adequate feedback, such information could be missed.
- *Identify internal considerations.* Finally, feedback from the international marketplace can greatly assist in identifying problems or loopholes in your company's operation, structure, and strategy. Given all of the challenges associated with effectively supporting international sales, your international customers can be a critical source to help you identify internal issues. From the input of your foreign buyers, you may find that particular aspects of your company structure are working while others are not. Their input also may help identify sales or customer support strategies that need improving.

Feedback Mechanisms

So what are the most effective ways to create reliable international feedback mechanisms? An ideal program will comprise a number of ideas, some more suited for smaller companies, others for larger ones. From the following list, you need to identify those that fit your company's corporate style, culture, and budget:

- *Market visits*. The single most effective feedback mechanism to use in the international marketplace is to simply keep visiting each market. Nothing can replace the depth and accuracy of information attained through face-to-face meetings with buyers, consumers, the media, and government officials. Each has a unique perspective and agenda. To attempt to sustain your international success through limited direct contact with your international customers and opinion makers will ultimately limit, if not jeopardize, your international success. Yet too many times, especially during domestic economic downturns (the driving force behind profits and thus the cash flow to fund travel), companies retrench and reduce international travel. This is understandable and perhaps necessary if the company's cash flow is really at risk. Yet it seems that the reduced international travel is less a symptom of cash flow problems and more one of top management's apathy toward international priorities. Unless the company's health is truly at risk, keep international market visits a priority. It is the best way to really learn what is happening, internally and externally.

- *International distributor meetings*. A more formal method is to hold international distributor/agent meetings. These can be wonderfully effective mechanisms to gather new ideas, introduce products, conduct brainstorming sessions, and listen to internal and external critiques - essentially the ideal forum for feedback in a single location within a single time frame. These meetings are often held in conjunction with international trade shows so that travel costs are minimized. It is also common to hold these meetings away from other distractions so you have the full attention of the participants. Wherever they are held, the key is to bring your international distributors together so you can receive valuable input as well as provide them with product details and company updates.

- *Monthly international reports*. Another formal mechanism is to implement monthly reports from your international sales staff. Essentially, the task would be to contact each distributor on a monthly basis to identify any potential problems (or opportunities) and receive sales forecasts. Though I always found this a particularly tedious process and my distributors seemed to resent my calls for sales forecasts, it is a good discipline and probably worth implementing even if all the other feedback mechanisms are in place. Monthly reports keep the flow of information going between your foreign visits. They are also a good means of making sure important information is written down and available to all interested parties. By the same token, do not think that these reports will tell you all that is happening. They should not replace other feedback mechanisms. Reports should simply augment other techniques to help you better determine what is really happening in the international markets.

- *Press*. Consistent contact with international press is also important. This is most effectively done during international travel, but can also done by telephone or through email. The key is to constantly utilize the perspective and experience of the press as a source for insights and trends that might otherwise be missed by customers or sales staff. Editorial staff are probably the most important contacts, but advertising staff can also be useful. Editorial contacts are more likely to provide industry trends and data, while advertising representatives can be particularly helpful with competitive information (as long as the relationship is nurtured by buying some advertising space from them!).

- *Warranty registration*. Direct feedback from consumers via warranty registration is an old trick, but useful internationally as well. Consider having international consumers register their products directly through your website. Consider adding foreign language options especially if your end-user are consumers rather than businesses. Include marketing related feedback such as how did they hear of the product and which features were most important. If you do have direct registration to your website you may need to discuss with your foreign distributors who may see such actions as an attempt to bypass them.

- *Websites/email/social media*. The Internet is an ideal feedback mechanism, especially for direct response from consumers. The best part about the Internet, besides being cheap, is that it can target not only current customers and representatives but also potential consumers. For example, because the Internet is available globally (as opposed to local advertising or trade shows), you may receive feedback from a specific country or market in which you do not have representation. This can be a good indication that perhaps you should consider appointing a distributor in that market. Such unsolicited feedback can also provide insights into the unique needs and requirements of a particular market. For example, you may find pricing issues are a concern in one region and quality or features in another.

Responding to Feedback

When feedback is received from the international marketplace, you must not discount it. We all like to think our input matters and international buyers and consumers are no different. In some respects, acknowledging their input is even more important, because they have no way of knowing if their inquiries got to you.

This is particularly important when dealing with international distributors. You may think you always know what is best. Even if you are right, you should not impose your will on international buyers. I have always believed that the essential cultural challenge facing international business is not learning the specific details of each culture, but conveying a sense of respect for other cultures. Part of this respect is listening with an open ear to your buyers. Always support feedback from your distributors by taking it seriously and making sure others in your company do too.

An effective and reliable feedback mechanism will not only help sustain your international success but also lay the groundwork for continued expansion and growth.

Make good feedback a priority. When done properly, it will become a competitive advantage that your competitors will find difficult to duplicate.

• MANAGING CHANGE TO SUSTAIN SUCCESS

Success seems to have its own challenges, and international success is no exception. International success can lead to new and unforeseen challenges that hopefully do not lead to failure. Some of these issues, such as cash flow constraints, are not unique to a company's international growth, but others are and may represent some concerns never faced by your company before.

Cash Flow Constraints

Whenever a company experiences steady growth, particularly if it occurs at a fast pace, it can place a burden on the company's cash flow. Unless the company is in the unique position of not needing significant working capital to generate product and sales, it will face cash flow problems.

The challenge lies in the fact that suppliers and employees have to be paid for raw materials and labor weeks before money is received for the goods produced with those materials and labor. Bridging the gap between payments for inputs and income from outputs is what working capital is all about. Sounds a bit like Business 101.

But isn't this what banks are for - to solve cash flow problems? The problem is that not all banks are comfortable with cash flow problems associated with international growth. For example, if your balance sheet contains any foreign receivables risk, many times, the amount of the receivables is completely taken out of the analysis affecting the health of the company. Banks feel that because foreign receivables are riskier than domestic debt it is unlikely that bad debt will ever be collected and it is better to view the receivables as bad from the beginning. This may sound conservative until you go through the unpleasant experience of collecting an international bad debt. You will begin to agree with the bankers!

Even if the issue is not financing international receivables, gathering working capital to finance future international orders may cause problems. Proof of this is the fact that banks are reluctant to loan money against an international letter of credit. It seems strange because the letter of credit is supposed to be a guarantee of payment - money in the bank as they say - so why won't a bank loan against it? The reality is that no matter how comfortable you are with your international business, your banker may not share your optimism. Bankers have learned from experience that problems happen - especially internationally.

Fortunately, there are two terrific government programs aimed at assisting with such internationally related problems. The first is the Export Working Capital Program from the U.S. Small Business Administration. It offers loan guarantees to banks against loans made for the purpose of working capital related to international expansion. The second is a family of products available from the Export-Import Bank, including long-term financing options and foreign receivables insurance. Both programs are discussed in Chapter 16.

Domestic Resources Become Maxed Out

This second issue is similar to the cash flow problem in that a valuable resource is constrained. However, the issue is not money but people and nonfinancial resources. Essentially the problem is that all of the nonspecific international support functions, such as R&D, customer service, order fulfillment, accounting, and logistics, all become overwhelmed as the workload increases due to international sales. This is a particularly sensitive issue if the employees are not part of the international expansion effort. They feel outside the loop, see no direct benefit to them, and effectively shut down as a result of the extra work.

I've seen this a number of times in companies with fast international growth. The shipping department complains that it didn't receive enough notice about the order and freight arrangements can't be organized in time to meet customer demands. The accounting department complains that it doesn't have time to keep checking if an overseas wire transfer has cleared. The order fulfillment department complains it has not had enough training about international documentation to complete the documents accurately. R&D complains it is under too much pressure from new product development deadlines to have to deal with stupid international questions from buyers using broken English. And the international sales department complains that no one supports it and all it wants to do is make money for the organization. Sound familiar?

It can happen faster than you might think, and before you know it, your domestic business is affected. The answer to these problems is good planning and internal communication, which will be discussed later in the chapter.

International Becomes the "Golden" Department

Directly related to the previous issue is the potential that the international department can become the favored department and become alienated and resented by the other departments. It happens easily. After a few high profile trips to Paris and Hong Kong, followed by some spectacular sales results and press mentions, those on the outside soon realize their work is boring and less important to the company. (If you laugh as you read this, it is a sure sign that the problem already exists!)

Again, this is an issue related to international activities pressuring support departments, though a bit more subtle. In this case, the enemy is internal rather than external. It is one thing to feel overworked as a team, but quite another when one department is having all the fun while the others are doing all the work.

Part of the solution is improved communication. But another aspect of the solution is to change the organizational structure. Companies tend to begin their international expansion by appointing one or two individuals to be responsible for the whole task. These would probably be the international sales manager and the international customer support manager. Both may have other domestic responsibilities, especially with customer support. But as the international sales grow and responsibilities increase, a true, independent international department becomes necessary. This is when the "golden department" is developed and domestic resources become maxed out. The problem is a result of success - increased growth means more work and a heightened profile for the international staff.

But how should you deal with these organizational problems? Do you add additional staff to each department or to the international department? As you add new international markets, do you begin to separate international regional focus into separate divisions, such as European sales versus Latin America sales? Such organizational design issues have long been the topic of research, writing, and teaching. There is no simple answer. Like many difficult business decisions, the answer depends on your company's current structure and product offerings, your industry, and your corporate culture. New models of organizational design are continually introduced, such as those in the '90s with increased emphasis on team building and matrix structures.

If you believe your company is struggling with its current organization structure, consider bring in outside assistance to analyze your current structure and offer an outside perspective. Designing an effective organizational structure is not a natural talent, nor is it easily acquired, which is why outside assistance is probably the best solution.

If you would like to investigate the issue, there are a number of books written on the subject. One of the classics is *Structure in Fives* by Henry Mintzberg (Prentice Hall). It presents the characteristics of five different structures. Though the issue of the international challenge is not directly addressed, the book does an excellent job of clarifying which structure best suits particular management styles, cultures, and industries. Chapter 17 also presents some international structures.

If you are not ready to completely redesign your corporate structure, but you are facing some of these internal challenges, my advice is to work on improved communication within the company. Frustrations and mistakes often can be simply traced to poor communication. Creating mechanisms for good internal communication is not easy, but it should be an ongoing goal.

International Success Creates Complacency

Having discussed these three internally focused problems, let's look at some external issues. The first is the potential for initial international success to create a false sense of security, leading to complacency.

Though most international sales programs take years to mature, it is possible that extremely successful results will be achieved quickly. It is not impossible to imagine a number of scenarios in which a company is able to break even on its international sales in less than a year, especially small to mid-sized companies with low overhead. A company that participates in an overseas trade show at a cost of less than $5,000 can make a few distributor appointments and begin to receive export orders, with no further travel or direct investment in the market. It would not take many orders to receive back only $5,000 in expenses.

But the concern I'm addressing here is more one of the potential for a company to lose sight of its long-term international strategy for the sake of short-term gain. For example, a company might reduce its international travel simply because international sales are strong. Or it might not schedule an international distributor meeting because there do not seem to be any problems or concerns with the distributors. It may even delay the international launch of a product so it doesn't impact the sales of existing products, while launching the product domestically and hoping international channels will pick up the old inventory.

These are all examples of a company either discriminating against its international sales, or simply losing sight of the ongoing investment that is required for strong, future sales. International business, just like a company's domestic business, requires investment in time, money, and resources. This should be obvious to everyone, but I have personally experienced the opposite so I feel the point is worth emphasizing.

Drawing Attention from Competitors

A good secret is hard to keep, especially when lots of people know about it. If you have tried to keep your international activities (and success) hidden from your competitors, it probably will not last long. Not only can they find out on their own what you are doing, but many of your routine activities will draw attention to your international expansion.

It is natural to want to keep your international profile low, especially in the beginning. I know of a software company in England that by accident hit upon an amazing market in Finland. Given the relative size of the market, you might assume France or Germany would be more productive, but due to a number of unique circumstances, including the remote nature of the many of the hotels which were part of their customer base, Finland was an extremely successful market. Naturally, the company didn't want its primary competitor to learn of this market and it routinely listed "various locations" as its reference site for Finland.

Finding good foreign markets (and distributors and agents) takes time and money, and with some luck, you get there before your competitors. But once you are there, it would be nice to have the market to yourself for awhile. Thus, companies routinely mask their international activities. Many companies hesitate to provide complete listings of their international distributor network because they serve as a guide to not only their international market selection strategy, but also as a hit list for competitors.

Company Becomes Too Dependent on One Market or Region

A final concern of how success can lead to problems is that companies may find such strong success in one international market or region that they forsake expanding into other markets and regions. The most likely scenario is that the company would like to expand into other markets but distractions from the domestic market or generally limited resources keep the company limited to one or two international markets. The company's international business is good enough to justify ongoing support but not expansion beyond the initially successful markets.

CHAPTER 22

The Internet and International Trade

The world has seen a tremendous increase in the level of global trade. Three factors have been particularly important in impacting this growth. The first is the end of the Cold War, the decline of communism, and the need for trade, especially from the west to the east. The second is the facilitation of international trade by governments through trade agreements that have reduced trade barriers. The third, and most important for this discussion about the Internet, is the role of technology and its impact on communication.

Technology has fundamentally affected all aspects of business. However, its impact on international trade, specifically through the Internet, is as great as on any other area of business. Who would have imagined just a few years ago that U.S. manufacturers would have the ability to communicate with their international customers through email or Skype? Or that an international sales manager in the U.S. can read the same-day issue of any number of international newspapers from the computer in his office for free?

The power of today's technology to support the activities of a global entrepreneur is awesome. Best of all, the technology is not expensive, which makes it a particularly powerful tool for small to mid-sized companies. In many ways, technology has become a leveler because it helps level the playing field between small and large international companies. For example, for a very reasonable price a small company's website can be just as impressive as the website of a large company. That is not true of traditional international advertising. A small company can unlikely afford to sponsor the International Olympics or purchase a 30 second spot during the Super Bowl.

As a topic for a book, the Internet and its application to international trade runs the risk of being out-of-date as soon as the book is published. Thus, the goal of this chapter is to discuss the broad considerations for companies as they design their websites for use internationally.

I will begin by addressing why the Internet is so well suited for international trade, followed by a discussion of its advantages. Next, I will look at the special considerations of using the Internet to support trade, including issues of language. Finally, I will review potential problems companies face as they expand their presence on the Internet.

• THE INTERNET - THE DREAM INTERNATIONAL TRADE TOOL

You may use the Internet so much that you forget about an important fundamental issue that separates the Internet from other support tools to build international trade - time and distance do not matter or impact cost. In other words, you never have to worry about how far away a customer is or what time of day it is in his or her local time zone. On the Internet, all communication is immediate and distance has no impact on cost. In addition, the duration of the communication has no impact on cost. Clearly, this is not true of many other communication tools such as:

- *Phone*. Phone usage is bound by time and cost factors.
- *Fax*. Because a fax can be sent and received at any time of the day, it is not bound by cost factors but is impacted by distance in that the farther away the recipient, the greater the cost to send the fax. Also the longer the document, the greater the cost.
- *Air mail/overnight delivery services*. Distance typically increases cost, size (weight) increases cost, and delivery is subject to delays which increase as the distance increases or the destinations are difficult to access.

The full impact of the advantages of the Internet over other forms of communication is only just being understood by international companies. Today, product manuals, technical updates, international price lists, software patches, training materials, and even real-time audio and video are only a click away. Best of all, it is demand driven - users have the option of getting the information when needed. If lost or misplaced the same information can be requested and received immediately, all without the help of the manufacturer. (Remember the Eger Manufacturing illustration in Chapter 20? Perhaps a technical support website could have solved the problem immediately if Eger had had the option of checking a website for information relating to its problem.)

Specific Advantages of the Internet

Beside the issues of time and distance already mentioned, the Internet offers these other key advantages:

- Low capital investment. Getting starting on the Internet can be as inexpensive as simply getting access to the World Wide Web, which costs less per month than dinner at most restaurants. Even establishing a website with full implementation of features such as graphics, downloadable documents, and email can cost less than developing a new brochure. Though the cost can eventually become significant, it will probably always rank lower than most of the other international sales and marketing items.
- Small can be big. With the Internet, a company's website becomes its public image. The difference between creating an impressive, quality website and one that is poor and ineffective is only the difference of a few thousand dollars. Thus, even a small company can afford a website equal to one offered by a

much larger competitor. Best of all, the user of the website will not be able to distinguish between the two, which is why I mentioned that the Internet is a leveler.

- Updates are easy and immediate. By its very nature, information on a company's website can be updated easily and quickly which makes it the perfect tool for maintaining marketing and technical information. Though desktop publishing has also improved the ease of maintaining such materials by eliminating the need to rely on outside printing companies, the Internet is an ideal publishing tool. Need to tell distributors about a technical update? No problem, email does it immediately and at no added cost. Need to correct a translation error in a marketing spec sheet? At little to no cost, the error is fixed.

- Translating is less expensive. Speaking of translations, the Internet is an excellent medium in which to translate. Because it is always in electronic format, the text is maintained separately from backgrounds and graphics and can be easily translated and integrated into the overall Web site. Compared to traditional printing, no special films and plates are required to change the language of a Web site. Plus, languages can be added as needed without worrying about batching print runs together as is needed in traditional printing to reduce costs.

    This is not to say the cost of the translating is less expensive because the time required to do the actual translating is still the same. Nor should all comparisons regarding cost savings be done only between the Internet and traditional printing, because companies produce many technical and marketing materials internally using desktop publishing tools which are also electronic. However, the Internet is at least as competitive as other options, and in many cases, less expensive.

- More reliable. This is an evolving issue as other countries catch up to the U.S. in their levels of Internet support. However, generally speaking, the Internet provides a very reliable mechanism of communicating with overseas contacts, considering the cost. And given that it is not subject to customs, freight, or distance-related delays, it can be seen as more reliable than mail. Even if something is not received, it can be transmitted again at no cost, unlike other communication options.

- Audit trail. Depending on the structure and capability of your Web site, all transactions such as email and the downloading information can be documented by time and user. Thus, companies have a full audit trail of all transactions via the Internet. Though companies also have audit trails of other communication means, such as faxes and mailings, they are not available automatically and are subject to human error. (Though to imply the computers never make mistakes would clearly be naive!)

- Control over information flow. Companies have full control over what can and cannot be sent over the Internet by the structure and controls put into place when the website was developed. Websites can be structured so levels of information can only be accessed by authorized users. In cases where maintaining a distinction between public and private information is particularly important, separate websites can be developed that do not share the same home page. However, companies always need to consider the impact of competitors or other malicious users breaking through these technical security barriers. Arguably, no information that could be damaging, such as proprietary R&D data, should be maintained on an Internet website. (This issue should be discussed between your technical staff and management.)

• USING THE INTERNET TO EXPAND INTERNATIONAL TRADE

The many ways in which the Internet can be used as an effective tool to increase international trade is evidenced by the fact that the Internet has already been mentioned in previous chapters. From downloading harmonized codes to communicating with foreign buyers, seemingly every topic associated with going global is in some way impacted by the Internet. The importance of the Internet in international business cannot be overemphasized. The Internet can be used to perform the following business functions:

- *Market research.* The Internet is a critical research tool when you need information to expand international trade. The Internet has an abundance of sites specifically designed for international marketing research, many of which involve little to no cost. Refer to Chapter 6 for examples.
- *Expanding representation.* As with manufacturers and service providers, distributors and agents have also established a presence on the Internet. While not a substitute for travel to the foreign market, the Internet can greatly assist you in identifying, profiling, and communicating with potential agents and distributors.
- *Customer and marketing support.* Once representation is established, and sales begin, the majority of the communication between manufacturers and their overseas representatives involves customer and marketing support information such as product updates, pricing, technical information, and day-to-day communication. This is where the use of the Internet really shines. It's fast, inexpensive, and not bound by distance or time, which makes it an ideal communication tool.
- *Advertising.* Companies seeking international distributors and customers have access to the millions of Internet users at no increased cost other than the cost of establishing and maintaining a Web site. When using traditional advertising, include your website address so potential customers can view more details if they desire.
- *Trade leads.* From the start, the Internet was seen as the ideal mechanism to generate international trade leads. Spanning distance and time constraints, the Internet is better suited than the phone or even fax. In fact, manufacturers report new business from the Internet that they would have otherwise not received. Though nothing is as effective as a strong network of agents, distributors, or overseas offices, the Internet is a great additional tool to use to generate leads.
- *Logistics.* There is a growing use of the Internet as a logistics support tool.

Shipping lines, airlines, and freight companies have developed Internet tools to support their customers. From pricing freight movements to tracking the status of a specific package, the Internet is slowly replacing other traditional options as the preferred communications method.

• SPECIAL CONSIDERATIONS WHEN USING THE INTERNET

As the role of the Internet for international companies continues to increase, so do the challenges of effectively using it. Without adequate planning and execution, the strengths and benefits of the Internet may only result in a huge burden and distraction to the company.

For the remainder of this chapter, I will address the needs and concerns of using the Internet as an external communication tool for buyers, prospective buyers, and other interested parties. While the Internet also has a role as a research tool for your staff, I will be focusing on considerations that should be taken when developing your website if it will be accessed by international Internet users.

Developing an Internet plan. One of the keys to successfully exploiting the power of the Internet is to properly plan. It should not be approached on an ad hoc basis where departments explore options independently. The whole company's Internet effort needs to be coordinated so when the technical discussions begin, the full scope of the opportunity (and its impact) will be clarified.

This is not easy. There is a natural tendency to simply create a website so something is out there. However, speaking from experience, the use of the Internet must be planned. A plan should be developed that outlines the overall goals and framework of the company's use of the Internet. The types of issues and questions to consider are detailed on the next page. The result of planning will be a stronger indication of your short-, medium-, and long-term needs, some initial cost estimates, and identification of staff responsibilities. This information is extremely helpful when you work with your Internet provider and/or Webmaster to develop your Web site.

The integration of the Internet into company activities. When a company develops its Internet plan, it should also decide which aspects of the seller/buyer relationship will be implemented on the Web site. For example, is the Internet only to be used to disseminate information from the seller to the buyer or will the buyer be able to place orders through the Internet? Will the buyer be able to check the status of an order via the Web site?

Keeping the site current. As detailed in Chapter 18, foreign agents and distributors often have to act as though they are actually the manufacturer of the product they sell. When problems occur, they will likely turn to the Internet for information and support assistance. This is why your site needs to be maintained and kept current with the

Issues to Be Discussed Prior to Developing an International Plan

- What are the goals for the company's use of the Internet and social media?

- Which departments need to be directly involved in the planning?

- Is there a need for an Internet website (for external users) and an Intranet website (for internal users)?

- Is there a need for a protected area of the Internet website for use by customers such as foreign agents and distributors?

- How should the Internet goals be prioritized and what time frame is appropriate for their implementation?

- Who in the company will be specifically in charge of the management of the Internet project, website(s), social media, and access?

- What budget will be allocated for the development of the Internet use? How will these costs be shared by departments?

- What training is needed for company staff to ensure the use of the Internet is appropriate and efficient?

- How will our needs for the Internet and social media change as our international business changes?

- What is the current connectivity of our international buyers? Do they all have access to email? Do they have browsers? If so, which ones and what versions? What connection speed do our foreign buyers have?

- What specific issues regarding the Internet are a priority for our foreign buyers?

latest product or service support information. Nothing is more frustrating for your buyers than to go to your site only to find outdated manuals or product support notices. This also is true of marketing information such as new product release information and corporate activities. Make it a priority to keep your site up to date with the most current product and company information.

Technical Considerations

Aside from the implementation issues and development of an Internet plan, there are also technical issues that should be considered. Each of these should be discussed in detail with the Webmaster because he or she is in the best position to make the appropriate decisions. Many of these issues will not be expensive to implement, but will increase the effectiveness of your Web site.

Mobile users. One of the most important technical considerations is that international users may access your website through mobile devices more often than a traditional computer. Though this is a trend globally, it is particularly important in markets such as China where users with no phone access went directly to cell phones skipping land lines. If your website is not adapted to recognize mobile users and make the appropriate adaptations, your international users may become frustrated. And as discussed in the prior chapter, the use of social media can play an important role in supplementing the traditional role of your website.

User statistics. Most companies that host websites offer the option to track the usage of the site. The option to track who accessed your website and when may increase your costs, but the data may be helpful to understanding where the hits (users accessing your Web site) are coming from. This data may be useful in tracking the effectiveness of a marketing campaign or to gauge the interest of your products from a country or region where you do not yet have representation.

Site registration requirements. Websites that will be used as a marketing/sales tool should probably have a provision that the Internet user register prior to advancing into the site. Consider having a number of initial pages to the site and then a registration if a user wants full product details. Competitors will probably offer false information, so you will not be able to always consider the information valid. However, most users are honest and the resulting data will be very useful in tracking global interest in your company and products.

Site security. If your site will have any type of sensitive information, such as pricing or technical manuals, be sure that the webmaster develops some type of security to keep nonauthorized users off the site. There are a number of schemes, such as passwords or the use of a hardware key, often called a dongle. However, most schemes are still open to abuse if an authorized user is befriended by a competitor and offers the competitor access. Even with a secure site, you still may want to keep particularly sensitive information off the site under the assumption that anything online will make its way into the hands of a competitor.

Language. An international Internet site should offer some non-English options. Though English is considered the language of international business, you should not assume that all potential buyers will know English. Consider having the most important pages translated into other languages, especially those of the markets where you have established representation. Your foreign agent or distributor may be able to assist with the translation. Professional translators also are a good option.

• THE POTENTIAL DOWNSIDES OF THE INTERNET

Given all the benefits offered by the Internet, it is clear that all companies need to use it in some way to enhance their international expansion. However, as with most powerful tools, there are potential pitfalls and concerns:

- *Dangerous substitute for travel.* There may be a concern that companies will become so dependent on the Internet that they will see it as a substitute for international travel. This is particularly likely due to the increased use of audio and video on the Net. Ultimately, there is no substitute for foreign travel. It must remain part of your company's overall international business plan. Regardless of how effective a tool the Internet becomes, you must maintain regular and effective face-to-face contact with your distributors and customers. The quality and accuracy of personal contact cannot be replaced by emails and Internet video conferences. Having said that, use of the Internet can reduce the necessity for foreign travel, but it won't replace it entirely.
- *Imposters.* If websites are anonymous in regards to who is the owner of the website (big, small, successful, or near bankruptcy), the same is true of the user at the other end. Emails from a potential distributor may actually be from a competitor. Thus, companies must always treat all Internet correspondence with a certain level of scrutiny, especially regarding decisions such as appointment of representation or financial issues. There is a strong potential for fraud on the Internet with new schemes being invented daily.
- *Open to misuse.* Given the previous concern and the fact that most websites are fully open to the public, companies should always remember that any information on their websites is just as likely to help as hurt them. The more detailed the technical specifications of a product, the more competitors know about those products. The more detailed your pricing policy, the easier for competitors to obtain pricing details. However, as long as companies always remain vigilant and keep controls and security measures in place, much of the opportunity for the data to be misused will be removed.

A company should keep these potential pitfalls in mind during the planning, creation, and maintenance of its Web site. However, do not let these issues dissuade you from creating a website for international use. The importance of the Internet as a tool to increase international trade cannot be overstated. It is an awesome tool and one that years down the road will probably be credited as a significant influence in increased trade of the 21st century.

Search Engine Optimization (SEO): You also need to invest in your search engine optimization so that your company or products have a strong presence from internet searches. If you have never had a professional review your search engine rankings, there is no better time than when you internationalize. This is because your website as supported by social media, can become your most important marketing communication platform – but only if a potential buyer or representative finds it. We offer SEO advice within our

Turner Center for Entrepreneurship at Bradley University and I am always taken back by how impressive the tools are that support SEO. I'm also impressed with the impact a relatively small budget can have on improving SEO such as buying Google search terms or rankings on Facebook searches. At the very least don't take this for granted: get outside input to benchmark your strengths and weaknesses and discuss options to enhance your SEO.

• CONGRATULATIONS!

You have made it to the end of the book, but I hope your journey to expand your international business continues for a long time! If you just got a few tips and resources from this book that were new to you, I hope you feel it has been worth your time reading. But also remember what I wrote in the forward: you now have to mentor someone else. Be sure and pass on the tips you have learned to others. And if you want to share ideas with me, please email me at jff@bradley.edu.

Want even more tips and insights? Between the second and third edition of this book I worked on an interesting project to update a landmark international marketing text first written by Vern Terpstra. The current publishers brought me in to revise the 9th edition which resulted in a new, tenth edition. It is quite different from this text in that the Terpstra International Marketing goes into much more detail on specific topics such as new product development, international sales promotion, exporting services, and the whole global business environment. Yet we kept a very practical tone to the book so it is direct and easy to read. It was also 100% aligned with the NASBITE CGBP marketing domain. For more information, check it out at:

http://internationalmarketing.naperpublishing.com/

Good luck and go global! / Jim Foley

Sample International Distribution Agreement

Below is a sample international distribution agreement. This is intended to be used as an illustration of the various issues and concerns that should be addressed in a real contract. It represents a fairly biased perspective in that the contract highly favors the exporter. It has been written as an exclusive contract. Companies should use the services of an attorney to develop an actual contract that will address the specific concerns of the company. An attorney also can advise you of the legality of such an agreement for a specific country. There are provisions in Figure A.1 that are not legal in some countries.

Figure A.1 International Distributor Agreement

THIS AGREEMENT is made (date), between _____, hereafter referred to as the COMPANY, a corporation with its principal office at
_____, and _____, hereafter referred to as the DISTRIBUTOR, a corporation with its principal offices at
_____.

RECITALS

A. The COMPANY is engaged in the business of manufacturing and marketing _____ and desires that the sale and use of such products be actively and diligently promoted; and

B. The DISTRIBUTOR desires to actively and diligently promote the sale and use such products in _____.

(continued)

Figure A.1 Continued

COVENANTS

In consideration of their mutual covenants and agreement contained herein, and the mutual benefits to be derived herefrom, the parties hereby covenant and agree as follows:

ARTICLE I. DEFINITIONS

1.1 AGREEMENT. The term "AGREEMENT" when used herein means this document and any annex, appendix, exhibit, attachment, schedule, addendum or modification hereto, unless the context otherwise indicates.

1.2 CUSTOMER. The term "CUSTOMER(S)" when used herein means any purchaser of PRODUCTS other than the DISTRIBUTOR.

1.3 PERFORMANCE TARGET. The term "PERFORMANCE TARGET" when used herein shall be according to the terms found in APPENDIX 1.

1.4 PRODUCT. The term "PRODUCT" when used herein means those products of the COMPANY which are specifically identified in Appendix 2 hereto, and as modified from time to time by COMPANY in writing.

1.5 TECHNICAL INFORMATION. The term "TECHNICAL INFORMATION" when used herein means and includes all know-how, designs, drawings, patents, specifications, catalogs, data sheets, sales and technical bulletins, service manuals, mechanical diagrams and all other information, whether or not reduced to writing, relating to the design, manufacture, use, and service of the PRODUCTS, as well as any other information relating to the business of the COMPANY which may be divulged to the DISTRIBUTOR in the course of its performance of this AGREEMENT and which is not generally known in the trade.

1.6 TERRITORY. The term "TERRITORY" when used herein means the territory described in APPENDIX 3.

ARTICLE II. APPOINTMENT AND SCOPE

2.1 Appointment. Subject to terms and conditions and for the term of this AGREEMENT, the COMPANY hereby appoints the DISTRIBUTOR as the exclusive independent distributor in the TERRITORY. The DISTRIBUTOR hereby accepts such appointment and agrees to devote such time and attention to the performance of such duties as may be reasonably necessary.

2.2 Distribution Outside Territory. The DISTRIBUTOR shall limit its sales activity with respect to PRODUCTS to CUSTOMERS located in the TERRITORY, and shall not be permitted to market or sell PRODUCTS outside the TERRITORY.

(continued)

Figure A.1 Continued

2.3 Independent Purchaser Status. The DISTRIBUTOR is to be considered an independent purchaser and seller of the PRODUCTS. The DISTRIBUTOR shall not be considered an agent or legal representative of the COMPANY for any purpose, and neither the DISTRIBUTOR nor any director, officer, agent or employee of the DISTRIBUTOR shall be, or be considered, an agent or employee of the COMPANY. The DISTRIBUTOR is not granted and shall not exercise the right or authority to assume or create any obligation or responsibility, including without limitation contractual obligations and obligations based on warranties or guarantees, on behalf of or in the name of the COMPANY.

2.4 Noncompetition. Unless previously authorized in writing by the COMPANY, the DISTRIBUTOR shall not sell, or offer for sale, or act as sales agent for the solicitation of order for any products which are competitive, as deemed by COMPANY, with any of the PRODUCTS.

ARTICLE III. TERMS AND CONDITIONS OF SALE

3.1 Purchase Orders. All orders for PRODUCTS shall be evidenced by the DIS-TRIBUTOR'S written purchase orders and shall be subject to all of the provisions set forth in this Article III and in the terms provided in APPENDIX 2, or as agreed upon by the parties from time to time. By placing each order hereunder, the DISTRIBUTOR confirms its agreement with and acceptance of all such terms and conditions.

3.2 Prices. The prices charged to the DISTRIBUTOR for PRODUCTS purchased hereunder shall be in accordance with the terms in APPENDIX 2 or as notified by COM-PANY with thirty (30) days written notice. The COMPANY may change its prices, dis-counts or terms and conditions of sale by providing written notification to DISTRIBUTOR, thirty (30) days prior to such change.

3.3 Payment. The DISTRIBUTOR shall make payment to the COMPANY in ac-cordance with payment terms specified in APPENDIX 2, or by terms agreed to by the parties.

3.4 Delivery. Delivery of PRODUCTS shall be EX Works _____, unless oth-erwise mutually agreed. For the purposes of the AGREEMENT, the term "EX Works _____" shall have the meaning ascribed thereto in INCOTERMS 1990 as pub-lished by the International Chamber of Commerce, Paris, France.

3.5 Warranty. All sales to the DISTRIBUTOR shall be subject to the COMPANY'S standard warranty as contained in its terms and conditions of sale in effect at the time of shipment. The COMPANY shall provide the DISTRIBUTOR with copies of any changes or modifications thereto during the life of this AGREEMENT. The DISTRIBUTOR may grant the COMPANY'S warranty to CUSTOMERS in connection with sales of the PROD-UCTS; provided, however, that such PRODUCTS have not in any way been altered by

(continued)

Figure A.1 Continued

the DISTRIBUTOR and provided further that such PRODUCTS are used in strict conformity with the COMPANY'S specifications. The DISTRIBUTOR hereby agrees that it shall not in any way alter the PRODUCTS (nor the parts or components thereof) without the prior written authorization of the COMPANY, nor grant any warranty nor make any representations other than those contained in the COMPANY'S then current warranty. Any warranty given by the DISTRIBUTOR with respect to PRODUCTS which have been altered without prior authorization, or any such additional warranty or representation, shall be void. Claims by the DISTRIBUTOR in regard to any defects in the PRODUCTS shall be made pursuant to claim procedures set forth in the COMPANY'S then current terms and conditions of sale.

3.6 No Other Warranties. The foregoing warranties are exclusive and in lieu of all other express and implied warranties whatsoever, including but not limited to implied warranties of merchantability and fitness for particular purpose. Under no circumstance shall the COMPANY be subject to any consequential, incidental, indirect, or contingent damages whatsoever with respect to claims made hereunder or by any purchaser or user of products.

3.7 Claims Procedures. Any claim against the COMPANY for shortages in or damages to the PRODUCTS shipped to DISTRIBUTOR shall be made in accordance with the COMPANY'S Damaged Cargo procedures and other written instructions conveyed to the DISTRIBUTOR by the COMPANY from time to time. Any other claims against the COMPANY arising out of PRODUCTS sold to DISTRIBUTOR shall be made within sixty (60) calendar days after DISTRIBUTOR first knows or has reason to know of such claim. Failure of DISTRIBUTOR to submit a claim within said sixty (60) day period shall act as a waiver of the DISTRIBUTOR'S right to submit such a claim. All such claims shall be submitted to the COMPANY in writing and shall set forth in full the details, basis, and amount of such claim against the COMPANY. Failure by the DISTRIBUTOR to provide proper documentation to support an insurance claim resulting in total or partial denial of coverage shall render the DISTRIBUTOR liable to the COMPANY for amounts not paid by such insurance claim.

3.8 Offsets. Any credit, allowances, or other amounts payable or creditable to by the COMPANY to the DISTRIBUTOR shall be subject to offset for any claims or other amounts owed by the DISTRIBUTOR to the COMPANY pursuant to the provisions hereof or otherwise.

ARTICLE IV. DISTRIBUTOR'S COVENANTS AND REPRESENTATIONS

4.1 Sales Promotion. The DISTRIBUTOR shall use its best efforts to promote the sale and use of the PRODUCTS by all existing and potential CUSTOMERS within the TERRITORY and will cooperate with users of the PRODUCTS within the TERRITORY.

4.2 Levels of Inventory. Within ninety (90) days following the date of the AGREEMENT and continuing thereafter until the termination hereof, the DISTRIBUTOR

(continued)

Figure A.1 Continued

shall maintain a minimum inventory of PRODUCTS necessary to fulfill the PERFOR-MANCE TARGET.

4.3 Facilities and Personnel. The DISTRIBUTOR shall maintain, at its own expense, such office space and facilities, and hire and train such personnel, as may be required to perform its obligations under this AGREEMENT.

4.4 Promotional Materials. The DISTRIBUTOR shall maintain an adequate inventory of the COMPANY'S current sales material and samples and shall use such materials and samples in an efficient and effective manner to promote the sale of the PRODUCTS in the TERRITORY. The DISTRIBUTOR shall at its own expense prepare translations of the COMPANY'S sales literature into the languages utilized in the TERRITORY.

4.5 Performance Target. The DISTRIBUTOR shall maintain the minimum sales volume for PRODUCTS to CUSTOMERS located within the TERRITORY as established in APPENDIX 1. In the event that the DISTRIBUTOR fails to meet such performance target, the COMPANY may terminate this AGREEMENT by giving DISTRIBUTOR written notice of default and thirty (30) days to cure such default. Failure to cure the default within such thirty (30) day period shall, at the option of the COMPANY, result in termination of this AGREEMENT.

4.6 Sales Policies. The DISTRIBUTOR shall comply, and shall cause its employees and agents to comply, with all sales policies established by the COMPANY from time to time, as well as with all the COMPANY'S education, commercial, and engineering instructions respecting the PRODUCTS.

4.7 Aftermarket Support. Subject to the provisions of Section 4.8 hereof, the DISTRIBUTOR shall provide full and complete service incident to the sale of the PRODUCTS in the TERRITORY in accordance with the COMPANY'S Aftermarket Service Procedures. Such aftermarket support shall include, without limitation, necessary installation, inspection, testing, and customer support.

4.8 Service. The DISTRIBUTOR shall assist the COMPANY in arranging for warranty, maintenance, and repair service with respect to all CUSTOMERS located in the TERRITORY. The DISTRIBUTOR shall not provide such service with respect to PRODUCTS sold by it except pursuant to the terms of a Service Agreement between the COMPANY and the DISTRIBUTOR.

4.9 Import Licenses, Exchange Controls, and Other Governmental Approvals; Compliance. The DISTRIBUTOR shall, at its expense, obtain any and all import licenses and governmental approvals which may be necessary to permit the sale by COMPANY and the purchase by the DISTRIBUTOR of PRODUCTS hereunder, comply with all registration requirements in the TERRITORY, obtain such approvals from the banking and other governmental authorities of the TERRITORY as may be necessary to guarantee payment of all amounts due hereunder to come in U.S. Dollars, and comply with any and all governmental laws, regulations, and order which may be applicable to the DISTRIBUTOR by reason of its execution of this AGREEMENT including any requirements to be

(continued)

Figure A.1 Continued

registered as the COMPANY'S independent distributor with any governmental authority, and including any and all laws, regulations or orders which govern or affect the ordering, export, shipment, import, sales (including government procurement), delivery, or redelivery of PRODUCTS in the TERRITORY. The DISTRIBUTOR shall furnish the COMPANY with such documentation as the COMPANY may request to confirm the DISTRIBUTOR'S compliance with this article 4.9 and agrees that it shall not engage in any course of conduct which, in the COMPANY'S reasonable belief, would cause the COMPANY to be in violation of the laws of any jurisdiction.

4.10 Local Laws. The DISTRIBUTOR shall notify the COMPANY of the existence and content of any mandatory provision of law in the TERRITORY or any other applicable law which conflicts with any provisions of this AGREEMENT at the time of its execution or thereafter. Failure to do so shall constitute a breach of this AGREEMENT for which the COMPANY may terminate this AGREEMENT pursuant to article 7.2 A hereof.

4.11 Safety Standards. The DISTRIBUTOR agrees to advise the COMPANY fully with respect to all safety standards, specification, and other requirements imposed by law, regulations, or order in the TERRITORY and applicable to the PRODUCTS. The COMPANY shall be entitled to increase the price charged to the DISTRIBUTOR immediately by the amount of any increase in the COMPANY'S cost of manufacturing attributable to compliance with any such safety standards, specifically or other requirements.

4.12 Indemnifications. The DISTRIBUTOR agrees to indemnify and hold the COMPANY, its officers, directors, employees, successors, and assigns harmless against all losses, damages, or expenses of whatever form or nature, including attorney's fees and other costs of legal defense, whether direct or indirect, which they, or any of them, may sustain or incur as a result of any acts or omissions of the DISTRIBUTOR or any of its directors, officers, employees, or agents, including, but not limited to, (i) breach of any the provisions of this AGREEMENT, (ii) negligence or other tortuous conduct, (iii) representations, warranties, or statements not specifically authorized by the COMPANY herein or otherwise in writing, or (iv) violations by the DISTRIBUTOR (or any of its directors, officers, employees, or agents) of any applicable law, regulation, or order in the TERRITORY or of the United States.

ARTICLE V. COMPANY'S COVENANTS AND REPRESENTATIONS

5.1 Sales Support. The COMPANY shall provide the DISTRIBUTOR with sales and marketing information applicable to PRODUCTS and shall furnish at reasonable cost such catalogs, specifications, promotional literature, and other materials pertaining to PRODUCTS as are available from time to time. Unless otherwise expressly agreed by the COMPANY, all such information will be furnished in the English language.

5.2 Notifications of Changes. The COMPANY shall notify the DISTRIBUTOR in writing of any changes in or affecting the PRODUCTS or prices, terms and conditions of sale policies, projected delivery dates, schedule changes and other matters which the

(continued)

Figure A.1 Continued

COMPANY determines may affect the business of the DISTRIBUTOR, thirty (30) days prior to such change.

5.3 Assistance. The COMPANY shall provide the DISTRIBUTOR with reasonable access to and assistance of its technical, sales, and service personnel as the COMPANY deems appropriate. Such assistance shall be without charge to the DISTRIBUTOR, exclusive of travel expenses, except as may otherwise be mutually agreed.

5.4 Training. The COMPANY shall conduct, and the DISTRIBUTOR shall cause its personnel to attend, such technical, sales, and service training sessions with respect to the PRODUCTS as the COMPANY deems necessary in order to allow the DISTRIBUTOR to effectively market and sell the PRODUCTS. Such training shall be provided without charge to the DISTRIBUTOR.

ARTICLE VI. CONFIDENTIALITY AND PROPRIETARY RIGHTS

6.1 Confidentiality of Technical Information. The DISTRIBUTOR shall hold in strict confidence the TECHNICAL INFORMATION supplied to it by the COMPANY and shall not divulge the same to any other person, firm, or corporation without the prior written permission of the COMPANY, except as reasonably required to perform its obligations under the AGREEMENT.

6.2 Use of Technical Information and Proprietary Rights. The DISTRIBUTOR shall not, without the COMPANY'S prior written consent use for any purpose other than implementation of this AGREEMENT any portion of the TECHNICAL INFORMATION supplied by the COMPANY hereunder or any patent, trademark, or other industrial property rights of the COMPANY nor copy any COMPANY design of any of the PRODUCTS. Acknowledging that the damages sustainable by the COMPANY as a consequence of any breach of the DISTRIBUTOR'S obligations under this Article 6.2 may be difficult to measure in monetary terms, the DISTRIBUTOR hereby agrees that the COMPANY shall be entitled (i) to have the continuance of any such breach permanently enjoined and (ii) to an award of actual and exemplary damages in an appropriate amount determined by arbitration as provided in Article 8.2.

6.3 Trademarks and Trade Names. The DISTRIBUTOR shall not directly or indirectly use any of the COMPANY'S trademarks or part thereof, or any mark or name confusingly similar thereto, as part of its corporate or business name or in any other manner, except that (i) the DISTRIBUTOR may identify itself as an authorized distributor of the COMPANY and (ii) the DISTRIBUTOR may use the COMPANY'S trademarks relating to the PRODUCTS, for display purposes in connection with solicitation of orders for PRODUCTS, from CUSTOMERS in the TERRITORY and in any other manner previously approved by the COMPANY in writing. In addition, the DISTRIBUTOR shall not register any of the COMPANY'S trademarks or any mark or name closely resembling them, unless requested to do so by the COMPANY in writing, nor shall the DISTRIBUTOR remove or

(continued)

Figure A.1 Continued

efface any of the COMPANY'S trademarks affixed to the PRODUCTS.

6.4 Protection of Proprietary Rights. The DISTRIBUTOR agrees to cooperate with and assist the COMPANY, at the COMPANY'S expense, in the protection of trademarks, patents, or copyrights owned by or licensed to the COMPANY, and shall inform the COMPANY immediately of any infringements or other improper action with respect to such trademarks, patents, or copyrights which shall come to the attention of the DISTRIBUTOR.

ARTICLE VII. TERM AND TERMINATION

7.1 Term. Unless terminated as provided in Section 7.2 below or mutual written consent, this AGREEMENT shall continue in full force and effect for an initial term expiring one (1) year after the date hereof and thereafter may be renewed by the COMPANY for successive one (1) year terms by written notice to the DISTRIBUTOR at least thirty (30) calendar days prior to the expiration of the initial term or any renewal term hereof.

7.2 Termination. This AGREEMENT may be terminated prior to expiration of the initial or any renewal term, as provided in Article 7.1 above, by prior written notice to the other party as follows:

A. With the exception of the termination provisions contained in Article 4.5 above, by either party in the event the other party should fail to perform any of its obligation hereunder and should fail to remedy such nonperformance within 90 calendar days after receiving written demand therefor;

B. By either party, effective immediately, if the other party should become the subject of any voluntary or involuntary bankruptcy, receivership, or other insolvency proceedings or make an assignment or other arrangement for the benefit of its creditors, or if such other party should be nationalized or have any of its material assets expropriated;

C. By the COMPANY, effective immediately, if the DISTRIBUTOR should attempt to sell, assign, delegate, or transfer any of its rights and obligations under this AGREEMENT without having obtained the COMPANY'S prior written consent thereto, or if there should occur any material change in the management, ownership, or control of the DISTRIBUTOR;

D. By the COMPANY, effective immediately, if any law or regulation should be adopted or in effect in the TERRITORY which would restrict the COMPANY'S termination rights or otherwise invalidate any provision hereof;

E. By the COMPANY, effective immediately, in accordance with provisions of Article 4.11;

F. By the COMPANY, effective immediately, if the DISTRIBUTOR knowingly makes any false or untrue statements or representations to the COMPANY herein or in the performance of its obligations hereunder.

(continued)

Figure A.1 Continued

7.3 Rights of Parties Upon Termination. The following provisions shall apply upon the termination or expiration of this AGREEMENT.

A.   The DISTRIBUTOR shall cease all sales and other activities on behalf of the COMPANY and shall return to the COMPANY and immediately cease all use of TECHNICAL INFORMATION previously furnished by the COMPANY and then in the DISTRIBUTOR'S possession. The DISTRIBUTOR shall take such action as is necessary to terminate the DISTRIBUTOR'S registration as the COMPANY'S sales representative with any governmental authority.

B.   All indebtedness of the DISTRIBUTOR to the COMPANY shall become immediately due and payable without further notice or demand, which is hereby expressly waived, and the COMPANY shall be entitled to reimbursement for any reasonable attorney's fees that it may incur in collecting or enforcing payment of such obligation.

C.   The DISTRIBUTOR shall remove from its property and immediately discontinue all use, directly or indirectly, or trademarks, designs, and markings owned or controlled, now or hereafter, by the COMPANY, or of any word, title, expression, trademarks, design, or marking which, in the opinion of the COMPANY, is confusingly similar thereto. The DISTRIBUTOR shall further certify in writing to the COMPANY that the DISTRIBUTOR has completely terminated its use of any and all such trademarks, designs, or markings, or any other word, title, or expression similar thereto which appeared in or upon any devices or other materials used in conjunction with the DISTRIBUTOR'S business. The COMPANY shall have no obligation to repurchase or to credit the DISTRIBUTOR for its inventory of the PRODUCTS at the time of termination of the AGREEMENT. The COMPANY may, at its option, repurchase from the DISTRIBUTOR, at the COMPANY'S then current list prices less any applicable then current discounts or at the net prices paid by the DISTRIBUTOR, whichever are lower, any or all inventory of PRODUCTS originally purchased by the DISTRIBUTOR from the COMPANY and remaining unsold by the DISTRIBUTOR.

7.4 Sole Remedy. The COMPANY'S repurchase of the DISTRIBUTOR'S inventory of PRODUCTS pursuant to Section 7.3 hereof, or the DISTRIBUTOR'S right to sell such inventory if not so repurchased by the COMPANY shall constitute the DISTRIBUTOR'S sole remedy for the termination or nonrenewal of the AGREEMENT and shall be in lieu of all other claims that DISTRIBUTOR may have against the COMPANY as a result thereof. Under no circumstance shall the COMPANY be liable to the DISTRIBUTOR by reason of termination or nonrenewal of this AGREEMENT for compensation or damages for:

A.   Loss of prospective compensation;

B.   Goodwill or loss thereof; or

C.   Expenditures, investments, leases or any type of commitment made in connection with the business of such party or in reliance on the existence of this AGREEMENT.

(continued)

Figure A.1 Continued

ARTICLE VIII. CONCILIATION AND DISPUTE RESOLUTION

8.1 Choice of Forum: All disputes arising between the parties concerning the validity, construction, or effect of the AGREEMENT, or the rights and obligations created hereunder, that cannot be resolved voluntarily by the parties shall be decided by the United States District Court for the _____ district of _____ (state).

8.2 Applicable Law. This AGREEMENT shall be construed, enforced, and performed in accordance with the law of the State of _____, United States of America.

ARTICLE IX. GENERAL PROVISIONS

9.1 Entire Agreement. This AGREEMENT, including the Appendixes hereto, represents the entire agreement between the parties on the subject matter hereof and supersedes all prior discussions, agreements, and understandings of every kind and nature between them. No modification of this AGREEMENT will be effective unless in writing and signed by both parties.

9.2 Notices. All notices under this AGREEMENT shall be in English and shall be in writing and given by registered airmail, cable or telex addressed to the parties at the addresses immediately below their respective signatures hereto, or to such other address of which either party may advise the other in writing. Notices will be deemed given when sent.

9.3 Force Majeure. Neither party shall be in default hereunder by reason of any failure or delay in the performance of any obligation under this AGREEMENT where such failure or delay arises out of any cause beyond the reasonable control and without the fault or negligence of such party. Such causes shall include, without limitation, storms, floods, other acts of nature, fires, explosions, riots, war or civil disturbance, strikes or other labor unrest, embargoes and other governmental actions or regulations which would prohibit either party from ordering or furnishing PRODUCTS or from performing any other aspects of the obligations hereunder, delays in transportation, and liability to obtain necessary labor, supplies, or manufacturing facilities.

9.4 Severability. Subject to the provisions of Article 7.2D above, the illegality or unenforceability of any provisions of the AGREEMENT shall not affect the validity and enforceability of any legal and enforceable provisions hereof.

9.5 Nonassignment. This AGREEMENT shall be binding upon and inure to the benefit of the successors and assigns of the business interest of the COMPANY, and may be assigned by the COMPANY but only to the acquirer of substantially all the COMPANY'S assets in conjunction with such an acquisition. The DISTRIBUTOR shall not sell, assign, delegate, or otherwise transfer any of its rights or obligations hereunder without the prior written consent of the COMPANY.

9.6 Language. The English language version of this AGREEMENT shall govern and control any translations of the AGREEMENT into any other language.

(continued)

Figure A.1 Continued

9.7 Waiver. The DISTRIBUTOR agrees that the failure of the COMPANY at any time to require performance by the DISTRIBUTOR of any of the provisions herein shall not operate as a waiver of the right of the COMPANY to request strict performance of the same like provisions, or any other provisions hereof, at a later time.

9.8 Compliance with U.S. Export Regulation. DISTRIBUTOR hereby agrees to comply in full with provisions of the Foreign Corrupt Practices Act and applicable regulations, the export regulation provisions of the Internal Revenue Code, the Export Administration Act and the implementing Commerce Department Regulations, and to hold the COMPANY harmless and indemnify for any such violations.

9.9 Headings. Any headings used herein are for convenience in reference only and are not a part of this AGREEMENT, nor shall they in any way affect the interpretation hereof.

IN WITNESS WHEREOF, the COMPANY and the DISTRIBUTOR have caused this instrument to be executed by their duly authorized employee, as of this day and year first above written.

DISTRIBUTOR: COMPANY:

BY:_____   BY:_____

Its: _____ (Title) Its: _____ (Title)

ATTEST   ATTEST

BY: _____   BY: _____

Its: _____ (Title) Its: _____ (Title)

NAME AND ADDRESS NAME AND ADDRESS

APPENDIX 1: Performance Targets (minimum volume requirements)

APPENDIX 2: Product Description and any General Sales Terms

APPENDIX 3: Description of Territory Covered

The Nine Basic Export Documents - Sample Forms and Instructions

For each of the following documents, refer to the appropriate section in Chapter 15 for additional information.

This appendix discusses nine documents in more detail:

1) Quotation and quotation checklist
2) Pro forma invoice
3) Commercial invoice
4) Packing list
5) Electronic Export Information filing
6) Ocean bill of lading
7) Certificate of origin (NAFTA Certificate discussed in Appendix C)
8) Insurance certificate
9) Drafts

• QUOTATION CHECKLIST

The following worksheet is a sample quotation form that can be adapted to your business. The quotation worksheet is the foundation for the pro forma invoice and should be used to double check calculations.

The following 45 items are generally included in a quotation:

1. Client's name
2. Number of units being quoted
3. Description of item being quoted
4. Specification(s) of item being quoted
5. Number of shipping units (pallets, slip sheets, skids, etc.) being quoted*
6. Width of item*
7. Length of item*
8. Height of item*
9. Total cubic inches of item divided by 1728^2 (the number of cubic inches in a cubic foot)*
10. Total cubic feet of item divided by unit of revenue tons, as determined by the steamship company (usually 40 or 35 cubic feet)*
11. Total number of pay or revenue tons in measure*
12. Number of shipping units (pallets, slip sheets, skids, etc.) being quoted*
13. Weight of each shipping unit*
14. Number of pounds*
15. Unit of revenue tons, as determined by the steamship company [usually long tons (2240 pounds) or metric tons (2204.6 pounds)]*
16. Total number of pay or revenue tons in weight* (Steamship companies usually charge by the units of weight or measure, whichever brings the greatest revenue to the steamship company.)
17. Number of units to a pallet, such as cases, if goods are on pallets*
18. Number of pallets to a container, if shipping in ocean or air containers*
19. Basic cost of the goods
20. Percentage of add-on for the broker
21. Dollar value of add-on for the broker
22. Total EXW cost of the goods
23. Export packaging costs (such as pallets, crates, etc.) if required
24. Special labeling, printing, and translation costs, if required
25. Inland freight to the port or airport
26. Ocean terminal handling charges or terminal receiving charges, or any charges levied at the port (This could also be airline transfer or handling fees.)
27. Dollar rate levied by steamship company
28. Weight or measure, whichever is greater
29. Dollar rate levied by airline company
30. Units of weight or measure, whichever is greater
31. Total ocean or air freight charges
32. Handling charges, if required

33. Documentation charges (such as freight forwarder's documentation charges, or internal charges for preparing documentation)
34. Fees for legalizing documents or notarization fees
35. Fees for inspection certificates
36. Courier or postage charges
37. Banking charges for L/C costs, freight forwarder banking charges, etc.
38. Currency adjustment factor (CAF), if applicable (for ocean shipments only)
39. Fuel adjustment factor (FAF) or bunker surcharges, if applicable (for ocean shipments only
40. Destination delivery charge (DDC) or container service charge (CSC) if applicable (for ocean shipments only)
41. Harbor maintenance fee, based upon .125% (.00125) of the FAS value of the shipment (for ocean shipments only)
42. Other charges, such as special over-the-road fees, or specific industry charges
43. CFR quotation
44. Insurance premium, if CIF quotation
45. CIF quotation

*These items may or may not be included. This is determined by the product and the method of shipment. For example, if a product is being shipped in a container, item numbers 5 through 16 would not be applicable. Conversely, if the product is not being shipped in a container, items 17 and 18 would not be applicable.

Figure B.1 Sample Quotation Checklist

CLIENT'S NAME: _____ 1 _____

Number of Units: _____ 2 _____   Description/s: _____ 3 _____

Specifications: _____

4

_____

_____ 5 _____ number of units x _____ 6 _____ x - _____ 7 _____ x _____ 8 _____ = _____ 9 _____
                                         Width   Length   Height   total cubic inches

Cubic inches _____ 9 _____ = _____ 10 _____ cubic feet divided by 40/35' = _____ 11 _____
                  (Divided by 1728 cubic inches) (1728" = 1 cubic foot)

                                                                    Pay tons/measure

OR _____ 12 _____ number of units x _____ 13 _____ weight = _____ 14 _____ number of lbs.

Wt. _____ 14 _____ number of lbs. divided by _____ 15 _____ lbs. in ton = Total tons   _____ 16 _____
                        (2204.6/2240.0/2000.0 = Metric/Long/Short)   *Pay tons/weight*

_____ 17 _____ Number units to pallet/container _____ 18 _____ Number pallets/container   U.S. DOLLARS

Product Cost: . $ _____ 19 _____

(Percentage/add on _____ 20 _____ %) $ _____ 21 _____
(Brokers only)   **TOTAL EX-WORKS (EXW)** $ _____ 22 _____ •
Other Costs:

Export Packaging $ _____ 23 _____ •
 (including pallets, shrink wrap, banding, stowing container, slip sheets, skids, etc.)

Special labeling, translation, printing $ _____ 24 _____ •

Inland freight *(drayage to warehouse and/or to port of exit)* $. _____ 25 _____ •

THC/TRC/stevedore/wharfage/dock charges, off-load, etc. $ _____ 26 _____ •

Ocean freight *(weight or measure)*   OR *Air freight (weight or measure)*

  Rate $ _____ 27 _____ per _____ 28 _____   Rate $ _____ 29 _____ per _____ 30 _____ $ _____ 31 _____

Handling $ _____ 32 _____ ••

Documentation fees *(freight forwarder, L/C document preparation)* $ _____ 33 _____ •

Legalization *(Chamber of Commerce, Consulates, etc.)* $ _____ 34 _____ •

Inspection fees or Health/Phytosanitary Certificates $ _____ 35 _____ •

Courier/Postage charges $ _____ 36 _____ •

Banking charges *(L/C CAD)* $ _____ 37 _____ •

Other   CAF   _____ 38 _____ $ _____ 38 _____

                         FAF/BAF   _____ 39 _____ $ _____ 39 _____

                         DDC/CSC   _____ 40 _____ $ _____ 40 _____

                         Harbor Maintenance Fee _____ 41 _____ $ _____ 41 _____ ••
                         (.125% of FAS value)
                         Other   _____ 42 _____ $ _____ 42 _____ ••

                         SUBTOTAL CFR $ _____ 43 _____

                         Insurance *(plus 10%)* $ _____ 44 _____

 * Charges included in the FAS value of the goods   **TOTAL EXW/FAS/CFR/CIF** $ _____ 45 _____
 ** Charges may be included in the FAS value of the goods

• PRO FORMA INVOICE

The following 27 items must be included in a pro forma invoice:

1. Shipper's company letterhead
2. "Pro forma invoice" in words
3. Buyer's name, address, city, and country
4. Pro forma invoice number
5. Date pro forma invoice is offered
6. Other reference numbers (e.g., fax number)
7. Quantity of items quoted
8. Model number of items quoted
9. Description of goods quoted
10. Unit price in U. S. dollars (USD)
11. Extended price in USD
12. Subtotals and listing of various shipping, insurance, handling, documentation, and other charges
13. Total price including terms of sale, port of entry, and validity date
14. Type of export packaging or containerized, special packaging
15. Type of freight specified
16. Port of exit to port of entry
17. Gross and net weight(s), usually in metric measure
18. Number of pieces, cubic feet of each piece, and total
19. Country of origin
20. Payment terms
21. U.S. bank information, address, branch number, cable number
22. Amount of the pro forma invoice in words
23. Beneficiary's (shipper/seller) name and address
24. Requested conditions
25. Documentation and legalization to be supplied by shipper
26. Time of shipment and request with a minimum 30 day L/C expirary date
27. Authorized party name and title

• COMMERCIAL INVOICE

The commercial invoice specifically lists the quantity, description, and price of the product(s). There is no specific order, but the following 30 items must be included:

1. Name and address of the buyer
2. Name and address of the seller
3. Name and address of the consignee
4. Marks
5. Invoice number

Figure B.2 Pro Forma Invoice – Items

1 COMPANY LETTER HEAD

2   PROFORMA INVOICE

TO: BUYER'S NAME   PROFORMA INVOICE NO.   **4**
       ADDRESS   **3**   DATE: **5**
       CITY, COUNTRY   REFERENCE NO.   **6**

QUOTATION AS FOLLOWS:

QUANTITY   MODEL   DESCRIPTION   USD   USD

  7   **8**   **9**   **10** UNIT PRICE   TOTAL PRICE   **11**

NO. OF ITEMS/MODEL NO./DESCRIPTION OF GOODS   UNIT PRICE   EXTENDED PRICE

TYPE OF EXPORT PACKAGING   **14**   SUBTOTAL (EXW SITE)
SHIPPED VIA AIR OR OCEAN   **15**   EXPORT PACKAGING
                                           INLAND FREIGHT   **12**
SHIPPED FROM PORT OF EXIT **16**   DOCUMENTATION, LEGALIZATION
  TO PORT OF ENTRY   & FREIGHT FORWARDER'S FEES
TERMS OF SALE: (CIF/CFR)   **13**   OCEAN FREIGHT & TERMINAL HANDLING CHARGES
QUOTE VALIDITY DATE   INSURANCE
                                           TOTAL (STATE TERMS OF SALE CIF/CFR)   **13**

NET WEIGHT AND GROSS WEIGHT   **17**
NO. OF PALLETS/ NO. CUBIC FEET EACH/ NO. CUBIC FEET TOTAL   **18**

COUNTRY OF ORIGIN   **19**

TERMS AND CONDITIONS

PAYMENT: SIMPLE, IRREVOCABLE (AND CONFIRMED) LETTER OF CREDIT, PAYMENT AT SIGHT,   **20**
            CABLED TO, ADVISED AND PAYABLE THROUGH:

            U.S. BANK
            ADDRESS/CITY/BRANCH/TELEX/SWIFT, ETC.   **21**

(IF REQUESTING A CONFIRMED LETTER OF CREDIT ADD "PLEASE INSTRUCT OPENING BANK TO RE-
QUEST U.S. BANK TO ADD ITS CONFIRMATION".)

IN THE AMOUNT OF U.S. DOLLARS IN WRITING AND FIGURES   **22**

TO ORDER OF BENEFICIARY
          CORRECT COMPANY NAME/ADDRESS/CITY   **23**

PARTIAL SHIPMENTS ALLOWED   **24**
TRANSSHIPMENT ALLOWED

BENEFICIARY AGREES TO PROVIDE:
LIST DOCUMENTS, CERTIFICATES, AND ANY LEGALIZATION OR CERTIFICATION, IF REQUIRED   **25**

SPECIFY THE NUMBER OF DAYS WHEN SHIPMENT WILL OCCUR, AFTER THE RECEIPT OF AN   **26**
ACCEPTABLE LETTER OF CREDIT AND STATE LETTER OF CREDIT EXPIRARY DATE AT LEAST 30 DAYS
AFTER SHIPMENT

AUTHORIZED PARTY NAME & TITLE   **27**

Figure B.3 Sample Pro Forma Invoice

moocow feeder company, esq., ltd.
1234 curds way
grazine, ca 99999
[999]269-2697

PROFORMA INVOICE

TO: AL-Sheik Development Corporation
P.O. Box 999
Dammam, Saudi Arabia

PROFORMA INVOICE NO. 001
DATE: 04/13/98
ADC REFERENCE NO. FAX 798-88

QUANTITY	MODEL	DESCRIPTION	USD UNIT PRICE	USD TOTAL PRICE
100,000	1234	MooCow Hoses	$0.50 EACH	$50,000.00
100,000	4321	MooCow Bands	$0.10 EACH	10,000.00

Packaged for export
Shipped via ocean freight
  in one (1) 20 ft. container
Shipped from Port of Los Angeles, CA
  to Dammam, Saudi Arabia
Terms of sale: CIF Dammam, Saudi Arabia

Gross weight: 44,000 LBS.
Net weight: 43,500 LBS.

Subtotal EXW Grazine, CA	$60,000.00
Inland freight	550.00
Export packaging	100.00
Documentation	200.00
Freight Forwarder's fees	125.00
Ocean freight	4,125.00
Handling	150.00
Insurance	394.77
Total CIF Dammam, Saudi Arabia	$65,644.77

Country of Origin: USA
Transshipment allowed
Partial shipments allowed
This quote valid for 30 days
Shipment within 30 days of receipt of an acceptable letter of credit
Letter of credit Expiration Date 30 days after shipment

Terms and Conditions

Payment: Simple, irrevocable letter of credit cabled to, advised, confirmed, and payable through:
    Bank of United States
    1111 Main Street
    San Francisco, California 99998
    Branch No. 4444
    Telex No. CCI 1717171
    Swift No. BOFUS US 7D

Please instruct your bank to request Bank of United States to add its confirmation.

In the amount of U.S. dollars sixty-five thousand six hundred forty-four and seventy-seven cents ($65,644.77)
To Order of Beneficiary:
    MooCow Feeder Company, Esq., Ltd.
    1234 Curds Way
    Grazine, CA 99999

Beneficiary agrees to provide:
Commercial Invoice
Certificate of Origin
Packing List
Ocean Bill of Lading
Insurance Certificate for 110% of full Invoice value, irrespective of percentage

----
JuDee Benton, President

6. Number of pages
7. Date
8. Name and address of the notify party
9. Date shipped
   NOTE: The word "about" followed by the date of sale allows a 10% over or under for the date shipped. If the word "about" does not appear in front of the listed shipping date, the date must exactly match the bill of lading.
10. Transportation details: This section should actually include a number of details regarding the mode of transportation including: carrier, vessel, voyage number, and bill of lading (for ocean); air carrier and air waybill number (for air)
11. From the port of exit
12. Freight prepaid or collect
13. Terms of sale (CIF port of entry)
14. Quantity and description of the goods
15. Unit price
16. Extended price
17. Subtotal prices, usually EXW
18. Description of all charges (charges can also be combined including insurance, inland freight, ocean freight, handling, freight forwarder's fees, other charges)
19. Listing of all charges
20. Manufacturer's or producer's name and address
21. Total charges and terms of sale (total CIF port of entry)
22. Gross and net weights of packages or units
23. Total cubic and individual measure of each package or unit
24. Country of origin of goods
25. Beneficiary statement
   NOTE: This statement is not set in concrete, and the import country, buyer, bank, or letter of credit can determine the correct wording.
26. Reference to letter of credit, if required
27. Shipment from port of exit to the port of entry
28. Certification statement
   NOTE: This statement is determined by the import country. The exact wording can be acquired from a freight forwarder, the import country consulate or embassy, or the Exporter's Encyclopedia.
29. Signature (make copies first, then sign each individually)
   NOTE: A signed document should be presented to a bank for negotiation or to an embassy or consulate for legalization with the signature page on the top. If you have a lengthy invoice, say 10 pages, the last page, page 10, should be on top followed by page 1Ð9.
30. Notary Jurat, if required
    Also add the export control statement as described in Chapter 15.

Figure B.4 Moocow Feeder Company Invoice, Page One

moocow feeder company, esq., ltd.
1234 curds way, grazine, ca 9999
INVOICE

BUYER: 1	BUYER'S NAME BUYER'S ADDRESS BUYER'S CITY/COUNTRY	INVOICE NO. PAGE NO.	INVOICE NO. 1 OF 2	5 6
		DATE:	INVOICE DATE	7
SHIPPER: 2	SELLER'S NAME SELLER'S ADDRESS SELLER'S CITY/STATE/ZIP			
CONSIGNED TO: 3	"CONSIGNED TO ORDER OF" OPENING BANK OR ASSURED'S NAME ASSURED'S ADDRESS ASSURED'S CITY/COUNTRY	NOTIFY: 8	"NOTIFY PARTY" BUYER'S NAME BUYER'S ADDRESS BUYER'S CITY/COUNTRY	
MARKS: 4	BUYER'S NAME BUYER'S ADDRESS BUYER'S CITY/COUNTRY NO. OF PIECES	DATE SHIPPED: SHIPPED VIA: 10 FREIGHT: TERMS OF SALE:	"ABOUT" DATE OF SAIL 9 CARRIER, VOYAGE NO. VESSEL NAME, B/L NO. SHIPMENT FROM PORT OF EXIT 11 OCEAN FREIGHT PAID 12 CIF PORT OF ENTRY 13	

DIMENSIONS AND DESCRIPTIONS	UNIT USD PRICE EACH	USD TOTAL
COVERING SHIPMENT OF: DESCRIPTION OF THE GOODS, AS PER THE L/C 14	UNIT PRICE 15	TOTAL PRICE 16
SUBTOTAL		SUBTOTAL AMOUNT 17
EXPORT CHARGES DESCRIPTION 18		LISTED AMOUNTS 19
MANUFACTURED BY: MANUFACTURER'S NAME MANUFACTURER'S ADDRESS 20 MANUFACTURER'S CITY		21
SUBTOTAL OR TOTAL: CIF PORT OF ENTRY		TOTAL QUOTE

Figure B. 5 Moocow Feeder Company Invoice, Page Two

DIMENSIONS AND DESCRIPTIONS	UNIT (USD) PRICE EACH	USD TOTAL
INVOICE NO. **INVOICE NO.**		
PAGE NO. **2 OF 2**		
DATE: **INVOICE DATE**		

DIMENSIONS AND DESCRIPTIONS	UNIT (USD) PRICE EACH	USD TOTAL
BALANCE FORWARD		TOTAL QUOTE

GROSS WEIGHT   **NET WEIGHT**   22
CUBIC FEET   **CUBIC FEET TOTAL**   23

COUNTRY OF ORIGIN:
    UNITED STATES OF AMERICA   24

25

N.B. ALL ITEMS LISTED ON
COMMERCIAL INVOICE NO.   **INVOICE NO.**
CONSTITUTE THE TOTAL SHIPMENT AND ALL ITEMS
COMPLY WITH THE TERMS AND CONDITIONS OF

    OPENING BANK'S NAME
    L/C REF. NO.   **26**
AND
    ADVISING U.S. BANK'S NAME
    U.S. BANK'S REF. NO.

SHIPMENT VIA OCEAN FREIGHT
SHIPMENT:
    SHIPMENT FROM PORT OF EXIT   27
    TO THE PORT OF ENTRY

WE CERTIFY THAT THE ABOVE INFORMATION IS TRUE
AND CORRECT AND THAT THE ORIGIN OF THE PRODUCT
IS THE UNITED STATES OF AMERICA (U.S.A.) I HEREBY   28
SWEAR THAT THE PRICES STATED IN THIS INVOICE ARE
THE CURRENT EXPORT MARKET PRICES, AND I ASSUME
FULL RESPONSIBILITY FOR ANY INACCURACIES THEREIN.

            29

JuDee Benton
President

TOTAL: **CIF PORT OF ENTRY**   TOTAL QUOTE

Sworn to before me: **30**

Dated at: **CITY, STATE**   on the   **DATE**   day of   **MONTH**   1999

    this   **DATE**   day of   **MONTH**   1999

PACKING LIST

The packing list is used by customs in the importing country and by the buyer for inventory control. The description of goods on the packing list is often identical to the listing of goods on the commercial invoice. A copy of the list is attached to the outside of one of the packages or is included in a packet of information supplied to a carrier.

The following 19 items are generally included on the packing list:

1. Name and address of the buyer
2. Name and address of the consignee
3. Name and address of the notify party
4. Invoice number
5. Number of pages of packing list
6. Date
7. Mode of transportation (shipped via vessel or line)
8. Date shipped ("About")
9. Terms of sale (CIF port of entry)
10. Freight prepaid or collect
11. Port of exit to port of entry
12. Shipping marks
13. Number of packages
14. Gross and net weight of packages or units and total cubic and individual measure of each package or unit
15. Description of the goods
16. Manufacturer's or producer's name and address
17. Country of origin of goods
18. Reference to letter of credit, if required
19. Signature
    Note: A signed document should be presented to a bank for negotiation or an embassy or to a consulate for legalization with the signature page on the top. If you have a lengthy packing list, the last page should be on top of the document followed by page 1 through the remaining.

You may also include a beneficiary statement. A packing list beneficiary statement generally states as follows: "I certify that all the above information is true and correct to the best of my belief and knowledge." A letter of credit can also require a statement, such as, "All items of United States manufacture."

• ELECTRONIC EXPORT INFORMATION FILING

The website at U.S. Census is the best way to preview the EEI filing. Even more helpful is to download the AES Direct User Manual because it details all the fields

Figure B.6 Sample Packing List

Moocow	Feeder	Company

SOLD TO:		INVOICE NO.	INVOICE NO.	4
1	BUYER'S NAME BUYER'S ADDRESS BUYER'S CITY/COUNTRY	PAGE NO.	1 OF 1	5
		DATE:	INVOICE DATE	6
CONSIGNED TO:		MODE:	OCEAN CARRIER VOYAGE NO. VESSEL NAME B/L NO. 7
2	CONSIGNED TO ORDER OF OPENING BANK OR ASSURED'S NAME ASSURED'S ADDRESS ASSURED'S CITY/COUNTRY	DATE OF SHIPMENT:	"ABOUT" DATE OF SAIL 8
		TERMS OF SALE:	CIF PORT OF ENTRY 9
NOTIFY:		FREIGHT:	OCEAN FREIGHT PAID 10
3	NOTIFY BUYER'S NAME BUYER'S ADDRESS BUYER'S CITY/COUNTRY	SHIPMENT:	SHIPMENT FROM PORT OF EXIT TO THE PORT OF ENTRY 11

SHIPMENT VIA OCEAN FREIGHT

Marks & Numbers	No. of Pieces	Weight Gross and Net Cubic Feet	Description
BUYER'S NAME BUYER'S ADDRESS BUYER'S CITY/COUNTRY NO. OF PIECES	NO. OF PIECES	GROSS WEIGHT NET WEIGHT CUBIC FEET CUBIC FEET TOTAL	DESCRIPTION OF THE GOODS, AS PER THE L/C
12	13	14	15
MANUFACTURED BY: 16 MANUFACTURER'S NAME MANUFACTURER'S ADDRESS MANUFACTURER'S CITY			
17			REFERENCE: OPENING BANK'S NAME L/C REF. NO. 18
ALL GOODS OF U.S.A. ORIGIN			AND ADVISING U.S. BANK'S NAME U.S. BANK'S REF. NO.
19			

required on the Electronic Export Information filing.

- ## OCEAN BILL OF LADING

    The ocean bill of lading will be prepared by the steamship line. However, the information is supplied to the steamship line by the freight forwarder. The shipper must know and understand all of this information for the purposes of reviewing for costs and, if applicable, complying with a letter of credit. The following 26 items are included:

    1. Shipper/exporter (the seller or consignor)
    2. Consignee (the shipper, buyer, bank, agent, or other party). Must state "To Order Of" to be negotiable.
    3. Notify party (the buyer, an agent, a bank, or other party)
    4. Bill of lading number (assigned by carrier)
    5. Export references (a shipper's reference number, invoice, or order number)
    6. Forwarding agent references (the name and address of the freight forwarder and the Federal Maritime Commission (FMC) license number)
    7. Point and country of origin
    8. Freight forwarder's agent or contact person
    9. Pier/terminal at a particular port
    10. Vessel name and voyage number
    11. Port of loading (port of actual loading and exit)
    12. Port of discharge (port of entry where goods are landed)
    13. For transshipment to (routing in the event a transshipment is necessary)
    14. Special information, such as the letter of credit reference number, terms of sale, etc. as required by the terms and conditions of a letter of credit
    15. Marks and numbers (the labeling as it appears on the goods and as stated in a L/C)
    16. Number of packages (total number of units and the type of units such as cases, containers, and pallets)
    17. Description of goods (description which complies with a L/C import license)
    18. Gross weight (the gross weight in pounds and kilos, not always required; a net weight may also be stated in this column)
    19. Measurements (in feet, inches, cubic feet or meters, and any fractions thereof)
    20. Other statements; for example, "As per Commercial Invoice Number"
    21. Freight paid (as required by a L/C or to indicate shipment is not freight collect)
    22. Clean on board (statement that the goods were not received damaged)
    23. Date on board bill of lading
    24. Freight charges (any freight and other related charges levied against a shipment)
    25. Declarations by steamship company or NVOCC
    26. Number of bills of lading

Figure B.7 Sample Ocean Bill of Lading

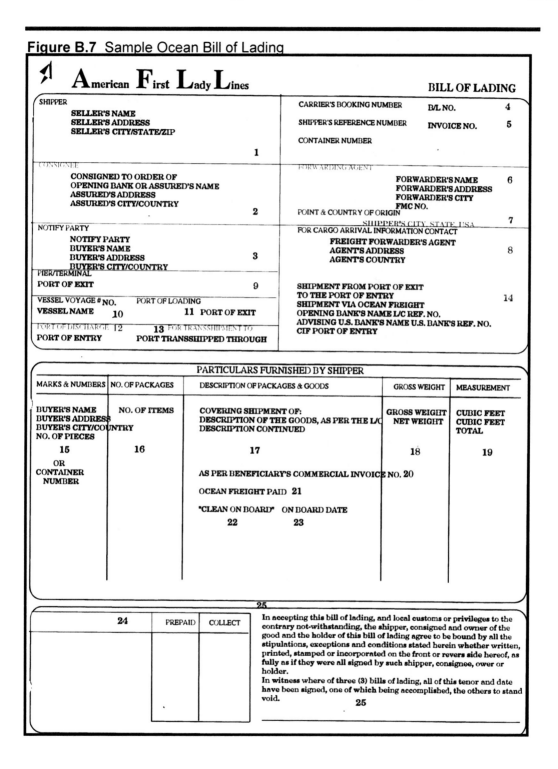

• CERTIFICATE OF ORIGIN

Not all countries require a certificate of origin for imported goods. Some countries accept the listing of the country of origin on the commercial invoice, thereby making it a combined document. Most governments accept a generic certificate of origin form that is available at stationery stores, or that which can be replicated by a word processor. However, certain countries, such as Canada and Israel, require and will only accept a specific form. The certificate of origin may or may not be issued by the seller. It usually must be certified by a chamber of commerce, or the consulate of the importing countries, or both.

The Certificate of Origin should include the following 23 items:

1. Name and position of agent or executive issuing the certificate
2. Name and address of the seller
3. Carrier and bill of lading or air waybill number
4. Date shipped ("About")
5. Name and address of the buyer
6. Name and address of the consignee
7. Name and address of the notify party
8. A statement attesting to the origin of the goods. Note: This statement is generally found in the wording of the certificate of origin, and is generally worded to the effect of, "are the product of the United States of America and are wholly of domestic origin."
9. Shipping marks and numbers
10. Number of packages
11. Gross and net weight of packages or units
12. Total cubic and individual measure of each package or unit
13. Description of the goods
14. Terms of sale (CIF port of entry)
15. Freight prepaid or collect
16. Manufacturer's or producer's name and address
17. Country origin of goods
18. Invoice number
19. Reference to letter of credit, if required
20. Mode of shipment
21. Port of exit to port of entry
22. Signature
23. Notary jurat

You may also include a beneficiary statement, if required. A letter of credit can require a beneficiary statement to acknowledge specific requirements, such as: "All items are of United States manufacture and the goods are indigenous of U.S.A. origin." Chamber of commerce certification can be used if certificate is not issued by seller.

Figure B.8 Sample Certificate of Origin

CERTIFICATE OF ORIGIN

FOR THE GENERAL USE AND FOR THE FOLLOWING COUNTRIES

Austria, Brazil, Columbia, Egypt, England, Finland, Germany, Greece, India, , Italy, Lebanon
Malaysia, Republic of Singapore, Netherlands, Saudi Arabia

THE UNDERSIGNED _____ NAME AND TITLE   **1**
TITLE

FOR _____ SELLER'S NAME, SELLER'S ADDRESS, SELLER'S CITY/STATE   **2** _____ declares
NAME AND ADDRESS OF SHIPPER

that the following mentioned goods shipped on: _____ OCEAN CARRIER, VOYAGE NO., VESSEL NAME   **3**
NAME OF VESSEL

_____ B/L NO. _____ on the date _____ "ABOUT" DATE OF SAIL   **4**

sold to _____ BUYER'S NAME, BUYER'S ADDRESS, BUYER'S CITY/COUNTRY   **5**

and consigned to _____ OPENING BANK NAME , ASSURED'S ADDRESS, ASSURED'S CITY/COUNTRY   **6**

and "Notify Party" _____ BUYER'S NAME, BUYER'S ADDRESS, BUYER'S CITY/COUNTRY   **7**

are the product of the United States of America and are wholly of domestic origin.   **8**

Marks & Numbers	No. of Pieces	Weight Gross and Net Cubic Feet	Description
9	**10**	**11**	**13**
BUYER'S NAME BUYER'S ADDRESS BUYER'S CITY/COUNTRY NO. OF PIECES	NO. OF PIECES	GROSS WEIGHT NET WEIGHT CUBIC FEET CUBIC FEET TOTAL **12**	DESCRIPTION OF THE GOODS, AS PER THE L/C

14
TERMS OF SALE:
    CIF PORT OF ENTRY
FREIGHT: **15**
    OCEAN FREIGHT PAID
MANUFACTURED BY:
    16
MANUFACTURER'S NAME
MANUFACTURER'S ADDRESS
MANUFACTURER'S CITY
    17
ALL GOODS OF U.S.A. ORIGIN
    22
 	
JuDee Benton
President
			REFERENCE
			INVOICE NO. INVOICE NO. **18**
			
			REFERENCE:
			OPENING BANK'S NAME
			L/C REF. NO.
			AND **19**
			ADVISING U.S. BANK'S NAME
			U.S. BANK'S REF. NO.
			SHIPMENT VIA OCEAN FREIGHT **20**
			SHIPMENT: SHIPMENT FROM PORT OF
			EXIT TO THE PORT OF
			ENTRY **21**

    23
Sworn to before me: Dated at: **CITY, STATE** _____ on the **DATE** _____ day of **MONTH** _____ 1998

this _____ **DATE** _____ day of _____ **MONTH** _____ 1998

• INSURANCE CERTIFICATE

Insurance certificates vary from company to company; therefore, the placement of information and even types of information will vary accordingly. If the certificate is not completed properly:

- no payment will be received from the bank if the insurance certificate was part of the letter of credit,
- no payment will be received from the insurance company in the event of the loss, or
- there could be a delay or reduced claim in the event of a settlement.

The following 18 items are generally listed on a certificate of insurance.

1. Policy number
2. Individual insurance certificate number
3. The dollar amount in numbers (usually valued at the CIF value plus 10%)
4. Shipper's reference number
5. City where certificate is issued
6. Date coverage begins
7. Insured
8. Port of exit
9. Port of entry
10. Dollar value in words
11. Description of the goods shipped
12. Shipped per mode of transportation, vessel, bill of lading number, date of sail
13. Payable to assured
14. Marks and numbers
15. Special conditions
16. Policy clauses
17. Countersigned
18. Endorsed on back, if required by a letter of credit

Figure B10 shows a sample insurance certificate.

Figure B.9 Sample Insurance Certificate

MUTUAL RISK
INSURANCE COMPANY
Trash-Bond Building, 4444 Skid Row, Hidden, CA 99998

U.S. **3** _____   Policy No: **1** POLICY NO.   **2** Certificate No: CERTIFICATE NO.

$ POLICY AMOUNT IN NUMBERS Ref.   **4** INVOICE NO.   **5** CITY OF POLICY HOLDER   EFFECTIVE DATE   **6**

7 NAME OF INSURED (SHIPPER)   City   Date

By this special policy of insurance

do make insurance and cause to be insured lost or not lost, for account of whom it may concern, at and

from: PORT OF EXIT   **8**

to: PORT OF ENTRY   **9**

in the sum of: POLICY AMOUNT DOLLARS IN WORDS   **10**
DOLLARS IN WORDS, CONTINUED

goods: DESCRIPTION OF THE GOODS, AS PER THE L/C   **11**
DESCRIPTION CONTINUED

Valued at the sum insured. Shipped per: OCEAN CARRIER, VESSEL NAME, VOYAGE NUMBER, "ABOUT" DATE OF SAIL   **12**
BILL OF LADING OR AIR WAYBILL NUMBER

Loss, if any, payable to: NAME OF ASSURED (USUALLY BANK) **13**

Marks & Numbers

BUYER'S NAME
BUYER'S ADDRESS
BUYER'S CITY/COUNTRY
NO. OF PIECES

14

or order, upon the surrender of this policy in the office of this Company in the U.S.A., or at the office of its nearest settling agents, as per back hereof, in funds current in the U.S.A. computed at the current rate of exchange on the date of payment of the claim, and on the payment being made, liability under this insurance shall be thereby discharged.

This special policy is subject to the following terms and conditions and also those printed on the reverse side hereof.

This insurance attaches from the time the goods leave the warehouse and/or store at the place named in the policy for the commencement of the transit and continue during the ordinary course of transit, including customary transhipment, if any, until the goods are discharged over side from the overseas vessel at the final port. Thereafter, the insurance continues while the goods are in transit and/or awaiting transit until delivered to final warehouse at the destination named in the policy or until the expiry of 15 days (or 30 days if the destination to which the goods are insured is outside the limits of the port) whichever shall first occur. The time limits referred to above to be reckoned from midnight of the day on which the discharge over side of the goods hereby insured from the overseas vessel is completed. Held covered at a premium to be arranged in the event of transhipment, if any, other than as above and/or in the event of delay in excess of the above time limits arising from circumstances beyond the control of the Assured.

Where this insurance by its terms covers while on docks, wharves, or elsewhere on shore, and/or during land transportation, it shall include the risks of collision, derailment, overturning or other accident to the conveyance, fire, lightning, sprinkler leakage, cyclones, hurricanes, earthquakes, floods (meaning the rising of navigable waters), and or collapse of docks or wharves, even though the insurance be otherwise F.P.A.

Where goods are shipped under a Bill of Lading containing the so-called "Both to Blame Collision" Clause, this Company agrees as to all losses covered by this insurance, to indemnify the Assured for this policy's proportion of any amount (not exceeding the amount insured) which the Assured may be legally bound to pay to the shipowners under such clause. In the event that such liability is asserted, the Assured agree to notify this Company who shall have the right at its own cost and expense to defend the Assured against such claim. Warranted free from Particular Average unless the vessel or craft be stranded, sunk or burnt, but notwithstanding this warranty this Company is to pay any loss of or damage to the interest insured which may reasonably be attributed to fire, collision, or contact of the vessel and/or craft and/or conveyance with any external substance (ice included) other than water or to discharge of cargo at port of distress. The foregoing warranty, however, shall not apply where broader terms of Average are provided for herein or endorsed hereon.

American Institute Clauses: This insurance, in addition to the foregoing is also subject to the following American Institute Cargo Clauses (1949): 1: Craft, etc. 2: Deviation 3: General Average 4: Explosion 5: Bill of Lading, etc. 6: Inchmaree 7: Warehousing & Forwarding Charges 8: Constructive Total Loss. Warranted free of claim for loss of market or for loss, damage or deterioration arising from delay, whether caused by a peril insured against or otherwise unless expressly assumed in writing herein

The following clauses shall have precedence of all others if in conflict therewith.

Approved General Merchandise, except while on deck of ocean vessel under On Deck Bill(s) of lading are insured. Against all risks of physical loss or damage from any external cause irrespective of percentage (but excluding those risks excepted by F.C. & S. and S. R. & C. C. Option is granted to insure as below, provided appropriate box is checked prior to shipment

16   F.P.A E.C. Institute Clause

Subject to particular average Irrespective of percentage

Including theft and/or non-delivery of an entire shipping package

This policy covers unboxed automobiles and household goods and personal effects, except while on deck of ocean vessel under an On Deck bill(s) of lading. Terms and conditions as per back hereof.

This policy is not transferable unless countersigned by:

COUNTERSIGNED

SIGNATURE
DATE SIGNED   **17**

18

15

SHIPMENT FROM THE PORT OF EXIT
TO THE PORT OF ENTRY
SHIPMENT VIA OCEAN OR AIR FREIGHT
OCEAN OR AIR FREIGHT PAID
OPENING BANK'S NAME L/C REF. NO.
ADVISING U.S. BANK'S NAME AND
U.S. BANK'S REF. NO.
CIF PORT OF ENTRY

In witness whereof, this policy is made and accepted upon the above express conditions, the date and date first written above.

• DRAFT

The draft is an unconditional order in writing from one party to another party (drawer to the drawee). The draft directs the drawee to pay a specified amount to the drawer at a specific time. Each letter of credit gives specific instructions as to how the draft is to be drawn.

The following 12 items are included on the draft.

1. Date of presentation to the bank, or before
2. Place where draft is drawn, which is usually the remitting bank's city
3. Type of draft, sight, or usance, and the terms of payment (either sight or specific time when payment will occur)
4. Drawer, usually the beneficiary or the negotiating or remitting bank
5. Type of currency and amount of drawing in figures
6. Amount of drawing in numbers
7. "Drawn under" party, clauses, and letter of credit reference number(s)
8. Drawee, the party payment is demanded of (a bank)
9. Address of drawee
10. Beneficiary or drawer (the party who signs an order directing the draw to pay a specific amount)
11. Authorized signature of beneficiary or drawer
12. Endorsement

See Figure B11 for a sample draft.

Figure B.10 Sample Bank Draft

BANK OF UNITED STATES

DATE: **1** DAY OF PRESENTATION

PLACE OF DRAWING: **2** REMITTING BANK'S CITY

AT: SIGHT OR TIME **3** Sight of this Bill Exchange

PAY TO THE ORDER OF **4** BENEFICIARY OR NEGOTIATING OR REMITTING BANK

6
WRITTEN LEGAL AMOUNT

US$ **5** AMOUNT IN FIGURES

VALUE RECEIVED AND CHARGED TO ACCOUNT OF: **7** DRAWN UNDER, LETTER OF CREDIT NUMBER REFERENCE NUMBER

TO: **8** DRAWEE (PARTY PAYMENT IS DEMANDED OF)

10 BENEFICIARY
DRAWER

AT: **9** CITY OF DRAWEE

11 BENEFICIARY'S SIGNATURE
AUTHORIZED SIGNATURE

12
BENEFICIARY'S ENDORSEMENT ON BACK OF DRAFT

The NAFTA Certificate of Origin

In Chapter 15, the background to the NAFTA certificate of origin was presented. This appendix is intended for readers who wish to learn more about the specifics of using the preference criterion and the completion of the certificate. The first section discusses each criterion in detail. The second section explains how to prepare the document.

• THE PREFERENCE CRITERION

Preference criterion A. There is a joke among NAFTA specialists that preference criterion A stands for audit! In reality, criterion A is not used except in a few industries, so a company that uses it will surely have its shipment and NAFTA certificate of origin inspected. Yet surprisingly, criterion A is one of the most common criteria used on certificates, though usually wrong.

Why the confusion? Manufacturers misunderstand criterion A because it seems to fit their goods perfectly. In the NAFTA agreement, criterion A is described as goods "wholly obtained or produced entirely in the territory of one or more of the Parties, as defined in Article 415"1.# The phrase "produced entirely in the territory" leads to the confusion. Produced implies manufactured. But in fact, as explained in Article 415, it actually means only very specific goods such as minerals, vegetables, and live animals born and raised, hunted and fished. (For more details, the full text of the agreement is available online at www.sice.oas.org).

Wholly obtained literally means obtained from the earth or sea, or grown on NAFTA land. There is one unusual exception which you can use as a trivia question on your next international flight. Goods taken from outer space such as moon rocks could qualify under criterion A. As long as the moon rocks are taken by U.S., Canadian, or Mexican astronauts, they qualify for NAFTA preferential treatment!

Be aware that criterion A will only be used by farmers, hunters, fishermen, and astronauts. Not manufacturers.

Criterion B. Most manufactured goods qualify for NAFTA preferential treatment through criterion B. This should be the first place you look when trying to qualify your products. Products qualify under criterion B through one of two methods: (1) transformation or (2) regional value content. In some cases, products must meet both conditions.

The first concept to understand is transformation. Transformation occurs when significant manufacturing is applied to materials such as a completely new product being created. But what constitutes significant manufacturing? This is defined in the agreement that effectively states a product has undergone significant manufacturing when the harmonized codes of the raw materials change into a different harmonized code for the final product. The agreement uses the words "change in tariff classification" to mean a change in harmonized code. The nice thing about qualifying under transformation is that the country of origin of the raw materials doesn't matter. As long as transformation occurs, the final good is considered of NAFTA origin.

Figure C.1 illustrates the principle of transformation. The final product is a cherry kitchen table. It is made from cherry wood, acrylic varnish, and hinges, each of which was purchased outside of NAFTA countries. It would seem likely that cherry wood, varnish, and hinges are different enough from a finished table that significant manufacturing must occur. But under NAFTA, the process of determining if significant manufacturing has occurred is defined by specific rules. The rules are contained in the second volume of the agreement known as Annex 401. It lists, by harmonized code, which harmonized codes qualify as being different enough to indicate that transformation has occurred.

Figure C.1 Example of NAFTA Transformation

Finished Product – Cherry Kitchen Table	Raw Materials
9403.40.9500 – Wooden furniture of a kind used in the kitchen	4407.99.0040 – Sawn cherry wood from Brazil
	3208.20.0000 – Acrylic varnish from Germany
	8302.10.4060 – Hinges suitable for furniture from the U.K.

Annex 401 Rules of Origin for 9403.40.9500: "A change to subheading 9403.10 through 9403.80 from any other chapter."

The table is made from materials all of which have harmonized codes outside of Chapter 94, which is the chapter that contains kitchen tables. Even though the raw material are not from NAFTA countries, they transform into a table which becomes a NAFTA good.

The rule for harmonized code 9403.40.9500, which is actually the rule for all harmonized codes between 9403.10 and 9403.80, states that a product will qualify as being of NAFTA origin if the following occurs:

- A change to subheading 9403.10 through 9403.80 from any other chapter; or
- A change to subheading 9403.10 through 9403.80 from subheading 9403.90, whether or not there is also a change from any other chapter, provided there is a regional value content of not less than:
    - 60 percent where the transaction method is used, or
    - 50 percent where the net cost method is used.2

This rule states two things. The first is the rule for transformation. "A change to subheading 9403.10 through 9403.80 from any other chapter" means that if all materials used to make the final product come from any chapter other than 94, regardless of their origin, the good qualifies. It can be considered as having originated in a NAFTA country. In other words, because 9403.10 through 9403.80 includes wooden furniture for the kitchen, as long as the materials used to make the table are not from Chapter 94 (Furniture), the table qualifies. In fact, each of the three materials - wood, varnish, and hinges - are indeed classified in chapters other than 94, as shown in the example.

You might think that it is obvious that all the components that make up a kitchen table are different than a kitchen table, so the table would qualify. But there could be an important exception: what if the table was made from parts of a table? For example, what if the manufacturer of the cherry kitchen table purchased parts of cherry tables from Brazil and simply assembled them? Remember that all nonoriginating materials have to be outside of Chapter 94. If the wood used to make the table is classified within Chapter 94, the good would not qualify for transformation because not enough manufacturing has occurred. This means that the good cannot qualify.

This is where the second part of the rule comes into effect. The harmonized code for parts of a kitchen table is 9403.90.7000. In Annex 401, the rule states that the good will still qualify if the regional value content is either 50 or 60 percent depending on the method. The rule states that a good that starts out as 9403.90 (parts) and is manufactured into a 9403.10-9403.80 (which includes kitchen tables) will qualify if the percentage of originating goods is enough to satisfy the regional value content threshold. This raises the issue of clarifying transaction value versus net cost methods of calculating regional value content.

Transaction value and net cost calculations. There are generally two situations where the regional value content of a product must be calculated. The first is when the product is unable to pass the transformation test, such as the above example of making a table from parts of a table. In these types of cases, the product may still qualify under the regional value content test if the rules in Annex 401 allow the option.

The second situation is when the rules in Annex 401 require the use of regional value content calculations. There are a number of products that must represent both significant manufacturing and regional value content. For example, boats of heading 8903 must fulfill both the transformation and regional value contents tests. In these cases, use of the regional value content calculation is not an option, it is a requirement.

When regional value content is either required or an option, there are two methods of calculating the RVC. Both are intended to determine what percentage of the final good is made from originating materials, and what percentage is from nonoriginating materials. The calculations can be performed in two ways: the transaction method and the net cost method.

Transaction Method

$$RVC = \frac{(TV-VNM)}{TV} \times 100$$

Where   RVC   = regional value content
              TV   = transaction value
              VNM   = value of nonoriginating materials used by the producer in the production of the good

Net Cost Method

$$NC = \frac{(NC-VNM)}{NC} \times 100$$

Where   RVC   = regional value content
              NC   = net cost of the good
              VNM   = value of nonoriginating materials used by the producer in the production of the good

The main difference between the two methods is that the transaction method includes gross profit in the calculation whereas the net cost method does not. Thus, the threshold that must be met is higher for the transaction method (60 percent) than the net cost method (50 percent). Figure C.2 shows the calculations for the cherry table.

The example in Figure C.2 demonstrates how regional value content can be used to qualify a good that otherwise would not qualify under transformation. The table does not qualify for transformation because the manufacturer purchases table parts to make a table, which is not enough to be considered significant manufacturing. However, the table does qualify under the transaction method of calculating regional value content because the RVC is greater than 60 percent. Only one method is needed to qualify.

Figure C.2 also shows how a product can qualify by one method but not the

---

Figure C.2 Calculation of Regional Value Content for a Cherry Kitchen Table

Cost and Price Assumptions

Brazilian cherry wood table parts	$ 35
German varnish	$ 3
English hinges	$ 1
Labor per table	$ 16
Factory overhead per table	$ 5
Total net cost	$ 60
Total value of nonoriginating goods	$ 39 (wood, varnish, hinge)
Invoice price (transaction value)	$100

Regional Value Calculations

Transaction Method (at least 60% needed to qualify):

$$RVC = \frac{(\$100 - \$39)}{\$100} \times 100 = 61\% \text{ (qualifies)}$$

Net Cost Method (at least 50% needed to qualify):

$$NC = \frac{(\$60 - \$39)}{\$60} \times 100 = 35\% \text{ (does not qualifies)}$$

---

other. The gross profit from the table, $40 ($100 less net cost of $60), when added to the value of originating costs (labor and overhead), is enough to make the transaction value 61 percent. However, under the net cost method, the kitchen table would not have qualified because 35 percent is less than the 50 percent required. Fortunately, the product only needs to meet one of the methods of calculating the regional value content. Be aware that a manufacturer cannot always choose which method to use. In some cases only one of the methods is allowed.

If it seems confusing that profit can be used in the calculation to determine the origin of a product, think of the profit as being local in nature. In other words, because the profit is earned by a NAFTA company, it is considered as having originated in the NAFTA territory.

To summarize, a product most easily qualifies under criterion B if it meets the transformation test. In these cases, it does not matter what country the materials used in the product come from because all the components transform into a NAFTA product on the basis of significant manufacturing. In cases where transformation does not occur, the regional value content can be calculated to determine if enough local materials have been used to qualify the product. In this case, the origin of the input materials does matter. Not all products have the option of choosing the calculation method and some require both.

Criterion C. This is the second most common criterion. It simply states that the final product is wholly made of materials that are already of NAFTA origin. Because only NAFTA materials were used, clearly the manufactured (or more likely assembled) product qualifies as a NAFTA product. Using the example of the cherry kitchen table, if the wood, varnish, and hinges had all been from the U.S., Canada, or Mexico, then the table would qualify under criterion C because the finished good is made wholly from originating materials.

When a manufacturer uses criterion C, it should obtain written evidence that the input materials are indeed from a NAFTA country. Such documents are needed in case of an audit by one of the customs agencies of a NAFTA country.

Criterion B or C? This raises the question: which should the manufacturer use, criterion B or C, if all input materials originate in the NAFTA territory? There is no right or wrong answer. Either B or C would be correct. However, manufacturers should understand that if they choose C, they should obtain some written evidence from their suppliers that indeed the materials are of U.S., Mexican, or Canadian origin, whereas with B, the manufacturer only has to get such evidence if it is using the regional value content calculation. If the product qualifies under transformation, no written evidence is required because the origin of the input materials is not relevant to the issue of qualifying for NAFTA.

Thus, the paperwork requirement is less of a challenge under B using transformation, which seems to indicate that B would be the preferred criterion. Be aware, however, that even though there is not a requirement to obtain written evidence of the origin of input materials, it is possible customs will ask for such documents during an audit. Thus some NAFTA specialists suggest that if a product qualifies under B or C, it is safest to use C and obtain all the required evidence of the origin of all input materials. From my perspective, unless a company has only a few suppliers, use B if a product qualifies through transformation and Annex 401 allows it.

• COMPLETING THE NAFTA CERTIFICATE OF ORIGIN

Now that you have a better understanding of how a product qualifies for NAFTA preferential treatment, you can concentrate on the NAFTA certificate of origin document, which can be equally confusing. I will stress that you should not attempt to complete your NAFTA documents without further training beyond this text. There are too many issues specific to particular products and situations for me to cover here. It would be dangerous and potentially expensive to not seek outside assistance. Having said that, I will at least give you a good idea of how to complete the document.

A blank NAFTA certificate of origin can be found in figure C.3. The form is broken down into 11 sections which I will address individually.

Figure C.3 NAFTA Certificate of Origin

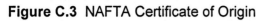

Box 1: Exporter's name and address. If you are the exporter, put your company's name, address, and country. For the tax identification number, use your FEIN (federal employers identification number, issued by the IRS). If your company is small and you don't have one, use your Social Security number.

If you are not the exporter, and are preparing the document for another company, put the name of the exporter, if known, or simply put "Unknown."

Box 2: Blanket period. This is one of those areas often misunderstood. A NAFTA certificate of origin can be valid for one year, but not more. If you are shipping the same product repeatedly, you can create one NAFTA certificate of origin for each year and then copy the document for each shipment or request.

The one year period can be of your choosing. Many companies simply complete all their certificates to be valid from January 1 through December 31. Others have them on a cycle throughout the year so the work of creating the certificates is spread throughout the year.

Box 3: Producer's name and address. If you are the manufacturer, put your name, address, and country in this box, along with your FEIN or Social Security number. You can also put "Same" if you are both the exporter and producer.

If you are not the manufacturer, you can either list the name of the manufacturer or put "Available to customs upon request." The second option is popular with distributors that do not want their customers to know where they purchased the product. This can also be true for some manufacturers who simply OEM the product - buy a product and put their name on it. If the certificate covers products for more than one producer, you can list additional producers on a separate piece of paper.

Box 4: Importer's name and address. This is the information of the foreign buyer in Mexico or Canada who will be importing the products. Put its name, address, and country, if known. For a blanket certificate, which will be used by some importers, put "Various." In cases where the certificate is prepared for use by another exporter and you do not know the name of the importer, put "Unknown."

Box 5: Description of good(s). For each product covered by the certificate, put a full description of the product. Be sure that the description matches the harmonized code wording for the product. Don't use extra words which can confuse customs. For example, in the case of our cherry kitchen table, the description would be wooden kitchen table, which is the phrase used in the harmonized code listing. However, the description also needs to be linked to the invoice. This is important if more than one type of kitchen table is manufactured. One way to do this would be to include a model number that also is used on the invoice.

Box 6: HTS tariff classification number. This is where you will list the harmonized code (HTS) for each product listed in the certificate. Generally, only write the first six digits of the code. The exception is for a few products in Annex 401 that specify the use of the eight-digit harmonized code rules of origin.

Box 7: Preference criterion. This box will indicate which criterion was used to qualify each product. As previously discussed, for most companies this will be either B or C. Agricultural companies tend to use A, and under certain circumstances, D, E, or F may be used by other companies.

If you are not the manufacturer, and you have a certificate of origin from the manufacturer, use the same criterion the manufacturer listed on its certificate. If you do not have a certificate from the manufacturer, put the criterion that you used to determine that the good qualifies. (Be aware, though, that you really should have a certificate from the manufacturer because you do not have firsthand knowledge of how the product was produced.)

Box 8: Producer. For each product, put a "yes" if you are the manufacturer of the product. If you did not manufacture the product, put a "no" followed by a 1, 2, or 3. Each number is used to indicate the basis upon which you have determined the good qualifies, even though you did not manufacture the product:

1. Your knowledge of whether the good qualifies as an originating good
2. Your reliance on the manufacturer's written representation (other than a NAFTA certificate of origin) that the good qualifies as an originating good
3. A completed and signed NAFTA certificate of origin for the good, voluntarily provided to the exporter by the manufacturer

It should be made clear that your strongest position in the case of an audit will be to have a NAFTA certificate of origin from the manufacturers of the products you sell but don't produce (you would put No-3 in Box 8). Your weakest position will be to use No-1, in which you have no written evidence. You should avoid using No-1 at all times by at least getting something in writing so you can put No-2.

Box 9: Net cost. This is the box where most mistakes are made. Some companies think they should put a dollar figure here to represent their net cost. This makes sense due to the title of the box, but this would mean disclosing your cost.

In fact, there are only two options: No and NC. If the good has a regional value content requirement, and you use the net cost method to qualify the product, put "NC." Otherwise put "No." A "No" means either the good qualified through some test other than regional value content, or the transaction value test was utilized. If the RVC is calculated according to the net cost method over a period of time, further identify the beginning and ending dates (DD/MM/YY) of that period. (See Articles 402.1, 402.5 of the agreement for more information.)

Box 10: Country of origin. Because this is a NAFTA certificate of origin, the only countries allowed are Canada, Mexico, and the U.S. Use the following abbreviations:

- US - for products from the U.S.
- CA - for products from Canada
- MX - for products from Mexico
- JNT - for joint Mexican/U.S. production

Refer to the specific rules of determining the origin as listed in Annex 302.2 of the agreement.

Box 11: Signatures. The certificate should be signed and dated by the exporter. When a certificate is created by a manufacturer for use by an exporter, the manufacturer should sign the certificate. The exporter will then create a certificate to use for the export shipment, putting No-3 in Box 8.

The person who signs the NAFTA certificate of origin should have sufficient responsibility within the company to be able to warrant that the certificate is correct. Notice that the certification in Box 11 contains the words "I certify that . . . the information on this document is true and accurate and I assume the responsibility for proving such representations." Many times I see clerks who may not be in a position to accurately know the proper steps to NAFTA certification signing the NAFTA certificates of origin. This is dangerous for two reasons. First, the certificate clearly states that the person signing the document can attest to the accuracy of the document. During an audit, if the person who signed it cannot demonstrate such knowledge, there could be a problem. Second, and more important, fines can be given both to the company and the person who signed the certificate. Because the person who signs the certificate is also taking on a personal financial risk in the form of potential fines, the person should have adequate responsibility in the company to warrant such a risk. (This is why the certificate should not be completed by an outside company, such as a freight company.)

There are a number of other issues relating to the NAFTA certificate of origin that are outside the scope of this book, for example, how to handle the calculation of net cost or country of origin when raw materials are purchased throughout the year with different costs or origin, and the materials are mixed together in the same inventory (referred to as fungible goods). There is also the issue of how to handle an audit.

These can be significant issues depending on your export activity, manufacturing processes, and industry. All companies exporting to Canada or Mexico should seek outside training on how to prepare the NAFTA certificate of origin. Workshops are held both nationally and locally.

• NOTES

1. The North American Free Trade Agreement, 1993, Volume I: 4-1.
2. The North American Free Trade Agreement, 1993, Volume II: Annex 401-154.

CPSIA information can be obtained
at www.ICGtesting.com
Printed in the USA
FFOW02n2109230117
31701FF